KEY TOPICS

NEUROLO(

C000318820

The KEY TOPICS Series

Advisors:

T.M. Craft *Department of Anaesthesia and Intensive Care, Royal United Hospital, Bath, UK*
C.S. Garrard *Intensive Therapy Unit, John Radcliffe Hospital, Oxford, UK*
P.M. Upton *Department of Anaesthetics, Royal Cornwall Hospital, Truro, UK*

Anaesthesia, Second Edition

Obstetrics and Gynaecology, Second Edition

Accident and Emergency Medicine

Paediatrics, Second Edition

Orthopaedic Surgery

Otolaryngology

Ophthalmology

Psychiatry

General Surgery

Renal Medicine

Trauma

Chronic Pain

Oral and Maxillofacial Surgery

Oncology

Cardiovascular Medicine

Neurology

Neonatology

Gastroenterology

Forthcoming titles include:
Respiratory Medicine
Thoracic Surgery
Critical Care
Orthopaedic Trauma Surgery
Accident and Emergency Medicine, Second Edition

KEY TOPICS IN
NEUROLOGY

PHILIP E.M. SMITH
MD, FRCP

*Consultant Neurologist, Department of Neurology, University
Hospital of Wales, Cardiff, UK*

βIOS
SCIENTIFIC
PUBLISHERS
Oxford • Washington DC

© BIOS Scientific Publishers Limited, 1998

First published 1998

A CIP catalogue record for this book is available from the British Library.

ISBN 1 85996 261 0

BIOS Scientific Publishers Ltd
9 Newtec Place, Magdalen Road, Oxford OX4 1RE, UK
Tel. +44 (0)1865 726286. Fax. +44 (0)1865 246823
World Wide Web home page: http://www.bios.co.uk/

Important Note from the Publisher
The information contained within this book was obtained by BIOS Scientific Publishers Ltd from sources believed by us to be reliable. However, while every effort has been made to ensure its accuracy, no responsibility for loss or injury whatsoever occasioned to any person acting or refraining from action as a result of information contained herein can be accepted by the authors or publishers.

The reader should remember that medicine is a constantly evolving science and while the authors and publishers have ensured that all dosages, applications and practices are based on current indications, there may be specific practices which differ between communities. You should always follow the guidelines laid down by the manufacturers of specific products and the relevant authorities in the country in which you are practising.

Production Editor: Jonathan Gunning.
Typeset by Chandos Electronic Publishing, Stanton Harcourt, UK.
Printed by T.J. International Ltd, Padstow, UK.

CONTENTS

[a]Contributed by C.E.M. Hillier, Specialist Registrar in Neurology, University Hospital of Wales, Cardiff, UK
[b]Contributed by B.N. McLean, Consultant Neurologist, The Royal Cornwall Hospital, Treliske, Truro, UK
[c]Contributed by T.A.T. Hughes, Stroke Research Fellow, Western General Hospital, Edinburgh, UK

ABBREVIATIONS

AC	air conduction
AChR	acetylcholine receptor
ACTH	adrenocorticotrophic hormone
ADCA	autosomal dominant cerebellar ataxia
AF	atrial fibrillation
AIDS	acquired immune deficiency syndrome
AION	anterior ischaemic optic neuropathy
ANCA	anti-neutrophil cytoplasmic antibody
APCA	anti-Purkinje cell antibody
BBB	blood–brain barrier
BC	bone conduction
BIH	benign intracranial hypertension
BPPV	benign paroxysmal positioning vertigo
BSE	bovine spongiform encephalopathy
CADASIL	cerebral autosomal dominant arteriopathy with subcortical infarcts and leucoencephalopathy
CAPN	chronic axonal peripheral neuropathy
CFS	chronic fatigue syndrome
CIDP	chronic inflammatory demyelinating polyradiculoneuropathy
CJD	Creutzfeldt–Jakob disease
CK	creatine kinase
CMV	cytomegalovirus
CNS	central nervous system
CoQ	coenzyme Q
CPAP	continuous positive airways pressure
CPEO	chronic progressive external ophthalmoplegia
CSF	cerebrospinal fluid
CT	computed tomography
CVT	cerebral venous thrombosis
DNET	dysembryoplastic neuroepithelial tumour
DRPLA	dentato-rubro-pallido-luysian atrophy
ECG	electrocardiogram
EEG	electroencephalogram
ELISA	enzyme-linked immunosorbent assay
ESR	erythrocyte sedimentation rate
FA	Friedreich's ataxia
FBC	full blood count
FHM	familial hemiplegic migraine
FLAIR	fast fluid-attenuated inversion recovery
GBS	Guillain–Barré syndrome
GCS	Glasgow Coma Scale

GFAP	glial fibrillary acidic protein
HCG	human chorionic gonadotrophin
HD	Huntington's disease
HIV	human immunodeficiency virus
HMSN	hereditary motor and sensory neuropathy
HNLPP	hereditary neuropathy with liability to pressure palsies
HOCM	hypertrophic obstructive cardiomyopathy
HRT	hormone replacement therapy
HSE	herpes simplex encephalitis
ICP	intracranial pressure
ISC	intermittent self-catheterization
KF	Kayser–Fleischer
KSS	Kearns–Sayre syndrome
LACS	lacunar syndrome
LEMS	Lambert–Eaton myasthenic syndrome
LHON	Leber's hereditary optic neuropathy
LMN	lower motor neurone
MAG	myelin-associated glycoprotein
MELAS	mitochondrial encephalopathy with lactic acidosis and stroke-like episodes
MERRF	myoclonic epilepsy with ragged-red fibres
MG	myasthenia gravis
MGUS	monoclonal gammopathy of uncertain significance
MLF	medial longitudinal fasciculus
MMSE	Mini-Mental State Examination
MND	motor neurone disease
MNGIE	mitochondrial neurogastrointestinal encephalopathy
MRCP	Member of the Royal College of Physicians
MRI	magnetic resonance imaging
MRV	magnetic resonance venography
MS	multiple sclerosis
MSA	multiple system atrophy
NADHCoQ	nicotinamide adenine dinucleotide coenzyme Q
NARP	neuropathy, ataxia and retinitis pigmentosa
NF	neurofibromatosis
$PaCO_2$	arterial partial pressure of CO_2
PACS	partial anterior cerebral syndrome
PCR	polymerase chain reaction
PD	Parkinson's disease
PET	positron emission tomography
PML	progressive multifocal leucoencephalopathy
PMN	polymorphonuclear leucocyte
PNET	primitive neuro-ectodermal tumour
POCS	posterior cerebral syndrome
PP	periodic paralysis

PPRF	paramedian pontine reticular formation
PrP^c	prion protein
PrP^{sc}	proteinase-resistant prion protein
REM	rapid eye movement
SAH	subarachnoid haemorrhage
SCA	spinocerebellar ataxia
SCLC	small cell lung carcinoma
SLE	systemic lupus erythematosus
SLR	straight leg raising
SMA	spinal muscular atrophy
SNHL	sensorineural hearing loss
SOD1	superoxide dismutase 1
SPECT	single photon emission computed tomography
SSPE	subacute sclerosing pan-encephalitis
SSRI	selective serotonin re-uptake inhibitor
SSS	superior sagittal sinus
SUNCT	short-lasting unilateral neuralgiform headache with conjunctival injection and tearing
TACS	total anterior cerebral syndrome
TIA	transient ischaemic attack
UMN	upper motor neurone
VC	vital capacity
VDRL	venereal disease research laboratory

PREFACE

The review topics in this book have been selected for their topicality and interest and form a broad overview of neurology for trainees and MRCP candidates. However, in this format and with this approach, some aspects will inevitably have been omitted; for these I apologize in advance. Each of the topics gives suggestions for further reading, but not all of the source material is directly referenced. Many of the ideas are built upon my notes from various neurology meetings where there is no published material to cite.

I am grateful to those colleagues who have contributed topics, and to Miss Pat Havard for her secretarial help.

P.E.M. Smith

APHASIA

Aphasia is an acquired disorder of language caused by focal brain lesions. It implies previously normal language and excludes congenital language disorders. Language disorders must be distinguished from disorders of speech, e.g. dysarthria, dysphonia, or of thought, e.g. schizophrenia or confusion.

Glossary

- Naming disturbance (anomia): inability to name objects that are seen and understood by the patient.
- Paraphasias (errors in speech output):
    Literal (phonemic) paraphasias, involving substitution of an incorrect sound, e.g. life for light.
    Verbal (semantic) paraphasias, involving substitution of an incorrect word, e.g. dog for cat.
    Neologisms, where brand new words are invented.
    Speech heavily contaminated by paraphasias is known as 'jargon speech' or 'word salad'.
- Fluency
    Fluent speech has a normal rate of production, sentence length, and melody (prosody) and is spoken without undue effort.
    Non-fluent speech is slow with short sentences, impaired melody (dysprosody) and requires obvious effort.
- Impaired repetition: inability to repeat words or phrases offered by the examiner.
- Impaired auditory comprehension: inability to understand word sounds.

Assessment

Six facets of language should be examined:

- Spontaneous speech with attention paid to fluency and content of speech.
- Naming of bedside objects.
- Auditory comprehension: ability to follow a two- or three-stage command, e.g. 'pick up a piece of paper, fold it and put in on the table'.
- Test of repetition, e.g. 'repeat "no ifs, ands or buts"'.
- Reading.
- Writing.

Neuroanatomical correlations

Although localizations of aphasia syndromes overlap, several principles apply:

- The large majority of language disturbance arises from left hemisphere disease (even in left handed individuals).
- Aphasias with impaired repetition are associated with lesions around the Sylvian fissure; aphasias with normal repetition are associated with lesions outside the peri-Sylvian area.
- Aphasias which are non-fluent, usually with preserved auditory comprehension, are associated with more anterior lesions; aphasias which are fluent, usually with impaired auditory comprehension, are associated with more posterior lesions.

Aphasia types

All true aphasias are characterized by paraphasias and anomia, and so these are of poor localizing value. Aphasia syndromes (each with localizing value) are distinguished by patterns of fluency, repetition and auditory comprehension.

Broca's (expressive or motor) aphasia

1. Language
- Fluency impaired.
- Repetition impaired.
- Auditory comprehension preserved.

Patients present a markedly non-fluent aphasia, speaking few words with frequent pauses and laboured speech. Syntax is often disturbed. Auditory comprehension appears superficially intact but is often mildly defective on formal testing.

2. Associated features
- Right hemiparesis is an almost invariable accompanying feature, greatly aiding correct diagnosis.
- Depression is common, since insight into the disability is preserved.

3. Anatomy. It localizes to the lower postero-lateral left frontal lobe (left frontal operculum).

Wernicke's (receptive or sensory) aphasia

1. Language
- Fluency preserved.
- Repetition impaired.
- Auditory comprehension impaired.

Wernicke's aphasia is the classical example of a fluent aphasia; speech is well articulated but with frequent paraphasias, both verbal and literal. Syntax is less disturbed. Because auditory comprehension is defective patients have little insight into their difficulty and continue to speak, often excessively, even though their speech makes little sense to others. Patients sound confused and, because there are often no other neurological signs, may be misdiagnosed as confused.

2. Anatomy. It localizes to the posterior aspect of left superior temporal gyrus.

Conduction aphasia

1. Language
- Fluency preserved.
- Repetition impaired.
- Auditory comprehension preserved.

This rare disorder is of theoretical interest, since its existence is predictable anatomically through disconnection of the auditory cortex from Broca's area. Speech is fluent but unlike Wernicke's aphasia, less abundant and with only minor comprehension problems. Repetition, though, is profoundly impaired; attempts to repeat provoke literal paraphasias, particularly when using words other than nouns.

2. Associated features
Right sided facial or arm weakness is common.

3. Anatomy. It localizes to the left peri-Sylvian region, involving the primary auditory cortex.

Transcortical motor aphasia

1. Language
- Fluency impaired.
- Repetition preserved.
- Auditory comprehension preserved.

Patients have non-fluent speech with paraphasias and have prominent echolalia with perseveration; it is distinguished from Broca's aphasia by intact repetition, emphasizing the need to test repetition in every patient.

2. Anatomy. It localizes to a small lesion anterior or superior to Broca's area, above the left frontal operculum.

Transcortical sensory aphasia

1. Language
- Fluency preserved.
- Repetition preserved.
- Auditory comprehension impaired.

Patients present similarly to Wernicke's aphasia although again with preserved repetition.

2. Anatomy. Posterior to Wernicke's area in the left parietal or occipito-temporal region.

Global aphasia

1. Language
- Fluency impaired.
- Repetition impaired.
- Verbal comprehension impaired.

A mixed Broca's and Wernicke's aphasia, almost invariably associated with right hemiparesis and hemianopia.

2. Anatomy. It localizes to a large lesion in the left peri-Sylvian region, usually associated with middle cerebral artery infarction.

Related conditions

1. Alexia with agraphia. A left parietal lesion damages connections between the Wernicke's area and the visual association cortex, leading to a marked impairment of both reading and writing ability.

2. Alexia without agraphia (pure alexia). A lesion confined to the left visual association cortex results in inability to read but with preserved writing ability.

3. Pure word deafness. This is not a true aphasia since there is normal fluent speech, but it is characterized by profound loss of auditory comprehension and complete impairment of repetition. It is caused by bilateral lesions of the superior temporal gyrus.

4. Aphemia. A rare variant of Broca's aphasia, where the patient is mute but with preservation of other language functions, including writing. It results from very small lesions in Broca's area.

5. Mutism. Although patients with severe aphasia may be completely mute, other conditions must be considered. Medial frontal lobe lesions involving the supplementary motor area may give rise to akinetic mutism, where patients show no spontaneous speech or motor function but if sufficiently stimulated may be able to repeat gestures and speech normally, and show preserved comprehension.

Causes of aphasia

1. Vascular lesions. The commonest cause of aphasia, particularly ischaemic strokes, giving abrupt onset of aphasia with associated neurological deficit in patients with vascular risk factors.

2. Trauma. Following head injury, particularly with cerebral contusion, depressed skull fracture or intracerebral bleeding, aphasia may accompany other neurological deficits.

3. Tumours. Those involving the left hemisphere may present with gradual onset aphasia.

4. Infections. Some conditions, including abscess or herpes simplex encephalitis, may be complicated by aphasia.

5. Degenerative. Although aphasia may accompany advanced Alzheimer's disease, progressive language dysfunction may occur in isolation (primary progressive aphasia) or as part of focal disorders, e.g. Pick's disease or Creutzfeldt–Jakob disease (CJD).

6. Epileptic aphasia. Landau–Kleffner syndrome is a childhood disorder manifesting as seizures with progressive aphasia.

Further reading

Sarno, MT. *Acquired Aphasia*, 2nd edn. New York: Academic Press Inc., 1991.

Related topics of interest

Coma and disorders of consciousness (p. 37)
Dementia (p. 57)
Epilepsy classification and syndromes (p. 73)
Stroke in young adults (p. 275)

ATAXIA

Hereditary ataxias

Improved genetic knowledge has allowed recent improvements in ataxia classification.

Autosomal recessive cerebellar ataxia

Friedreich's ataxia (FA) is the commonest progressive childhood-onset ataxia. Typically, onset is before age 20 years (mean age 10 years) with cerebellar ataxia, variously accompanied by dysarthria, pyramidal weakness, absent or reduced reflexes, extensor plantar responses and impaired position sense. Electrocardiogram (ECG) is abnormal in most and half develop cardiomyopathy. All show absent or reduced amplitude sensory nerve potentials. A few develop deafness, optic atrophy or diabetes. There is a very large expansion on chromosome 9 (200–1000 GAA repeats) in the first non-coding region (intron) of a gene called frataxin. Larger repeats correlate with earlier age of onset. Gene recognition has included hitherto 'atypical forms' within the definition. Thus, cases presenting up to age 50 years, families with 'pseudodominant' inheritance, cases with retained reflexes or some presenting initially with chorea may all now be classified as FA.

Ataxia with vitamin E deficiency presents as childhood-onset progressive ataxia with areflexia and diminished position sense. There is profound vitamin E deficiency without malabsorption; high dose vitamin E may prevent progression. A vitamin E transporting protein is abnormal, coded on chromosome 8q13.

Autosomal dominant cerebellar ataxia (ADCA)

This is a varied group of disorders, usually of adult onset. The classification is moving from descriptive to genetic as genetic knowledge advances.

- ADCA type I: the onset is usually aged 20–60 years, with progressive truncal ataxia, dysarthria, hyperreflexia and nystagmus; there may be ophthalmoplegia, optic atrophy, peripheral neuropathy, dementia or extrapyramidal features. The four genotypes (spinocerebellar ataxia (SCA) types 1–4, caused by expansions of triplet repeats on different chromosomes), are clinically indistinguishable.

- Machado–Joseph disease presents with progressive ataxia, pyramidal and extrapyramidal signs, occasional peripheral neuropathy and sometimes staring eyes, facial and tongue contraction fasciculations and peripheral muscle wasting. It is classifiable as a variant of ADCA I since the genetic abnormality is in the SCA 3 gene. It is nearly exclusive to people of Portuguese or Azorean descent.
- ADCA types II (genotype SCA 7) and III (genotype SCA 5) refer respectively to ADCA with pigmentary macular dystrophy and ADCA as a pure cerebellar syndrome.
- Hereditary olivopontocerebellar atrophy is the term describing cases with the ADCA I phenotype whose genetic basis remains undetermined.

Autosomal dominant episodic ataxia

These rare genetically heterogeneous conditions manifest as childhood or adolescent-onset attacks of ataxia, dysarthria, vertigo and nystagmus. There are two main types:

1. Type 1. Episodic ataxia/myokymia is a disorder of voltage-gated potassium channels mapping to chromosome 12p, and presents with brief ataxic attacks (seconds to minutes). Myokymia (muscle rippling) without cerebellar signs persists between attacks.

2. Type 2. Acetazolamide-responsive hereditary paroxysmal cerebellar ataxia is a familial calcium channel disorder mapping to chromosome 19p (gene encoding α1 subunit of a brain specific calcium channel), and presents with attacks of ataxia and sometimes vertigo lasting between hours and weeks, often with mild cerebellar signs and nystagmus persisting between attacks. It is closely associated with familial hemiplegic migraine (chromosome 19p13.1) and often there are accompanying symptoms of headache, drowsiness, fever and vomiting. Acetazolamide can reduce the attack frequency.

Ataxia in other hereditary disease

Mitochondrial disorders   See Mitochondrial disorders.

Huntington's disease   Huntington's disease is a triplet repeat disorder manifesting as gradual onset dementia and chorea, occasionally with a young onset akinetic-rigid syndrome. Ataxia occasionally dominates the clinical picture. (See Chorea.)

Dentato-rubro-pallido-luysian atrophy   This triplet repeat disorder (chromosome 12p), first described in Japanese families but increasingly recognized elsewhere, presents with chorea, ataxia, myoclonic epilepsy and dementia. It is now considered the commonest cause of adult-onset hereditary chorea after Huntington's disease.

Wilson's disease   This rare but treatable condition must be considered in any young onset ataxia. (See Chorea.)

Roussy–Lévy syndrome   Roussy–Lévy syndrome is hereditary motor and sensory neuropathy where associated postural tremor is sufficiently severe to resemble cerebellar ataxia. (See Peripheral neuropathy (hereditary).)

Prion diseases   Gerstmann–Sträussler disease and familial CJD may present with ataxia.

Hartnup disease   This and other rare enzyme deficiencies may present as intermittent ataxia.

Leucodystrophies   See Parkinsonian (akinetic rigid) disorders.

Acquired ataxias

Vascular   Strokes affecting the brainstem or cerebellum present with abrupt-onset and often lateralized ataxia. A stuttering onset ataxia with other brainstem signs is seen in basilar artery thrombosis.

Drugs and toxins   • Alcohol is the commonest cause of ataxia. Long-term alcohol use may lead to Purkinje cell damage and permanent ataxia.

- Drugs: phenytoin and other anticonvulsants are commonly associated with ataxia in toxic doses.
- Biological toxins such as that acquired from the marine toxin ciguatoxin, contaminating fish and shellfish, may lead to an acute ataxic illness through sodium channel blockade.

Inflammatory

1. Infections
- Viral encephalitis may involve predominantly the brainstem and cerebellum (rhombencephalitis), especially in *Mycoplasma* infections.
- HIV disease may also present as ataxia.

2. Demyelination
- Multiple sclerosis is the commonest cause of chronic ataxia in neurological practice (and postgraduate examinations).
- The Miller Fisher variant of Guillain–Barré syndrome presents with ataxia, external ophthalmoparesis and areflexia without weakness. Anti-Gq1b ganglioside antibody is almost invariably present and is probably pathogenic.
- Bickerstaff's encephalitis is a post-infectious brainstem demyelination presenting as rapidly progressive brainstem dysfunction with cranial nerve palsies. No specific organism has been identified. Anti-Gq1b ganglioside antibodies are often found suggesting it is part of Miller Fisher syndrome.
- Central pontine myelinolysis is a rare brainstem syndrome usually seen in alcoholics and occasionally associated with rapid correction of hyponatraemia from any cause. Demyelination is seen in the central pons.

Structural causes

1. Neoplastic
- Posterior fossa tumours may be:
(a) Primary, usually in children, e.g. cystic astrocytoma, medulloblastoma, ependymoma or haemangio-blastoma.
(b) Secondary, usually adults, e.g. melanoma, bronchus, breast.
- Paraneoplastic syndromes: breast and ovarian malignancies may present with ataxia.

2. *Communicating hydrocephalus.* See Dementia.

3. *Chiari malformation*
- This is an important treatable cause of ataxia, often with headache and downbeat nystagmus.

Deficiency states

- Vitamin E deficiency presents as ataxia with areflexia and is seen in conditions with malabsorption of fat-soluble vitamins, e.g. coeliac disease, cystic fibrosis.
- Wernicke's encephalopathy: thiamine deficiency may arise through alcoholism or by repeated vomiting, e.g. hyperemesis gravidarum. Mamillary body haemorrhages lead to the triad of confusion, ataxia and external ophthalmoparesis. A low red cell transketolase is a useful marker of thiamine deficiency rapidly reversed with thiamine supplements.

Prion diseases

Sporadic CJD may present with ataxia (Brownell–Oppenheimer variant).

Endocrine

Hypothyroidism presents a rare reversible ataxia, although usually the other features are then obvious.

Functional

Occasionally, no cause for ataxia can be found and psychological causes suspected.

Sensory ataxia

Ataxia may also occur through defective feedback from peripheral sensory pathways. Altered position sense in the hands is characteristic of a high cervical myelopathy; rarer causes of sensory ataxia include subacute combined degeneration of the cord from vitamin B_{12} deficiency, tabes dorsalis and subacute sensory neuropathy (either post-viral or paraneoplastic).

Postural instability

This is a characteristic feature of Parkinson's disease and of some akinetic-rigid syndromes, e.g. Steele–Richardson syndrome.

Further reading

Harding AE. Inherited ataxia. *Current Opinion in Neurology*, 1995; **8**: 306–309.

Related topics of interest

Chorea (p. 31)
Dementia (p. 57)
Encephalitis (p. 68)
HIV neurology (p. 136)
Mitochondrial disorders (p. 146)
Multiple sclerosis (p. 164)
Paraneoplastic neurological syndromes (p. 215)
Parkinsonian (akinetic rigid) syndromes (p. 220)
Prion diseases (p. 246)

AUTONOMIC DISORDERS

The autonomic nervous system

Central

The hypothalamus, under the influence of cortex and limbic system (olfactory, hippocampus, amygdaloid, cingular cortex and septal area) controls the autonomic nervous system via descending pathways through the pons and to the spinal cord.

Peripheral

The (efferent) autonomic nervous system comprises sympathetic and parasympathetic pre-ganglionic neurones in the brain and spinal cord.

- Sympathetic myelinated fibres emerge at the thoracic and upper lumbar cord level and synapse in paravertebral ganglia and then in other ganglia, e.g. stellate, superior and inferior mesenteric.
- Parasympathetic fibres travel with cranial nerves III, VII, IX and X and also emerge with sacral roots 2,3 and 4.

Causes of dysfunction

Primary

1. Acute and subacute. Acute (or subacute) autonomic neuropathy, a variant of Guillain–Barré syndrome, presents usually following a febrile illness over days or weeks with autonomic symptoms, particularly postural hypotension, loss of sweating, sphincter dysfunction, impotence, dry mouth and eyes. Cerebrospinal (CSF) protein may be elevated and recovery occurs gradually over months or years. Autonomic dysfunction and liability to brady- and tachyarrhythmias is a characteristic feature of Guillain–Barré syndrome, with implications for mortality in this condition.

2. Chronic
- Pure autonomic failure results from discrete loss of intermediolateral column cells (the final common pathway for the sympathetic system). It occurs in

middle aged or elderly patients presenting initially with impotence or loss of libido, reduced sweating and disabling postural dizziness over months or years.
- Multiple system atrophy is commonly associated with autonomic failure (Shy–Drager variant).

Secondary

1. Autonomic neuropathy. The commonest causes of autonomic neuropathy are diabetes mellitus, alcohol toxicity, amyloidosis, and paraneoplastic disease.

2. Spinal cord lesions. Autonomic dysreflexia is a characteristic feature of high cord lesions (above T6); loss of blood pressure control can lead to recurrent hypertensive crises with drowsiness and even coma.

3. Medications. These may lead to autonomic dysfunction directly acting on central autonomic neurones (alcohol or tricyclic antidepressants), on peripheral autonomic neurones (vasodilators) or indirectly through damage to neuromuscular junctions, e.g. organophosphates.

Clinical features

The range of autonomic manifestations is very broad.

Cardiovascular

Failure of cardiovascular autonomic innervation gives the most characteristic picture of autonomic neuropathy, and particularly the manifestations of postural hypotension. In contrast to the active vasodilatation and bradycardia of reflex (vasovagal) syncope, here there is failure to vasoconstrict in response to hypotension. It results from dysfunction, often age related, of the autonomic nervous system. The effects of postural hypotensive ischaemia in various organs are:

- Brain: dizziness, visual blurring, fainting, weakness, lethargy and fatigue.
- Muscle: shoulder and neck 'coat hanger' pain; low back and buttock aching.
- Heart: exertional chest pain.
- Kidney: diurnal oliguria, nocturnal polyuria.

Pre-syncope and syncope occur within seconds or minutes of assuming the upright posture. Patients are particularly vulnerable after rising from lying and after meals; the hour after breakfast is the most likely time for syncope. Unlike in reflex syncope, the skin may be warm, the pulse rate unchanged and sweating absent.

The main risk factors for orthostatic (postural) syncope are:

- Elderly related autonomic dysfunction.
- Autonomic neuropathy, especially from diabetes or alcohol.
- Medication, especially antihypertensives, phenothiazines, tricyclic antidepressants, anti-Parkinsonian treatment and diuretics.

Sudomotor

Disordered sweating may lead to anhydrosis and heat intolerance.

Alimentary

Xerostomia, dysphagia, constipation and (particularly in diabetic neuropathy) nocturnal diarrhoea.

Urinary

Urgency and urge incontinence may be exacerbated by nocturnal polyuria.

Reproductive

Erectile and ejaculatory failure are early features of autonomic disease.

Respiratory

Peripheral autonomic involvement may lead to stridor and sleep apnoea. Disturbed central control of breathing may lead to involuntary inspiratory gasps or 'cluster' breathing and rarely to autonomous (involuntary) breathing.

Ocular

Horner's syndrome resulting from disturbed sympathetic supply to the eye results in the triad of small pupil, partial ptosis and enophthalmos, occasionally with ipsilateral facial anhydrosis. It follows lesions anywhere in the anatomical 'U' which runs from the hypothalamus via the brain stem (e.g. posterior inferior cerebellar artery infarct) emerging from the cord at T1 and 2 (Pancoast tumour) and ascending in the carotid plexus (carotid dissection) to relay in the ciliary ganglion before innervating the pupil. Atonic (Adie) pupils are due to post ganglionic parasympathetic lesions giving a pupil unreactive to light and only poorly responsive to accommodation. There is denervation super-sensitivity to topical pilocarpine. Adie syndrome is a benign condition combining Adie pupil and lost deep tendon reflexes.

Management

Orthostatic syncope

1. Non-pharmacological
- Avoidance of provoking manoeuvres and postures, e.g. sudden standing from lying, straining, Valsalva manoeuvre, strenuous exercise, hot baths, large carbohydrate meals, alcohol and vasodepressor drugs (e.g. L-dopa).
- Night time head up tilt reduces renal perfusion and so limits night time polyuria and morning hypotension. Small frequent meals, increased salt intake and gentle exercise, particularly swimming, are helpful. Certain manoeuvres reduce peripheral pooling and enhance venous return: standing cross legged whilst activating calf and thigh muscles or kneeling with the head below the level of the heart. Elastic stockings are rarely helpful.

2. Pharmacological
- Mineralocorticoids, e.g. fludrocortisone acetate 50–200 µg nocte may help to maintain blood pressure but often gives supine hypertension and ankle oedema.
- Sympathomimetics, e.g. ephedrine or midodrine may help.
- Peptide release inhibitors, e.g. octreotide can reduce splanchnic pooling.
- Vasopressin analogues, e.g. desmopressin, are particularly useful for nocturnal polyuria.

Specific conditions
- Provoking drugs should be removed.
- Carotid sinus sensitivity may require a cardiac pacemaker.
- Acute and subacute dysautonomia may be limited by immunoglobulin treatment.
- Amyloid autonomic neuropathy may respond to liver transplantation.
- Diabetic autonomic neuropathy may respond to pancreatic transplantation.

Further reading

Bannister R, Mathias CJ, eds. *Autonomic Failure. A Textbook of Clinical Disorders of the Autonomic Nervous System,* 3rd edn. Oxford: Oxford University Press, 1992.

Related topics of interest

BENIGN INTRACRANIAL HYPERTENSION

Benign intracranial hypertension (BIH), formerly known as 'pseudotumour cerebri' or 'otitic hydocephalus', is a condition of unknown aetiology, occurring particularly in obese young women, in which intracranial hypertension leads to headaches, papilloedema and potential visual loss. It is an important preventable cause of blindness in young people and is not as benign as its title suggests.

Aetiology

In most cases the cause is unknown. There is an imbalance between CSF production (choroid plexus) and its absorption (arachnoid granulations) in a mechanism similar to glaucoma in the eye.

Underlying causes

1. *Hormonal.* It is more common in obese women with menstrual irregularity. The contraceptive pill has been implicated (without definite evidence) and danazol may provoke BIH. Elevated human chorionic gonadotrophin (HCG) levels in testicular tumour is a rare cause in men. Addison's disease and long term corticosteroid treatment (paradoxically since steroids are sometimes used in its treatment) may also provoke BIH. Hypoparathyroidism (primary or secondary) may lead to BIH.

2. *Drugs.* BIH may be associated with certain treatments including antibiotics (especially tetracycline, nalidixic acid and nitrofurantoin), vitamin A, retinoids, lithium, steroids, indomethacin and danazol.

3. *Venous sinus thrombosis.* This may present as BIH and itself is associated with proliferative haematological disease such as polycythaemia rubra vera, essential thrombocythaemia, paroxysmal nocturnal haemoglobinuria and myeloma.

Clinical features

1. *Patient characteristics.* The overall incidence is 1 per 100 000 per year but among obese women of childbearing age it reaches 19 per 100 000.

- Female to male ratio is 8:1.
- Mean body weight is 40% overweight for height.

2. *Presenting features*
- Headache of pressure type, worse on lying flat, stooping or straining, often with vomiting.
- Visual obscurations, e.g. dark patches or flashes may

occur on straining; occasionally diplopia from VI palsy occurs.
- Papilloedema with associated enlarged blind spots on visual field testing.

Investigations

The diagnosis of BIH is based upon:

- Brain imaging (CT or MRI) normal except for small ventricles and occasional empty sella.
- Cerebrospinal fluid opening pressure exceeds 250 cm H_2O with normal constituents.
- Visual fields showing peripheral field encroachment with blind spots enlargement.

Visual acuity may be deceptively well preserved in the early stages but visual loss may occur:

- Early through macular oedema or haemorrhage.
- Late through encroachment of the constricted peripheral field or enlarged blind spot on to the central field of vision.

Management

1. *Remove underlying causes.* These should be sought, excluded and treated. BIH in a man or in a thin woman is sufficiently rare to prompt a thorough search for an underlying cause. A careful drug history, a thrombophilia screen, and search for malignancy, hormonal factors or hypoparathyroidism are particularly important.

2. *Medication*
- Weight loss should be encouraged through sensible dieting.
- The carbonic anhydrase inhibitor, acetazolamide, or the loop diuretic, frusemide, may depress CSF production and so lower intracranial pressure.
- Corticosteroids are often used though their mechanism of benefit is unclear and their side effects troublesome.
- Repeated lumbar punctures are unnecessary except in the acute situation where rapid temporary relief of symptoms is needed.

3. *Monitoring.* Regular monitoring (e.g. monthly) is recommended in the early stages. Collaboration with an ophthalmologist is useful.

- Visual fields must be monitored by perimetry.
- Visual acuity must be carefully assessed.
- Fundal photographs give an objective assessment of the disc appearance.

4. Surgery. If, despite medical treatment, there is progressive visual field deterioration or a reduction of visual acuity not due to macular oedema, a surgical procedure may be indicated.

- Optic nerve sheath fenestration sets up a chronic CSF filter into the orbit and removes pressure from the optic nerve; it is regarded by ophthalmologists as the procedure of first choice.
- Lumbo-peritoneal shunt will effectively lower the CSF pressure but there may be complications including blockage or infection and the need for re-operation.
- Subtemporal decompression is now rarely used owing to its high complication rate of seizures and stroke.

Prognosis   Overall, the prognosis with careful monitoring and timely intervention is very good but it is essential not to underestimate the potential risk to vision.

Further reading

Corbett JJ, Thompson S. The rational management of idiopathic intracranial hypertension. *Archives of Neurology* 1989; **46:** 1049–51.

Related topics of interest

CEREBRAL VENOUS THROMBOSIS

Cerebral venous thrombosis (CVT) is a relatively rare disorder with an estimated incidence of four per million per year. The diagnosis is often missed or delayed due to its heterogeneous presentation and failure to consider it as a possible differential.

Anatomy

Cerebral veins contain 70% of the total cerebral blood volume and are arranged into the superficial and deep venous system.

The superficial system drains blood from the outer 2 cm of cerebral cortex into the superior sagittal sinus (SSS). The sinus follows the falx cerebri towards the occiput where it drains into the transverse sinuses (usually the right, but there is wide anatomical variation). From here venous blood drains from the transverse sinuses into the sigmoid sinuses, into the right and left internal jugular veins.

The deep cerebral veins drain blood in a centripetal direction from deep brain structures into the great cerebral vein of Galen. From here blood drains into the straight sinus and then into the torcula (confluence of the superior sagittal sinus and the right and left transverse sinuses) and leaves the head in the internal jugular veins.

Clinical features

Clinical features of CVT are extraordinarily variable and depend upon the site and extent of involvement of cerebral veins or venous sinuses. Most often, cerebral veins and venous sinuses are affected together.

- Cerebral vein thrombosis frequently leads to cerebral venous infarction. This differs from arterial occlusion infarction in that it is not confined to any one arterial distribution, there is associated oedema, sometimes haemorrhage, and seizures are a common presenting feature. Thus, patients present with subacute onset of focal neurological signs, e.g. hemiparesis, together with headache, altered consciousness and partial or secondarily generalized seizures.
- Sinus thrombosis: if thrombosis is restricted to the superior sagittal or lateral sinuses the clinical picture is dominated by raised intracranial pressure (headache and papilloedema). Clinically this can be indistinguishable from benign intracranial hypertension.

- Although headache is the commonest symptom there are no distinguishing characteristics that help one think of CVT. At one extreme of the spectrum the headache may be acute and severe suggesting a diagnosis of subarachnoid haemorrhage and at the other a chronic daily headache suggestive of tension type headache. The most striking feature about headache in CVT is its association with clinical signs which occur in the majority and would prompt further investigation (*Table 1*).

Table 1. Symptoms and signs of CVT

Symptoms/signs	% Frequency
Headache	41–100
Papilloedema	39–66
Motor or sensory deficit	34–40
Seizures	29–45
Mental state changes	26–50
Aphasia	10–16
Cranial nerve deficits	2–12
Cerebellar signs	Rare
Nystagmus	Rare
Hearing loss	Rare
Bilateral or alternating cortical signs	Rare

Causes

- Local infection (ears, sinuses, tonsils, teeth), the commonest cause until the arrival of antibiotics, now rarely causes CVT.
- Pregnancy, puerperium and the oral contraceptives are the commonest causes.
- Inherited thrombophilia: protein C, Protein S, or antithrombin III deficiency and Factor V Leiden.
- Malignancy (direct infiltration of the venous sinuses or associated thrombophilia).
- Acquired haematological: thrombocythaemia, iron deficiency anaemia, primary polycythaemia, paroxysmal nocturnal haemoglobinuria, disseminated intravascular coagulation, lupus anticoagulant, anticardiolipin antibodies.
- Connective tissue and inflammatory: Behçet's disease, systemic lupus erythematosus, sarcoidosis,

Wegener's granulomatosis, polyarteritis nodosa, ulcerative colitis.
- Iatrogenic: intracranial surgery, neck vein cannulation, danazol, L-asparaginase, methotrexate.
- Other: closed head injury, dehydration, congestive heart failure, congenital heart disease, nephrotic syndrome, homocystinuria.

There is much interest in the interaction between inherited and acquired risk factors.

Investigations

- CT (computed tomography) brain scan is unfortunately normal in 5–42% of patients with CVT. Small ventricles, focal hypodensity and focal hyperdensity (haemorrhage) are each seen in some cases. The 'empty delta' sign (or empty triangle sign) occurs in <35% of contrast CT examinations in CVT. The SSS walls enhance with contrast whilst the lumen (full of thrombus) remains hypodense giving a 'ring' appearance. If one is considering the diagnosis, a normal CT is insufficient for exclusion and further imaging with formal angiography or magnetic resonance imaging (MRI) is required.
- Intra-arterial angiography has been the definitive 'gold standard' investigation but is invasive and venous thrombosis can be missed if the entire venous phase is not visualized. MRI together with magnetic resonance venography (MRV) are set to take over as the investigation of choice as MRI becomes more available.
- MRI/MRV, although safe, is difficult in certain situations, e.g. if the patient is restless or ventilated. However, unless contraindicated, MRI/MRV should now be the first-line investigation in suspected CVT.
- General investigation: There are no specific markers; routine haematological and biochemical investigation are often normal. Cerebrospinal fluid examination may show elevated protein or white cell count but is non-specific. An extended thrombophilia screen, indicated in all proven CVT cases, often reveals an inherited thrombotic tendency. The contraceptive pill may be a factor that reveals an hitherto latent inherited prothrombotic tendency.

Management

This follows three lines; symptomatic, antithrombotic and aetiological.

1. Symptomatic. This is directed at seizure control and reducing raised intracranial pressure.

• Symptomatic seizures should be treated appropriately. The likelihood of acute symptomatic seizures is sufficiently high to justify prophylactic antiepileptic medication. Any first line anticonvulsant can be used; phenytoin is rapidly acting and is widely used in the acute situation. Seizure recurrence following the acute illness is unlikely and antiepileptic medication can safely be withdrawn 6 months to a year after diagnosis if the patient remains seizure free.

• Raised intracranial pressure management depends upon its severity. All patients with thrombosis of a major sinus will be expected to have some raised pressure. Minor brain swelling does not require treatment. A decreased conscious level or rapidly deteriorating vision implies significantly raised pressure and is usually treated with 20% mannitol and dexamethasone. Repeated lumbar puncture, optic nerve fenestration, lumbar peritoneal or ventriculo-peritoneal shunting are used for resistant cases.

2. Antithrombotic. Treatment is with heparin, warfarin and/or thrombolysis with urokinase or recombinant tissue plasminogen activator. There has only been one randomized controlled trial of heparin in CVT, with small patient numbers ($n = 20$) but with a definite reduction in both morbidity and mortality with intravenous heparin compared to placebo. The evidence for the benefit of oral anticoagulation comes from case series only. Most patients are anticoagulated with warfarin for 3 months to 1 year unless there is an underlying disorder requiring a longer period of anticoagulation. Thrombolysis, intravenously or locally, may be beneficial in some cases but the evidence for its efficacy is based on scattered case reports. Randomized trial data are needed before widespread use of thrombolysis can be recommended.

3. Aetiological. The underlying cause of the CVT, if identified, should be treated or the provoking factor withdrawn.

Outcome

This has improved due to widespread use of antibiotics, early diagnosis and the detection of less severe cases which previously would have gone undiagnosed. However, mortality still ranges from 5–30%.

Conclusion

Although rare, CVT is treatable and should be added to the differential diagnosis of anyone presenting with headache associated with clinical signs. Unless the diagnosis is considered cases will be missed.

Further reading

Bousser M-G, Ross Russell R. *Cerebral Venous Thrombosis. Major Problems in Neurology,* Vol. 33. London: WB Saunders, 1997.

Related topics of interest

CEREBROSPINAL FLUID

Physiology

There are 150 ml of cerebrospinal fluid (CSF); 20 ml are ventricular. Daily production is 300–500 ml, giving a 2–3 times daily turnover. Two-thirds of the CSF derives from the blood–CSF barrier; one-third from the blood–brain barrier (BBB).

CSF circulation begins from the choroid plexus and interstitium, passes through the ventricles to the surface of the brain and spinal cord and is reabsorbed by arachnoid granulations.

The lumbar area is a cul-de-sac, where turnover is slower.

Constituents

These derive from:

- Filtration from serum on the basis of charge and size.
- Active transport of some components.
- Synthesis within choroid.
- Brain tissue.

1. *Normal values*
- Protein 0.24–0.54 g/l (varies between laboratories).
- Glucose: >50% serum value.
- Cells: <4 white blood cells/mm^3.
- Pressure is generated by arterial and interstitial pressures:
    Lumbar = 40–200 mm H$_2$O.
    Ventricular = 50–180 mm H$_2$O (adult); 120–150 mm H$_2$O (child).

2. *Abnormalities*
- Disruption of blood–brain–CSF barrier results in CSF changes. This can occur at several levels: vascular endothelium, spinal roots, meninges and brain. Differing protein content patterns can differentiate levels of barrier disruption.
- Serum changes result in CSF changes, hence BBB function assessments use serum parameters.
- Primary brain disorders may release proteins, occasionally disease specific.

Lumbar puncture

Technique

Correct positioning is vital. The patient adopts a left lateral position flexed into a fetal posture with one pillow between the legs and one under the head. Shoulders and hips are aligned at right angles to the bed. The L3,4 interspace is perpendicularly below the iliac crest. The spinal needle should be no larger than a 23 gauge and ideally 26 gauge. It is inserted perpendicular to the skin and aimed at 20 degrees towards the head. Advance in a single movement, removing the stylet after resistance eases, to allow CSF to flow. Five ml can safely be removed. A fine atraumatic 'blunt' needle gives less likelihood of post LP headache as does replacement of the needle stylet before final needle withdrawal.

Complications

- Low pressure headache (see below).
- Traumatic tap: this is indicated by declining red cell counts in serial samples. Spectrophotometry may help to differentiate subarachnoid haemorrhage with xanthrochromia.

Measurements

1. *Proteins.* These may be measured in three ways:
- Quantified. This requires reference to serum values and normal ranges for age and site of CSF sampling, e.g. ventricular CSF has a high pre-albumin level.
- Semi-quantified. The use of ratios and indices to correct for BBB damage.
- Qualitative. Using electrophoresis, particularly isoelectric focusing for IgG, antigen immunoblotting and antibody affinity studies offer highly specific and sensitive results.

2. *Cells.* The number and morphology are assessed. Function measurements, e.g. cytokine responses, are research tools only.

3. *Organisms.* Viral recovery is poor from CSF, bacterial recovery is better. Antigen detection is more sensitive using polymerase chain reaction (PCR) and enzyme linked immunosorbent assay (ELISA).

CSF in disease states – general principles

Blood–brain barrier function

- Total protein is a crude measure, the albumin ratio is better, i.e. CSF protein divided by serum albumin. Protein electrophoresis is the most sensitive. Barrier function may reflect disease activity and treatment response. It may be correlated with other measures, e.g. MRI scanning.
- Immunoglobulin analysis. IgG measurement using isoelectric focusing looking for oligoclonal banding is best. IgM quantified analysis is difficult but IgM may be an early marker for infection, e.g. Lyme disease. IgA is rarely measured but is elevated in multiple sclerosis (MS) and infections.

Disease associated proteins/antigens

- Specific. Viral and bacterial antigens detected by PCR, immunoblotting or ELISA.
- Non-specific associated with tumour, inflammatory or degenerative disorders.

Oligoclonal IgG

- Local intrathecal synthesis of oligoclonal IgG is predominantly found in MS but is associated with other demyelinating disorders, CNS infections, post infectious disorders (e.g. acute disseminated encephalomyelitis), paraneoplastic disturbances and CNS inflammatory disorders including vasculitis.
- Oligoclonal IgG is not found in degenerative, vascular, psychiatric, metabolic or neuromuscular disorders.
- An identical pattern of oligoclonal IgG in serum and CSF (leak pattern) occurs in response to any systemic disorder producing peripheral lymphocyte activation, e.g. Guillain–Barré syndrome.

CSF in specific disorders

Meningitis and encephalitis   These are detailed elsewhere.

Multiple sclerosis

- Locally synthesized oligoclonal IgG is found in 95% of clinically definite MS.
- BBB function is abnormal in acute relapses and in chronic progressive disease. CSF total protein is modestly elevated (usually <1 g/l).

- Cell count: 50% have between 5 and 35 white cells/mm^3, usually lymphocytes; >50 cells is unusual.
- Free light chains, tumour necrosis factor alpha and myelin basic protein are elevated in CSF during acute relapses and the latter two (to a lesser extent) in chronic progressive disease. These are not specific findings. Non-specific immune system activation results in production of viral specific antibodies and cytokine release but none of these have obvious aetiological significance nor are they useful diagnostically.

Inflammatory disorders

1. Systemic lupus erythematosus. Elevation of CSF anti-neuronal antibodies occurs. 25% have locally synthesized oligoclonal IgG and disrupted BBB correlating with disease activity. CSF ribosomal P antibody (a serum marker for neuropsychiatric disease) is not elevated.

2. Sarcoidosis. Disease activity does not correlate with CSF angiotensin converting enzyme values. 50% have locally synthesized oligoclonal IgG. Kveim reacts with some CSF IgG clones and is specific for neurological sarcoidosis.

3. Behçet's. Oligoclonal IgG is an infrequent finding and no specific CSF changes occur.

4. Stiff man syndrome. This is an autoimmune disorder with circulating anti-glutamate receptor antibodies resulting in pancreatic damage and diabetes and spinal cord damage. All patients have oligoclonal IgG in the CSF with specific immunoreactivity to the glutamate receptor.

Paraneoplastic disorders

- Antineuronal nuclear antibodies (anti-Hu) are associated with small cell lung carcinoma producing sensory neuropathy and encephalomyelitis. These rarely occur with breast and prostatic carcinoma.
- Anti-Purkinje cell antibodies (anti-Yo) are associated with ovarian and gynaecological malignancies and produce cerebellar degenerations. They rarely occur with breast carcinoma and Hodgkin's.

- Locally synthesized oligoclonal IgG is associated with paraneoplastic disease but not primary or secondary tumour deposits.

Creutzfeldt–Jakob disease (CJD)

A CSF marker protein, 14-3-3, has been reported in new variant CJD, but is not sensitive, and may not be specific. CSF protein is elevated in 29%, and one case of oligoclonal IgG is reported.

Dementia

Tau protein is elevated in Alzheimer's and other degenerative dementias, but has a low sensitivity.

Abnormal CSF pressure

High pressure

Several conditions cause elevated CSF pressure with a normal or non-diagnostic MRI or CT brain scan, e.g. meningitis, encephalitis, benign or idiopathic intracranial hypertension, dural sinus and venous thrombosis, hepatic and metabolic encephalopathies, Guillain–Barré syndrome, lead encephalopathy, hyponatraemia and water intoxication, spinal cord tumours.

Low pressure

- Iatrogenic. Post lumbar puncture, where risk increases with needle size and multiple punctures, and intracranial or spinal trauma or surgery with CSF leakage.
- Spontaneous intracranial hypotension (Schallen-brand's syndrome) follows spontaneous rupture of a spinal arachnoid cyst.

1. Clinical features. Headache increased by the erect posture or straining and reduced by supine position. Tinnitus and auditory phenomena, VI nerve palsies (uni- or bilateral), and nausea, vertigo, vomiting on postural change all occur.

2. Investigations. MRI brain scanning shows dural enhancement due to compensatory filling by blood to equalize intracranial pressure. The appearances can be mistaken for diffuse meningeal infiltration by tumour. Subdural haematomas or hygromas also occur. CSF may be blood stained as a consequence of rupture of bridging cortical vein.

3. Management. Post lumbar puncture leaks usually respond to conservative management and settle within hours to days. Surgical and traumatic CSF leaks may require surgical repair. Identification of leaking site can be problematical but fine cut CT, MRI or isotope cisternography can localize. Spontaneous intracranial hypotension may take months to resolve, but even when no leak is identified, epidural blood patch may help.

Further reading

Thompson EJ. Cerebrospinal fluid. *Journal of Neurology, Neurosurgery and Psychiatry*, 1995; **59:** 2349–57.
McLean BN. Lumbar puncture. *Medicine*, 1996; **24** (4) 29–30.

Related topics of interest

CHOREA

'Chorea' derives from the Greek for 'dance'. It is defined (World Federation of Neurologists) as 'a state of excessive, spontaneous movements, irregularly timed, randomly distributed and abrupt'. Severity varies from restlessness with mild, intermittent exaggeration of gesture and expression, fidgeting movements and unstable dance-like gait to a continuous flow of disabling, violent movements. Its anatomical basis remains uncertain.

Causes

Many inherited and acquired conditions may be associated with chorea and the list below is not exhaustive.

1. Hereditary
- Huntington's disease.
- Benign hereditary chorea.
- Neuroacanthocytosis.
- Paroxysmal choreoathetosis.
- Dentato-rubro-pallido-luysian atrophy (DRPLA).
- Wilson's disease.
- Machado–Joseph disease.
- Ataxia telangiectasia.
- Tuberose sclerosis.
- Hallevorden–Spatz disease.
- Lesch–Nyhan syndrome.
- Lysosomal storage disorders.
- Amino acid disorders.
- Leigh's disease.
- Porphyria.

2. Acquired
- Drugs (neuroleptics, antiparkinsonian drugs, phenytoin, amphetamines, tricyclics, oral contraceptives).
- Pregnancy.
- Alcohol.
- Anoxia.
- Carbon monoxide, manganese, mercury, thallium, toluene.
- Hyperthyroidism, hypoparathyroidism.
- Hyponatraemia, hypocalcaemia, hypomagnesaemia.
- Hypo- or hyperglycaemia.
- Sydenham's chorea.
- Systemic lupus erythematosus.
- Cerebrovascular disease.

- Tumours.
- Polycythaemia rubra vera.

Huntington's disease (HD)   First described in 1872, HD is a progressive disease combining chorea with psychiatric illness and dementia. It is autosomal dominant with complete penetrance.

1. Genetics. The gene responsible for HD maps to chromosome 4p16.3, coding a protein termed huntingtin. The gene contains an expanded trinucleotide (CAG) repeat translated into an expanded polyglutamine tract which may itself be pathogenic. All cases have >30 repeats, the larger repeats being inherited paternally.

2. Clinical features. Symptoms start at any age but usually in the 4th and 5th decades. Chorea may be the presenting feature but the first symptoms are often mental changes first noticed by the family. The clinical course is relentless with death occurring 10–20 years after symptom onset. Younger patients who present with a parkinsonian (akinetic-rigid) syndrome (the Westphal variant), are usually paternally inherited, and have a poorer prognosis than adults. Conversely, the presentation in elderly patients may be with a mild motor condition and little cognitive impairment.

A known family history of HD is clearly important in making the clinical diagnosis. Without a clear family history one should enquire about premature death in family members, psychiatric illness and deviant behaviour.

Clinical signs include chorea, ataxia and cognitive impairment. Saccadic eye movements are often slowed and jerky.

3. Investigations. Genetic testing on blood is available. Disease confirmation testing is relatively straightforward but pre-symptomatic testing of unaffected family members is undertaken only after appropriate and prolonged counselling.

CT and MRI may demonstrate caudate nucleus atrophy.

At post-mortem the brain is of reduced weight with generalized atrophy; the basal ganglia, especially the caudate nuclei, are particularly atrophic.

4. Management. This is supportive, there is no cure. Medical treatment for chorea includes the neuroleptic drugs, especially tetrabenazine, but depression can be a troublesome side effect. Psychiatric disease should be treated traditionally.

5. Support group. Huntington's Disease Association, 108 Battersea High Street, London SW11 3HP, UK.

Benign familial chorea

This condition, also known as chronic juvenile hereditary chorea or familial essential chorea, was first described in 1967. It is autosomal dominant and presents in infancy or childhood with generalized chorea but does not progress. Mild mental retardation has been described. Confusion with HD is resolved by genetic testing.

Neuroacanthocytosis

Common in Japan, but in practice an extremely rare disease, this condition may be inherited as an autosomal recessive. Its hallmark is peripheral blood acanthocytes, due to defective membrane lipids.

1. Clinical features. Symptoms begin in the third and fourth decade with orofacial dyskinesias including tongue protrusion and biting, vocal and motor tics. Patients may develop generalized chorea, cognitive changes, parkinsonism, a motor peripheral neuropathy and seizures. Its progression is variable with death usually within a few years.

2. Diagnosis. A fresh blood smear should be examined for acanthocytes comprising >10% of the peripheral blood film. Serum creatine kinase is usually elevated. Nerve conduction studies confirm a motor neuropathy. Late in the disease, CT may demonstrate caudate nucleus atrophy. Post-mortem confirms atrophy of the striatum (putamen and caudate).

3. Management. There is no cure. Treatment is supportive and aimed at treating chorea and controlling seizures.

Paroxysmal choreoathetosis

These conditions are thought to be potassium channelopathies.

1. Kinesigenic. Paroxysmal kinesigenic choreoathetosis, shows autosomal dominant inheritance in 50% of cases and affects males to females 4:1. Paroxysms of chorea or dystonia are precipitated by sudden movement or startle. The duration of these episodes is usually seconds but rarely more than 5 minutes. They may occur up to a hundred times per day. Treatment is with low doses of anticonvulsants.

2. *Non-kinesigenic.* Paroxysmal non-kinesigenic choreoathetosis is autosomal dominant and affects males to females 3:2. Onset is usually during infancy. Attacks are precipitated by fatigue, stress, alcohol and caffeine and last 5 minutes to 4 hours; frequency varies from several times daily to every 3 months. It is difficult to treat and does not respond to anticonvulsants.

Dentato-rubro-pallido-luysian atrophy (DRPLA)

This rare autosomal dominant disease is due to an expansion of a trinucleotide (CAG) repeat on chromosome 12. As more cases become recognized so the clinical phenotype of this disease broadens. Clinical features include ataxia, dystonia, choreoathetosis, dementia, myoclonus and epilepsy. It is worth looking for this mutation in families with the HD phenotype who test negative for the HD gene.

Wilson's disease (hepatolenticular degeneration)

This autosomal recessive disease of copper metabolism results from a defect in a copper-transporting ATPase coded on chromosome 13. The actual pathogenesis remains unclear but copper accumulates in the liver eventually resulting in liver failure from cirrhosis.

1. *Clinical features.* It presents in children or young adults with either tremor, chorea, dysarthria, dysphagia, drooling, psychiatric disturbance, seizures, dementia or just cirrhosis. When cerebral dysfunction is present the patient invariably has Kayser–Fleischer (KF) rings (yellow-brown copper deposition in Descemet's membrane of the cornea). Untreated, death occurs within 10 years.

2. *Diagnosis.* If the diagnosis is suspected, slit lamp examination looking for KF rings is mandatory. Liver function tests are abnormal. Serum caeruloplasmin and serum copper are both reduced and 24 hour urinary copper is increased. For practical purposes if these are normal, Wilson's is excluded. However, because of the

importance of the diagnosis, liver biopsy dry copper level is needed for certainty.

3. Management. This is a treatable condition and although rare should be considered in any young person with unexplained psychiatric or neurological disease. Treatment is with D-penicillamine.

Sydenham's chorea (rheumatic chorea, St Vitus' dance)

Sydenham's chorea is a major manifestation of acute rheumatic fever but may be the sole manifestation of a group A ß-haemolytic streptococcal infection. The suspected aetiology is autoimmune, with cross-reactivity of antibodies between streptococcus and striatal neurones.

1. Clinical features. With the introduction of antibiotics, Sydenham's chorea has virtually disappeared from developed countries but remains endemic in the third world. Chorea develops months after streptococcal infection and usually affects girls aged 5–15 years. The chorea is usually generalized but hemichorea may occur. Chorea develops insidiously, progresses over weeks and then gradually resolves spontaneously. Psychological disturbances are common, ranging from emotional lability and decreased attention span to obsessive compulsive symptoms and remit shortly after the chorea subsides. Twenty per cent suffer recurrence, usually within 2 years.

2. Diagnosis. When associated with carditis, the diagnosis is easy. Antistreptolysin-O titres are usually raised.

3. Management. The chorea may be treated with haloperidol or valproate. Anecdotal reports suggest plasma exchange and intravenous immunoglobulin are useful. Patients should be given long-term penicillin and avoid the oral contraceptive pill which may induce relapse.

Further reading

Harper PS. *Huntington's Disease*, 2nd edn. *Major Problems in Neurology 31*. London: WB Saunders, 1996.

Bradley WG. *Neurology In Clinical Practice*, 2nd edn. Boston: Butterworth-Heinemann, 1995.

Related topics of interest

COMA AND DISORDERS OF CONSCIOUSNESS

Consciousness

Consciousness is 'the state of awareness of self and environment when provided with adequate stimulation' and has two components:

- Level of consciousness, or arousal, is determined by the brainstem reticular activating formation (dorsal midbrain and pons). Thus, brainstem disease either intrinsic, e.g. haemorrhage, or extrinsic, e.g. compression may lead to unconsciousness.
- Content of consciousness, the integrated activity including sensations, emotions and mental activity, is determined by the cerebral cortex. Cortical lesions give unconsciousness only if the whole cortex is affected, e.g. hypoxaemia or hypoglycaemia.

Causes of coma

- Head injury.
- Drug overdose.
- Medical coma.
    Hypoxic-ischaemic, from hypotension, respiratory or cardiac arrest.
    Cerebrovascular, from stroke or subarachnoid haemorrhage.
    Metabolic, from hepatic failure or hypoglycaemia.

Clinical presentation

- No focal signs, no meningism, e.g. poisoning, hypoxia, infection, hypothermia or epilepsy.
- No focal signs with meningism, e.g. subarachnoid haemorrhage, meningitis or encephalitis.
- Focal signs, e.g. space occupying lesion or cerebral infarction.

Clinical assessment

1. Emergency. This includes attention to airway, breathing, circulation (ABC), a search for trauma and checking the blood glucose level.

2. History. History details may need to be obtained from relatives, bystanders, the patient's wallet, or by telephoning the family doctor. The patient's medical history, medication and social background are important and empty bottles must be sought.

3. *General examination.* Assessment includes temperature, pulse, respiratory rate and blood pressure.

4. *Head and neck.* A search for depressed skull fracture, laceration, haematoma and meningism and an examination of the optic fundi and ears.

5. *Limbs.* Assessment of spontaneous movements, lateralizing signs, asymmetry of tone and reflexes and evidence of focal seizures.

6. *Level of consciousness (Glasgow Coma Scale (GCS))*
(a) Eye opening:
    1 None.
    2 To pain.
    3 To command.
    4 Spontaneously.
(b) Best motor response:
    1 None.
    2 Extension.
    3 Abnormal flexion (shoulder adducted).
    4 Normal flexion (shoulder abducted).
    5 Localizing pain.
    6 Spontaneous movements.
(c) Best verbal response:
    1 Unresponsive.
    2 Incomprehensible sounds.
    3 Words, confused.
    4 Words, orientated.
    5 Talking normally.

Coma is defined as 242 or worse on the GCS:
    2 No eye opening to command.
    4 Not localizing pain.
    2 Not uttering words.

7. *Pupils.* The pupils are small in metabolic coma and after opiate poisoning. Following most poisonings, the pupils are normal; with anticholinergics they are large.

8. *Corneal reflexes*
• In poisoning, corneal reflexes are lost early: lost corneals in light coma suggests overdose and therefore a good prognosis.
• For other causes, corneal reflexes are character-

istically retained until deep coma: lost corneals in non-overdose coma indicates a poor prognosis.

9. *Eye position*
- Mild eye divergence is normal in coma.
- Gaze away from a hemiparesis suggests a hemisphere cause; gaze towards a hemiparesis suggests a pontine lesion.
- Fixed downgaze indicates a metabolic cause or midbrain tectum lesion.

10. *Spontaneous eye movements*
- Roving eye movements (as in sleep) or periodic alternating gaze, is non-localizing and indicates an intact brainstem.
- Spontaneous nystagmus uncommon in coma since it requires functioning of both cortex and brainstem.
- Ocular bobbing occurs rarely in metabolic coma and in lesions of the low pons. (See Nystagmus.)
- Uniocular nystagmoid jerking suggests a mid or low pontine lesion.

11. *Induced eye movements*
- Oculocephalic (doll's eye) movements disappear if pons is depressed or damaged.
- Oculovestibular movements assessment is the most reproducible clinical test in coma. Fifty to two hundred ml of iced water is injected into a clear auditory canal. The normal response, seen in wakefulness or feigned coma, is nystagmus with fast phase away.
- Tonic deviation towards the stimulus indicates a supratentorial lesion; no response or dysconjugate gaze indicates a brainstem lesion. Tonic upward deviation may follow poisoning.

12. *Breathing pattern.* The localizing value of various breathing patterns is probably overstated.
- Cheyne–Stokes breathing generally suggests a diencephalic lesion but can be seen with a sluggish circulation, e.g. left ventricular failure.
- Central neurogenic hyperventilation suggests a low midbrain or upper pontine lesion.
- Ataxic breathing suggests a medullary lesion.
- Yawning and hiccup non-specifically indicate a brainstem lesion.

Investigations

1. Brain scan. In coma with focal signs or meningism, it is essential to exclude a mass lesion.

2. Lumbar puncture. This is indicated in coma (especially with meningism) but only having excluded a mass lesion on brain scan.

3. Electroencephalogram (EEG). This can identify a lateralized lesion, diagnose non-convulsive status epilepticus, and distinguish feigned from real coma. Metabolic causes may be distinguished on EEG from toxic causes by:

• Diffuse slowing of EEG rhythms in metabolic coma.
• Triphasic complexes present in hepatic coma.
• Diffuse fast (beta) waves suggesting coma from sedative drugs.

Alpha coma describes coma with an abnormal and unresponsive alpha rhythm. It indicates either diffuse hypoxic damage (present in 25% of post cardiac arrest coma) or an intrinsic brainstem lesion. The prognosis depends upon the underlying cause.

Prognosis

1. Aetiology. The proportion of patients returning to an independent existence after coma (>6 hours) depends upon the cause:

• Drugs 99%.
• Hepatic 30%.
• Trauma 20%.
• Hypoxic-ischaemic 10%.
• Stroke and subarachnoid haemorrhage 5%.

2. Traumatic coma. The prognosis following traumatic coma depends upon:

• Depth (GCS 3 on admission 80% mortality; GCS >8, mortality 3%).
• Duration (patients >48 hours in coma have an 80% mortality).
• Shock (BP <90 mmHg, heart rate >150 beats per minute). Coma + shock has a 95% mortality.
• Whether cardio-pulmonary resuscitation was needed.
• Whether neurological signs are present.

Differential diagnosis

• Brain death.
• Locked-in syndrome.

- Vegetative state.
- Abulia.
- Catatonia.
- Feigned coma.

Brain death

1. *Preconditions*
- Apnoeic coma.
- An identified irremediable structural cause.
- No drug-induced, hypothermic or metabolic cause for coma.

2. *Clinical tests of brainstem function*
- Absent cranial nerve responses and no gag response.
- Absent respiratory movement after discontinuing ventilation and despite $Paco_2 > 6.7$ kPa.

Vegetative state

1. *Preconditions*
- An established cause.
- No persisting effects of sedative, anaesthetic or neuromuscular blockade.
- No persisting causative metabolic disturbance.

2. *Clinical criteria*
- Unawareness of self and environment.
- No volitional response to visual, auditory, tactile or noxious stimuli.
- No language expression or comprehension.
- Presence of cycles of eye closure and opening resembling sleep and wakening.
- Spontaneous breathing.
- Stable circulation.

3. *Clinical signs*
- Preserved pupillary and corneal reflexes.
- Oculovestibular response is tonic with no nystagmus.
- Roving eye movements are present without visual fixation or blink to menace.
- Some inconsistent non-purposeful movements.

Continuing vegetative state

This is where a vegetative state has existed for 4 weeks or more.

Persistent vegetative state

This diagnosis implies irreversibility and must be unhurried and made with great care. Two experienced physicians separately assess the patient taking account of additional observations made by staff and carers. Persistent vegetative state is diagnosed only where the vegetative state has persisted:

- \>12 months following head injury.
- \>6 months following other causes.
- From birth in anencephaly.

Locked-in syndrome
Although not a disorder of consciousness, this tragic syndrome may easily be mistaken for coma. Carers of patients apparently in coma must be aware that patients may be alert despite apparent coma. Locked-in patients are conscious but paralysed (de-efferented) owing to a lesion at the base of the pons impairing every voluntary movement except vertical eye movements. It presents major management and communication problems.

Further reading

Pallis C, Harley DH. *ABC of Brainstem Death*, 2nd edn. London: BMJ Publishing Group, 1996.
Royal College of Physicians Working Group on Persistent Vegetative State. *Journal of the Royal College of Physicians*, 1996; **30:** 119–21.
Zeman A. Persistent vegetative state. *Lancet,* 1997; **350:** 795–99.

Related topics of interest

DEAFNESS (SENSORINEURAL)

Recent years have seen major advances in the understanding of the aetiology of deafness. Heredity plays a role in most cases of hearing impairment. Genetic causes account for half of childhood cases and also present in adults, often labelled degenerative.

Hereditary

1. Non-syndromal

- Otosclerosis: stapedial otosclerosis is the commonest hereditary conductive deafness. Sensorineural hearing loss (SNHL) may also occur through cochlear sclerosis, sometimes preceding stapedial sclerosis. Otosclerosis is autosomal dominant with incomplete penetrance though some are X-linked (Xq21). The prevalence is 2%; (female:male 2:1). Its probable aetiology is autoimmune enzyme release, damaging the inner ear and resulting in deposition of woven bone (more vascular and cellular than lamellar bone) in the oval window niche causing stapes footplate fixation. Stapedectomy is sometimes indicated.
- Isolated: SNHL at various frequencies occurs in several inherited conditions, sometimes presenting late in life. The commonest genes are: recessive (11q and 13q); dominant (1p and 13q).

2. Syndromal. These are mainly childhood-onset syndromes with extra-otological features:

- Alport's syndrome: this is either X-linked dominant (Xq22) or autosomal dominant. It presents with progressive renal failure, deafness and cataract. A defect of the type IV collagen molecule results in abnormally fragile ears and kidneys, vulnerable to progressive degeneration.
- Usher syndrome: this autosomal recessive condition presents with SNHL and retinitis pigmentosa. There are three genetic loci of the gene encoding myosin (11q), necessary for stereociliary function.
- Refsum's disease: this autosomal recessive condition of abnormal phytanic acid storage presents in childhood with retinitis pigmentosa, polyneuropathy and, in 80% of cases, cochlear deafness. There may be collapse of Reissner's membrane, degeneration of stria vascularis and disorganization of the organ of

Corti. A low phytanic acid diet sometimes halts the hearing loss.

- MELAS syndrome (see Mitochondrial disorders). This multisystem mitochondrial disorder, like related disorders, e.g. Kearns–Sayre syndrome, may show progressive bilateral SNHL.
- Jervell and Lange–Nielsen syndrome of prolonged electrocardiographic QT interval with SNHL.
- Pendred's syndrome of SNHL with thyroid goitre.
- Waardenburg's syndrome of deafness with telecanthus and pigment disorder (20% white forelock; 45% heterochromic iris).

Degenerative

The commonest elderly-onset deafness is presbycusis (or 'presbyacusis' = the hearing of an old man). It is defined as an otherwise unexplained high tone SNHL, usually of gradual onset, in an elderly person. Genetic factors and noise exposure play a role. Patients have poor speech discrimination with particular difficulty in hearing against background noise, e.g. other conversation, and often withdraw socially. Unlike in conductive hearing loss, discrimination is not helped by shouting.

Infections

1. Viral. Viral infections damage hearing either by:
- Cochlear involvement (viral endolymphatic labyrinthitis), e.g. mumps, measles, influenza, adenoviruses.
- VIII nerve involvement (viral neuronitis), e.g. Ramsay Hunt syndrome of facial palsy, hearing loss and auricular herpes zoster, giving deafness in about 30%.

SNHL in AIDS is often due other infections, e.g. cytomegalovirus or syphilis as well as to HIV itself.

2. Bacterial. Bacterial infections represent important preventable causes of deafness, e.g. Lyme disease and syphilis. Bacterial meningitis, especially pneumococcal, may result in hearing loss in up to 30% of children. Cryptococcal meningitis in immunosuppressed people may lead to sudden SNHL. Chronic suppurative otitis media may impair hearing. A major cause of deafness in bacterial infection is aminoglycoside toxicity (see below).

Ischaemia	Conditions threatening the blood supply of the inner ear may damage hearing. Age-adjusted hearing loss correlates with cardiovascular disease. Arterial loops may compress the VIII nerve in the posterior fossa, e.g. ipsilateral deafness with hemifacial spasm. Vasculitis (especially Wegener's granulomatosis) and coagulopathies may also impair hearing.
Brainstem lesions	*1. Bilateral.* Deafness caused by brainstem lesions is usually bilateral and complete. This is because when the VIII nerves enter the brainstem they divide into two tracts and each sends fibres bilaterally. Thus only a severe and widespread central lesion e.g. brainstem encephalitis, can cause deafness, inevitably bilateral.
	2. Unilateral. Unilateral brainstem deafness can be caused only by a very peripheral lesion at the VIII nerve entry zone, e.g. by a multiple sclerosis plaque or unusual stroke, e.g. Foville syndrome.
Tumours	*1. Vestibular Schwannoma.* Fifteen percent present with sudden deafness as the initial symptom. This may occur as a unilateral and isolated problem or may be bilateral as part of neurofibromatosis type 2 (see Neurocutaneous syndromes).
	2. Leukaemia. Malignant infiltration of the cochlea and labyrinthine system with associated haemorrhage may occur in leukaemia.
Trauma	• A longitudinal fracture (80%) parallel to the petrous ridge through the tympanic membrane, ossicles and middle ear roof, may result from a blow to the temple and lead to conductive hearing loss. • A transverse fracture (20%) crossing the petrous ridge and involving the internal auditory canal and labyrinth may result from blows to the occipital or frontal regions and result in SNHL often with facial nerve palsy.
Acoustic trauma	Noise-induced hearing loss is very common (*c.* 1 in 30 prevalence). It may result either from prolonged exposure to excessive levels of noise or from short intense periods of impact noise.

Drugs	Ototoxicity, causing either tinnitus, deafness or vertigo, may occur following exposure to aminoglycosides, salicylates, non-steroidal anti-inflammatories, loop diuretics and beta-blockers. Predisposition to aminoglycoside ototoxicity is a genetically determined mitochondrial disorder.
Ménière's disease	This is an uncommon but frequently diagnosed cause of progressive low-tone SNHL in middle age, associated with tinnitus and episodic vertigo. (See Vertigo).
Sudden deafness	This is defined as SNHL developing over hours to a few days. It is usually unilateral and usually associated with tinnitus. Overall, about 70% of cases recover. The major causes are:

- Viral infection: viral endolymphatic labyrinthitis is the commonest suspected cause (25% have a viral infection at the time of deafness) but is usually a diagnosis of exclusion.
- Vascular or haematological: ischaemic end organ damage may result from blood vessel narrowing, hypercoagulability, or embolus, e.g. from open heart surgery or vasculitis, e.g. systemic lupus erythematosus (SLE). Predisposing factors include diabetes, arteriosclerosis, hypertension, hyperlipidaemia and smoking. A tortuous vessel e.g. posterior inferior cerebellar artery may compress the VIII nerve leading to unilateral deafness, often in conjunction with hemifacial spasm.
- Toxic causes especially aminoglycoside antimicrobials.
- Inflammatory or neoplastic causes may lead to deafness by inflammation or infiltration of the inner ear or cranial nerves. Multiple sclerosis may lead to deafness by inflammation in the brainstem itself.
- Trauma: either fracture (see above) or following single exposure to an intense sound.
- Post-lumbar puncture deafness follows in 0.2%. It is a temporary low frequency deafness due to patent cochlear aqueducts allowing reverse flow of perilymph.

Further reading

Roland NJ, McRae RDR, McCombe AW. *Key Topics in Otolaryngology*. Oxford: Bios Scientific Publishers, 1995.

Yeoh LH. Causes of hearing disease. In: Stephens D, ed. *Adult Audiology*. Oxford: Butterworth-Heinemann, 1997; 1–28.

Related topics of interest

Mitochondrial disorders (p. 146)
Neurocutaneous syndromes (p. 179)
Peripheral neuropathy (hereditary) (p. 236)
Vertigo (p. 307)

DEGENERATIVE DISC DISEASE

Lumbar disc disease

Anatomy and mechanics

The lumbar intervertebral discs comprise 20% of the vertebral column's height and form a strong bond and cushion between vertebral bodies necessary to transmit the body's weight. Large forces act upon the lumbar discs, highest when seated (10–15 kg/cm^2), lower when standing (7–12 kg/cm^2), lowest when lying (5–8 kg/cm^2). Standing is thus more comfortable than sitting in disc disease.

Discs comprise:

- Nucleus pulposus, the semi-fluid gelatinous inner substance.
- Annulus fibrosus, the fibrous outer ring, thinnest and weakest posteriorly as the nucleus pulposus lies off centre.
- End plates, hyaline cartilage with bony rims separating discs from vertebral bodies and permitting blood supply and nutrition.

Age-related degeneration

Normal ageing produces:

- Disc dehydration.
- Loss of elasticity (more annulus; less nucleus).
- Reduced blood supply.
- Fissuring of annulus and nucleus.

This predisposes to disc protrusion in young and middle age. Elderly disc herniation is rare as advanced degeneration leaves a firm, calcified fibrocartilage plate.

Lumbar disc prolapse

The annulus may bulge postero-laterally and, with sufficient forces, nucleus pulposus is extruded as loose material: 'sequestered disc'. Most protrusions are posterior, giving symptoms by:

- Stretching the (innervated) posterior annulus and posterior ligament.
- Compression of nerve roots.

1. Which disc, which root? Each lumbar root relates to two intervertebral discs. Each root branches from the cauda equina to pass infero-laterally and emerge at its respective foramen.

- The L5 root branches from the cauda equina at the L4,5 disc level and exits via the L5,S1 foramen. It is compressed shortly after its origin by a L4,5 disc posterolateral protrusion and only rarely by a large lateral L5,S1 protrusion.
- The S1 root (origin at L5,S1 disc level; exit via S1,2 foramen) is compressed by a L5,S1 posterolateral protrusion.
- Large L5,S1 fragments may compress both the S1 root posteriorly and the L5 root laterally.
- Large central protrusions compress the whole cauda equina, especially with a narrow canal.

Ninety five per cent of lumbar disc protrusions are at L5,S1 (S1 nerve root) or L4,5 (L5 nerve root) because:

- These discs spaces have more movement.
- These discs are crossed by roots destined for their exit foramina.

2. Clinical features. Young adults, especially males and manual workers, are most affected. Often there is an acute strain history. Root compression pain is worse on movement, especially upright and exacerbated by coughing, sneezing and straining. Additional leg pain strongly suggests a sequestered disc with improvement likely following surgery. Pain confined to the back (i.e. no leg pain) is often less helped by surgery.

- Straight leg raising (SLR): increased tension in the lower lumbar roots on SLR provokes pain and spasm in the hamstrings when there is root compression. Ankle dorsiflexion exacerbates it and knee flexion reduces it. 'Sitting straight leg raising' with knees extended ('please sit forward so I may look at your back') helps to verify a positive test.
- S1 root syndrome: this comprises 55% of lumbar disc prolapses and presents with:
    Pain: posterior thigh, lateral calf, foot and positive SLR.
    Paraesthesiae and numbness: lateral foot and two toes.

Weakness: ankle plantar flexion and eversion.
Reflexes: ankle jerk reduced or absent.
- L5 root syndrome: This comprises 40% of lumbar disc prolapses and presents with:
  Pain: posterolateral thigh and lateral calf, positive SLR.
  Paraesthesiae and numbness: lateral calf and dorsomedial foot.
  Weakness: ankle dorsiflexion and inversion; toe dorsiflexion; hip abduction.
  Reflexes normal; possible reduced medial hamstring reflex.

Lumbar canal stenosis

1. Clinical features. This affects older patients, especially men, with symptoms that differ from lumbar root compression:

- Gradual onset.
- Exercise induced symptoms (neurogenic claudication), e.g. heaviness, fatigue, weakness and tingling of feet, legs, buttocks, perineum.
- Relief by rest.
- Improvement by leaning forward, e.g. cycling.
- Occasional unwanted erection.
- Few physical signs except occasionally following exercise.

2. Mechanism
- Limitation of exercise-induced increased blood flow by a narrow canal.
- Congestion, compression and friction on the lumbar roots when exercising upright (lumbar spine extended).

Arachnoiditis

This presents as gradual onset progressive neuropathic pain in one or more dermatomes without root tension signs. There are many causes and a wide clinical spectrum. It is attributed to previous meningitic reaction from haemorrhage, trauma, surgery, meningitis or oil-based contrast medium, e.g. Myodil, and follows a latent interval of <10 years.

MRI shows nerve root thickening. The pain responds poorly to analgesia, amitriptyline being the most successful.

Cervical disc disease

Degeneration affects predominantly C5,6 and C6,7, the most mobile part of the cervical spine. It differs from lumbar disease in that:

- Acute disc herniation is rare.
- Osteophyte formation accounts for the majority.
- Root compression occurs at the same level as the corresponding exit foramen. Thus, the C6 nerve root is compressed at C5,6.

Cervical disc prolapse

This presents in young people with sudden neck and arm pain, worse on neck movement (especially ipsilateral flexion) and coughing, and may follow neck injury. As in lumbar disease, there is a soft extruded disc fragment or annulus bulge. It usually responds to conservative treatment (collar and analgesia), but if surgery is undertaken for persistent pain the results are usually good.

Cervical spondylosis

This is a very common degenerative condition with advancing age, manifesting as tissue encroachment into the intervertebral foramina compressing nerve roots (radiculopathy) or spinal canal compressing the cord (myelopathy).

1. Cervical spondylitic radiculopathy. It presents in older persons with gradual onset progressive symptoms but only mild pain; there is corresponding dermatomal sensory loss and weakness with reflex loss in the corresponding myotome. It may resolve spontaneously over several months and is usually managed conservatively.

- C5 root syndrome (C4,5 foramen):
    Pain: neck and lateral upper arm.
    Numbness: shoulder and lateral upper arm.
    Weakness: deltoid, biceps, brachioradialis.
    Reflexes: reduced or absent biceps or supinator.
- C6 root syndrome (C5,6 foramen):
    Pain: neck, shoulder, lateral arm, thumb and index finger.
    Numbness: thumb and index finger.
    Weakness: biceps and wrist extensors.
    Reflexes: reduced or absent biceps and supinator.
- C7 root syndrome (C6,7 foramen):
    Pain: often severe in neck, scapular area, shoulder, lateral arm and little finger.

Numbness: middle finger.
Weakness: triceps.
Reflexes: reduced of absent triceps.

2. Cervical spondylitic myelopathy. Cervical spondylosis is a frequently diagnosed cause of cervical cord compression in the elderly. The classical syndrome is C5,6 radiculo-myelopathy, giving both:

• Lower motor neurone (LMN) signs at C6 with lost biceps and supinator reflexes.
• Upper motor neurone (UMN) signs at C7 and below giving brisk triceps and long finger flexor reflexes and spastic paraparesis.

This combination gives an 'inverted supinator' where, on tapping the supinator reflex, there is finger flexion (UMN C7) without elbow flexion (LMN C6).

The mechanism of cervical spondylitic myelopathy is less clear than it seems. Several features suggest that chronic progressive cord compression by osteophytes is not the only cause:

• The clinical course is often more rapid than would be expected.
• Spontaneous improvement may occur.
• The clinical-radiological correlation is poor in that severe spondylosis may be apparent without any myelopathy.
• Surgery often gives only slow and incomplete recovery quite unlike surgery following spinal meningioma cord compression.
• Often at surgery there is only minor cord compression.

These factors suggest that some cases of apparently spondylitic myelopathy are due to normal ageing changes, to vascular problems and to demyelination; this limits the scope of surgery in this common condition.

Further reading

McCormack BM, Weinstein PR. Cervical spondylosis. An update. *Western Journal of Medicine*, 1996; **165:** 43–51.

Related topic of interest

Spinal cord injury (p. 263)

DELIRIUM (ACUTE CONFUSIONAL STATES)

Delirium is an organic mental syndrome. It is often caused by treatable or preventable conditions and so its diagnosis is important. The clinical manifestations of delirium are similar no matter what the cause of disruption of the integrative function of the brain.

Clinical features

The following are present in delirium:

- Impaired concentration and attention.
- Global disturbance of cognition (thinking, remembering, perceiving).
- Psychomotor disturbance.
- Disturbed sleep/wake cycle.
- Emotional disturbance.

Clues to the diagnosis are:

- Sudden onset.
- Worse at (and often beginning at) night.
- Sharp fluctuations in severity.
- Paranoid misinterpretations.
- Relatively brief duration (hours to weeks).

There is usually laboratory evidence of widespread cortical dysfunction: the EEG, for example, showing diffuse changes.

Differential diagnosis

Delirium is often missed in patients who have:

- A pre-existing psychiatric label, e.g. an Alzheimer's disease patient who develops constipation or urinary retention.
- A rare disease where common treatable causes are missed, e.g. AIDS patient with a urinary tract infection.

Delirium is distinguished from dementia by its abrupt onset, impaired consciousness, its variability, the marked involvement of the sleep/wake cycle and the presence of an underlying physical illness.

Causes

1. Predisposing factors
- Age over 60 years.
- Pre-existing brain damage: delirium is the commonest psychiatric disturbance in the elderly. Predisposing factors include age-related involutional brain changes, accompanying brain damage, e.g. Alzheimer's disease, reduced resistance to stress,

increased susceptibility to infection, multiple underlying disorders and medications, poor nutrition and impaired vision and hearing. Thus, the most susceptible group are the demented elderly population.
- Drug addiction.
- Psychosocial stress, including bereavement, relocation to an unfamiliar environment, sleep deprivation, sensory underload or overload, e.g. intensive care, and immobilization.

2. Precipitating factors. Several disorders precipitate delirium in susceptible individuals.

- Primary cerebral disease such as head trauma, epilepsy (either ictal, e.g. complex partial status or post ictal), cerebrovascular disease, or space occupying lesion, e.g. tumour or abscess.
- Secondary cerebral disease may result from underlying systemic disease including metabolic disturbance (e.g. hypoxaemia, hypoglycaemia, liver failure), vitamin deficiency, fluid or electrolyte imbalance, intracranial infection (e.g. meningitis, encephalitis), extracranial infection (e.g. septicaemia), or physical injury (burns or trauma).
- Intoxications: most important are medications, especially steroids, cytotoxics, antipsychotics, anti-epileptics, anti-Parkinsonian treatment and anticholinergics; any drug in overdose may potentially cause confusion. *A detailed drug history is essential in every confused patient.* Alcohol, illicit drugs and solvents are important to consider in confusion at any age.
- Withdrawal: alcohol withdrawal may pass unsuspected in hospital inpatients, particularly the elderly. Withdrawal of sedation, e.g. benzodiazepines, may also cause confusion.
- Cardiovascular disorders or anaemia.

3. Modifying factors. Certain additional factors determine the likelihood and severity of delirium. These include:

- Two or more provoking factors together, e.g. a severe burn with infection.
- Rate of change of provoking factors, e.g. rapid alcohol withdrawal, rapid electrolyte change.

- Duration of exposure, e.g. prolonged versus brief hypoglycaemia.
- The extent of exposure, e.g. focal versus generalized cerebral problem.

Management

- Specific.
(a) Remove underlying cause(s) if identified.
(b) Correct nutritional deficiency.
(c) Vitamin supplements (especially thiamine).
(d) Appropriate fluid balance.
- Symptomatic and supportive.
(a) Optimize the sensory and social environment to give adequate rest and sleep. Confused patients show the adaptive behaviour of wandering and exploring. Their ideal environment (difficult to achieve in a general medical ward) has constant lighting, room to wander and the minimum number of people.
(b) Avoid additional patient anxiety by backing off from confrontation, not arguing, and trying to negotiate and temporise.
- Sedation
(a) Sedation is sometimes needed to avoid serious or even lethal self injury; sedation must be avoided in hepatic encephalopathy. If a decision is made to take charge over an acutely confused patient, it is essential that the management is firm and not half-hearted, that there are enough people present and enough sedation is given.
(b) Haloperidol 20 mg is the first choice treatment for acute agitation in an adult. Important side effects include acute dystonia, hypotension and prolongation of the electrocardiographic QT interval with risk of sudden cardiac death. It must be avoided in acute withdrawal of alcohol or drugs.
(c) Lorazepam intramuscularly is indicated if a more rapid response is needed.
(d) Chlordiazepoxide (with thiamine and high calorie, high fluid intake) is first choice for alcohol or drug withdrawal. The dose must be monitored several times daily and is titrated against arousal level (sweating, pulse rate). Chlormethiazole should be avoided. Patients should not be discharged with this sedation.

Prognosis   This depends upon the cause. The most likely outcome from delirium is full recovery but some cases progress to persistent organic neurological disorder, coma or death.

Further reading

Lipowski, ZJ. *Delirium: Acute Confusional States*. Oxford: Oxford University Press, 1990.
Jacobson, SA. Delirium in the elderly. *Psychiatric Clinics of North America*, 1997; **20:** 91–110.
Marsh, CM. Psychiatric presentations of medical illness. *Psychiatric Clinics of North America*, 1997; **20:** 181–204.

Related topics of interest

Coma and disorders of consciousness (p. 37)
Dementia (p. 57)

DEMENTIA

Dementia is the acquired loss of cognitive ability sufficiently severe to interfere with daily functioning and quality of life. Its prevalence is markedly age specific, being 1% aged 60 and doubling every 5 years to 30–50% by age 85 years. Although the common forms are untreatable, dementia management concentrates principally on identifying potentially treatable causes.

Alzheimer's disease

This primary degenerative brain disease comprises 70% of dementias. The progressive decline in cognitive function varies between individuals; average survival is 8–10 years.

Clinical features
- Progressive memory impairment is the usual presenting feature. Episodic (autobiographical) memory, e.g. for everyday events is lost early. Attention span is initially preserved but disorientation in time and space is inevitable in advanced disease.
- Progressive language impairment advances with the disease giving difficulty with spontaneous speech and word finding. Early language preservation may initially mask the cognitive impairment. Speech contains automatic phrases and clichés. Impaired naming ability and verbal comprehension are frequent.
- Visuospatial disability progresses with the disease giving difficulty recognizing faces and becoming lost through impaired topographical memory.
- Dyspraxia: disordered skilled movement and tool use gives difficulty with activities of daily living, e.g. dressing and using cutlery.
- Problems with complex tasks, such as meal preparation and personal hygiene, owing to impairment in several cognitive areas, particularly frontal lobe dysfunction.
- Personality changes: passivity or aggression commonly lead to management problems.
- Depression and anxiety occurs in 40%, particularly early on.
- Delusions and hallucinations: paranoid delusions occur in <50% of patients; hallucinations, particularly visual, including of people and animals, occur in <25%.

Physical signs	These are rare until late. Frontal release signs (grasp reflex, pout response and palmo-mental reflex) are common but non-specific. Rigidity, tremor and sometimes myoclonic jerking are seen in up to 30% of patients with advanced disease.
Genetics	• A family history is reported by up to half of patients, but only <10% have definite autosomal dominant inheritance. These include genes encoding amyloid precursor protein (chromosome 21), pre-senilin 1 (chromosome 14) and pre-senilin 2 (chromosome 1).
	• Patients with Down's syndrome (trisomy 21) almost invariably develop Alzheimer's disease in the 5th and 6th decades.
	• Genetic variation in apolipoprotein E (apo E) status (chromosome 19) confers differing probability of developing late onset Alzheimer's disease. Heterozygotes for the apo E4 allele (prevalence 25%) are at substantially increased risk, but among homozygotes, (prevalence 2–3%), 90% develop Alzheimer's disease. Even patients with other dementia types, e.g. vascular dementia or dementia pugilistica (*vide infra*) have a greater than normal chance of possessing the apo E4 allele, indicating a causative link between Alzheimer's disease and other dementia types.
Investigations	• MRI brain scan may demonstrate quantifiable medial temporal atrophy.
	• Single photon emission computerized tomography (SPECT) may show reduced blood flow in the posterior biparietal and bitemporal areas.
	• EEG shows non-specific slowing.
	• Cerebrospinal fluid is normal but Tau protein levels may be elevated.
	• Serum melanotransferrin (P97) is higher in Alzheimer's disease than controls.
	• apo E4 genotype is associated with increased risk of Alzheimer's disease with occurrence at an earlier age but is unreliable as a predictive test.
Pathology	• Neurofibrillary tangles: these develop within the cell body adjacent to the nucleus and are seen best on silver stains or immunocytochemistry to ubiquitin or

tau. They are most numerous in the association neocortex, hippocampus and nucleus basalis of Meynert.

- Senile plaques: these comprise dystrophic axons and dendrites around a core of amyloid protein (ß-amyloid or A4 protein).
- Neurochemistry: a cholinergic deficit resulting from damage to the cortical cholinergic projection from the basal forebrain (nucleus basalis of Meynert) gives potential for cholinergic therapy.

Vascular dementia

This comprises 10–20% of dementias. Its severity and prognosis depends upon the nature of the underlying cerebrovascular disease.

Clinical features
- Ninety per cent have had clinical vascular events, e.g. acute unilateral motor or sensory dysfunction.
- A fluctuating course is characteristic.
- Urinary and gait dysfunction may be seen early.
- Pseudobulbar palsy with bradykinesia, rigidity but extensor plantar responses are common late in the disease.

Investigations
CT brain scan shows discrete infarcts or leucoaryosis (diffuse white matter disease). Central atrophy, including third ventricular enlargement, may occur.

Dementia of frontal lobe type

This group of disorders represents 1–5% of dementias. The term Pick's disease, previously applied to this group, is reserved for those with specific pathology.

Clinical features
- Disordered executive function (impaired initiation, goal setting and planning).
- Relatively preserved cognitive functioning.
- Preserved visuospatial function.
- Disinhibited behaviour.
- Poor insight.
- Language impairment may occur with progressive aphasia, unfocused speech, echo-like spontaneous repetition and compulsive repetition of phrases.

Lewy body dementia

A fluctuating dementia of the elderly, characterized by motor features (akinesia and rigidity), affective disorder especially depression, confusional episodes and hallucinations (see Parkinson's disease).

Prion dementia

See Prion diseases.

Huntington's disease

See Chorea.

Communicating hydrocephalus

Clinical features	• Gait dyspraxia. • Cognitive decline. • Urinary incontinence. • CT brain scan shows ventricular system enlargement. Each is relatively common in the normal elderly leading to frequent over-diagnosis. Cortical symptoms (aphasia, dyspraxia) and psychosis are rare.
Management	A CSF drainage procedure may be indicated. • Removing 30 ml of CSF can give temporary improvement and predicts a good result from CSF drainage procedure. • Ventriculo-peritoneal shunting is most helpful when the cognitive impairment is of short duration. • Neuro-endoscopic third ventriculostomy is less often complicated by subdural haematoma and may become the treatment of choice.

Rare but treatable dementias

• Bilateral subdural haematomas may present in the elderly as a diffuse cognitive decline often without an obvious trauma history.
• Complex partial status epilepticus gives a variable cognitive impairment with associated altered consciousness and characteristic EEG findings.

- Cerebral neoplasm, e.g. frontal lobe tumours, especially meningioma, may present with progressive dementia. Neoplastic meningitis especially lymphoma, may present as a rapid onset cognitive decline.
- Cerebral vasculitis presents with stroke-like episodes and characteristic scan appearances.
- HIV dementia is associated with psychomotor slowing and focal neurological signs.
- Hypothyroidism: patients may show depression, irritability and mental slowing.
- Vitamin B$_{12}$ deficiency is often associated with psychiatric symptoms or myelopathy and neuropathy, and usually haemopoietic abnormalities.
- Neurosyphilis often presents with psychiatric symptoms and frontal lobe dementia.
- Whipple's disease: this rare multisystem chronic granulomatous disorder presents with progressive dementia, ophthalmoparesis, seizures, myoclonus, gait disturbance, hypothalamic dysfunction and later coma. The pathognomonic finding is oculomasticatory myorhythmia in which the eyes move in time with involuntary jaw movement. The intestinal lipodystrophy is due to infection with the Gram positive bacillus *Tropherema whippelii*.

Differential diagnosis

- Age-associated cognitive decline, insufficient to affect daily function, is normal in the healthy elderly.
- Medications commonly contribute to cognitive impairment in the elderly; medication withdrawal may reverse the impairment.
- Depression is common and essential to exclude. It is distinguished from dementia in several ways:
    It is the patient and not the family that reports the cognitive difficulty.
    The duration is shorter (weeks or months).
    The onset may be sudden.
    There is often a previous or family history of depression.
    There is evidence of psychomotor slowing and poor effort on testing ('I don't know' answers).
    It may respond to a therapeutic trial of antidepressants.

Management

General   Important measures are:

- Stopping unnecessary medications.
- Controlling alcohol intake.
- Excluding contributing causes especially depression.
- Treating any identified underlying condition.

Specific   Drug treatment to enhance brain acetylcholine levels
                      using anticholinesterases, e.g. tetrahydroaminoacridine
                      and more recently donepezil, leads to significant short-
                      term improvement in cognitive function in Alzheimer's
                      disease, but does not halt the underlying progressive
                      disorder.

Further reading

Geldmacher DS, Whitehouse PJ. Evaluation of dementia. *New England Journal of Medicine*, 1996; **335:** 330–36.
Piccini C, Bracco L, Amaducci L. Treatable and reversible dementias: an update. *Journal of the Neurological Sciences,* 1998; **153:** 172–81.
Rossor M. Alzheimer's Disease. *British Medical Journal,* 1993; **307:** 779–82.

Related topics of interest

DYSTONIA

Dystonia, or involuntary posturing, is characterized by sustained postures, spasms, jerks, or tremor. It is predominantly action-induced and so improves with muscle relaxation or sleep.

Abnormally executed motor programmes result from dysfunction in the brain stem and basal ganglial circuits controlling movement. The normal organization of agonist and antagonist muscle activity is replaced by chaotic co-contraction.

Dystonia is mostly idiopathic but occasionally symptomatic. It is either generalized or focal. Segmental dystonia refers to focal dystonia involving more than one adjacent muscle group.

Generalized dystonia

Idiopathic torsion dystonia This condition, formerly dystonia musculorum deformans, begins in childhood with lower limb involvement, triggered by movement, e.g. running. It progresses to involve all four limbs and is characterized by sustained dystonic posturing and often by a family history (autosomal dominant).

Dopa responsive dystonia This condition, Segawa's disease, is rare but treatable. Onset is in childhood, usually with toe walking, postural instability and falls. There may be marked diurnal fluctuation with particular benefit following sleep. Other features include parkinsonism and apparent lower limb spasticity and it must be considered in the differential diagnosis of hereditary spastic paraparesis. It must be excluded as a cause of athetoid cerebral palsy. Deficiency of a cyclohydrolase from one of several mutations prevents endogenous dopa production. There is a dramatic and sustained response to L-dopa, usually low dose and without risk of late dystonic side effects. Since the phenotype may be indistinguishable from idiopathic torsion dystonia, a trial of L-dopa is essential in all cases of generalized or childhood onset dystonia.

Paroxysmal dystonias • Paroxysmal kinesigenic dystonia is a familial disorder in which brief dystonic posturing, lasting seconds to minutes, may follow abrupt voluntary movement. It responds well to low dose carbamazepine.

- Paroxysmal dystonic choreoathetosis is much rarer. Episodic abnormal movements occur (choreoathetosis, ballism or dysarthria) lasting several days, often provoked by stress, tiredness and alcohol, with little response to treatment. It is often misdiagnosed as hysteria but is an autosomal dominant condition with genetic heterogeneity.
- 'Paroxysmal nocturnal dystonia' is now recognized as a frontal lobe epilepsy and not a dystonia; most cases are identical to autosomal dominant nocturnal frontal lobe epilepsy.

Symptomatic dystonia

1. Neuroleptics. Neuroleptic agents may cause three forms of dystonia:
- An acute dystonic reaction to neuroleptics may occur as an idiosyncratic reaction in young people, e.g. following metaclopramide or prochlorperazine. Acute retrocollis, oculogyric crisis and limb dystonia may be seen. It resolves spontaneously after 12–48 hours but an anticholinergic treatment is sometimes necessary.
- Tardive dystonia evolves as a late effect of long term neuroleptic medication in young or middle aged patients. It is characterized by opisthotonus, oculogyric movements and limb dystonia, may persist after drug withdrawal and is poorly responsive to medications.
- Tardive dyskinesia is characteristically seen in elderly patients on long-term neuroleptic medication and manifests as disfiguring involuntary orofacial and lingual movements. The movements may worsen on drug withdrawal and respond poorly to medication.

2. Parkinson's disease. This may be associated with dystonia, e.g. 'striatal toe' even before medication is begun; anti-Parkinsonian medications, particularly L-dopa, cause dose related dystonic posturing as a late effect in patients with Parkinson's disease.

3. Structural and metabolic brain disease. Multiple sclerosis may be associated with tonic spasms (resembling acute painful hemidystonia) which are strikingly responsive to carbamazepine. Other structural causes of dystonia include brain tumour, cerebrovascular disease, head trauma, encephalitis and cerebral palsy. Metabolic causes include Wilson's disease, Niemann–Pick disease Type C and GM_2 gangliosidoses.

4. Trauma. In susceptible individuals, i.e. non-manifesting carriers of a dystonia gene, trauma (surgery, injury) or other physical stress may be sufficient to provoke the appearance of dystonia.

Focal dystonias

These are usually of adult onset, manifesting mainly in the upper body and remain focal.

Spasmodic torticollis
Prevalence is 1 per 10 000 with a mean age of onset in the early 40s. Patients develop involuntary lateral rotation and/or extension of the neck, often with jerky movements. Left-sided rotation is more common than right. Pain over the tense muscles may be the dominant feature. Up to 15% of patients report previous significant head injury. The major symptom is of social embarrassment leading to withdrawal and isolation.

Idiopathic blepharospasm
This condition manifests as involuntary blinking, sometimes with sustained eye closure. Prevalence is 1 per 5000. It develops insidiously in the fifth to seventh decade affecting women more than men. Often for many years patients have blinked excessively or experienced eye discomfort. The symptom is variable, being worse in bright lights and with fatigue or anxiety.

Oromandibular dystonia
This rare condition gives involuntary jaw and/or tongue movements. At its most mild it manifests as bruxism (jaw grinding) but may go on to give major facial distortions with involuntary jaw opening.

Limb dystonia
The majority are occupational (craft palsies). They may complicate certain repetitive activities requiring good coordination, e.g. writing, violin playing, dart throwing, golf putting. The best known is *writer's cramp*, where attempts to write lead to involuntary posturing of the hand and arm. Violinists' finger or golfers' 'yips' are other examples.

Aetiology of dystonia

The majority of idiopathic generalized and focal dystonia are genetic. Severely affected individuals may show childhood onset lower limb and subsequently generalized dystonia; more mildly affected individuals show an adult onset of cranial and neck dystonia.

There is genetic heterogeneity but most cases map to chromosome 9q32-34 (DYT1 locus) where the deletion of one glutamate leads to an abnormality of Torsin A, an ATP binding protein. Dystonia is commonest among Ashkenazi Jews; 1 in 2000 of New York Jews carry the DYT1 dystonia gene.

Diagnosis

Despite the advances in the understanding of the genetics, the diagnosis remains essentially clinical.

Management

1. *General measures*
- An explanation to the patient often comes as a relief as often such symptoms were dismissed as psychological.
- Exclusion of an underlying cause for symptomatic dystonia is essential.

2. *Medications*
- A trial of L-dopa (Sinemet 275 twice daily, for 2 months) is necessary, at least in childhood onset generalized dystonia, to exclude dopa responsive dystonia.
- Anticholinergics, e.g. benzhexol, improves dystonia in about 40% of cases but the doses used are limited by side effects, particularly dry mouth and urinary dysfunction.
- Botulinum toxin is now the treatment of choice for focal dystonia. It permanently damages the motor end plates and function is restored only as new nerve terminals grow over 2–3 months. Botulinum toxin A is injected into the affected muscles; after 2–3 days benefit is seen which may be sustained for 2–3 months before repeat injection is required. Side effects may include 'flu-like symptoms, and local muscle weakness. Injections for spasmodic torticollis may be associated with transient dysphagia and injections for blepharospasm may lead to temporary ptosis. Antibodies to botulinum toxin may result in treatment failures. The antigenically distinct botulinum toxin type 'F' may be an alternative.

3. *Surgery.* Stereotactic thalamotomy is an alternative for disabling dystonia unresponsive to medical therapies. The anterior portion of the ventrolateral nucleus is deliberately damaged. Surgical results are less impressive than for dystonia of Parkinson's disease and is a treatment of last resort.

4. *Genetic counselling.* It is important to warn patients of the genetic risk of autosomal dominant disorder but precise counselling is impeded by the relatively low gene penetrance, i.e. not all gene carriers manifest the disorder.

Further reading

Moore P. *Handbook of Botulinum Toxin Treatment.* Oxford: Blackwell Science, 1995.
Nygaard TG. Dopa-responsive dystonia. *Current Opinion in Neurology*, 1995; **8:** 310–13.

Related topics of interest

ENCEPHALITIS

Acute encephalitis is an inflammatory disorder of the brain parenchyma, an unusual complication of common viral infections. The reasons for patient susceptibility are unknown. It represents the severe end of a spectrum of viral CNS infection:

- Viral meningitis (common and mild).
- Meningoencephalitis (meningitis with mild brain involvement).
- Encephalitis (rare and severe).

The forms of encephalitis are:

- Acute viral encephalitis.
- Post-viral syndromes.
- Chronic viral encephalitis.

Acute viral encephalitis

Viruses spread to the brain either:

- Neuronally, e.g. herpes simplex encephalitis (HSE) or rabies.
- Haematologically, e.g. arthropod-borne infection.

The encephalitides are broadly divided into those that are:

- Focal, e.g. HSE.
- Generalized, e.g. arthropod-borne encephalitis.

Investigations
- Brain imaging may demonstrate focal abnormalities, e.g. high signal on MRI.
- Electroencephalogram (EEG) shows a diffuse abnormality with specific changes in HSE (see below).
- CSF examination is essential, showing a mononuclear pleocytosis ($5-200/mm^3$) and elevated CSF protein ($0.4-2.0$ g/l) with normal glucose. 5% have normal CSF. Virus-specific IgG ratio of CSF:serum may identify a causative agent. PCR for viral DNA is very sensitive but can identify only a small number of agents. Viral cultures are unhelpful.
- Culture of respiratory secretions, throat swabs, blood, urine and stools.
- Paired sera for viral antibody remains the mainstay of diagnosis.
- Brain biopsy is now rarely required but exceptionally is performed in patients unresponsive to acyclovir.

Pathology
- Vascular: endothelial inflammation of cortical

vessels and capillaries, particularly involving the grey matter or grey/white matter junction.

- Perivascular and grey matter lymphocytic infiltration is usual. Astrocytic proliferation occurs later.
- Viral inclusions: e.g. Cowdry Type A inclusions (herpes simplex) or Negri bodies (rabies).

Herpes simplex encephalitis (HSE)

This is the commonest viral encephalitis in the UK (incidence of 1/million/year). The acute focal inflammation is caused by reactivation of latent herpes simplex virus type 1 (HSV1) infection. It occurs sporadically at any season and any age, 30% aged <20 years and 50% aged >50 years. It affects apparently immuno-competent individuals, though has an increased incidence in AIDS.

Clinical features

After a vague prodrome, patients develop an acute febrile illness with headache, altered consciousness, disorientation, bizarre behaviour, clinical signs, e.g. hemiparesis, and seizures. Mild meningism may be present.

It affects predominantly the temporal lobes (sometimes with haemorrhagic necrosis) giving features including aphasia, agnosia and temporal lobe epilepsy.

Investigations

- EEG characteristically shows periodic high voltage spike and wave complexes (2–3 Hz periodicity) particularly over the temporal leads.
- MRI shows focal (especially temporal) increased signal appearing between days 5–10 of the illness. Haemorrhage and infarction may occur.
- CSF: PCR is highly sensitive for HSV1; virus-specific IgG may be identified.

Management

- Early specific treatment (intravenous acyclovir 30 mg/kg/day for 14 days) significantly reduces mortality. It is often administered on a presumptive diagnosis, e.g. acute brain dysfunction with CSF pleocytosis.
- Steroids do not influence the prognosis.
- Anticonvulsants may be necessary.

Prognosis

This depends mainly upon age and level of consciousness. The overall mortality without treatment is 70% but in patients aged <30 years it is 25%.

Arthropod-borne (Arbo) viral encephalitides

These sporadic and epidemic infections are transmitted by mosquitoes and ticks:
- Flavivirus infections include:
(a) Mosquito-borne: Japanese B (see below), St Louis and Western Nile encephalitis.
(b) Tick-borne: Kyasanur forest encephalitis.
- Alphaviruses include Eastern, Western and Venezuelan equine encephalomyelitis.
- Bunyaviruses including Lacrosse virus.

Japanese B encephalitis This is the commonest serious Asian epidemic infection; 20 000 cases occur annually. It is transmitted by the Culicina mosquito breeding in rice fields and epidemics coincide with their life cycle. Following inoculation there is blood-borne spread to the brain with particular basal ganglia involvement. It may give a poliomyelitis-like picture. Virus-specific CSF IgM gives the diagnosis.

Rabies

Rabies remains endemic in wild animals in many parts of the world, including USA. It is transmitted by the bite of a rabid animal, especially dogs. The virus causes a pure encephalitis without meningeal involvement and particularly affects limbic neurones.
  The clinical stages are:

- Incubation: 90–350 days.
- Prodrome: lethargy, anorexia and malaise.
- Hyperexcitability (furious rabies) with convulsions provoked by external stimuli, 'hydrophobia' (spasmodic pharyngeal contraction accompanying attempts to eat or drink), and high pyrexia.
- Comatose: generalized paralysis and multi-organ failure.
- Death is invariable.

Prevention is by urgent vaccine and antiserum following suspected exposure.

Poliomyelitis

Poliomyelitis (Gk: 'grey marrow of the spinal cord') is now rare in developed countries following vaccination programmes but still occurs in underdeveloped areas. It is caused by infection of the motor neurones of the spinal cord and brainstem with associated marked inflammatory response. Only 1–2% of those infected develop the typically asymmetrical flaccid paralysis affecting limbs or bulbar musculature.
  Cocksackie, echoviruses and Japanese B encephalitis may give an identical picture.

Others

- Herpes viruses. The herpes simplex virus type 2 (genital) may infect neonates, giving a blood-borne multi-organ disorder with diffuse brain involvement and poor outcome. Cytomegalovirus, Epstein–Barr virus or varicella zoster may each cause encephalitis. Varicella zoster in younger people may lead to a mild post-infectious encephalomyelitis (see below) with ataxia. In older persons (e.g. following ophthalmic zoster) it may produce cerebral vasculitis and stroke.
- Paramyxoviruses, e.g. mumps, measles.
- Arena viruses, e.g. lymphocytic choriomeningitis virus and Lassa fever.

Post-viral syndromes

These autoimmune phenomena, commoner in children than adults, are initiated by common viral infections. World-wide, measles is the usual cause. Following a latent interval of 5–15 days, patients develop an acute brain and spinal cord syndrome with evidence of widespread demyelination.
- Post-infectious encephalomyelitis (inflammation of the brain and spinal cord) comprises 30% of acute encephalitis.
- Acute disseminated encephalomyelitis is a more severe form associated with a multifocal neurological disorder (resembling acute multiple sclerosis). The mortality approaches 25%.
- Acute haemorrhagic leucoencephalitis is the severest form, usually diagnosed at autopsy.

Treatment is supportive and with high-dose steroids as appropriate.

Chronic viral encephalitis

- Acquired immunodeficiency syndrome (AIDS), including HIV encephalitis and progressive multifocal leucoencephalopathy (PML) (see HIV neurology).
- Subacute sclerosing pan-encephalitis (SSPE) is a progressive condition developing 5–15 years after early childhood measles. Deteriorating school performance, personality change and dementia are followed by myoclonus, seizures, spasticity, chorioretinitis, akinetic mutism and death. The EEG characteristically shows background attenuation and periodic bursts every 5–7 seconds (burst-suppression). CSF measles antibody is elevated. SSPE results from defective measles virus M protein production, preventing virus budding from host cells; spread is achieved only slowly by cell fusion accounting for the long incubation period. Intrathecal interferon-α may induce remissions.
- Progressive rubella panencephalitis is similar to SSPE, invariably fatal and with no effective treatment.

- Rasmussen's encephalitis causes a progressive medication resistant, localization-related epilepsy syndrome in young children. Inflammatory cell infiltrates occur in one or both hemispheres. The responsible agent is unknown, but cytomegalovirus is occasionally isolated. Treatment is with acyclovir or ganciclovir, possibly immunoglobulins and sometimes surgical resection.

Differential diagnosis

This is important as most acute encephalopathies (brain dysfunction without inflammation of brain parenchyma) are potentially treatable.

- Non-viral infections: brain abscess, subdural empyema, infective endocarditis, tuberculosis, atypical organisms.
- Toxins and drugs: heavy metals (especially lead in children), salicylates, barbiturates.
- Metabolic: electrolyte disturbance, hypo- or hyper-glycaemia, porphyria, phaeochromocytoma.
- Systemic disease: vasculitis, connective tissue disease, sarcoidosis.
- Mitochondrial disorders including Reye's syndrome (a subacute encephalopathy sometimes precipitated by salicylates).
- Others: subdural haematoma, cerebral infarction, hypertension, acute psychosis, complex partial status epilepticus.

Encephalopathy in immunodeficient patients

The causes of encephalitis differ in immunodeficient patients, e.g. AIDS. The major causes of encephalopathy, either singly or in combination, in immunosuppressed patients are:

- Cytomegalovirus
- Toxoplasma
- Papovavirus, e.g. JC virus, causing PML
- Herpes simplex viruses
- Primary CNS lymphoma

Further reading

Whitley RJ. Viral encephalitis. *New England Journal of Medicine,* 1990; **323:** 242–49.
Jubelt B, Ropka S. In: Rosenberg RN, ed. *Atlas of Clinical Neurology.* Boston: Butterworth-Heinemann,1997.

Related topics of interest

Cerebrospinal fluid (p. 25)
Coma and disorders of consciousness (p. 37)
Delirium (acute confusional states) (p. 53)

HIV neurology (p. 136)
Meningitis (p. 140)
Multiple sclerosis (p. 164)

EPILEPSY CLASSIFICATION AND SYNDROMES

Seizure diagnosis

Seizure classification is clinical (including witness description), based upon its site of origin and whether the consciousness is altered. EEG criteria are used for childhood typical absences.

Site of seizure origin
- Generalized seizures appear to begin in all of the brain at once, e.g. tonic-clonic, absence or myoclonic seizures.
- Partial seizures begin in a specific brain area, e.g. motor, sensory, autonomic or psychomotor seizures. Secondarily generalized seizures begin as partial but become generalized.

Conscious level
- Simple partial seizure: consciousness is retained.
- Complex partial seizure: consciousness is altered or lost.

Epilepsy diagnosis

Epilepsy, the propensity to recurrent seizures, encompasses a vast spectrum of clinical presentation ranging from an otherwise normal adult with two previous minor sleep-related attacks to a totally dependent, intellectually impaired child with frequent, intractable seizures of various types.

A seizure diagnosis, e.g. 'complex partial seizures', is made in most patients at presentation but merely describes a symptom. It may help the anti-epileptic medication choice but does not imply aetiology or prognosis.

It is therefore helpful to make an 'epilepsy diagnosis' taking account, not only of the main seizure type, but also of the likely aetiology, age of onset, neurological signs and investigations results such as EEG. Epilepsy classification is based upon a description of site of origin of the predominant seizure type and the presumed aetiology of the seizures.

Site of seizure onset
- Partial: termed localization-related epilepsy and is further refined by stating probable site of origin, e.g. temporal, frontal.
- Generalized; termed generalized epilepsy.

Aetiology
- Symptomatic: cause known.

- Cryptogenic: cause thought to be known but unproven.
- Idiopathic: cause unknown and/or genetically determined.

These terms are combined, giving an epilepsy diagnosis, e.g. cryptogenic localization-related epilepsy (R temporal).

Syndrome diagnosis

Certain syndromes can be defined showing characteristics helpful in directing clinical management. An epilepsy syndrome diagnosis might allow meaningful predictions of treatment response, seizure provoking factors, and prognosis. Some diagnoses allow departures from epilepsy management conventions, e.g. in juvenile myoclonic epilepsy, initiating medication after a single seizure, continuing treatment lifelong despite seizure freedom, and maintaining valproate during preconception and pregnancy.

Epilepsy syndromes

1. Idiopathic. Most patients with idiopathic epilepsies can be assigned into epilepsy syndromes.
(a) Idiopathic localization-related
- Benign childhood epilepsy with centro-temporal spikes, formerly benign rolandic epilepsy, is the commonest childhood localization-related epilepsy. An otherwise normal child presents aged 5–7 years with facio-brachial simple partial seizures from sleep. The EEG is strikingly abnormal with frequent centro-temporal spike and waves; cerebral imaging (not always necessary) is normal. Treatment, if needed, is carbamazepine usually with complete control. Spontaneous remission occurs at puberty. Developmental dyslexia is common among these children.
- Benign childhood epilepsy with occipital paroxysms presents in children and teenagers with episodic involuntary eye deviation and unformed coloured visual hallucinations, sometimes with a secondarily generalized seizure. EEG shows occipital paroxysms and imaging is normal. Carbamazepine or valproate usually controls the seizures.
- Autosomal dominant nocturnal frontal lobe epilepsy presents as childhood-onset, predominantly sleep-related, seizures with marked intra-family variation in severity. Seizures include nocturnal tonic spasms, posturing, bizarre movements, often with retained

consciousness, leading to suspicion of hyperventilation or psychogenic attacks. Physical examination and brain scan are normal; the EEG may be normal, occasionally even remaining so during brief attacks. Carbamazepine is usually the most effective medication. Some families map to chromosome 20q.13.2, the region coding for the neuronal nicotinic acetylcholine receptor alpha 4 subunit.

(b) Idiopathic generalized epilepsy

- Benign familial neonatal convulsion is rare but has a good neurodevelopmental prognosis.
- Familial cases are dominantly inherited, most mapping to chromosome 20q and some to 8q. Frequent generalized seizures first occur on day 2 or 3, resolving by 1 to 6 months; 15% later develop epilepsy.

  Non-familial cases show frequent clonic, often partial seizures, on day 4–6 ('5th day fits'), sometimes progressing to status but remitting after a few days. The diagnosis is through exclusion but once established, the syndrome has a good prognosis.

  Childhood absence epilepsy, formerly 'petit mal', is characterized by very frequent sudden onset and offset of altered consciousness with regular 3 Hz generalized spike and wave on EEG and provocation by hyperventilation. It responds well to valproate or ethosuximide and usually remits at puberty.

- Eyelid myoclonia with absences shows the triad of: eyelid myoclonia associated with brief absences; polyspike and wave on EEG induced by eye closure; photosensitivity. Onset is around aged 6 years (other photosensitive epilepsies occur first in the early teenage years). Eyelid myoclonia manifests as rapid (4–6 Hz) eyelid jerking with upward eyeball deviation. The absences are brief (2–5 seconds) with mildly impaired consciousness. Valproate is the preferred treatment although complete response occurs in only 60%.

- Juvenile myoclonic epilepsy is common and presents at puberty with myoclonic jerks on wakening, sometimes culminating in tonic-clonic seizures. Seizures are often provoked by sleep deprivation and alcohol. There may be a history of atypical childhood absences and 30% are photosensitive. EEG shows generalized polyspike and wave (especially if sleep-deprived) and brain imaging is normal. Valproate is the treatment of choice; carbamazepine may exacerbate the myoclonus. Treatment is indicated even after a single tonic-clonic seizure. It often needs to be continued lifelong and continued during pregnancy (with prior folate supplementation). Advice on regular sleep pattern is important. It is autosomal dominant with incomplete penetrance with links to chromosomes 6p and 15q.

2. Symptomatic/cryptogenic. Symptomatic and cryptogenic (secondary) epilepsies are more heterogeneous and more difficult to classify and to treat than idiopathic (primary) epilepsies.

(a) Symptomatic/cryptogenic generalized

These are serious epilepsies with many possible aetiologies usually with learning disability, multiple seizure types and resistance to medication.

- West syndrome has infantile onset of repetitive spasms ('salaam attacks'); developmental delay; 'hypsarrhythmia' (*Gk* hyps, high) on EEG. The poor prognosis for treatment response, epilepsy remission and subsequent intellectual handicap reflects the underlying cause. Vigabatrin is the treatment of choice, especially if caused by tuberose sclerosis.
- Lennox–Gastaut syndrome, often developing from West syndrome, occurs between aged 1 and 5 years. The main seizure type is the axial tonic type although atypical absences ('stares'), myoclonus ('jerks') and atonic attacks ('falls') are seen. EEG shows diffuse 2 Hz spike and wave with 10 Hz bursts in sleep. Mental development is slow and medication resistance usual.
- Myoclonic astatic epilepsy is similar to Lennox–Gastaut syndrome, the main differences being that myoclonic seizures and atonic seizures predominate and the overall prognosis is better.
- Progressive myoclonus epilepsy is characterized by myoclonic and tonic-clonic seizures, progressive neurological decline, resistance to medication and a poor overall prognosis. There are five likely causes: Unverricht–Lundborg disease (Baltic myoclonus);

Lafora body disease; ceroid lipofuscinosis; sialidosis and mitochondrial encephalomyopathy.

(b) Cryptogenic localization-related

Most cryptogenic localization-related epilepsies, the commonest adult presentation, are not classifiable into syndromes. Nevertheless, syndromic features aid treatment decisions and prognosis assessment.

- Medial temporal lobe epilepsy is the best defined adult cryptogenic localization-related epilepsy. Characteristically there is an event (e.g. infection, trauma or febrile seizure) before the age of 4 years that is crucial to the expression of the disorder. After a variable latent period, temporal lobe seizures develop. Seizures are complex partial with rare tonic clonic but are relatively resistant to medication. An epigastric aura, often in isolation, is described by 80%. EEG shows anterior temporal interictal spikes, bilateral and independent in 50%. MRI shows hippocampal atrophy and often mesial temporal sclerosis. Ipsilateral hippocampal atrophy correlates with surgical resection success. Pathology shows pyramidal cell loss in hippocampal zones CA1 and CA3 with mesial temporal sclerosis; surprisingly some change is bilateral in up to 80%.

3. Undetermined. Some syndromes show seizures unclassifiable as partial or generalized:

- Landau–Kleffner syndrome (acquired epileptic aphasia). A rare childhood-onset acquired aphasia with multifocal spike and wave EEG discharges, often with clinical seizures and learning/behavioural difficulties. The seizures may remit but aphasia persists.

Further reading

Hopkins A, Shorvon S, Cascino G, eds. *Epilepsy*, 2nd edn. London: Chapman Hall Medical, 1995.

Related topics of interest

EPILEPSY MANAGEMENT IN ADULTS

General

Diagnostic certainty

There are many possible causes of blackouts and certainty of the diagnosis of epilepsy is essential before specific treatment is begun. The diagnosis rests largely upon the history given by the patient and any witness, though may be reinforced by appropriate investigations. Having established epilepsy as the cause of blackouts, a more precise epilepsy diagnosis and possibly an epilepsy syndrome diagnosis should be sought (see Epilepsy classification and syndromes), since this will influence management strategy.

Lifestyle measures

1. Information. Patients with epilepsy should have access to information about their condition; ideally this should be written, unbiased, clear and patient-orientated.

2. Driving. There are legal requirements to comply with the driving authority regulations. In the UK, all drivers with undiagnosed blackouts or epilepsy must inform the licensing authority and their insurers; they are likely to be required to be free from blackouts for one year before an ordinary licence can be issued, or for 10 years seizure-free and off medication before a heavy goods licence can be granted.

3. Avoiding injury. Aside from driving, people with epilepsy should generally aim to lead normal and fulfilling lives. Advice on restrictions must balance potential physical hazards against the possible psychological and social damage that follows such restrictions. Most doctors advise that people with frequent seizures should:
(a) Bathe in shallow water and never swim alone.
(b) Take care with cooking, hot saucepans etc.
(c) Take care with young babies, e.g. feed while sitting on the floor, avoid carrying on stairs etc.
(d) Take appropriate precautions with cycling, use of open machinery etc.

4. Risk. Living with epilepsy inevitably involves living with a degree of risk – the doctor must point out such risks but not legislate for their complete avoidance.

5. Alcohol. Sensible drinking (2 to 4 units per day) is fine for adults with epilepsy. More than this increases the risk of seizures either:
(a) Directly through toxic epileptogenic effects and potential problems of alcohol withdrawal.
(b) Indirectly through interaction with certain antiepileptic medications, forgetting tablets and disrupting sleep quality.

Medication

Is drug treatment needed?

Antiepileptic treatment implies a secure diagnosis of epilepsy and so carries important long-term implications for driving, employment and social opportunity, as well as its potential for toxicity and teratogenicity. Points to remember are:

- It is easier to start medication than to withdraw it.
- Diagnostic certainty is essential before drug treatment is begun.
- Antiepileptic medication is usually withheld following a single seizure.
- There is no place for a trial of antiepileptic medication.
- Do not start antiepileptic treatment on the basis of an abnormal EEG unless such findings match the history.

If drug treatment is needed

- Epilepsy treatment is long term and should be as simple as possible.
- Most epilepsy can be controlled on a single drug.
- Aim for the lowest effective maintenance dose.
- Once or twice daily dosing is preferable; a midday dose is best avoided.

Which drug?

1. First line. Established treatments are usually first choice:

- Valproate for adults with any seizure type.
- Carbamazepine for partial seizures only.

- Phenytoin especially for partial seizures.

2. *Second line.* Adding or substituting a second drug if the first is ineffective or inappropriate:

- Lamotrigine for any seizure type.
- Gabapentin, vigabatrin, topiramate or tiagabine, especially for partial seizures.

Important interactions

- Enzyme inducers, especially carbamazepine or phenytoin, hasten the metabolism of, and are affected by, other liver-metabolized drugs.
- Contraceptive pill: a 50 μg oestrogen pill is necessary with enzyme inducers including topiramate.
- Codeine phosphate and erythromycin increase carbamazepine levels.
- Valproate slows lamotrigine metabolism and so a lower lamotrigine dose is needed: this combination must be used with caution.
- Carbamazepine and phenytoin increase lamotrigine metabolism and so a higher lamotrigine is needed.

Blood levels

Antiepileptic blood levels are much overused in clinical practice.

1. Indications
- Unpredictable optimal dose: the saturation kinetics of phenytoin leave a narrow therapeutic window between effective and toxic blood levels; fine adjustment is required to optimize the dose.
- Unreliable symptom reporting: children and those with learning disability are less reliable in reporting toxicity symptoms.
- Suspected overdose, non-compliance or malabsorption.
- Pregnancy: occasionally necessary since blood levels change with physiological changes. Free drug levels are little changed, however and medication changes are still best made upon clinical grounds.

2. Drawbacks
- An individual's 'therapeutic range' may differ from the laboratory 'guidance range'.
- Acting upon a blood level alone is potentially harmful:

Provoking seizures in well controlled patients.
Denying patients adequate dosing for fear of provoking toxicity.

- Valproate and newer antiepileptic drug levels are unnecessary except in suspected overdose, poor compliance, malabsorption or drug-related encephalopathy.

Teratogenicity

All antiepileptic medications are potentially teratogenetic. It is important to stress to the patient that:

- Ninety per cent of infants exposed to anticonvulsants are normal.
- Major birth defect occurs in 3% of pregnancies independent of drug exposure or genetic history.

More is known about the more established drugs. Particular risks are:

- Spina bifida in 1.5% of babies exposed to valproate *in utero*.
- Spina bifida in <1% exposed to carbamazepine.
- Phenytoin and phenobarbitone give a 4–5 times risk of cleft lip/palate and congenital heart disease.

The teratogenetic potential may be reduced by:

- Using a single drug at the lowest effective dose.
- Using slow-release formulations to avoid unnecessary peak plasma levels.
- prescribing folate 4–5 mg for 3 months before conception and throughout pregnancy.
- Vitamin K supplementation throughout pregnancy if using phenytoin.

Medication withdrawal

There is no right time to withdraw antiepileptic medication. In children, the need for such treatment needs frequent review. In adults, lifestyle considerations such as driving and pregnancy are likely to influence the patient's decision.

The following favour a better prognosis following withdrawal:

- Long duration seizure-free.
- Control on only one medication.
- Seizure free since starting medication.
- Long seizure-free intervals before medication.

- Having never had a major convulsion (tonic-clonic seizure).
- Idiopathic generalized epilepsy (except myoclonic epilepsy).
- Normal inter-ictal EEG (a weak predictor only).

Status epilepticus

Definition

Seizures continuing for 30 minutes without regaining consciousness between.

Differential diagnosis

Consider pseudostatus (<50% of hospital admissions for status).

Management

- Emergency: airway, breathing, circulation.
- Supportive.
- Specific.
    Benzodiazepine (e.g. lorazepam) by bolus and infusion; phenytoin infusion or fosphenytoin bolus.
    Carbamazepine or valproate by nasogastric tube.
    Sedation and assisted ventilation if indicated.

The mortality is 5–10%, though relates more to the underlying cause than the nature of the seizures.

Surgery

Curative epilepsy surgery is occasionally possible and still under used in clinical practice. For best results there must be:

- Certainty of the site of the epileptogenic focus.
- Excellent concordance between clinical features, neurophysiology, and radiological evidence of structurally abnormal tissue.
- Minimal risk to memory and speech.

To meet these criteria, a rigorous pre-surgical evaluation is necessary with detailed MRI, depth electrode ictal recording and Wada testing (or functional MRI) with psychometric assessment of each hemisphere.

Other treatments

Stress control Stress, resulting from seizures or the threat of seizures, may affect epilepsy in several ways:

- Hyperventilation lowering seizure threshold or mimicking seizures.
- Increased alcohol consumption.
- Impaired sleep quality.

Relaxation techniques (meditation, aroma therapy) are often surprisingly effective in improving seizure control.

Diet A ketogenic diet can be a useful though unpleasant adjunct in childhood absence epilepsy.

Vagal stimulation A novel and invasive treatment whose effectiveness remains to be proven.

Immune modulation Steroids and/or immunoglobulin treatment are effective for some childhood-onset epilepsies (e.g. Rasmussen's encephalitis).

Further reading

Hopkins A, Shorvon S, Cascino G, eds. *Epilepsy,* 2nd edn. London: Chapman Hall Medical, 1995.

Related topics of interest

EXAMINATION OF COGNITIVE FUNCTION

Background

- Higher mental functions comprise those that are:
  (a) Distributed, e.g. attention, memory.
  (b) Localized, e.g. language.
- A distinction between cortical and subcortical disorders is useful:
  (a) Cortical damage is best illustrated by Alzheimer's disease where, early on, there is isolated loss of a localized cortical function, e.g. language.
  (b) Subcortical implies damage to deep structures, e.g. basal ganglia or thalamus, causing loss of integration and organization of localized cortical functions.
- In general, the frontal lobes (i.e. brain anterior to the central and lateral sulci) are motor, while the temporal, parietal and occipital lobes are sensory. Large areas of frontal and parietal cortex are concerned with processing motor and sensory information.
- The further from the central sulcus, the more complex the brain activity, e.g. sensory cortex moves from pin prick appreciation to three dimensional colour vision; the motor cortex from simple movements to personality, planning and expression of thoughts on the meaning of life.
- Integrated cortical functioning, essential for complex tasks, depends upon large tracts (inter-hemispheric, e.g. corpus callosum; intra-hemispheric, e.g. arcuate fasciculus). The arcuate fasciculus connects Wernicke's to Broca's area (see Aphasia) and when damaged causes difficulty with spoken word repetition but relative sparing of comprehension and spontaneous language (conduction aphasia).
- A large variety of organic pathologies present as focal or diffuse brain failure. Depression and other psychiatric disease may mimic dementia.

Assessment

- It is essential to speak to a relative or carer alone; this often reveals the most important history.
- Cognitive testing can be difficult and time-consuming; detailed assessment is appropriate only for highly selected patients. In clinical practice, a more superficial assessment comprising a few simple

questions and tasks can detect important higher mental function deficits sufficient to:

(a) Localize the lesion and suggest possible underlying diagnoses.

(b) Establish the need for more detailed testing.

(c) Help the patient, relatives and staff to understand the problems.

- Clinicians should not be deterred from cognitive testing just because they cannot remember terminology and anatomical associations; these can be looked up later. Inability to remember the different types and causes of dyslexia is no reason to omit testing reading ability.

- To be effective the clinician must memorize a short series of questions and tasks and become familiar with some of the reasons (there are many) why patients cannot complete them.

- The Mini-Mental State Examination (MMSE) is easy to use and forms a useful basis for supplementary questions and tests. It is weighted towards verbal skills and, in isolation, cannot localize the lesion. MMSE points (**total 30**) are given in the following text.

- Adding numbers together can give the deceptive impression of having precisely quantified the cognitive deficit, e.g. 20/30 implying 1/3 demented. Adding differing cognitive functions together is as meaningless as adding other physical signs, e.g. brisk reflexes, ataxia, nystagmus. The quantified result must always be qualified, e.g. 27/30, with mistakes on orientation... etc.

Distributed functions

Distributed functions include not only orientation, attention, concentration but also memory (temporal lobe, thalamus, cerebellum) and 'frontal' functions (reliant upon temporal and other cortical functioning).

1. Orientation. The questions relate to:

- Time: day, date, month, season, year (**5 points**).
- Place: building, ward, city, county, country (**5 points**).
- Person (name, age, birthday).

2. Attention/concentration. Tests include:

(a) Attention alone:

- Months of the year or the days of the week backwards.
- Digit span (repeating <7 numbers forwards or <5 backwards).

(b) Attention and calculation together:
- Serial 7s, i.e. subtracting 7 from 100 and continue subtracting 7 from the product. In the MMSE, one point is given for each correct answer (**5 points**).

3. Memory

(a) Anterograde memory concerns new memory formation.
- Verbal: repeating three objects named by the examiner, e.g. dog, blackboard, lettuce, on first hearing them (immediate recall or working memory) (**3 points**) and after a 5 minute interval (delayed recall) (**3 points**). Recalling a name and address is an alternative.
- Non-verbal: recall of diagrams, e.g. the Rey–Osterrieth complex figure, tests visual memory.

(b) Retrograde memory concerns established memory and is not formally tested in the MMSE. It divides into:
- Episodic memory (past experiences, e.g. that holiday in Blackpool).
- Semantic memory (previously learned facts, e.g. the capital of Wales, the causes of angina).

4. Frontal lobe. Cognitive dysfunction from frontal disease is often difficult to recognize and frequently passes unnoticed on routine testing. It is not specifically assessed in the MMSE. Frontal lobe function tests include:

(a) Initiation
- Category fluency: e.g. generating names of animals (normal >15 in 1 minute).
- Letter fluency: e.g. generating words beginning with the letter 'f' (normal >15 in 1 minute).

(b) Similarities: e.g. what is similar about an apple and a banana?

(c) Abstraction: e.g. proverb interpretation ('look before you leap').

(d) Cognitive estimates: asking the patient to give an estimated answer, e.g. how fast do racehorses gallop?

Localized functions

1. Dominant hemisphere
(a) Language.
Aphasia contaminates cognitive assessment and must be considered in every case before testing. (See also Aphasia.)

- Spontaneous language (not scored in the MMSE) is assessed either during the history or by asking the patient to describe a scene in a picture.
- Naming is tested with two objects, e.g. watch, pencil (**2 points**).
- Repetition is tested by sentence repetition, 'No ifs, ands, or buts' (**1 point**).
- Comprehension is tested by asking the patient to complete a three-stage command 'Pick up this paper, fold it, and put it on the floor' (**3 points**). A more extensive test uses three objects (e.g. pen, key, watch); the patient points as the examiner names them, then names them on request, then uses them as instructed (e.g. 'Pick up the watch and touch the key with it') and finally demonstrates an understanding (e.g. 'Which would you use to write?').
- Dyslexia (difficulty reading) and dysgraphia (difficulty writing) may be associated with spoken language disorders. The patient reads and obeys a written command (CLOSE YOUR EYES) (**1 point**) and writes a simple sentence without help or prompting (**1 point**).

(b) Calculation
Oral or written calculation may be assessed by serial 7s (see above) or simple mental arithmetic (e.g. 7+4, 11–3).

2. Non-dominant hemisphere. These disorders are very disabling, but more difficult to appreciate because language and memory are usually normal; impaired visuospatial skills are prominent with right parietal lobe damage.

- Constructional skills are assessed by copying intersecting pentagons (**1 point**).
- Dyspraxia is the inability to perform a task despite otherwise normal neurological function. Patients with upper limb dyspraxia have normal tone, strength and sensation etc., but cannot organize complex actions on command, e.g. wave good-bye.

- Agnosia implies impaired 'gnosis', the organization of sensory information allowing recognition of a shape, face or object. Anosognosia implies impaired insight into agnosia: 'don't know that they don't know'.
- Astereognosis is the inability to recognize an object or shape placed in the hand despite intact position sense, pin prick and two-point discrimination.
- Inattention or neglect is assessed by cancellation tests (e.g. crossing off all the stars in a picture), line bisection (finding a line's mid-point) or drawing a clock face.

Brief cognitive assessment   This 5-minute preliminary assessment is appropriate to a busy outpatients clinic, having first spoken to patient with carer (noting language content, memory for family's names etc.), and then to the carer alone. At each stage more detailed testing may be appropriate.

- If aphasia is suspected, test repetition, comprehension, reading and drawing (further cognitive testing difficult if patient aphasic).
- 'Name the months of the year backwards, starting with December.'
- 'Remember this name and address: Daniel Roberts, 35 West Register Street, Glasgow'; ask patient to repeat it until certain.
- 'Name every animal you can think of in one minute.'
- Serial 7s.
- Copy intersecting pentagons.
- News events, public figures' names.
- 'What was that name and address?'

Further reading

Hodges J. *Cognitive Testing for Clinicians*. Oxford: Oxford Medical Publications, 1994.

Related topics of interest

Aphasia (p. 1)
Delirium (acute confusional states) (p. 53)
Dementia (p. 57)
History taking in neurology (p. 131)

Non-organic neurology (p. 200)
Stroke (p. 269)

EXAMINATION OF THE CRANIAL NERVES

Before examining the cranial nerves, note, and, if appropriate, examine in detail:

- Attention and concentration.
- Conscious level (Glasgow Coma Scale).
- Frontal disinhibition reflexes (pout, palmo-mental and grasp reflexes).
- Scalp (including temporal arteries).
- Skull size (consider measuring skull circumference), shape, scars, irregularities and cranial bruits.
- Neck stiffness, especially with altered consciousness or headache.
- Spine, including craniovertebral junction (low hairline, short neck), masses, hairy patch, tenderness or bruit.

In practice, the cranial nerve examination does not progress sequentially from I to XII.

Olfactory (I)

'Is your sense of smell normal?' If not, sample aromas with each nostril individually.

Optic (II), Oculomotor (III), Trochlear (IV) and Abducens (VI)

Acuity	<ul><li>'Are there problems with your vision?'</li><li>Use a standard reading chart with varying sized prints.</li><li>'Do you wear reading glasses?' Acuity measurement is meaningless unless there is optimal refraction (clean reading glasses or pin hole).</li><li>'Read aloud the smallest print that you can see'.</li><li>Assess and record separately for each eye.</li></ul>
Fields	<ul><li>Brief assessment if no abnormality suspected: With both eyes open. Hold up both hands with palms towards the patient. 'Look at my eyes'. 'Can you see both of my hands?' 'Which finger am I moving?' (right, left, and both).</li><li>Detailed assessment if an abnormality found or suspected. The room's light should be behind the patient. Compare your right visual field with the patient's left field and vice versa.</li></ul>

Shut your left eye and cover patient's right eye: 'look into my eye'.

Bring a red pin along the diagonal of each of the four visual quadrants.

Compare the size of blind spots and red perception in the central field.

Document fields labelled right and left from the patient's (not the examiner's) viewpoint.

Pupils

- Light response.
  Use a bright light, not ophthalmoscope.
  Assess direct and consensual response in each eye.
- Accommodation
  This is assessed during eye movements (see below).

Eye movements

Movements should be complete, conjugate, without nystagmus and with no diplopia.

1. Pursuit
- With one hand on the patient's forehead.
- 'Follow my finger and tell me if you see double'.
- Move finger right and left, vertically up and down, then in towards the nose, observing pupillary response with convergence.

2. Saccades. Look quickly to the left; to the right; look up; look down.

Fundi

Ophthalmoscopical examination is an opportunity to observe the only nerve and the only blood vessels that are directly visible.

- 'Look up at that object and try to keep looking at it even though I get in your way'.
- For the right eye, hold the ophthalmoscope in the right hand, look with the right eye, and examine from the patient's right side (and vice versa).
- First focus on the iris from 10–20 cm away, looking for cataract etc.
- With the lens on 0, move close to the patient's eye (the closer in, the better the view).
- First examine the disc, then the vessels, then the macula.

- When in an exam situation, be prepared to comment immediately, i.e. take a few seconds whilst looking at the fundi to think what to say.

Facial (VII)

- Observe for facial symmetry, especially brow furrowing and nasolabial folds.
- 'Close both eyes tightly' noting extent of lash burial; try to pull the eyelids apart.
- 'Close your lips tightly together': try to pull them apart.

Trigeminal (V)

Sensory

- Light touch. Using cotton wool to touch a point in each of the three trigeminal dermatomes on each side, ask, 'Does this feel normal?'
- Pinprick. Using a disposable pin, again in each division on each side, ask, 'Does this feel sharp like a pin?'
- Corneal reflex:
  'Look up there'(up and away).
  Touch the cornea (over the iris) with a wisp of cotton wool.
  Note direct and consensual blink.
  Care with interpreting findings in contact lens wearers.

Motor

- Note bulk and symmetry of temporalis and masseter muscles.
- 'Open your mouth and keep it open' noting opening in midline and whether opening can be overcome.

Vagus (X)

- Note quality and clarity of speech.
- 'Open your mouth and say, "Aah"'.
- The soft palate should elevate in the midline.
- Observe the midline raphe as the uvula may not be central.

Glossopharyngeal (IX)

This nerve is sensory to the posterior pharyngeal wall.

- Say, "Aah".
- As the palate elevates touch the posterior pharyngeal wall on each side with an orange stick.
- 'Does it feel the same on each side?'

Hypoglossal XII

- With tongue resting in the floor of the mouth, note tongue bulk and observe for fasciculation.
- 'Put your tongue out', noting movement in the midline.
- 'Push your tongue into your cheek', assessing tongue strength on each side by pushing it back.

Taste (chorda tympani travelling with VII)

- Assess each side individually, and so done without mouth movements.
- Three flavours (salt, sweet, sour).

Auditory (VIII)

Brief
- 'Do you hear this noise?'
- Rub your fingers in front of each ear.

Detailed
- 'Repeat these numbers after me'.
- Whisper numbers at increasing amplitude into each ear whilst tapping a finger in the opposite ear.

Rinné's test (modified)
- With a vibrating tuning fork on the mastoid process: 'Tell me when the sound has gone'.
- Move the fork in front of the ear: 'Can you hear it now?'

Note:
- 'Rinné positive' = air conduction (AC) better than bone conduction (BC). This can be normal or found in sensorineural loss.
- 'Rinné negative', BC > AC in conductive loss.

Weber's test
- Place the vibrating tuning fork on the midline forehead.
- 'Which ear do you hear this in?'
- Louder in affected ear (conductive); louder in normal ear (sensorineural).

Vestibular   Hallpike's manoeuvre (see Vertigo).

Accessory (XI)

- Note sternomastoid and trapezius bulk.
- Place one hand on the forehead and the other behind the patient's head.
- 'Push your head forwards as hard as you can'.

Assess sternomastoids individually by lateral neck rotation. Note: left sternomastoid turns head to right and vice versa.

- 'Shrug your shoulders' and try to overcome this movement.

Further reading

Fuller GN. *Neurological Examination Made Easy*. Edinburgh: Churchill Livingstone, 1993.
Patten J. *Neurological Differential Diagnosis*, 2nd edn. London: Springer, 1996.

Related topics of interest

Coma and disorders of consciousness (p. 37)
Eye movement disorders (p. 100)
Nystagmus (p. 206)
Optic nerve disorders (p. 210)
Vertigo (p. 307)

EXAMINATION OF THE LIMBS (NEUROLOGICAL)

Inspection

1. General
- Burns, scars, wasting, fasciculation, tremor, hemi-smallness.
- Pes cavus and other foot deformity.
- Pressure sores, e.g. buttocks and heels.
- Diabetic ulceration, e.g. soles of feet.
- A catheter, which may be obscured by clothing or a sheet.

2. Muscle inspection. Full limb muscle exposure is essential:

- Upper limbs includes inspection of the shoulder and scapular muscles, e.g. scapular winging, periscapular fasciculation and the small hand muscles (first dorsal interosseous and thenar eminence). Holding the arms out straight with the palms uppermost and eyes closed is useful for assessing mild UMN weakness (downward drift with pronation and elbow flexion) and altered position sense (finger or arm movements: 'pseudochorea').
- Lower limb inspection includes inspection of buttocks. Extensor digitorum brevis in the lateral foot is useful for assessing foot muscle wasting. The patient's walking must be observed.

Tone

Note the resistance to passive limb movements.

- Reduced (flaccid) muscle tone is difficult to determine without weakness.
- Increased muscle tone may be either:
(a) Spasticity (pyramidal; 'clasp knife' hypertonia) varies with speed and direction of movement. Sudden passive movements help to prevent the patient 'helping'. It is best felt in the arms as a 'spastic catch' on forearm supination and in the legs as a catch on knee flexion. Initial resistance is replaced by 'giving way' (compare opening a 'clasp knife' or penknife: the first movement is difficult before suddenly it opens easily).
(b) Rigidity (extrapyramidal; lead pipe or cogwheel) is

unchanged by speed or direction of movement. It is best felt in the arms on wrist extension and flexion and can be brought out by the patient being asked to concentrate on movement of another limb.

(c) Gegenhalten (= holding against) hypertonia is involuntary active resistance to passive movements and indicates frontal lobe dysfunction, e.g. dementia.

Strength testing

'Strength' (force) is not the same as 'power' (rate of force production).

1. Method
- Ask the patient to make a movement and then see if you can overcome it.
- Assess one muscle group at a time, i.e. not two limbs together.
- Select muscle groups carefully: inherently weaker muscles are preferred, e.g. extensors in the arms, flexors in the legs, toe dorsiflexion and finger abduction.

2. Which muscles? Selected groups (with muscle, nerve and root innervation) include:

- Shoulder abduction (from 90 degrees), deltoid, axillary, C5.
- Elbow extension, triceps, radial, C7.
- Finger extension, extensor digitorum, posterior interosseous, C7.
- Index abduction, first dorsal interosseous, ulnar, T1.
- Hip flexion, iliopsoas, femoral, L1,2.
- Knee flexion, hamstrings, sciatic, S1.
- Ankle dorsiflexion, peroneals, common peroneal and sciatic, L4,5.
- Hallux dorsiflexion, extensor hallucis longus, common peroneal, L5.

3. Points
- Strength can be quantified using the MRC Scale 1–5. However, it is often more meaningful to describe weakness as normal, mild, moderate or severe.
- Patients occasionally need encouraging to maximum effort. The patient should look at the limb while the examiner's raised voice exhorts one big effort.
- The first dorsal interosseous muscle (index finger abduction) is the best muscle in which to assess ulnar function. It is the last muscle the ulnar innervates; if

strength and bulk are preserved here then an ulnar lesion is unlikely.

- Abductor pollicis brevis is the best muscle in which to assess median function. The patient must lift the thumb vertically against resistance (a common mistake is to test extensor and not abductor).
- Neck flexion strength (sternomastoids) is important in distinguishing generalized weakness (e.g. motor neurone disease, myasthenia, polymyositis) from cervical myelopathy.

4. Patterns. Weakness is rarely generalized; pattern recognition helps in diagnosis.

- Pyramidal weakness (of extensors in the arms and flexors in the legs) characterizes an upper motor neurone lesion.
- Proximal weakness suggests myopathy or Guillain–Barré syndrome.
- Distal weakness suggests peripheral neuropathy.

Reflexes

1. Tendon
- Observe the muscle being tapped as well as the movement.
- Reinforce apparently absent reflexes by the patient pulling apart clasped hands (Jendrassik's manoeuvre) or teeth clenching.
- Elicit ankle jerks either by tapping the Achilles or by tapping the hand over the metatarsal heads.
- Their root innervation is easily remembered: S1,2 (ankle), L3,4 (knee), C5,6 (biceps, supinator), C7,8 (triceps).

2. Superficial
- Plantar response: 'I'm going to scratch your foot: try to keep the toes still'. Scratch the lateral sole with an orange stick and observe the first movement of the great toe.
- Superficial abdominals: useful only in the young and nulliparous. Stroke each abdominal quadrant with an orange stick, observing for localized muscle contraction. They are lost early in multiple sclerosis but often preserved in degenerative conditions, e.g. hereditary spastic paraparesis and motor neurone disease.

| **Coordination** | Cerebellar signs comprise a triad (of Charcot): dysarthria, nystagmus, limb ataxia. Limb ataxia manifests as intention tremor, dysdiadochokinesis and gait ataxia. |

- Intention tremor is assessed in the arms by finger to nose testing and in the legs by heel to shin testing; observe for tremor just before touching the finger or nose. Ensure the shoulder is abducted and the hand turns between touching finger and nose; the tremor can be exaggerated by reaching further forward, i.e. moving back the examiner's finger.
- Dysdiadochokinesis is assessed in the arms by rapidly tapping the thumb and index finger or rapid pronation/supination of the hand.
- Gait in cerebellar disease is broad based and unsteady. Minor problems can be brought out during 'tandem gait', i.e. 'look at your feet and walk as if on a tightrope'.

Sensory testing

- Ask the patient to delineate any patches of sensory loss before testing.
- Identify broad patterns of sensory loss; avoid being bogged down in minute areas of sensory loss.
- Patients (as well as doctors) become fatigued and increasingly suggestible during a prolonged examination.
- Sensory loss is rarely generalized; pattern recognition helps in diagnosis:
(a) Stocking and glove loss implies a peripheral neuropathy.
(b) A sensory level implies a cord lesion.
(c) Hemianaesthesia with other signs suggests a contralateral cerebral lesion.
(d) Hemianaesthesia without other signs implies non-organic disorder, often with hyperventilation.
(e) Dissociated sensory loss, e.g. spinothalamic lost but dorsal column preserved, suggests a hemicord lesion (e.g. anterior spinal artery syndrome; Brown–Séquard syndrome) or syringomyelia.
(f) Dissociated and suspended sensory loss 'cape and balaclava' characterizes syringomyelia.

1. Pinprick
- Use disposable pins, never hypodermic needles.

- Demonstrate normal pinprick sensation, e.g. on the forehead.
- Over affected areas, ask, 'Does this feel normal?' rather than, 'Can you feel this?'

2. Light touch
- Use cotton wool.
- Demonstrate normal light touch feeling in an uninvolved area.
- Over affected areas, ask, 'Does this feel normal?'

3. Position sense
- Demonstrate the test with the patient's eyes open and big movements of the finger or toe.
- 'Close your eyes and say whether your toe moves up or down.'
- Make small (2–3 mm) toe or finger movements, holding the digit at its sides.
- Romberg's sign: The patient must be able to stand unaided feet together with the eyes open. Falling on eye closure is Romberg positive, but it adds nothing to position sense assessment on the bed.

4. Vibration
- Demonstrate normal vibration feeling on the sternum.
- 'Do you feel this buzzing or just pressing?' when placed on bony prominences, e.g. medial malleolus and tibial tuberosity.

5. Two point discrimination. A sensitive test, important if organic disease is suspected but no sensory changes otherwise identified, e.g. demyelination. 'Can you feel one or two points?' over the finger tips or toes. Use two points each time, but note the distance apart that can be distinguished.

Describing deficits

Neurology shorthand is often preferable to a lengthy description. Examples include:

- Spastic paraparesis (or paraplegia if complete) with sensory level at T10.
- Asymmetrical flaccid tetraparesis R > L.
- Left spastic hemiparesis.
- Flaccid monoparesis right arm.

Further reading

Fuller GN. *Neurological Examination Made Easy*. Edinburgh: Churchill Livingstone, 1993.
Patten J. *Neurological Differential Diagnosis*, 2nd edn. London: Springer,1996.

Related topics of interest

Examination of the cranial nerves (p. 89)
History taking in neurology (p. 131)

EYE MOVEMENT DISORDERS

Oculomotor (III) nerve

Anatomy

The third nerve nucleus comprises a complex series of subnuclei (see below). The third nerve fascicle passes ventrally through the red nucleus, emerging in the interpeduncular space to pass forward in the subarachnoid space parallel to the posterior cerebral artery. It pierces the dura lateral to the posterior clinoid and travels in the wall of the cavernous sinus, entering the orbit through the superior orbital fissure. It branches into:

- The superior division (motor to superior rectus and levator palpebrae superioris).
- The inferior division (motor to medial rectus, inferior oblique, inferior rectus and parasympathetic to the ciliary ganglion and iris sphincter).

Third nerve lesions

A complete third nerve palsy comprises:

- Depression and abduction of the globe ('down and out').
- Fixed dilated pupil.
- Complete ptosis.

1. Nuclear lesions. These reflect the complex anatomy of the third nerve nucleus. Inferior oblique, inferior rectus and medial rectus are supplied by uncrossed fibres, superior rectus supplied by crossed fibres and levator palpebrae muscles receive a shared projection from a midline central sub-nucleus. Thus, in a nuclear third nerve palsy:

- Ptosis is either bilateral or absent.
- Superior rectus is involved contralaterally but spared ipsilaterally.

2. Fascicular lesions. Fascicular (intra-brainstem) third nerve palsies often involve adjacent structures:
- Benedikt's syndrome: ipsilateral III with contralateral numbness (medial lemniscus) with

contralateral tremor and abnormal movement (red nucleus).
- Weber's syndrome: ipsilateral III with contralateral hemiparesis (cerebral peduncle).

3. Subarachnoid space lesions. This is the commonest site for a III lesion.

- A complete III palsy usually indicates a lesion of the peripheral nerve in the subarachnoid space, e.g. posterior communicating aneurysm or compression by tumour or uncal herniation.
- A partial III palsy with spared pupil usually indicates microvascular disease in this vicinity such as diabetes, where it may be accompanied by severe pain around the eye but a good prognosis for complete recovery.

4. Cavernous sinus lesions. Lesions here are associated with palsies of IV, VI and ophthalmic division of V.

Aberrant reinnervation of III

Aberrant third nerve reinnervation may follow a third nerve palsy, owing to regeneration but with 'faulty wiring'. This leads to:

- Upper lid elevation on attempted adduction or downgaze (pseudo Graefe phenomenon).
- Pupil constriction on attempted eye movement.

Aberrant reinnervation without previous third nerve palsy suggests a chronic intracavernous lesion such as meningioma or aneurysm.

Trochlear (IV) nerve

Anatomy

The trochlear nucleus lies caudal to, and continuous with, the oculomotor nucleus. Its fibres curve over the aqueduct to decussate completely and leave the dorsal brain stem, passing forward beneath the free edge of tentorium. The nerve pierces the dura and runs in the lateral wall of the cavernous sinus, entering the orbit through the superior orbital fissure to supply the superior oblique muscle.

Fourth nerve lesions

Superior oblique palsy gives vertical or oblique diplopia on attempted down gaze with the globe adducted.

Causes:

- Compressive causes are rare.
- Closed head trauma: its long subarachnoid course makes it vulnerable to injury.
- Vascular causes account for a minority.
- Congenital IV palsy is relatively common; some adult onset chronic cases are simply a decompensation of congenital palsy.

Abducens (VI) nerve

Anatomy

The nucleus lies in the floor of the fourth ventricle in the caudal pons; its fascicle passes downwards through the pons. The peripheral nerve passes upwards on the clivus in the subarachnoid space, piercing the dura to enter the inferior petrosal sinus and then travels within the cavernous sinus. It enters the orbit via the superior orbital fissure to innervate the lateral rectus.

Sixth nerve lesions

Lateral rectus palsy presents with horizontal diplopia on gaze to the affected side. Sixth nerve palsies have poor localizing value, being common in microvascular disease and following head trauma.

1. Nuclear lesions. This presents as gaze paresis rather than isolated VI nerve palsy, since the nucleus also projects to the contralateral medial rectus subnucleus of III.

2. Fascicular (intra brain stem) lesions. Here, VI nerve palsies are associated with other brain stem structure involvement:

- Foville's syndrome of ipsilateral VI with ipsilateral facial weakness, face pain, Horner's syndrome and deafness.
- Millard–Gubler syndrome of ipsilateral VI with contralateral hemiparesis (cerebral peduncle).

3. Subarachnoid space lesions. Involvement here is with tumours, e.g. nasopharyngeal carcinoma, chordoma etc., meningitic infiltration or raised intracranial pressure stretching the nerve.

4. Intra-sinus lesions
- Petrosal sinus: involvement by temporal bone fracture or infection (Gradenigo's syndrome of face pain and VI nerve palsy).
- Cavernous sinus: the VI nerve within the sinus is more vulnerable than the III or IV nerves lying in its wall.

Special sixth nerve syndromes
- Möbius syndrome: congenital bilateral VI with facial diplegia.
- Duane's syndrome: congenital sixth nerve nucleus hypoplasia leads to globe abduction failure with palpebral fissure narrowing on adduction.

Horizontal gaze syndromes

1. Anatomy. Voluntary horizontal eye movements are generated in the frontal lobe and project to the contralateral paramedian pontine reticular formation (PPRF) which in turn projects to the III and VI nuclei.

2. Horizontal gaze palsy
- Unilateral frontal lobe insults give contralateral gaze paralysis (look towards the lesion).
- PPRF or VI nucleus lesions give ipsilateral gaze paralysis (look away from the lesion).

3. Internuclear ophthalmoplegia. The medial longitudinal fasciculus (MLF) connects III, IV and VI and itself connects to the vestibular nuclei. In MLF lesions (e.g. multiple sclerosis)

- The ipsilateral eye adducts slowly and incompletely.
- The abducting eye shows coarse horizontal (ataxic) nystagmus.

4. Fisher's 'one and a half' syndrome. This localizes to a lesion involving:
- PPRF or VI nerve nucleus (giving ipsilateral gaze palsy – i.e. 'one') as well as
- MLF (giving ipsilateral medial rectus weakness i.e. 'half' of contralateral gaze).

The only remaining eye movement is contralateral eye abduction.

Vertical gaze syndromes

1. Vertical gaze palsy. The frontal eye fields and the superior colliculus project to the rostral interstitial nucleus of the MLF at the most rostral point of the midbrain; this in turn projects to III and IV nuclei influencing vertical gaze. Lesions here include pineal and other tumours, hydrocephalus, infarct or haemorrhage.

(a) Wernicke's encephalopathy

This is the most treatable of the gaze pareses. Thiamine deficiency presents as:

- Confusion and short-term memory loss.
- Ataxia.
- Nystagmus and impaired vertical gaze.

Red cell transketolase indicates thiamine deficiency; replacement is urgent and easy. Failure to diagnose may leave long-term morbidity (Korsakov's syndrome). Mamillary body haemorrhages are found in severe cases.

(b) Parinaud's syndrome

The complete syndrome of a pineal tumour is Parinaud's (periaqueductal) syndrome comprising:

- Upgaze (and occasionally downgaze) paralysis.
- Pupillary light-near dissociation.
- Convergence-retraction nystagmus.
- Papilloedema.

(c) Paramedian thalamic infarction

Lacunar infarcts in the posterior thalamus and rostral midbrain may give a discrete syndrome.

- Depressed conscious level.
- Impaired upgaze.
- Little or no motor or sensory disturbance.

Infarction may be bilateral since, in 30%, a single posterior cerebral artery branch supplies paramedian arteries to both sides. The lesion(s) may be seen only on MRI. Overall, the prognosis for recovery is good.

2. Supranuclear gaze palsy. Steele–Richardson–Olzsweski syndrome (progressive supranuclear palsy) manifests as:

- Slowed saccades.
- Impaired voluntary vertical eye movements (fronto-midbrain pathway).
- Preserved reflex eye movements (superior colliculus-midbrain pathway).

Similar problems occur in Huntington's, Wilson's, Parkinson's and Alzheimer's diseases.

Neuromuscular disorders

Impaired eye movements are associated with:

- Myasthenia gravis, an important differential diagnosis for any gaze paresis, particularly with ptosis (pseudo-internuclear ophthalmoplegia is a well known diagnostic trap).
- Mitochondrial cytopathy with chronic progressive external ophthalmoparesis, e.g. Kearns–Sayre syndrome.
- Oculopharyngeal muscular dystrophy.
- Orbital tumour or pseudo tumour (often from orbital myositis).
- Graves' disease.
- Ophthalmoplegic migraine.

Further reading

Slamovits TL, Hedges TR III, Kupersmith MJ, *et al. Neuro-ophthalmology. Basic and Clinical Science Course, Section 5*. San Francisco: American Academy of Ophthalmology, 1994.

Related topics of interest

Examination of the cranial nerves (p. 89)
Mitochondrial disorders (p. 146)
Muscle disorders (inherited) (p. 174)
Nystagmus (p. 206)
Parkinsonian (akinetic rigid) syndromes (p. 220)
Stroke (p. 269)

FATIGUE SYNDROMES

Chronic fatigue syndrome

Although persistent fatigue occurs in 50% of people at some stage in their life, chronic and persistent fatigue is much rarer. Chronic fatigue syndrome (CFS), popularly known as myalgic encephalomyelitis, has a prevalence of 0.5–1.5%. The patient's life is dominated by abnormally persistent or recurrent fatigue for which no physical basis can be determined. Symptoms are no less distressing or disabling for having no discernible cause and the frustrations of patients with this condition are understandable.

Definition

At least 50% loss of physical or social functioning, persisting for at least 6 months, together with four of the following:

- Sleep disturbance.
- Concentration impairment.
- Muscle pain.
- Multiple joint pains.
- Headache.
- Exacerbation of fatigue following exertion.
- Sore throat.
- Tender lymphadenopathy.

Although CFS is precisely defined for research purposes, it is likely to represent an arbitrary cut off point from one end of a fatigue spectrum rather than a discrete disorder. It is a clinical diagnosis since there are no abnormal pathological, clinical or laboratory findings, and no serious underlying organic cause or severe psychiatric disorder.

Aetiology

Its aetiology remains obscure and the reasons for its development and maintenance are likely to be heterogeneous. 50% of CFS cases follow a flu-like illness but any other acute stressors, including adverse life events or other psychological trauma may trigger the condition.

Associated factors

1. Physical. Major physical impairment is, by definition, excluded. Nevertheless, several treatable physical conditions must be considered either as differential diagnoses or as exacerbating factors of CFS. These might include obstructive sleep apnoea, hypothyroidism, anaemia, infection, polymyalgia rheumatica, Parkinson's disease, connective tissue disease, idiopathic hypersomnia, nocturnal limb movements and even temporal lobe epilepsy.

Prolonged rest may lead to superimposed symptoms of postural hypotension (dizziness and blacking of vision on standing) and to muscle wasting.

2. Psychiatric. Psychiatric symptoms are usual and accompany 70% of CFS cases.

(a) Depression. Depression presenting with somatic symptoms rather than low mood is difficult to diagnose. Such symptoms include:

> Non-specific: lethargy, generalized pains, headache and reduced libido.
> Anxiety related: tight feelings in the chest and throat, dry mouth, palpitation.
> Hyperventilation: breathlessness, tingling, blurred vision, light headedness.

The disability itself promotes further feelings of anxiety and depression, setting up a vicious cycle of symptoms. People with a history of depression are more likely to develop fatigue following a significant viral infection.

(b) Panic disorder. This manifests as sudden attacks of anxiety with physical symptoms, including those of hyperventilation and palpitation.

(c) Somatization disorder. Here, multiple physical symptoms occur with no organic explanation. Patients typically request repeated investigations and object to a psychological explanation for their symptoms. The definition includes the presence of 13 out of 30 medically unexplained symptoms, usually with onset under the age of 30, with persistence for several years and a sickness belief.

(d) Personality type. Differing responses to the same stress by different personalities may be one explanation for fatigue symptoms. Type A personalities, i.e. those who are perfectionists and 'action prone', are more prevalent among chronic fatigue populations. Whilst such a personality is advantageous when life is going well, it may be disadvantageous in adversity.

3. Endocrine dysfunction. CFS patients appear to have an abnormal biochemical stress response. The hypothalamic-pituitary axis, the long term mediator of the body's stress response, may be functioning sub-optimally. A consistent finding in CFS is mild centrally-mediated hypocortisolism, manifesting as reduced urinary free cortisol, lowered serum cortisol, reduced pituitary response to corticotrophin releasing hormone and enhanced adrenal cortical response to adrenocorticotrophic hormone (ACTH).

Management

The condition is often self limiting but the treatment strategy should include a clear explanation with emphasis on the treatable aspects of the condition (hyperventilation, avoiding lying flat during the daytime, avoiding excessive sleep) with appropriate reassurance.

1. Clinic setting. Patients with CFS are best assessed in clinics combining medical and psychiatric disciplines. Listening to the patient and giving time for detailed explanation and discussion are important. The physician must be explicit in assuring the patient that the symptoms are believed, real and disabling, but nevertheless potentially reversible. Patients need time to discuss their physical symptoms before any question of a psychological component is raised.

2. Exclude physical causes. In practice, these are rare unless there are physical signs or the patient is elderly. Baseline blood tests might include full blood count, erythrocyte sedimentation rate, C-reactive protein, rheumatology screen and thyroid function. Neurological investigations are normal and in particular muscle physiology and muscle strength (measured during electrical stimulation rather than relying on patient effort) is normal.

3. Lifestyle modification
- A routine of sleep and meals is important. Avoidance of lying in bed in the daytime and a resolve to rise at the same time each morning are helpful.
- Activity rather than rest is a major component of management of CFS. A sensible graded exercise programme keeping a diary of amounts of exercise done (rather than just resting) should be encouraged.

Agreement with the patient of short term goals and keeping of a diary are helpful in establishing a programme and monitoring progress.

- Information on and management strategies of hyperventilation may also be appropriate.

4. Medication. The use of antidepressant agents is often surprisingly helpful even in those patients not overtly depressed. Low dose tricyclic antidepressants, e.g. amitriptyline 10–25 mg at night, are aimed mainly at:

- Improving sleep pattern.
- Controlling muscle pain.
- Possible effect on dysregulation of 5-HT and hypothalamic-pituitary axis.

5. Cognitive behaviour therapy. Although time consuming, this has a demonstrated beneficial effect in CFS, aiming at altering beliefs and behaviours surrounding the condition. It is important to try to challenge or modify illness beliefs, negative cognitions, maladaptive coping strategies, anxiety and stress.

Prognosis

There is no excess mortality in CFS. Adverse prognostic factors are:
- Advancing age (the outcome in children is good).
- Long duration of symptoms.
- Associated psychiatric disorder, particularly depression.
- Belief in a physical cause (illness belief) which is often accompanied by expectation of failure and exercise avoidance.

Fibromyalgia syndrome

This is slightly more common than CFS, with a prevalence of 2–4%. There is overlap with chronic fatigue syndrome. It is commoner in females and rare in children. It is defined as more than 3 months of widespread, usually continuous pain, present above and below the waist, together with tenderness on palpation of 11 of 18 recognized sites, notably at the lower cervical area, elbows, medial fat pad of knee and greater trochanter of femur.

Common associated symptoms are fatigue, sleep disturbance, irritable bowel, headache and depression. Similar symptoms may be provoked in volunteers by sleep deprivation. Investigations are normal.

Management includes:

- Regularizing lifestyle, especially the sleep pattern.
- Adequate analgesia: a non-steroidal medication together with a low dose tricyclic antidepressant such as amitriptyline.

Further reading

Doherty M, Jones A. Fibromyalgia syndrome. *British Medical Journal,* 1995; **310:** 386–9.

Fukuda K, Straus SE, Hickie I, *et al.* The chronic fatigue syndrome: a comprehensive approach to its definition and study. *Annals of Internal Medicine,* 1994; **121:** 953–9.

Joyce J, Hotopf M, Wessely, S. The prognosis of chronic fatigue and chronic fatigue syndrome: a systematic review. *Quarterly Journal of Medicine,* 1997; **90:** 223–33.

Llewelyn, MB. Assessing the fatigued patient. *British Journal of Hospital Medicine,* 1996; **55:** 125–9.

Related topics of interest

Muscle disease (inflammatory) (p. 170)
Neurogenic pain (p. 189)
Neuromuscular junction disorders (p. 194)

GUILLAIN–BARRÉ SYNDROME

Guillain–Barré syndrome (GBS), or acute inflammatory demyelinating poly-radiculoneuropathy, is the commonest cause of acute generalized paralysis. The annual incidence is 1–2 cases per 100 000 population per year.

Clinical features

The typical first symptoms are fine paraesthesiae in the toes or finger tips. Within days, weakness in the legs ascends to involve arms, face and oropharyngeal muscles to a variable degree. Low back pain is common.

Examination may show symmetrical flaccid tetraparesis, often with bilateral facial and neck flexion weakness, reduced or absent deep tendon reflexes but only minimal sensory loss. In severe cases there may be weakness of ventilatory muscles, external ocular muscles and dysphagia. Autonomic dysfunction may occur with sphincter involvement and propensity to brady- and tachy-arrhythmias.

Typically the illness progresses over 1–3 weeks before plateauing and gradually improving. Complete recovery is usual but residual deficit and even death may occur.

Pathogenesis

Two-thirds of cases appear to follow a viral infection, usually non-specific flu-like illness but occasionally HIV, cytomegalovirus, Epstein–Barr virus, hepatitis or infectious mononucleosis. *Campylobacter jejuni* enteritis with diarrhoea is important and associated with more severe forms of GBS. GBS occasionally follows vaccination.

Investigations

1. Electrophysiology. Nerve conduction studies show evidence of demyelination:

- Conduction block: a reduction in amplitude of the muscle action potential after stimulation of the distal as compared to the proximal nerve.
- Slowed motor nerve conduction velocity.
- Delayed dispersed or absent late 'F' responses, reflecting demyelination in proximal nerves and roots.

A proportion of Guillain–Barré patients have axonal involvement with a worse prognosis for recovery.

2. *Cerebrospinal fluid.* This shows normal pressure, no excess of white cells but with a protein concentration elevated above 0.45 g/l after the first week. A normal CSF protein and elevated CSF lymphocyte count is occasionally seen early in the illness, but suggests alternative possibilities, e.g. HIV, neoplasia, sarcoid meningitis or Lyme disease.

3. *Immunology.* Antibodies to *C. jejuni* can be found in 30% of patients but in 70% of those with the axonal form of GBS. Antibodies to ganglioside GM_1 are found in 30% and generally reflect a worse prognosis. Some patients show myelin protein 2 antibodies.

4. *Nerve biopsy.* This is rarely necessary but would show severe demyelination, sometimes with an acute mononuclear cell infiltrate.

Clinical variants

1. *Axonal form.* 20% of cases have an acute motor and sometimes sensory axonal neuropathy which has:

- A more rapid onset.
- A higher proportion of preceding *C. jejuni* infection.
- More frequent GM_1 ganglioside antibodies.
- A generally worse prognosis.

2. *Miller Fisher syndrome.* This comprises:

- Acute ophthalmoparesis.
- Ataxia.
- Areflexia without weakness.
- Antibody to Gq1b ganglioside in almost all cases.

Overall it carries a very good prognosis and may not require specific treatment.

'Symptomatic' Guillain–Barré syndrome

This may accompany underlying systemic disease, particularly systemic lupus erythematosus, Hodgkin's disease, sarcoidosis or recently acquired HIV infection.

Differential diagnosis

This depends upon the pattern of weakness, the presence of deep tendon reflexes and the clinical setting but includes:

- Acute spinal cord disease, e.g. compression or transverse myelitis (especially with spinal shock).

- Myopathic or neuromuscular junction disorders, e.g. myasthenia gravis, polymyositis, metabolic myopathies, hypophosphataemia.
- Acute or subacute neuropathy, e.g. porphyria (particularly difficult to distinguish from GBS), critical illness neuropathy, vasculitic neuropathy, paraneoplastic neuropathy, neoplastic meningitis.
- Toxicity, e.g. heavy metal intoxication, neurotoxic fish poisoning.
- Infections, e.g. botulism, poliomyelitis, Lyme disease.
- Hysteria (often wrongly diagnosed in GBS).

Management

1. Assessment and supportive treatment. Almost all patients require observation in hospital for at least several days. Careful monitoring and supportive treatment may be life saving in GBS.

- Vital capacity must be monitored closely and elective ventilation instituted as necessary.
- Cardiac monitoring is advisable in the early stages as acute autonomic neuropathy may provoke cardiac arrhythmias.
- Prevention of deep vein thrombosis is very important.
- Acutely inflamed nerves may be unusually vulnerable to pressure palsies and foam elbow and knee supports are appropriate in the early illness.
- Attention to swallowing is important; some patients require nasogastric or percutaneous gastrostomy feeding.
- Depression, common in severely affected patients, may require medication.

2. Rehabilitation. Physiotherapy may help to prevent chest infections and contractures and aid mobility. Mobilization using a tilt table helps to avoid troublesome postural hypotension. As strength gradually improves resisted exercises are started to restore muscle strength and the patient mobilized. Persistent flaccid dropped foot requires ankle and foot orthoses. Fatigue may persist for 12–18 months. A few men have residual impotence.

3. Specific measures. Plasma exchange and intravenous immunoglobulin are each of proven benefit in GBS.

Immunoglobulin 0.4 g/kg/day for 5 days is easier and less invasive, and is now the treatment of choice. High dose corticosteroids are of no value in GBS.

Prognosis   The overall prognosis for complete recovery is good but death (approximately 10%) and long term disability (10%) still occur. Recurrence is rare. Subsequent vaccination is best avoided unless essential. Factors suggesting a poor prognosis are:

- Older age.
- Preceding *C. jejuni* infection.
- Evidence of axonal damage.
- Rapid onset of weakness.
- Assisted ventilation.

Further reading

Ropper AH. The Guillain–Barré Syndrome. *New England Journal of Medicine,* 1992; **326:** 1130–36.

Related topics of interest

Autonomic disorders (p. 12)
HIV neurology (p. 136)
Peripheral neuropathy (acquired) (p. 230)
Respiratory neurology (p. 251)

HEADACHE (MIGRAINE AND CLUSTER HEADACHE)

Migraine is an episodic headache accompanied by nausea and photophobia; focal neurological symptoms (aura) precede the headache in 10%.

Clinical features

The distinguishing features of migraine are that the headache is:

- Intermittent: the typical duration is 1–24 hours with freedom from headache between attacks.
- Often unilateral ('hemicrania').
- Vascular: throbbing, exacerbated by exertion or movement and eased by scalp pressure.
- With systemic upset: this includes nausea, vomiting, phonophobia, photophobia, fatigue, hyperaesthesia and autonomic disturbance.
- Aura precedes or accompanies the headache in about 10%. Aura sensory symptoms typically are positive (flashes, tingling) rather than negative (black spots, numbness). Visual auras are commonest, manifesting as blurring, rippling, spots or flashes characteristically in zigzag shapes, usually in both visual fields and sometimes slowly enlarging and moving across the visual field, impairing vision. Limb symptoms are usually unilateral, manifesting as tingling ± weakness spreading from one body part to another, characteristically having disappeared from the first site before developing fully at the second.
- Provoking factors include missing meals, losing sleep, stress, relaxation following stress, the premenstrual period, exertion, alcohol, strong smells and bright lights. Certain foods can trigger migraine but less commonly than generally supposed.

Migraine is classified according to the presence of an aura:

- Migraine without aura: 'common migraine'.
- Migraine with aura: 'classical migraine'.

Migraine variants

1. Familial hemiplegic migraine (FHM). A family history of migraine is common, especially in migraine with aura. It manifests as migraine with unilateral limb symptoms and dysphasia. FHM is associated with a chromosome 19 mutation. Mutations in the same gene can also cause episodic ataxia type 2, spinocerebellar degeneration type 6, and familial tremor, explaining frequent association of tremor and ataxia with FHM.

Migraine coma is a rare manifestation of FHM and commonly follows minor head trauma. It may be associated with fever and mild CSF pleocytosis giving confusion with encephalitis; the prognosis for full recovery is excellent though recurrences may occur.

2. Basilar migraine. Rarely, headache is preceded by brain stem symptoms, including diplopia, vertigo, ataxia, blacking of vision and altered consciousness. Migraine syncope is a recognized complication of basilar migraine giving diagnostic confusion with epilepsy.

3. Migraine equivalents. This describes recurrent migraine auras without headache. There is a particular association with pregnancy. Attacks may be terminated using oral vasodilators, e.g. biting a nifedipine capsule.

4. Ophthalmoplegic migraine. This unusual condition typically presents with migraine headache with a pupil-sparing third nerve palsy. It is usually diagnosed only following exclusion of other conditions including posterior communicating artery aneurysm.

5. Retinal migraine. Here, typical visual auras occur repeatedly often without significant headache and without resulting field defect. It responds well to aspirin.

6. Childhood periodic syndromes.
- Benign paroxysmal vertigo of childhood occurs between ages 4 to 8 years. The child experiences brief vertigo occasionally with migraine headache. It remits spontaneously.
- Alternating hemiplegia of childhood is an unusually severe variant of childhood-onset hemiplegic migraine.
- Abdominal migraine (periodic syndrome): childhood migraine often manifests as recurrent abdominal pain rather than headache.

7. Transient global amnesia. There is transient (several hours) anterograde memory loss characterized by acute amnesia and repeated questioning, which may be accompanied by migraine type headache. It has an excellent prognosis only rarely recurs. Presumably, it relates to transient ischaemia of mesial temporal structures.

Investigations

Cerebral imaging may be necessary if there are unusual features or an equivocal clinical history. Underlying structural lesions only rarely present with migraine symptoms.

Management

1. General measures
- An explanation of the symptoms is important in reassuring patients. A routine for meals and sleep must be emphasized. Control of caffeine consumption (which can cause rebound vascular headache and interfere with sleep pattern) and attention to stress (behavioural engineering to smooth peaks and troughs of stress) may be suggested, and avoidance of specific triggers if any are recognized.
- In treating childhood migraine, attention must be paid to family dynamics, bullying, school performance and studying conditions (desk height, lighting etc.).

2. Medications
(a) Acute. First line are non-steroidal preparations, e.g. aspirin, preferably soluble for rapid action. This may be combined with an anti-emetic or sometimes a sedative since sleep itself is often effective treatment. Ergotamine is helpful for short-term use but side effects and drug interactions necessitate caution; analgesic-induced headache commonly results from its frequent use. Specific medications, including 5-HT_1 agonists (sumatriptan, zolmitriptan) are very effective in typical migraine.
(b) Prophylaxis. Preventative treatment may be indicated if there are more than two migraine attacks per month; as with any long-term medication, caution is needed before prescribing. The wide choice of prophylactic treatments reflects their relative ineffectiveness (approximately 50% for each treatment) and propensity for side effects. Each must be used for several weeks before assessing their full

effect. $5HT_2$ antagonists, e.g. pizotifen, are often first choice but may cause fatigue and weight gain. Beta-blockers, e.g. propranolol, are commonly used but may exacerbate asthma and cause fatigue or impotence. 5HT uptake inhibitors (e.g. amitriptyline), calcium channel blockers (e.g. verapamil), and antiepileptic agents (e.g. sodium valproate (with folate 5 mg daily in women of childbearing potential)) are occasionally used. Clonidine and antihistamines are ineffective.

Cluster headache and variants (trigeminal-autonomic cephalgias)

These short-lasting primary headache syndromes comprise a group of unilateral facial headaches with varying degrees of autonomic involvement, distinct from and much less common than migraine.

Cluster headache

1. Clinical features. Attacks of short-lived (45 minutes to 4 hours), rapid onset (10–15 minutes), severe, unilateral orbital pain without aura occur typically from sleep. Attacks typically occur 1–2 times daily for 2–3 months; further clusters follow a mean remission of 2 years. Accompanying autonomic disturbances include ipsilateral tearing, redness, ptosis and meiosis, nasal congestion, facial flushing and sweating. During the episodes patients are typically restless, pacing and agitated, clearly distinguishing them from migraine.

2. Patient characteristics. The male:female ratio is 6:1. Typical patients are aged 20–50 years, type A personalities, driven, successful and hard working. Often there is a smoking history (80%) or excessive alcohol consumption (50%).

3. Investigations. Cerebral imaging is unnecessary if the history is typical. Exclusion of an ipsilateral cavernous sinus lesion may be necessary in chronic cluster headache.

4. Management. Acute attacks are rapidly relieved by inhaling oxygen (6–7 litres/min) or sumatriptan given by injection or nasal spray. Occasionally, relief is found in nasal local anaesthetic or capsaicin, or, in resistant cases, by radiofrequency thermocoagulation of the Gasserian ganglion.

Prophylaxis: the most effective are verapamil, lithium, prednisolone or methysergide.

Chronic cluster headache

This describes cluster headache occurring for one year without remissions of more than 14 days.

Chronic paroxysmal hemicrania

This variant of cluster headache is more common in women and manifests as very brief episodes lasting for 5–10 minutes occurring many times per day without the tendency for clustering. It may be strikingly responsive to indomethacin.

SUNCT syndrome

Short-lasting unilateral neuralgiform headache with conjuctival injection and tearing (SUNCT) manifests as very frequent (c. 5 per hour) brief attacks (5–20 seconds) of unilateral orbital pain with marked autonomic features of ipsilateral tearing and rhinorrhoea. It usually proves intractable to treatment. Occasional cases are symptomatic of brainstem or cerebello-pontine angle vascular malformations and it has also been described in AIDS.

Hypnic headache

This occurs in elderly males giving generalized short-lived headache without autonomic features occurring from sleep; it responds to lithium.

Hemicrania continua

A continuous unilateral moderately severe pain with occasional exacerbations and autonomic features which usually responds to indomethacin.

Further reading

Ferrari MD. Migraine. *Lancet*, 1998; **351:** 1043–51.
Goadsby PJ, Lipton RB. A review of paroxysmal hemicranias, SUNCT syndrome and other short-lasting headaches with autonomic feature, including new cases. *Brain*, 1997; **120:** 193–209.
Lance JW. *Mechanism and Management of Headache*. Oxford: Butterworth-Heinemann, 1993.

Related topics of interest

HEADACHE OTHER THAN MIGRAINE

The broad differential diagnosis of headache rests predominantly with the clinical history.

Benign syndromes

Tension type headache

This is the commonest form of headache. It is distinguished from migraine by its 'tight band' generalized discomfort without systemic upset, photophobia or aura. Often the headache occurs daily and there may be a feeling of pressure upon the vertex. It worsens at times of stress and towards the end of the day. There is a close association with musculoskeletal problems, particularly neck muscle tension which may occur in association with cervical spondylosis or neck trauma, e.g. following whiplash injury. Approximately one third of patients with tension headache have accompanying symptoms of depression and the individual symptoms themselves are commonly provoked by anxiety, stress, noise or glare.

Physical examination shows no specific signs though there may be evidence of inappropriate muscle contraction over the forehead and neck.

Tension vascular headache: tension headache may develop in association with migraine giving a continuous headache with episodes between of typical migraine. The distinction of tension type headache from migraine is not as clear cut as traditionally supposed and this overlap syndrome is very common.

1. Investigations. Cerebral imaging is not necessary unless the history is atypical.

2. Management. Reassurance as to the benign nature of the symptoms is important.

3. General measures. Any specific provoking factors of craniocervical muscle tension must be explained and addressed, e.g. poorly fitting dentures, a tendency to grind the teeth at night, refractive error are important. A programme of relaxation exercises is often very helpful and can reinforce to the patient the notion of scalp and neck muscle tension causing the headache rather than there being any serious intracranial cause. Hyperventilation may accompany tension headache and this may also be helped by explanation and specific measures.

4. Medication. These must be used with caution as often they are poorly effective if used in isolation; combined with relaxation therapy the symptoms can be overcome. A non-steroidal preparation is a preferable starting point. Low dose amitriptyline 10–25 mg at night can help to restore a regular sleep pattern as well as provide some analgesic effect and bring benefit even in those who are not depressed.

Cluster headache

See Headache (migraine and cluster headache).

Exploding head syndrome

This is a parasomnia of middle-aged or elderly patients who wake from sleep with a sensation of sudden explosion inside the head. It is a benign phenomenon which may recur but does not usually require any specific intervention with migraine prophylaxis.

Idiopathic stabbing (ice pick) headache

Occasional stabbing scalp sensations may occur as a benign phenomenon; when located to one site might require imaging to exclude an underlying structural lesion.

Ophthalmodynia

This is a variant of idiopathic stabbing headache where the repeated hot needle type discomfort is localized to one eye.

Ice cream headache

Ice in the mouth may provoke a dull aching discomfort over the nasal bridge and forehead; it is sometimes regarded as a clinical test of migraine susceptibility.

Exertional headache

Generalized headache following coughing, exertion or sexual intercourse are well recognized and may cause great concern and limitation of one's sexual activity. They are presumed to be migraine variants but no specific treatment is consistently helpful.

Serious syndromes

Giant cell arteritis

This condition presents over the age of 55 years and manifests as severe pain and tenderness over the scalp arteries, particularly the temporal area on one side. It is accompanied by systemic upset, muscular aching and weight loss and the erythrocyte sedimentation rate (ESR) is usually, but not always, very elevated (>100 mm/hour).

Temporal artery biopsy shows an arteritis with loss of internal elastic lamina and giant cells among the inflammatory infiltrate. Emergency treatment with high dose steroids (prednisolone 60–80 mg daily) is indicated to prevent permanent blindness through short posterior ciliary artery occlusion. The condition must be suspected in any elderly person presenting with headache. Cluster headache is occasionally confused with giant cell arteritis since both are steroid responsive.

Subarachnoid haemorrhage

This presents as an abrupt severe 'worst of my life' headache often with vomiting and loss of consciousness. It may require urgent investigation and surgical treatment to prevent life threatening recurrence of haemorrhage (see Subarachnoid haemorrhage).

Meningism

Headache with neck stiffness accompanies meningeal irritation from infection (e.g. bacterial or viral meningitis) or subarachnoid haemorrhage. Mild meningism without meningitis may accompany a flu type illness.

Raised intracranial pressure

The typical symptoms are bifrontal headache on waking, worsened on movement, exertion, coughing, stooping or straining, accompanied by vomiting and sometimes ataxia and visual disturbance. Cerebral imaging is indicated. An important cause in young obese women is benign intracranial hypertension, which may be complicated by progressive visual loss.

Symptoms of intermittently elevated intracranial pressure, particularly if associated with syncope, must prompt an urgent search for obstructive hydrocephalus from lesions such as a third ventricular colloid cyst or Chiari malformation (protrusion of low lying cerebellar tonsils through the foramen magnum) since these are potential causes of sudden death. A CT brain scan for intermittent headache must include views of the foramen magnum.

Intracranial hypotension

Here there is a generalized headache exacerbated by the upright posture, accompanied by nausea, vomiting, hearing loss, tinnitus, and sometimes neck stiffness and diplopia. The commonest cause is CSF leak following lumbar puncture though spontaneous intracranial hypotension may occur following CSF leaks around the mid thoracic spinal roots following exertion. Treatment is with bed rest and fluids and, occasionally, a blood patch to seal the spinal CSF leak. (See Cerebrospinal fluid.)

Headache in other medical problems

Medication and substances

Vasodilator preparations such as nitroglycerine and nifedipine may provoke vascular type headache. Abuse of vasoconstrictors such as ergotamine, caffeine or nicotine may lead to vasoconstriction sufficient to cause a chronic daily headache with rebound headache on withdrawal and further analgesic abuse (analgesic induced headache). Alcohol may provoke headache through its direct toxic effects leading to a vascular type headache (hangover) and also through provoking sleep apnoea.

Sleep apnoea

Morning headache may sometimes result from hypercapnia and hypoxaemia associated with repeated sleep apnoea in obese subjects.

Headache and epilepsy

A vascular type headache commonly follows seizures. Migraine episodes (especially basilar migraine) may be complicated by syncope and occasionally by seizures.

Further reading

Lance JW. *Mechanism and Management of Headache*. Oxford: Butterworth Heinemann, 1993.

Related topics of interest

Headache (migraine and cluster headache) (p. 115)
Meningitis (p. 140)
Subarachnoid haemorrhage (p. 280)
Vasculitis of the central nervous system (p. 301)

HEAD INJURY

Head injuries are common but most are mild, not requiring hospital admission. Hospitalized head injury incidence is 450 per 100 000 per year. Most are young and follow road traffic accidents; the male to female ratio in 2.5:1. Alcohol or drugs commonly complicate head injury.

Severity of brain injury

The extent of brain injury depends on the degree of immediate (primary) brain damage and the effects of subsequent (secondary) processes.

Primary

1. Local injury. Contusion or laceration at the impact site may, to the casual observer, appear to represent the extent of injury but is often its least severe component.

Skull fracture does not always imply a severe brain injury. Skull flexibility in children can permit severe brain injury without skull fracture. The likelihood and severity of skull fracture is greatly increased when crushed. A depressed skull fracture is not necessarily associated with lost consciousness since it is diffuse rather than local brain injury that determines brain injury severity.

The main significance of a skull fracture is its strong association with intracranial bleeding (see below) and the risk of infection and dural tear following a compound fracture.

2. Generalized injury. Acceleration or deceleration forces move the brain within the skull and dural envelope leading to two injury types:

- Polar: frontal and temporal lobe impact against the anterior and middle temporal fossa walls cause contusions on their tips and under surfaces.
- Diffuse: axons shearing within their myelin sheaths (diffuse axonal injury) can be widespread and severe. This is the main determinant of the duration of coma immediately following injury. Marked diffuse axonal injury leads to deep coma from the onset with extensor posturing and a high likelihood of progression to persistent vegetative state.

Secondary

The brain's high energy demands render it vulnerable to the effects of multiple injuries.

Systemic effects

- Hypoxaemia is present in 30% of head injured patients on admission, resulting from airway obstruction, aspiration, chest injury or coma apnoea.
- Hypotension usually follows blood loss, particularly from abdominal injury. Autoregulation normally maintains cerebral perfusion despite hypotension, but this may be lost following brain stem injury.
- Metabolic factors, including hyponatraemia and hypoglycaemia, potentiate brain damage. As in subarachnoid haemorrhage, hyponatraemia is usually due to cerebral salt wasting rather than dilution; patients with head injury should not be deliberately dehydrated.

Intracranial lesions

1. Haematoma
- Acute extradural haematoma results from arterial bleeding into the extra-dural space, particularly following fractures crossing the middle meningeal vessels on the temporal bone. The classical presentation is with brief unconsciousness followed by a lucid interval of partial or full recovery of consciousness and then secondary loss of consciousness (the preventable 'talk and die' head injury death). Most intracranial haemorrhage, however, occurs in patients unconscious from the outset. The risk of intracranial haematoma ranges from 1:1000 (orientated with no skull fracture) to 1:50 (disorientated without fracture or fracture but orientated) to 1:4 in patients with skull fracture and disorientation.
- Subdural haematoma: this results from tearing of the veins attaching the brain to the dura and presents less dramatically. It is particularly likely to occur with elderly atrophic brains.

2. Brain swelling and oedema
- Congestive brain swelling follows increases in cerebral blood volume.
- Vasogenic oedema results from protein-rich fluid exuding through damaged vessels.
- Cytotoxic (intracellular) oedema follows hypoxia.

3. Hydrocephalus. Blood or infection in the CSF pathways may provoke aqueduct obstruction or impaired CSF absorption, giving hydrocephalus.

Infection	Compound skull fractures and basal fractures into the perinasal sinuses or middle ear are associated with infection risk.
Vasospasm	Traumatic subarachnoid haemorrhage (SAH) with blood around vessels provokes vasospasm as in aneurysmal SAH.
Epilepsy	Early seizures (see below) following head injury further threaten the damaged brain by markedly increasing neuronal activity and metabolic demand.
Brain herniation	Bleeding and swelling into a rigidly enclosed space presses the brain towards the skull 'exits':

- Herniation of the uncus of the medial temporal lobe (tentorial pressure cone) over the tentorial free edge, compresses the ipsilateral midbrain peduncle and III nerve causing first a contralateral hemiparesis and then an ipsilateral third nerve palsy with dilated pupil.
- Downward displacement and compression of the medulla interferes with its basilar blood supply and may result in apnoea and brain death.

Genetic factors	It is likely that genetic factors including apo E status help to determine the extent of brain damage following trauma.

Post-traumatic amnesia

The best retrospective guide to the severity of diffuse brain damage is the duration of post-traumatic amnesia, i.e. how long before becoming aware of their surroundings. A broad estimate is sufficient to grade head injury severity (see *Table 1*).

Table 1. Guide to assessing the severity of head injury

Time before becoming aware of surroundings	Severity of head injury
<5 minutes	Very mild
5–60 minutes	Mild
1–24 hours	Moderate
1–7 days	Severe
1–4 weeks	Very severe
>4 weeks	Extremely severe

The duration of post-traumatic amnesia correlates with the outcome and the chances of returning to work and also influences the likelihood of developing post-traumatic epilepsy.

Post-traumatic epilepsy

This is broadly divided into early (traumatic) and late (post-traumatic) epilepsy.

- Early: seizures within a week (commonly within an hour) are particularly likely in young children. Although 75% have no further seizures, 25% develop post-traumatic epilepsy.
- Late: seizures after one week develop within a year in half of cases, after 4 years in 25%, and may even occur <40 years later.

Risk of late epilepsy
- Thirty five per cent (over 4 years) following surgery for acute intracranial haematoma.
- Twenty five per cent following early epilepsy.
- Twenty per cent following depressed skull vault fractures.
- Increased with other severe injury indicators, e.g. prolonged post-traumatic amnesia, dural penetration or focal neurological signs.
- Apparently uninfluenced by a family history of epilepsy.
- Unpredictable from the EEG.
- Low in mild or moderate injury, e.g. 1% if no haematoma, no depressed fracture and no early epilepsy; 2% if post-traumatic amnesia exceeds 24 hours.
- Underlying epilepsy tendency unchanged despite prophylactic antiepileptic medication.

Outcome

The outcome following head injury depends upon:

- Pre-injury status of the brain. If there is pre-existing brain disease, even trivial injury can lead to major deficit, e.g. head injuries in those on the verge of senile dementia.
- Total amount of immediate (primary) damage.
- Cumulative effects of secondary pathological processes on the injured brain.

Minor: post concussion syndrome
Symptoms following mild head injury, e.g. headache, dizziness, anxiety were previously considered

predominantly psychological. However, there is inevitable injury of cerebral neurones and axons in any head injury and this, together with mild vestibular damage, may lead to these symptoms.

Major
Following severe head injury, post concussion symptoms are unusual. Major social and physical handicap may result from the physical and mental impairments.

1. Physical. Hemisphere damage leading to hemiparesis, dysphasia and epilepsy, brain stem injury and cranial nerve involvement (notably olfactory nerve leading to anosmia).

2. Mental. Profound short-term memory loss commonly follows temporal lobe injury.

Personality changes are a common and disabling consequence of frontal lobe injury and are not amenable to treatment.

Pre-morbid psychological status plays a significant role in the subsequent social disability. Head injured patients are not a random sample of the population but contain a high proportion of social deviants, risk takers, drinkers, etc. and also of adolescents or otherwise healthy people unprepared for an invalid role.

Management

The principles of acute management are to minimize the primary impact damage and, often more importantly, to prevent secondary damage by various pathological mechanisms, e.g. intracranial haemorrhage, cerebral oedema, hypoxaemia etc.

Rehabilitation of post head injured patients is a major discipline aiming to influence favourably the natural process of recovery.

Further reading

Rosenthal M, Griffith ER, Bond MR, Miller JD, eds. *Rehabilitation of the Adult and Child with Traumatic Brain Injury*, 2nd edn. Philadelphia: FA Davis Co, 1990.

Related topics of interest

HISTORY TAKING IN NEUROLOGY

Making a diagnosis

Two questions lead to a neurological diagnosis:

- What is the site of the lesion?
- What is the most likely lesion at that site in this individual?

These questions are the basis of history taking, physical examination and subsequent investigations. Despite the emphasis placed upon physical examination in teaching and in postgraduate examinations, and notwithstanding the importance of neurological investigations, accurate and detailed history remains central to our art.

Points to cover

There is no right or wrong way to take a history but a basic routine ensures that important points are not omitted. It is usual in neurology to start with the patient's age and handedness, before asking 'what is the problem and when did it begin?' The presenting complaint is then refined by further questions:

- Each principal symptom is elicited; this may involve speaking to or telephoning a witness if altered consciousness or blackout is reported.
- Onset: did each symptom begin suddenly, e.g. vascular, or gradually, e.g. tumour?
- Time course: in what order did the symptoms appear? Has each symptom improved, worsened or continued intermittently? It is helpful to picture the time course mentally as a graph.
- Associated symptoms: what accompanies each of the major symptoms? e.g. in headache, were there zigzags in the vision, photophobia, nausea, etc.
- Pattern: do the symptoms comprise a recognizable pattern? In making a diagnosis, pattern recognition from experience is very important. No amount of book knowledge can substitute for having seen and dealt with a condition before.
- Severity: how severe is each symptom? Descriptions such as 'the worst headache of my life' are helpful in determining the nature of the problem.
- The presenting complaint is then placed in context by:
    Past medical history.

Family history.
Social history.
Medication history.

General principles

- During the history the clinician develops and tests diagnostic hypotheses using further questions and subsequently by physical examination and other investigations.
- Every patient has a different tale to tell and the clinician's task is to enable the patient to describe their individual story. Patients in practice rarely conform completely to text-book 'typical' descriptions. It is important not to be tempted to shape the patient's history to fit preconceived ideas.
- Patients should be allowed to tell their story in their own way; this means not interrupting too soon (if the history is being written down then earlier points can be clarified later).
- Some patients remember their details best by linking events to visits to the doctor. This can lead to a rather circumstantial history, often just second-hand reports of what various doctors are alleged to have said. Whilst not wishing to interrupt too soon for fear of the patient losing their thread, some compromise is needed to try to return to the specifics.
- A 'poor historian' often means an impatient or hurried doctor.
- Open questions, e.g. 'what was the first thing you noticed?' are greatly preferable to closed questions, e.g. 'did the headache begin suddenly?' The answers to open questions are much more powerful since they are given spontaneously. Closed questions are needed to refine the diagnostic hypothesis, e.g. specifically asking a patient with migraine about photophobia, nausea, aura, pain movement etc.
- Use patients' own words when documenting or describing the history. Reports of 'tingling', 'fizzing' or 'pricking' should be documented as such rather than as 'paraesthesiae'. Knowledgeable or medical patients may describe their symptoms in technical terms, e.g. paraesthesiae, and so may sometimes not give the clearest possible symptom description, and may inadvertently mislead the clinician.
- Non-specific terms used by the patient, e.g.

'dizziness' or 'numbness', must be clarified. The implications for 'light headedness' versus 'vertigo', or 'loss of feeling' versus 'weakness' are clinically very important.

- The answer to a puzzling case is far more likely to come by re-taking the history than by re-examining the signs or repeating investigations. Other people's histories never seem quite like one's own and it is surprising how a fresh airing of symptoms can give new answers.
- Red flags: seemingly throw away lines, 'it's probably not important but...', or the history detail accompanied by a small laugh, signal points of great importance to the patient and should be noted as such.
- Body language: important information often can be obtained from non-verbal signals such as the way the patient dresses and behaves. Clinicians requesting their patients undressed before the consultation lose both this opportunity and patient dignity; few of us would perform well in clinic whilst undressed.
- 'Do you have any other questions?' The last words in the consultation can be the most significant. After a discussion about the diagnosis with the doctor, and often through relief, underlying anxieties and important pieces of history are revealed, e.g. fear of brain tumour or of Alzheimer's disease. It is therefore important to give the opportunity for, and to note carefully, the contents of questions raised at the end of the consultation.

History versus examination
- The history is clearly far more important than the examination. Nevertheless, students, very junior doctors, and patients are more impressed by the examination and investigations. This is despite the fact that the diagnosis and management plan are usually clear from just the history.
- The physical examination rather than the history is emphasized in postgraduate clinical examinations. This is because it is easier to teach and assess physical examination than history taking.
- More than half of patients attending a neurology clinic have no abnormal neurological signs. This sometimes surprises non-neurologists who were taught only on cases with many signs.

- If a neurological diagnosis has not been reached by the end of the history, it is unlikely to be reached at all.
- It is better to spend more time on the history and less on the examination; why not more questions whilst examining?
- The examination is the first (and only essential) investigation.
- Neurological signs without associated symptoms are usually unimportant. Unexpected signs often imply an insufficiently detailed history, e.g. preceding sciatica explaining an absent ankle jerk; unilateral hearing loss not mentioned by the patient. It must be noted that this close association with signs to symptoms applies to neurology but not necessarily to other disciplines, e.g. cardiology where, for example, high blood pressure or heart murmurs usually are asymptomatic.
- Non-organic symptoms are very common in neurology. Neurological symptoms are themselves frightening (blackouts, headaches, tingling) and the very same symptoms often result from anxiety. Functional symptoms are real and not imaginary but arise through anxiety rather than disease. The problem is further complicated on examination because frightened patients with organic disease may subconsciously 'help' the doctor by exaggerating their problems, giving confusing signs such as 'give-way weakness' or 'non-anatomical sensory loss'.
- It is usually best to reserve discussion of a patient's problem until after the examination. Although the problem is often clear to the clinician at an early stage in the history, the patient (who values the examination very highly) might feel that the doctor is jumping to premature conclusions without having first performed an examination.
- Neurological examination without a history: This is reserved only for life or death situations, such as the patient found in coma or the MRCP clinical examination.

Further reading

Smith PEM. Neurological examination: why bother? *The Remedy,* 1995; **4**: 98–9.

Related topics of interest

HIV NEUROLOGY

The human immunodeficiency virus type 1 (HIV) targets mainly the cell-mediated immune system; in the process it damages nervous system cells with consequent morbidity and mortality. Almost all nervous system components are vulnerable.

Central nervous system (CNS)

Most HIV-related CNS complications occur during the late, or AIDS, phase, when immunosuppression is progressing and CD4 cell counts are low. The exceptions are the acute meningitis or encephalopathy that may accompany the initial infection with seroconversion, and a 'multiple sclerosis-like' illness which can be seen in the middle phase of the disease.

Meninges

1. Viral. Aseptic meningitis or mild meningo-encephalitis, caused by HIV itself, presents with headache and cerebrospinal fluid lymphocyte pleocytosis. It may present or recur as the ill-defined entity, 'HIV headache'.

2. Opportunistic
- Cryptococcal meningitis is the commonest and most treatable HIV-related meningitis. The fungus, *Cryptococcus neoformans*, grows in the subarachnoid space giving a truly cryptic illness with fever, malaise, headache and often mild CSF inflammatory changes; *Cryptococcus* must be specifically sought by Indian ink staining.
- Tuberculous meningitis accompanying HIV infection is serious with a high morbidity and mortality.

Brain

Cerebral complications of HIV infection may manifest as focal or diffuse disorders.

1. Focal disorders. The three conditions comprising most HIV-associated focal CNS disease are:

- Cerebral toxoplasmosis.
- Primary CNS lymphoma.
- Progressive multifocal leucoencephalopathy.

All present with focal hemispheric dysfunction (e.g. hemiparesis, hemisensory impairment, aphasia, apraxia, hemianopia) but are usually distinguishable by their speed of evolution, the radiological appearances, the response to a trial of treatment and by biopsy if necessary.

(a) Cerebral toxoplasmosis. Reactivation and haematogenous spread of latent infection by the protozoan *Toxoplasma gondii* results in a focal CNS disturbance progressing rapidly over several days with clouding of consciousness and constitutional symptoms. Cerebral imaging shows ring-enhancing mass lesions with surrounding oedema in the grey matter of the diencephalon or cerebral cortex. The mortality rate is 50%.

(b) Primary CNS lymphoma. Here the focal neurological deficit evolves over 1–2 weeks and cerebral imaging shows uniformly enhancing mass lesions with surrounding oedema in the deep periventricular white matter. The mortality rate is 70%.

(c) Progressive multifocal leucoencephalopathy (PML). This condition is due to CNS invasion by the papova virus, JC virus, (not to be confused with Creutzfeldt–Jakob disease) infecting oligodendroglial cells, so leading to demyelinating lesions. The focal deficits evolve more gradually over several weeks and include hemiparesis, visual loss, cerebellar disturbance and progressing to dementia and paralysis. Cerebral imaging shows white matter lesions adjacent to the cortex without mass effect or enhancement, the site of the lesions correlating with the clinical deficit. There is no effective treatment and mortality rate is 85%.

2. Diffuse disorders. These are broadly divided into two groups:

(a) Alertness impaired. Encephalopathy from systemic disease or opportunistic viral infection:
- Encephalopathy with impaired consciousness may result from systemic disease including metabolic and toxic disorders, sepsis and diffuse intravascular coagulation.
- Opportunistic viral encephalitis such as cerebral cytomegalovirus infection is very common at autopsy although uncommon as a clinically recognized cause of encephalitis. Zoster associated cerebral angiitis may rarely cause encephalitis in HIV. Herpes simplex type 1 encephalitis is more common in patients with HIV.

(b) Alertness preserved. AIDS dementia complex from HIV itself:

AIDS dementia complex (or HIV associated cognitive motor complex) is caused directly by brain HIV infection, but occurs only late accompanying severe immunosuppression. A progressive subcortical dementia with slowness and imprecision of thought occurs with impairment of motor control. Conscious level is not impaired. It presents as poor concentration, easy forgetting and slowed fine movements of the limbs and eyes. Later, more obvious motor features develop including frontal release signs (pout and palmomental reflexes) sometimes progressing to a spastic tetraparesis. Cerebral imaging shows PML-like lesions but with subcortical sparing; despite radiologically focal lesions, there are no corresponding focal clinical features.

Spinal cord

A vacuolar myelopathy may occur as part of AIDS dementia complex but usually only when there is already advanced brain dysfunction and cerebral atrophy.

Peripheral nervous system

This is a common form of morbidity in HIV infection. In contrast to CNS disease, an autoimmune aetiology is more common than disease from opportunistic infection.

Nerve and root

1. Autoimmune. Subacute (Guillain–Barré like) and chronic inflammatory demyelinating polyradiculoneuropathies (CIDP) may occur whilst the HIV disease is otherwise clinically latent, and resemble in their presentation and management similar neuropathies seen in patients without HIV disease; the main differences from sporadic forms are the higher CSF cell count and the poorer prognosis for recovery.

Brachial neuritis and multiple mononeuropathy may also accompany early HIV infection.

2. Unknown cause. A distal sensory neuropathy is common but rarely severe and presents as painful dysaethesiae in the feet upon walking and disturbed sleep. It is probably due to cytokine upregulation in response to HIV infection.

3. Opportunistic infection. Cytomegalovirus (CMV) infection is the commonest opportunistic infection in peripheral nerve in HIV. It occurs in the late (AIDS) phase of the illness and presents as a polyradiculoneuropathy or multiple mononeuropathy.

The polyradiculoneuropathy is subacute and progressive, presenting as pain starting in the lumbar root dermatomes, and gradually ascending; a CSF pleocytosis dominated by neutrophils is seen. The prognosis without treatment is very poor.

4. Drug toxicity. Antiviral nucleoside treatment may itself result in a painful peripheral neuropathy.

Muscle The myopathic complications of HIV infection occur late in the illness. Both inflammatory and non-inflammatory myopathies may occur. Treatment with zidovudine may lead to a mitochondrial myopathy with associated depletion of mitochondrial DNA. This occurs through incorporation of zidovudine into mitochondrial DNA inhibiting daughter strand synthesis; the myopathy improves following withdrawal of the drug.

Further reading

Price RC. Neurological complications of HIV infection. *Lancet*, 1996; **348**: 445–52.
Gendelman HE, Lipton SA, Epstein L, Swindells S. *The Neurology of AIDS*. London: Chapman & Hall, 1997.

Related topics of interest

MENINGITIS

Meningitis, inflammation of the meningeal coverings of the brain and spinal cord, is a common acute neurological problem. Most are benign with a good outcome, especially viral forms, but acute bacterial meningitis is a medical emergency with significant morbidity and mortality if untreated.

Acute bacterial meningitis

Subarachnoid space infection with a polymorphonuclear leucocyte (PMN) response usually follows blood-borne dissemination but occasionally follows local spread from ear, mastoid, skull trauma or lumbar puncture.

Organisms
- *Neisseria meningitidis* (meningococcus). Most are serogroup B, recently shifting to group C. Children and adults are affected, usually in winter epidemics. The illness is characterized by septicaemia, arthralgia and a purpuric rash on dependent or pressure-bearing skin. Nasopharyngeal carriage is common. Mortality is 3–5% in the gradual onset (meningitic) form but 15–20% in the abrupt-onset (septicaemic) form.
- *Streptococcus pneumoniae* (pneumococcus). Usually affects adults, especially if debilitated, e.g. alcoholism, hyposplenism, immunodeficiency. Pneumonia and mastoid disease are often the primary source. Onset can be abrupt and death rapid. Mortality is 20%, the prognosis being worse with coma presentation, seizures or low CSF white cell count.
- *Haemophilus influenzae*. Affects particularly neonates and small children, but is rare since the introduction of vaccination. An upper respiratory tract infection precedes an abrupt onset meningitis. The prognosis is good with a low mortality (<5%).
- *E. coli* and *Klebsiella pneumoniae*, are commonest in neonates.

Pathology
The subarachnoid space distends with purulent exudate, the pia-arachnoid becomes congested and hyperaemic. The exudate may organize at the base of the brain, giving cranial nerve palsies and obstructive hydrocephalus. Underlying brain parenchyma becomes oedematous and vessel involvement (vasculitis) produces thrombosis and infarction.

Clinical features

- Symptoms: a prodrome with myalgia, respiratory or ear involvement is followed by severe headache, neck stiffness and photophobia.
- Signs:
    - Meningeal irritation: neck stiffness, Kernig's sign (resistance to knee extension with the thigh flexed), Brudzinski's sign (neck flexion causing hip and knee flexion).
    - Impaired consciousness.
    - Systemic illness with fever.
    - Meningococcal skin rash.
    - Seizures, cranial nerve palsies (including deafness) and local cortical deficits.
- Septicaemic shock with disseminated intravascular coagulation, endocarditis and arthritis may occur.

Investigations

If meningococcal meningitis is suspected, especially with septicaemic shock, treat blindly (stat benzylpenicillin) before investigating.

- CT brain scan is mandatory for altered consciousness, papilloedema or focal neurology.
- Lumbar puncture (LP) should only proceed before a scan if there are no abnormal neurological signs or altered consciousness. CSF investigations include:
    - Gram staining (meningococcus–negative cocci; pneumococcus–positive cocci; *Haemophilus*–negative bacilli) and culture, as initial staining may be negative.
    - White cell count elevated >100/mm^3, mainly PMNs.
    - CSF:serum glucose ratio <50%.
- Blood culture identifies *Haemophilus* (80%), meningococcus (50%) and pneumococcus (<50%). Antibiotic pre-treatment reduces culture positivity significantly.
- Polymerase chain reaction on the earliest CSF and serum may identify bacterial DNA despite negative cultures.
- Skin biopsy of meningococcal rash demonstrates organisms in 63%.
- Nasopharyngeal swabs confirm meningococcal infection (40%) even after antibiotics.
- Serological markers for capsid antigens have a decreasing role in diagnosis.

- The infection source identified with chest, sinus, skull or mastoid radiographs.

Treatment

1. Antibiotics
(a) Before identifying the organism:
- Neonates: cefotaxime and ampicillin.
- Infants, children or adults: cefotaxime or benzylpenicillin.

(b) After identifying the organism:
- Meningococcus or pneumococcus: benzylpenicillin.
- *Haemophilus* and *E. coli*: cefotaxime.
- Chloramphenicol is an alternative for children and adults.

Treatment continues 7–10 days after patient is afebrile.

2. Corticosteroids. These remain controversial, the main indications being children with *Haemophilus* and adults with rapidly declining neurological function.

3. Primary infection. Treatment of source infection.

4. Contacts. Rifampicin 600 mg twice daily for 2 days (meningococcal), or 4 days (*Haemophilus*) with reduced doses for children.

Tuberculous meningitis

Less than 1% of tuberculous infection involves the CNS. Damage results from infection, exudation and vasculitis.

Clinical features
- Phase I, non-specific fever and lethargy.
- Phase II, confusion, cranial nerve palsies, meningism and vasculitis (giving paralysis, ataxia and dysarthria).
- Phase III, coma.

Atypical presentations include a slow onset (dementia) or rapid onset (mimicking acute bacterial meningitis).

Investigations
- CSF shows an acute PMN response changing to a predominantly lymphocytic picture. Protein is increased (1–4 g/l), glucose is reduced and 20% show acid and alcohol fast bacilli (more following CSF culture).
- Chest radiograph: 50–70% have a primary focus or recent infection.

- CT brain scan may show meningeal enhancement, hydrocephalus, infarction or tuberculomas.
- Polymerase chain reaction is unreliable for CSF and serum.
- Purified protein derivative: 90% show a positive skin response.

Treatment
- Triple therapy with isoniazid, rifampicin and pyrazinamide (2 months), then isoniazid and rifampicin (7 months) is the commonest regimen.
- Steroids for decreasing conscious level, neurological progression, or spinal block.
- Ventriculo-peritoneal shunting for hydrocephalus.

Outcome
Despite early treatment, mortality is 10%, but up to 50% with delayed treatment. Another 30% have residual neurological deficits.

Acute viral meningitis

These are the commonest CNS infections, and generally are benign.

Causes
Enteroviruses, mumps, herpes simplex virus type 2 and Epstein–Barr virus are the commonest. Lymphocytic choriomeningitis virus and HIV 1 and 2 are relatively rare.

Clinical features
Following a viral prodrome, the meningeal phase is a mild illness manifesting as meningism without prominent systemic symptoms or focal signs. Recovery occurs over 7–14 days.

Investigations
CSF shows increased lymphocytes or monocytes, mildly elevated protein and normal glucose. Viral serology, nasopharyngeal swabs and stool cultures may help. Often no organism is identified.

Aseptic meningitis

The differential diagnosis includes:

- Infections, e.g. tuberculosis, fungal, leptospirosis, partially treated bacterial meningitis and parameningeal infections.

- Granulomatous disease, e.g. sarcoidosis.
- Malignant meningitis.
- Drugs, e.g. immunoglobulins, ibuprofen.

Subacute/chronic meningitis

This heterogeneous group of disorders frequently requires extensive investigations for diagnosis.

- Very low CSF glucose suggests:
(a) Tuberculous meningitis.
(b) Fungal meningitides including cryptococcus and nocardia.
(c) Malignant meningitis from lung, breast or gastrointestinal carcinoma, leukaemia, lymphoma, cerebral glioma and medulloblastoma.
- Slightly low or normal CSF glucose suggests:
(a) Parameningeal infections: cerebral or epidural abscesses, sinus and mastoid infections.
(b) Bacterial infections including treponemal, brucellosis, leptospirosis, listeriosis and borreliosis.
(c) Miscellaneous: toxoplasmosis and connective tissue disorders including sarcoidosis, Behçet's and SLE.

Spirochaetal infection

Neurosyphilis

Although uncommon, it is increasing in susceptible communities paralleling the rise of HIV infection. Most are asymptomatic but 25% develop an acute meningitis within 2 years of primary infection.

1. Clinical features
- Aseptic meningitis presents as fever, malaise, neck stiffness and skin rash (50%).
- Acute basal meningitis may lead to hydrocephalus with cranial nerve palsies (especially VII and VIII) and papilloedema.

2. Investigations. The CSF shows lymphocytosis (100–2000/mm^3), elevated protein (0.5–2 g/l), low glucose and a positive reagin response (Venereal Disease Research Laboratories). CSF reactivity best indicates disease activity and repeat CSF is required to ensure successful treatment; CSF normal at one year is a cure.

3. Treatment. Penicillin G 2–4 megaunits IV 4-hourly for 10 days (alternatively, procaine penicillin or benzathine penicillin intramuscularly). A Jarisch–Herxheimer reaction following initiation of treatment may require steroids.

Lyme disease

Borrelia burgdorferi, a tick-borne organism, causes erythema chronicum migrans and a relapsing arthritis. After primary infection, secondary dissemination gives a mild meningitic illness with systemic disturbance lasting 3–4 weeks. Fifteen per cent develop neurological involvement, usually a subacute lymphocytic meningitis, sometimes encephalitis. Cranial nerve palsies are common, particularly VII (frequently bilateral). CSF shows a lymphocytosis with elevated protein and normal glucose. Specific serology usually provides the diagnosis. Tetracycline, penicillin or erythromycin are usually effective for the meningitic phase.

Leptospirosis

Leptospirosis is implicated in 4–17% of sporadic aseptic meningitis in the UK and USA. CSF pleocytosis develops in 90% during the second week of illness and an acute aseptic meningitis occurs in 50%. Headache, often severe, is usually the most prominent symptom. The CSF usually becomes abnormal only after the fifth day, initially neutrophils but later lymphocytes. CSF protein is increased. The illness is usually self-limiting but CSF changes persist for up to 10 weeks after clinical recovery.

Further reading

Cartwright K, Knoll S. Optimising the investigation of meningococcal disease. *British Medical Journal*, 1997; **315:** 757–8.
Kennedy PGE, Johnson RT, eds. *Infections of the Nervous System.* Oxford: Butterworth, 1987.
Lindsay KW, Bone I, Callander R. *Neurology and Neurosurgery Illustrated*, 3rd edn. Edinburgh: Churchill Livingstone, 1997.

Related topics of interest

MITOCHONDRIAL DISORDERS

Mitochondria (thread-like bodies) are cytoplasmic organelles which originated from intracellular bacteria early in evolution. They are essential for energy production and are most abundant in high energy-requiring cells. Mitochondrial diseases are a clinically and biochemically heterogeneous group of inborn metabolic disorders involving the mitochondrial respiratory chain.

Mitochondrial DNA

Most human DNA is nuclear but 1% is mitochondrial. Each mitochondrion contains 2–10 double stranded circular DNA molecules (mtDNA), 16 569 base pairs in length. mtDNA encodes subunits of the electron transport chain of the inner mitochondrial membrane and also components of ATP synthetase. Deletions, duplications and a large number of mtDNA point mutations may occur which are associated with human disease.

Characteristics of mitochondrial DNA

Two characteristics account for certain unusual features of mitochondrial diseases.

- Maternal transmission: mitochondria are found only in the cytoplasm. At fertilization, cytoplasm is derived only from the ovum since the spermatocyte contains only nuclear tissue. Thus, mtDNA and many mitochondrial diseases are maternally inherited. Some nuclear DNA encodes enzymes involved in mitochondrial respiratory chain and so a few mitochondrial diseases are autosomally inherited.
- Heteroplasmy: mtDNA is much more susceptible to mutation than nuclear DNA. Since there are several copies of mtDNA within each mitochondrion, a mutation in a single copy will lead to two populations (wild type and mutant) of mtDNA co-existing within a mitochondrion and within a cell. This is termed heteroplasmy. More than 85% mutant mtDNA heteroplasmy is needed to manifest clinically. The level of heteroplasmy varies between different tissues within the same individual (segregative replication) and between affected individuals in the same family. The consequences of this include:
  (a) Widely varying clinical expression (poor genotype/phenotype correlation).

(b) The clinical phenotype correlates with the level of heteroplasmy in affected tissues.

(c) Subclinical cases: some family members may be so mildly affected that they do not come to medical attention; the absence of a family history is therefore unreliable.

Mitochondrial biochemistry

The mitochondrial respiratory chain comprises five enzyme complexes embedded in the inner mitochondrial membrane which utilize products of carbohydrate and fatty acid metabolism. Disruption of these processes may cause cellular dysfunction resulting in disease.

Respiratory chain defects

In adults, the most common respiratory chain defects are in:

- Reduced nicotinamide adenine dinucleotide coenzyme Q (NADHCoQ) reductase (Complex I).
- Coenzyme Q (CoQ) cytochrome C reductase (Complex III).

A secondary carnitine deficiency occurs in some patients.

Classical mitochondrial syndromes

Chronic progressive external ophthalmoplegia (CPEO)

This is a common feature of mitochondrial disease presenting as ptosis and progressive impairment of eye movements with normal pupils. It may be misdiagnosed as myasthenia gravis. It is often associated with other features of mitochondrial disease such as skeletal muscle weakness, encephalopathy or pigmentary retinopathy.

Most cases are due to sporadic mtDNA deletions arising in germ cells; usually there is no family history.

Kearns–Sayre syndrome (KSS)

This describes patients presenting with CPEO and pigmentary retinopathy before the age of 20 years also showing one of:
- Ataxia.
- Complete heart block.
- CSF protein level exceeding 1 g/l.

It is associated with a mtDNA deletion detectable on muscle biopsy.

Pearson's syndrome

This disorder presents as neonatal exocrine pancreatic and hepatic insufficiency, refractory sideroblastic anaemia and pancytopenia with lactic acidosis. Surviving children may later develop KSS.

Myoclonic epilepsy with ragged-red fibres (MERRF)

This is one of the progressive myoclonic ataxias, presenting usually in the second decade with:

- Progressive myoclonus.
- Ataxia.
- Seizures.

Additional features may be short stature, hearing loss, optic atrophy, neuropathy, hypoventilation and migraine.

The disorder is maternally inherited and due to a mtDNA point mutation, particularly A to G transition at 8344 in the tRNA-Lys gene.

This syndrome may comprise the majority of cases formerly labelled Ramsay Hunt syndrome (dyssynergica cerebellaris myoclonica).

Mitochondrial encephalopathy with lactic acidosis and stroke-like episodes (MELAS)

MELAS usually presents in childhood with recurrent stroke-like episodes leading to hemiparesis, hemianopia and cortical blindness often accompanied by focal seizures. It may lead to progressive encephalopathy and premature death. CT brain scanning shows widespread low density areas involving grey and white matter. The condition is associated with mtDNA point mutations especially an A to G transition at 3243 on the tRNA-Leu (UUR) gene.

It must be considered as a cause of young onset stroke.

Leber's hereditary optic neuropathy (LHON)

LHON predominantly affects males presenting under the age of 30 years. It presents as sudden painless visual deterioration becoming bilateral within months with a capillary microangiopathy and subsequent optic atrophy on fundoscopy. It is associated with several mtDNA point mutations encoding subunits of Complex I (notably at 11778 in the ND4 gene) and is maternally inherited. Additional environmental and genetic factors influence disease expression.

Female carriers of these mutations may develop a multiple sclerosis like disorder (Harding's syndrome) with prominent visual involvement, characteristic MRI brain scan changes and positive oligoclonal bands.

Others

Rarer mitochondrial syndromes include NARP (neuropathy, ataxia and retinitis pigmentosa) and MNGIE (mitochondrial neurogastrointestinal encephalopathy). In addition to the classical syndromes, mild ptosis, limb weakness or fatigue, pigmentary retinopathy, hearing loss, diabetes, cardiomyopathy, ataxia, neuropathy and unexplained stroke-like episodes may also be attributable to mitochondrial cytopathy. Predisposition to aminoglycoside-induced sensorineural hearing loss is also a maternally transmitted mitochondrial disorder.

Investigations

Genetic analysis

Molecular genetic analysis of peripheral blood white cells or preferably muscle biopsy tissue may localize the pathological point mutation providing a rapid screening test for mitochondrial disease.

Pathology: muscle biopsy

The classical features of ragged-red fibres seen on muscle stained with Gomori Trichrome is characteristic. Clusters of red staining mitochondria in the periphery of affected muscle cells (subsarcolemmal aggregates) occur. Aggregates are sometimes better seen on NADH or succinate dehydrogenase stains but histological changes are not invariably present and are an imperfect marker of systemic mitochondrial disease.

Electron microscopy may demonstrate abnormal numbers and morphology of mitochondria sometimes with paracrystalline inclusions.

Biochemistry

1. Mitochondrial enzyme defects. Analysis of Complexes I to V on muscle biopsy tissue may give a more detailed understanding of an individual's condition.

2. Serum creatine kinase. This is only marginally increased and is unhelpful in diagnosis.

3. Lactate. Lactate levels in serum and CSF may be abnormally elevated particularly several hours after fasting or exercise. This follows impaired utilization of pyruvate in Krebs' cycle.

Neurophysiology   Electromyography may show only non-specific changes in mitochondrial myopathy.

Ageing and degenerative disease

Owing to the high mutation rate of mtDNA, somatic mtDNA mutations accumulate with normal ageing. This may lead to a progressive decline in oxidative phosphorylation and may contribute to normal ageing. Mitochondrial dysfunction may also underly certain neurodegenerative disorders, e.g. Alzheimer's, Parkinson's and Huntington's disease.

Management

Effective treatment remains limited. Acute exacerbations with severe lactic acidosis precipitated by infection, exercise or alcohol may be improved by slow infusions of sodium bicarbonate. Patients with secondary carnitine deficiency may improve with oral carnitine. Treatment with ubiquinone, ascorbic acid, menadione and steroids have given no consistent improvements.

Further reading

Servidei S. Mitochondrial encephalomyelopathies: gene mutations. *Neuromuscular Disorders,* 1997; **7**: XIII–XVIII.
Shapira AHV. Mitochondrial disorders. *Current Opinion in Neurology,* 1997; **10**: 43–7.
Sherrat EJ, Thomas AW, Alcolado JC. Mitochondrial DNA defects: a widening clinical spectrum of disorders. *Clinical Science,* 1997; **92**: 225–35.

Related topics of interest

MONONEUROPATHIES

Carpal tunnel syndrome

Anatomy

The median nerve passes with the flexor tendons beneath the transverse carpal ligament and entrapment here leads to the carpal tunnel syndrome. Women are more affected than men. It is often bilateral though worse in the dominant hand.

Causes

Often none is found. It is associated with repetitive movement occupations, arthritis, tenosynovitis, pregnancy, hypothyroidism, amyloidosis (including dialysis) and acromegaly.

Symptoms

- Pain in the first three digits, arm and shoulder.
- Tingling confined to the palmar first three digits.
- Symptoms characteristically develop from sleep and are relieved by hand shaking.
- Daytime symptoms provoked by use, e.g. knitting.
- The hand may feel weak.

Signs

There may be reduced sensation over the first $3\frac{1}{2}$ digits. Later there is wasting and weakness of the median-innervated intrinsic muscles (especially abductor pollicis brevis). Tinel's sign (wrist tapping) and Phalen's sign (wrist flexion) are unreliable.

Investigations

Nerve conduction studies are essential. The most reliable indicators are slowed sensory velocity and reduced amplitude of the median sensory action potential.

Differential diagnosis

- C6,7 radiculopathy presents as hand pain and tingling but differs in that:
    Waking at night and shaking the hand is unusual.
    Symptoms involve both dorsal and palmar finger surfaces.
    Symptoms are rarely bilateral.
    Neck movement may provoke pain.
    Weakness and reflex change in non-median-innervated muscles.
    Nerve conduction normal.

- Thoracic inlet syndrome (brachial plexus lower trunk compression by cervical rib or band) differs in that:
  Small hand muscle wasting begins in, but is not confined to, the thenar eminence.
  Sensory loss over the medial hand and forearm.

Management

- Consider underlying causes.
- Dorsiflexion wrist splints at night.
- Carpal tunnel corticosteroid injection.
- Surgical decompression needed for most with significant symptoms.

Ulnar nerve

Anatomy

At the elbow, the ulnar nerve lies in the condylar (ulnar) groove behind the medial epicondyle. Its main sensory branch leaves in the distal forearm to innervate the medial hand and fourth and fifth digits. In the wrist it passes between the pisiform bone and the hook of hamate (Guyon's canal) where it divides into:

- Superficial sensory branch supplying the distal medial palm and palmar aspect of $1\frac{1}{2}$ digits.
- Deep motor branch supplying the hypothenar muscles, then crossing the palm to innervate the other intrinsic muscles, ending at the first dorsal interosseous.

Elbow lesion

This is the commonest site, the nerve here covered only by skin and subcutaneous fat. It may follow a single injury or multiple minor trauma and there may be predisposing elbow deformity; often there is no apparent reason.

Symptoms: numbness and tingling on the fourth and fifth digits and medial palm (never forearm), often with hand weakness.

Signs: ulnar nerve palpation (axilla to wrist) may reveal a mass or tenderness. Tinel's sign at the elbow may give tingling but is only significant if very severe. A complete lesion gives:

- Numbness over the medial hand and $1\frac{1}{2}$ digits.

- Weakness and wasting of all ulnar-innervated intrinsic hand muscles plus flexor carpi ulnaris and flexor digitorum profundus (medial two digits).

Wrist and hand

Wrist lesions are rare, affecting only the intrinsic hand muscles and distal hand sensation.

Hand lesions, e.g. from repetitive trauma by tools or crutches, involve all the ulnar-innervated small hand muscles except the hypothenar eminence, often without sensory loss.

Differential diagnosis

- Pancoast's syndrome (tumour invasion of the lower brachial plexus) differs from ulnar neuropathy in that:

    Arm pain, tingling and numbness is over the medial arm/forearm.
    All small hand muscles are involved.
    Associated Horner's syndrome.
- Syringomyelia differs in that:
    All small hand muscles are involved.
    The sensory loss is dissociated.
- Motor neurone disease may be confused with an ulnar lesion in the hand, which spares sensation.

Investigations

Nerve conduction studies: here, motor conduction velocities are the most reliable. Ulnar nerve sensory action potential is commonly lost in manual workers.

Management

- Ulnar protection, e.g. foam elbow support at night.
- Surgery: though frequently undertaken its benefit is disputed.

Radial nerve

Anatomy

The nerve entwines the humeral shaft in the spiral groove. At the elbow it divides into:

- Posterior interosseous branch motor to the finger extensors.
- Superficial cutaneous branch sensory to the dorsal hand.

The wrist extensor motor supply leaves the nerve in the upper arm.

Axillary or upper arm lesions	Neuropraxis, e.g. from crutches or drunken sleep ('Saturday night palsy') presents as wrist drop (additional triceps weakness if axillary) but often no demonstrable sensory loss.
Posterior interosseous lesions	Compression by lipoma, ganglia, rheumatoid arthritis or proximal forearm fibrous band give finger drop without wrist drop or sensory loss.
Management	• Neuropraxis is managed conservatively, awaiting spontaneous recovery over weeks or months. • Posterior interosseous palsy may require imaging and surgical exploration.

Common peroneal nerve

Anatomy	This branch of the sciatic nerve is vulnerable to compression as it winds around the fibular neck. Here it divides into: • Superficial peroneal, motor to the peroneal muscles and sensory to the lower lateral leg and dorsal foot. • Deep peroneal, motor to foot and toe dorsiflexors, tibialis anterior, extensor hallucis longus and extensor digitorum brevis and sensory to the first interdigital web space.
Lesions	These follow local trauma during sleep, coma, general anaesthetic, plaster bandage etc. presenting as a foot drop with weakness of toe and foot dorsiflexion and ankle eversion; sensory loss involves the antero-lateral lower leg and dorsal foot. Deep peroneal neuropathy may accompany anterior compartment swelling, e.g. following exercise or trauma.
Nerve conduction studies	These show conduction impairment at the fibular neck and neuropathic changes confined to common peroneal-innervated nerve muscles.
Differential diagnosis	L5 radiculopathy presents as foot drop with dorsal foot sensory loss, but is distinguished by: • Back and leg pain.

- Gluteal muscle involvement (superior and inferior gluteal nerve) giving weak hip extension and abduction.
- Ankle inversion weakness (tibial nerve).
- With associated S1 compression, a reduced ankle jerk.

Management
- With a clear compressive history an expectant approach is justified; if not, imaging and possible exploration may be needed.
- Anterior compartment syndrome is a surgical emergency.

Femoral nerve

Anatomy

It arises from the lumbar plexus, passes between the psoas and iliacus (iliacus compartment), then deep to the inguinal ligament before dividing into the motor branch (to quadriceps) and cutaneous branch (to the anterior thigh), ending as the saphenous nerve (sensory to medial calf).

Causes

Usually in the iliacus compartment by haematoma, infiltration or operation.

Signs

Quadriceps wasting and weakness, reduced knee jerk, reduced antero-medial thigh and leg sensation.

Differential diagnosis

L2-4 plexopathy, e.g. diabetic amyotrophy, gives more extensive weakness, including hip adductors (obturator nerve) and psoas.

Lateral cutaneous nerve of the thigh

Anatomy

This passes through a small lateral split in the inguinal ligament and is purely sensory.

Clinical

Meralgia paraesthetica. In obese or pregnant patients or possibly kinked by tight clothing or unaccustomed exercise, nerve compression leads to pain and tingling in the lateral thigh, sensitivity to touch exacerbated by prolonged sitting or standing and sensory loss confined to the lateral thigh. It is sometimes bilateral.

Management Usually, it resolves spontaneously; analgesia is sometimes required.

Bell's palsy

Incidence is 25/100 000 and is commoner in patients with diabetes and hypertension.

Clinical Sudden unilateral lower motor neurone facial weakness, complete in 70%, together with ipsilateral mastoid pain (50%), reduced taste (chorda tympani) (30%), hyperacusis (stapedius) (30%), and excess tearing (10%). 'Facial numbness' is often described but none is found objectively.

Prognosis Recovery can be rapid and complete but in more severe cases spontaneous recovery begins at about 2 months and further improvement is rarely seen beyond 9 months. Adverse factors are:

- Greater age.
- Abrupt onset.
- Completeness of lesion.
- Taste involvement.

Management
- Steroids (short reducing course) are generally used if seen within 4 days of onset. Symptomatic treatment with heat and massage may help.
- Surgery: eye protection using tarsorraphy or botulinum toxin to close the lid may be needed acutely. Facial nerve decompression is not indicated. Cosmetic procedures, e.g. sling, may be undertaken when no further recovery is expected.

Differential diagnosis Ramsay Hunt syndrome with herpes zoster rash around the external auditory canal carries a poorer prognosis for recovery.

Acoustic neuroma and other cerebello-pontine angle lesions should be considered.

Further reading

Dyck PJ, Thomas PK. *Peripheral Neuropathy*, 3rd edn. Philadelphia: WB Saunders, 1993.

Related topics of interest

MOTOR NEURONE DISEASES

Motor neurone disease (MND) is characterized by progressive degeneration of both UMNs and LMNs.

Clinical features

The clinical features depend upon the extent and distribution of motor neurone involvement. The life expectancy depends upon the severity of bulbar and ventilatory muscle weakness.

Patients present with weakness, fatigue and muscle wasting, cramps and fasciculations. Dysphagia, dysarthria and dyspnoea frequently develop.

- LMN: muscle wasting, weakness and fasciculations.
- UMN: spasticity, hyper-reflexia and extensor plantar responses.
- Bulbar: dysarthria and slow swallow.
- Ventilatory: poor cough and tachypnoea.
- Cognitive function: dementia, particularly frontal, occasionally occurs ('MND plus').

The following are spared:

- External ocular muscles.
- Pelvic floor striated muscles (continence).
- Sensory: some non-specific sensory symptoms occur without signs.

Epidemiology

MND occurs predominantly in middle aged and elderly, the age-specific incidence rising to 1 in 10 000 when aged 65–85 years. The male to female ratio is 1.5 to 1.0. Less than 10% are familial.

Pathology

The characteristic pathology is motor neurone degeneration in the anterior horn of the spinal cord grey matter (anterior horn cells). The motor cranial nerves III, IV and VI (eye movements) are spared as is Onuf's nucleus in the sacral cord (governing sphincter control).

Inclusion bodies (Bunina bodies) occur in the degenerating motor neurones, staining immuno-cytochemically for ubiquitin.

Pathogenesis

The cause is unknown. Genetic factors are imputed in a minority. Environmental exposure to neurotoxins might explain the increased incidence among leather workers.

The theory that the damage is mediated by excitotoxic amino acids, e.g. glutamate, is supported by increased extracellular glutamate in MND. Also, abnormal copper-zinc superoxide dismutase 1 (SOD1) mutation in some familial cases suggests free radical damage in MND.

Types

Four forms are distinguished by varying extent of UMN and LMN involvement:

- Amyotrophic lateral sclerosis (80%): both UMN and LMN are affected with limbs, bulbar and ventilatory muscles involved.
- Progressive bulbar palsy (10%): combined LMN and UMN involvement gives signs respectively of bulbar palsy (tongue atrophy, weakness and fasciculation) and pseudobulbar palsy (slow tongue movements and brisk jaw jerk).
- Progressive muscular atrophy is predominantly LMN involvement of the limbs and trunk. Slower onset forms may resemble spinal muscular atrophy.
- Primary lateral sclerosis: a rare variant with clinical and pathological degeneration restricted to UMNs giving pseudobulbar palsy and spastic tetraparesis.

Variants

1. Familial MND. A heterogeneous group of disorders comprising 5–10% of MND. Generally they show a younger onset, shorter duration of illness and more widespread disease.

The copper-zinc SOD1 mutation (chromosome 21q22) is identified in 15% of familial cases.

2. X-linked bulbospinal neuronopathy (Kennedy's disease). This familial disorder is confined to males; longevity is surprisingly little affected. Bulbar weakness occurs with LMN limb signs, gynaecomastia and postural tremor. Facial fasciculations are characteristic. Its cause is an expanded triplet repeat (CAG) in the first exon of the androgen receptor gene (X chromosome).

3. Pacific MND. The combination of MND, parkinsonism and dementia characterizes the MND-like illness found in Guam (Marinas archipelago, South Pacific), Western New Guinea and the Japanese Kii Peninsula.

4. Amyotrophic Creutzfeldt–Jakob disease (CJD). Sometimes, apparent CJD shows prominent anterior horn cell neurone degeneration presenting as rapid onset MND with fronto-temporal dementia. It is probably not a prion disorder and is designated 'MND plus'.

Differential diagnosis

A confident diagnosis of MND is essential since several treatable conditions may mimic MND. The diagnosis can be difficult in aged people owing to co-morbidity, e.g. spinal degenerative disease giving fasciculations at any spinal level or cerebrovascular disease leading to bulbar signs.

1. Spinal muscular atrophy (SMA). This group of autosomal recessive conditions is associated with anterior horn cell degeneration. They resemble muscular dystrophy except for fasciculations and early loss of tendon reflexes. There are three clinical types:

- Werdig–Hoffmann disease (infantile).
- Kugelberg–Welander (juvenile).
- Adult onset.

These each map to chromosome 5q12-14. The early onset forms are homozygous and the juvenile and adult forms are heterozygous.

Distal SMA represents 10% of SMAs and mimics the Charcot–Marie–Tooth phenotype though is distinguishable by the normal sensation and sensory nerve action potentials.

Monomelic SMA is a rare adult-onset condition where wasting of one limb occurs, particularly in males. It is relatively benign and must be distinguished from MND. Some cases are focal CIDP and so are potentially responsive to immunoglobulin treatment.

2. Multifocal motor neuropathy with conduction block. This important treatable imitator of MND is diagnosed eletrophysiologically (multifocal partial conduction blocks). It presents with patchy asymmetrical predominantly distal muscle wasting, weakness and fasciculations often more in the upper limbs. Occasionally, sensory symptoms occur without signs. The reflexes are preserved but not brisk, CSF is normal and circulating anti-ganglioside antibodies are occasionally found. Neurophysiology studies usually give the diagnosis. It is usually treated with intravenous immunoglobulins.

3. Cervical spondylosis with myeloradiculopathy. This may give the combination of LMN signs (confined to the level of the compressed nerve roots) and UMN signs (below the level of cord compression). There are usually associated sensory changes in the corresponding spinal dermatomes.

4. Cramp-fasciculation syndrome. This is one of several conditions characterized by peripheral nerve hyper-excitability. It is a diagnosis of exclusion.

Investigations

The diagnosis is essentially clinical according to diagnostic criteria (El Escorial, 1994). Investigations aim to exclude conditions mimicking MND.

1. Neurophysiology. Motor nerve conduction velocity is normal though the compound muscle action potential amplitude is reduced. Electromyography shows evidence of chronic partial denervation with:

- Fibrillation potentials on needle insertion.
- Spontaneous fibrillation and fasciculation potentials in the resting muscle.
- Marked reduction in numbers of spikes on maximal muscle contraction.

2. Imaging. Brain and spinal cord imaging may be necessary to exclude structural causes of UMN and LMN lesions.

3. Cerebrospinal fluid examination. This is sometimes indicated to exclude inflammatory causes of neuronal degeneration.

4. Bloods
- Creatine kinase is often mildly elevated.
- VDRL is essential to exclude neurosyphilis.
- Anti-ganglioside antibodies may suggest multifocal motor neuropathy.
- SOD1 antibodies may be identified in some familial cases.

Management

1. Certainty of diagnosis. This implies:
- A positive clinical diagnosis.
- Exclusion of related conditions.

2. *Support*

(a) Giving the diagnosis. Careful thought must be given to planning the giving of the diagnosis (protected time, relative or carer present etc.).

(b) Support and counselling. Appropriate support, counselling and follow up must be provided after the diagnosis is given. The assistance of and telephone contact with nurse counsellors and MND association support workers are important.

(c) Symptomatic
- Cramps may respond to physical stretches and to quinine.
- Fasciculations: beta blockers or anticonvulsants, e.g. gabapentin.
- Spasticity.
- Depression.
- Sleep disturbance.

(d) Physical. Disability develops rapidly and aids to daily living must be provided promptly, e.g. walking stick, Zimmer frame or wheelchair, dropped foot splints, wrist dorsiflexors.

3. *Specific*

(a) Nutrition and swallowing. Swallowing difficulty and aspiration are particular problems in MND. Percutaneous endoscopic gastrostomy is considered:

- Electively while still relatively well nourished.
- To avoid the prolonged struggles to eat and maintain nutrition.
- To reduce the aspiration risk.

A gastrostomy still allows eating some foods for pleasure.

(b) Speech. Communication aids including portable typewriters should be available as dysarthria progresses to anarthria.

(c) Respiratory. Respiratory physiotherapy and assisted coughing are sometimes appropriate. Disproportionate diaphragmatic involvement provoking life-threatening breathlessness and orthopnoea may require nocturnal assisted ventilation (by mask) if the patient is still ambulant; the aim is relief of breathlessness, not correction of physical and biochemical abnormalities.

4. Drugs
- Anticholinesterases, e.g. pyridostigmine, occasionally improve weakness in early MND but increased salivation limit their usefulness.
- Anticholinergics, e.g. propantheline, dry secretions and prevent drooling.
- Glutamate modulators, e.g. riluzole prolongs life expectancy in MND.
- Nerve growth factors, muscle proteins mediating nerve regeneration after injury, can support anterior horn cell survival. Human insulin-like growth factor 1 injections appear effective in slowing MND.
- A trial of immunoglobulins is appropriate for purely LMN forms with the possibility of multifocal motor neuropathy being missed neurophysiologically.
- Narcotics are appropriate in terminal care.

Further reading

Leigh PN, Swash M, eds. *Motor Neurone Disease: Biology and Management.* London: Springer Verlag, 1995.
World Federation of Neurology Research Group on Neuromuscular Diseases. El Escorial World Federation of Neurology criteria for the diagnosis of amyotrophic lateral sclerosis. *Journal of the Neurological Sciences,* 1994; **124** (Suppl): 96–107.

Related topics of interest

MULTIPLE SCLEROSIS

Multiple sclerosis (MS) is the commonest cause of neurological disability in the UK. Demyelination is central to the pathogenesis, producing symptoms and signs of multiple areas of CNS involvement dissociated in time. The diagnosis is only made with certainty after death.

Epidemiology
- Most patients (90%) present aged 10 to 50 years.
- Female:male prevalence is 2:1.
- MS affects all races although is rare in Afro-Caribbeans and common in Caucasians.
- Prevalence in susceptible populations relates to latitude: the incidence increases further from the equator. The UK prevalence is 1 per 1000 compared to 0.06 per 1000 in Spain.

Aetiology
This is unknown. No definite infective cause has been demonstrated although some relapses are linked to infective episodes.

Genetics
- A multifactorial genetic component to susceptibility is likely.
- Monozygotic twins show 25% concordance for MS, dizygotic 3%, and first degree relatives 1%.
- Caucasians show linkage to HLA A3, A7, DR2(15) and DQ1 on chromosome 6.
- T-cell receptor loci and the immunoglobulin heavy chain gene are also associated.

Pathology
The hallmark is immune-mediated damage to the oligodendrocyte myelin complex in multiple CNS areas producing multiple plaques, often perivascular. Early blood–brain barrier breakdown in response to an unknown stimulus may trigger the cascade of events including:

- Inflammatory infiltrate (lymphocytes, plasma cells, macrophages) through a damaged blood–brain barrier.
- Oligodendrocyte damage and myelin stripping by astrocytes, microglia and macrophages.
- Complement, immune complex and cytokine release with local activation and subsequent release into CSF.

- Astrocyte proliferation.
- Damage to demyelinated axons.
- Limited and incomplete myelin repair.

Clinical types

- Relapsing-remitting (33%), dominated by symptomatic relapses with remissions either complete or leaving some disability.
- Secondarily progressive (22%) where an initial relapsing-remitting course subsequently develops into progressive disease, with or without superimposed relapses.
- Primary progressive (43%) where symptoms and signs progress from the onset.

Symptoms

Symptoms derive from sites of predilection for plaques. Presenting symptoms often begin focally then spread over hours to days, last for weeks before, in relapsing disease, resolving over weeks to months. The commonest symptoms at presentation are:

(a) Sensory: pins and needles, hyperaesthesia, dysaesthesia, unpleasant paraesthesias and painful paroxysmal disturbances.

(b) Visual: painful visual loss, blurred vision with loss of colour definition from optic neuritis, oscillopsia (visual image instability) from cerebellar involvement, and diplopia from cranial nerve or brainstem lesions.

(c) Motor: limb weakness, heaviness, stiffness and sometimes painful spasms.

(d) Brainstem/cerebellar: coordination difficulties, tremor, vertigo and gait disturbance. Sensory ataxia can occur from position sense loss particularly in the hands.

(e) Sphincter disturbance: urinary frequency, urgency, incontinence and hesitancy result from brain, spinal cord and autonomic involvement. Sexual dysfunction is common, bowel symptoms less so.

(f) Non-specific symptoms include fatigue and cognitive impairment.

(g) Paroxysmal symptoms: these last seconds to minutes, sometimes hours, and comprise:

- Uthoff's phenomenon: body temperature increase from exercise or hot environment, e.g. bath produce temporary increases or recurrence of symptoms.

- L'hermitte's phenomenon: neck flexion produces tingling electric shock-like sensations in the arms and legs. Caused by plaques in the cervical cord, the symptom also occurs in cervical cord compression and B_{12} deficiency.
- Paroxysmal dysarthria, ataxia, tonic spasms (paroxysmal dystonias), and trigeminal neuralgia.

(h) Age-related presentation:
- Optic neuritis is more likely if age of onset is <20 years.
- Insidious myelopathy is more likely if >40 years.

Signs

1. Motor. Spasticity, pyramidal weakness, brisk deep tendon reflexes and extensor plantars indicate upper motor neurone involvement.

2. Sensory. Altered sensory perception, e.g. hyperaesthesia follow patterns determined by plaque location. Cord lesions may produce dissociated or suspended sensory loss mimicking compression or syrinx. Position sense loss in the hands produces sensory ataxia 'the useless hand of Oppenheim'.

3. Visual. Acute optic neuritis produces impaired visual acuity sometimes with swollen, haemorrhagic discs. Optic atrophy with disc pallor may follow. Nystagmus with ocular palsies occur. Internuclear ophthalmoplegia is particularly associated with MS.

4. Cerebellar. Limb and gait ataxia, nystagmus, and dysarthria (Charcot's triad).

5. Brainstem. Cranial nerve palsies with motor, sensory, visual and cerebellar features occur.
Sensory symptoms without signs and motor signs without symptoms are characteristic of MS.

Investigations

- MRI is the most sensitive imaging technique.
Brain MRI (T2 weighted) shows typical periventricular high signal abnormalities; lesions enhance using gadolinium-DTPA. Other preferentially affected areas include optic nerve, corpus callosum, temporal lobes, brainstem and cerebellum. The FLAIR (Fast Fluid-Attenuated Inversion Recovery) MRI sequence increases sensitivity to 98%. MRI changes are non-specific

and accompany other CNS inflammatory disorders including SLE, sarcoidosis, vasculitis, infective and other demyelinating diseases. Clinically silent lesions are common.

Spinal MRI is much less sensitive and used only to exclude other pathology.

- CSF

  Oligoclonal bands: 95% of patients with clinically definite MS have locally-synthesized oligoclonal IgG resulting from clonal production by activated lymphocytes within the CNS. This is not specific for MS and occurs in other inflammatory, infective and demyelinating disorders.

  Cells: 50% have >5 white cells/mm^3 (predominantly lymphocytes) but rarely >50/mm^3.

  Protein: A mild increase is common.

- Electrophysiology: visual, auditory and brain stem evoked potentials help to identify subclinical lesions; with MRI brain scanning, however, they are now rarely needed for diagnosis.

- CT head scanning is no longer used in MS diagnosis.

- There are no clinically useful serological markers for MS though some have antinuclear antibodies of uncertain relevance.

Diagnosis

This is based upon an appropriate history and clinical signs.

- There must be clinical or paraclinical evidence of lesions at more than one site in the CNS and a history of two or more clinical relapses (symptom presentation or exacerbation lasting >24 hours), or evidence of continuous disease progression over 6 months.

- There must be no other explanation for the symptoms and signs.

Several diagnostic criteria have been used for research purposes, the most commonly used being the Poser criteria which incorporates MRI, CSF and electrophysiology results.

Differential diagnosis

Several other disorders present with symptoms and signs mimicking MS and are generally excluded by appropriate investigations.

- Autoimmune disorders including SLE, Sjögren's, Behçet's, polyarteritis and vasculitis and acute disseminated encephalomyelitis.
- Granulomatous disease including sarcoidosis and Wegener's.
- Infections including Lyme disease, syphilis and HIV.
- Miscellaneous disorders including mitochondrial cytopathy, Leber's hereditary optic neuropathy, adrenoleucodystrophy, cardiogenic emboli, Chiari malformation and cerebellar degenerative disorders.

Management

Symptomatic

- Painful sensory symptoms respond to carbamazepine, phenytoin and amitriptyline.
- Muscle spasms and spasticity respond to baclofen, dantrolene, diazepam and tizanidine. Intrathecal baclofen is used for some intractable cases.
- Bladder disturbances: detrusor instability responds to oxybutynin or imipramine. Intermittent self-catheterization and suprapubic vibrators are helpful for detrusor-sphincter incoordination. Reducing evening fluid intake and desmopressin nasal spray may reduce nocturia.
- Dystonias and hemiataxia may respond to thalamotomy.
- Tremor and cerebellar symptoms are poorly responsive but isoniazid, carbamazepine, clonazepam and gabapentin have been used.
- Sexual dysfunction may respond to papaverine (impotence) and yohimbine (ejaculatory failure).
- Physiotherapy and occupational therapy are important adjuncts.

Disease modification

1. Acute relapse. Intravenous or oral methylprednisolone 1g daily for 3 days shortens the relapse duration but does not influence either ultimate recovery or progression of first episodes to MS.

2. Disease progression
- ß-interferon benefits relapsing-remitting disease with ~50% reduction in severe relapses and a modest effect on disability. There is a dramatic reduction in development of new lesions on MRI brain scanning.

<table>
<tr><td>**Prognosis**</td><td>

- Copolymer I modestly affects relapse rate but not disability.
- Azathioprine or pulsed intravenous immunoglobulins help some patients; most other immunosuppressives are unsuccessful.

</td></tr>
</table>

Prognosis

- Thirty per cent of patients follow a benign course (infrequent relapses and mild disability). Good prognostic features include: onset with optic neuritis, isolated brainstem or sensory symptoms, onset age <40 years, relapsing-remitting disease, first attack of short duration, no family history.
- Ten to fifteen per cent have a bad prognosis. Poor prognostic features include onset age >40 years, multiple sites at onset or cerebellar/spinal cord involvement, first attack of long duration, progressive course from onset, family history of MS.
- The risk of progressing from a first episode (optic neuritis, brainstem or spinal cord syndrome) to MS over 10 years ranges from 10% (normal MRI at onset) to 80% (abnormal MRI at onset).
- CSF oligoclonal IgG at first symptom also strongly predicts MS development.

Further reading

Matthews WB, Compston A, Allen IV, Martyn CN. *McAlpine's Multiple Sclerosis*, 2nd edn. Edinburgh: Churchill Livingstone, 1991.
Matthews WB. *Multiple Sclerosis: The Facts*, 3rd edn. Oxford: Oxford University Press, 1993.
Miller DH. Demyelinating diseases. *Current Opinions in Neurology,* 1997; **10:** 179–214.

Related topics of interest

Neurogenic bladder (p. 184)
Nystagmus (p. 206)
Optic nerve disorders (p. 210)

MUSCLE DISORDERS (INFLAMMATORY)

Inflammatory muscle disorders comprise the major group of treatable myopathies. They comprise those with known cause (e.g. infection or drugs) and idiopathic/autoimmune types.

Known cause

Infectious myositis

- Viral. This presents, often in childhood, with painful generalized muscle weakness following a prodromal febrile illness. Occasionally there is rhabdomyolysis and myocarditis. The viruses most commonly associated are enteroviruses (especially Cocksackie), influenza B, HIV and HTLV1. The serum creatine kinase (CK) is elevated to 5–50 times normal. It is rare to isolate virus from the muscle but infection is inferred from blood viral titres. The condition usually resolves spontaneously with supportive treatment; occasionally chronic muscle infection (e.g. from HIV) can give a clinical picture indistinguishable from polymyositis.
- Bacterial. This presents, especially in tropical countries, as a suppurative myositis and is usually caused by *Staphylococcus aureus*.
- Parasitic. This is rare in the UK, the main causes being toxoplasmosis, cysticercosis and trichinosis.

Drug-induced

This can be seen with d-penicillamine and some lipid lowering agents.

Unknown cause/autoimmune

The idiopathic inflammatory myopathies are a heterogeneous group of disorders characterized by chronic lymphocytic and macrophage infiltration in muscle tissue. Polymyositis and dermatomyositis are often confused or considered as the same condition, but are distinct with different underlying mechanisms.

Polymyositis

1. Clinical features. A sporadic and often very chronic condition affecting predominantly older females. It presents with symmetrical weakness of proximal limb muscles occasionally with pain and muscle tenderness;

weight loss, neck weakness, dysphagia and voice change are common.

2. Mechanism. There is a T-cell-mediated cytotoxicity of muscle fibres. The muscle inflammatory infiltrate is composed of activated lymphocytes.

3. Investigations. The CK and the ESR are usually, though not invariably, elevated. Electromyography may show abundant brief low amplitude polyphasic potentials. Muscle biopsy shows endomysial infiltration by mononuclear inflammatory infiltrates (predominantly T8 lymphocytes), surrounding and invading muscle fibres. Anti Jo-1 antibody, found in 30% of cases, is associated with lung infiltrates and greater risk of cardiomyopathy. Antibody to signal recognition peptide, found in 5%, is associated with a fulminant course and resistance to treatment. Electrocardiogram occasionally shows heart block.

4. Management. With immunosuppression, usually daily prednisolone 40–60 mg daily initially, perhaps together with azathioprine 2.5 mg/kg/day, switching to alternate day prednisolone when there is clear clinical improvement. Cyclosporin, pulsed cyclophosphamide or intravenous immunoglobulin may be necessary if the steroid response is inadequate. Muscle strength measurements are important in monitoring treatment progress. The encouragement of mobility (especially in the elderly) and intensive physiotherapy aimed at preventing contractures is essential. A high protein diet is advisable. Attention to swallowing, adequacy of ventilation and precautions against deep venous thrombosis must be considered.

Dermatomyositis

1. Clinical features. The presentation is subacute and generally affects a younger population than polymyositis. Dermatomyositis comprises 95% of childhood myositis. Muscle pain and tenderness are usual; fever, weight loss and dysphagia are common. A heliotrope-coloured rash over the extensor surfaces and trunk occurs in 90% of cases but is not essential for the diagnosis.

2. Mechanism. The disease is mediated by humoral factors such as antibodies against capillary endothelial cells; it is thus a complement-mediated microangiopathy with the muscle inflammation occurring secondarily to focal ischaemia.

3. Investigations. In 15% of adults there is an underlying malignancy and some basic screening investigations in adults are required (rectal and vaginal examination, chest radiograph and abdominal ultrasound). CK and ESR are usually elevated. Muscle biopsy shows microvascular injury with perifascicular fibre atrophy, a perimysial inflammatory infiltrate dominated by B and T4 lymphocytes; deposits of membrane attack complex confirm the role of complement. Antibodies to Mi-2, an antinuclear antibody, are found in 20% of cases.

4. Management. As for polymyositis.

Inclusion body myositis

1. Clinical features. It usually occurs in older people and is the commonest myopathy of elderly men. The onset is slow and painless with a predominantly distal pattern of weakness though particularly involves the quadriceps and forearm flexors, especially flexor digitorum profundus. It can progress to severe generalized weakness and disability. Dysphagia occurs in one third of cases. There is no skin rash. Numbness and sensory symptoms may suggest an associated mild peripheral neuropathy.

2. Mechanism. The condition is a degenerative disorder, partly mediated by cytotoxic T cells, with a secondary inflammatory response to degenerating muscle. This explains why the amount of inflammation is variable and the response to immunosuppression is poor.

3. Investigations. Serum CK is usually normal. Muscle biopsy may show inflammation, predominantly an endomysially-located mononuclear infiltrate with cytotoxic T cells invading non-necrotic muscle fibres; rimmed vacuoles and filamentous inclusions in muscle are characteristic. The inclusions contain ubiquitin and tau protein, so are pathologically similar to Alzheimer neurofibrillary tangles.

4. Management. No specific treatment is available and management is supportive only.

Granulomatous myositis This is associated particularly with sarcoidosis, characteristic granulomata being seen on muscle biopsy.

Further reading

Walton JN, Karpati G, Hilton-Jones D, eds. *Disorders of Voluntary Muscle*, 6th edn. Edinburgh: Churchill Livingstone, 1994.
Lane RJM, ed. *Handbook of Muscle Disease*. Monticello: Marcel Dekker, 1996.

Related topics of interest

HIV neurology (p. 136)
Mitochondrial disorders (p. 146)
Muscle disorders (inherited) (p. 174)
Paraneoplastic neurological syndromes (p. 215)

MUSCLE DISORDERS (INHERITED)

The hereditary myopathies comprise the muscular dystrophies, hereditary dystrophic myotonias, and various inherited metabolic disorders including those caused by disorders of mitochondrial function.

Classification

- Muscular dystrophies.
  X-linked.
    Duchenne and Becker dystrophies.
    Emery–Dreifuss syndrome.
  Autosomal dominant.
    Facioscapulohumeral muscular dystrophy.
    Scapuloperoneal dystrophy.
    Oculopharyngeal dystrophy.
  Autosomal recessive.
    Limb girdle muscular dystrophy.
- Hereditary myotonias.
  Myotonic dystrophy.
  Channelopathies.
- Congenital myopathies.
  Nemaline myopathy.
  Central core disease.
- Metabolic.
  McArdle's disease.
  Phosphofructokinase deficiency.
- Mitochondrial disorders.

Clinical features

1. Duchenne dystrophy. Typically, a boy with previous mild delay in motor milestones presents aged 3–5 years with declining ability to climb stairs, a waddling gait and paradoxically large calves. The decline in mobility is remorseless to wheelchair confinement aged 9–12 years complicated by contractures. Death at 17–20 years results from ventilatory failure from progressive respiratory muscle weakness, compounded by scoliosis. Cardiomyopathy is common and ECG changes may even be seen in non-manifesting female carriers. Intelligence is marginally but consistently lower than the general population.

2. Becker muscular dystrophy. This presents with similar progressive muscle weakness but milder and of later onset. Calf hypertrophy and toe walking are characteristic.

3. Emery–Dreifuss syndrome. Progressive humero-peroneal muscle weakness develops from early childhood complicated by early contractures of Achilles tendons, elbow flexors and paraspinal muscles, and life-threatening cardiac conduction defects.

4. Facioscapulohumeral. As the name implies, there is a curious distribution of muscle involvement. The combination of scapular winging and facial weakness is characteristic. A wide spectrum of clinical severity, even within families, some with only minimal facial involvement and normal life expectancy, others wheelchair bound in childhood with ventilatory failure. An exudative retinopathy in one third of cases; photocoagulation therapy may be necessary to prevent retinal detachment.

5. Limb girdle dystrophies. A heterogeneous disorder presenting typically with progressive proximal wasting and weakness dating from childhood. Needs careful distinction from similarly presenting conditions such as Becker muscular dystrophy, spinal muscular atrophy, chronic polymyositis, mitochondrial cytopathy and adult-onset acid maltase deficiency. The autosomal recessive forms are designated type 2 and further divided into types A–F. Type 2A (calpain III deficiency) presents in the classical way; types 2 C, 2D, 2E and 2 F (g-, a-, b-, and d- sarcoglycan deficiency respectively) may present like a Duchenne dystrophy but with recessive inheritance.

6. Myotonic dystrophy. The most easily diagnosed of muscle diseases. Despite its name, it differs from the muscular dystrophies in its predominantly distal muscle involvement with wasting, weakness and myotonia (failure to relax a contracted muscle voluntarily). Facial and sternomastoid involvement are characteristic. Almost all cases show subcapsular cataracts. Men have frontal balding and hypogonadism and often there is sleep apnoea and somnolence. ECG abnormalities are common and sudden death risk relatively high.

7. 'Channelopathies'. Ion channels disorders are increasingly identified in neurology. Inherited neuromuscular forms are:

• Non-dystrophic myotonias: chloride channelopathies, e.g. myotonia congenita (Thompsen's disease (dominant) and Becker's disease (recessive)) and sodium channelopathies, e.g. paramyotonia congenita.

- Familial periodic paralysis (PP): hyperkalaemic PP results from mutations in the same sodium channel gene as paramyotonia congenita. Hypokalaemic PP is a calcium channelopathy.

8. Congenital myopathies. A group of childhood onset slowly progressive muscle weakness but often normal life expectancy. Skeletal abnormalities such as kyphoscoliosis, pes cavus and high arched palate are common. Their names derive from muscle biopsy appearances, e.g. of nemaline rods or central cores in muscle fibres.

9. Metabolic myopathies. Examples of these rare autosomal recessive enzyme deficiency conditions are McArdle's disease (myophosphorylase deficiency) and phosphofructokinase deficiency which present in childhood or early adult life with muscle pain and cramps on exertion. They are readily diagnosed on muscle biopsy. Carnitine palmatyl transferase deficiency can present as rhabdomyolysis following prolonged fasting or exertion. Acid maltase deficiency (adult Pompe's disease) can present with early diaphragm weakness at a time when the patient is still ambulant, and may do well with assisted nocturnal ventilation.

10. Mitochondrial disorders. See Mitochondrial disorders.

Genetics

1. Duchenne and Becker. There is deletion on short (p) arm of the X chromosome at Xp21, the gene coding for the muscle membrane protein, dystrophin. In Duchenne, dystrophin is absent; in Becker it is abnormal or reduced. Together they comprise the 'Xp21 myopathies' or 'dystrophinopathies'.

2. Emery–Dreifuss. There is a mutation on the long (q) arm of the X chromosome at Xq28 coding for the nuclear membrane protein, emerin.

3. Facioscapulohumeral. Most show large deletions of variable size at chromosome 4q35 but the molecular basis and gene product are unknown.

4. *Limb girdle*. Many childhood onset cases are autosomal recessive 'sarcoglycanopathies', with disorders of a- b- g- or d- sarcoglycan (in descending order of molecular weight), components of the dystrophin molecule.

5. *Myotonic dystrophy*. There is an unstable expansion of triplet repeats (CTG) in the myotonin protein kinase gene on chromosome 19q. With each generation, the repeat number increases with worsening clinical state (anticipation). Severe childhood cases result particularly from maternal transmission of the gene.

Investigations

1. *Creatine kinase (CK)*. The serum level of skeletal muscle derived CK (CK-MM) is a sensitive index of muscle disease. High levels occur in muscular dystrophy, especially Duchenne (e.g. 30 000 IU), declining with reduced mobility as the disease progresses. Lesser increases are seen in other muscle diseases including inherited metabolic muscle disorders.

2. *Electromyography*. A needle electrode inserted into relaxed muscle records 'insertional' and spontaneous activity, and then the discharges during a voluntary contraction (interference pattern). In muscle disease, damage to individual muscle fibres reduces the amplitude and duration of the motor potentials. Polyphasic discharges are increased and their high frequency content is heard over the loudspeaker as a high-pitched crackle. Reduced motor unit size means more must be recruited at a given force – the interference pattern is therefore complete at lower than expected force. Abnormal spontaneous activity is sometimes seen, especially in metabolic disorders. Repetitive discharges in myotonic dystrophy give a sound like a 'dive bomber'.

3. *Muscle biopsy*. This is an essential diagnostic tool in muscle disease. In muscular dystrophy, there is fatty and fibrous replacement of muscle, wide variation of fibre size usually with groups of contracted intensely staining fibres, fibre splitting and abnormal central nuclei. Immunocytochemistry for dystrophin and sarcoglycan are important in distinguishing conditions with the Duchenne phenotype. Various abnormalities such as glycogen deposition (acid maltase deficiency), enzyme deficiency disorders (e.g. McArdle's) and conditions with specific histological appearances (e.g. nemaline myopathy) can readily be diagnosed. Mitochondrial disorders may show 'ragged red fibres' on Gomori trichrome; additional electron microscopy is often helpful.

Management

There is no specific treatment for muscular dystrophy. Accurate diagnosis is essential to provide meaningful genetic advice to patient and 'at risk' family members. Diet and weight optimization can maintain mobility and self esteem. Reduced muscle bulk lowers the target weights and, at his ideal weight, a Duchenne boy might even appear too thin. Physiotherapy can prevent contractures and build morale. Surgery to prevent scoliosis helps to maintain posture and maintain vital capacity. Assisted ventilation is indicated for patients with selected diaphragm weakness and may be used, in selected cases, to relieve breathlessness from ventilatory muscle failure.

Future genetic treatment for Duchenne muscular dystrophy may be through increasing gene expression of utrophin, a sarcolemmal protein similar to dystrophin, but already present in Duchenne muscle.

Further reading

Dubowitz V. The muscular dystrophies – clarity or chaos? *New England Journal of Medicine,* 1997; **336:** 650–51.
Emery AEH. *Duchenne Muscular Dystrophy,* 2nd edn. Oxford: Oxford University Press, 1993.
Harper PS. *Myotonic Dystrophy*, 2nd edn. London: WB Saunders, 1989.
Lane RJM, ed. *Handbook of Muscle Disease.* Monticello: Marcel Dekker, 1996.

Related topics of interest

Mitochondrial disorders (p. 146)
Muscle disorders (inflammatory) (p. 170)

NEUROCUTANEOUS SYNDROMES

The neurocutaneous syndromes, formerly phakomatoses, comprise a group of disorders characterized by predominant involvement of the ectodermally-derived nervous system and the skin. The list of neurocutaneous conditions is very extensive; only the commoner autosomal dominant conditions are considered here.

Neurofibromatosis

There are two autosomal dominant conditions characterized by multiple neurofibromas.

Neurofibromatosis 1 (NF1)

The commoner form, (prevalence 1:5000), is also known as von Recklinghausen's disease or peripheral neurofibromatosis. The inherited abnormality is in a tumour suppressor gene (*nf1*) on chromosome 17.11.2; the gene product is known as neurofibromin.

Clinical manifestations

1. *Peripheral lesions of embryonic neural crest origin.*
- Café au lait spots. These are flat, light brown skin patches.
- Axillary freckling is a sign unique to neurofibromatosis.
- Neurofibromas. Cutaneous neurofibromas increase in number from the time of puberty. Plexiform neurofibromas are large and sometimes pedunculated. Intraspinal neurofibromas are common and may cause nerve or spinal cord compression.
- Lisch nodules. These multiple melanocytic hamartomas of the iris occur in up to 100% of adults when examined obliquely by slit lamp. Their smooth dome shapes distinguish them from naevi.

2. *Malignant tumours*
- Optic nerve glioma is found on MRI in up to 15% of NF1 cases; they are low grade pilocytic astrocytomas. Surgical excision is hampered by its frequent involvement of the chiasm and the other optic nerve.
- Others: neurofibrosarcomas and embryonic childhood tumours may also occur in the central nervous system. There is an increased incidence of

other systemic tumours, including chronic myelocytic leukaemia and phaeo-chromocytoma.

3. Skeletal lesions. These include scoliosis (usually mild), congenital bowing and long bone dysplasia.

4. Mild hearing deficits
- These, without excess prevalence of acoustic neuroma, are common.
- Incidental MRI brain scan findings. Scattered bright lesions occur in up to 60%, especially children, and are probably age-related myelination abnormalities.

Diagnosis

Consensus criteria for NF1 are met if a patient has two or more of the following:

- Café au lait patches (six or more) with maximum diameter >5 mm (pre pubertal) or >15 mm (post pubertal).
- Neurofibromas (two or more).
- Axillary or inguinal freckling.
- Optic nerve glioma.
- Lisch nodules (two or more).
- A characteristic bone lesion, e.g. sphenoid wing dysplasia, long bone cortex thinning.
- A first degree relative with NF1 by above criteria.

Neurofibromatosis 2 (NF2)

The rarer form (prevalence 1:50 000) is also know as central neurofibromatosis. The inherited abnormality is of a classical tumour suppressor gene (*nf2*) on chromosome 22q.12; the gene product is known as **merlin** (**m**oesin, **e**zrin and **r**adixin **li**ke prote**in**) or schwannomin.

Clinical manifestations

- Bilateral Schwannomas (acoustic neuromas), the hallmark, are present in 90%.
- Other CNS tumours occur, including meningioma (50%), other Schwannomas (30%), and spinal cord ependymomas, but there is no excess of optic nerve gliomas or hamartomas.
- Juvenile posterior capsular lens opacity, present in 85%, potentially causes serious additional hardship to patients with impaired hearing.
- Peripheral manifestations including neurofibromas and café au lait patches are only scanty.

Relatives frequently have acoustic neuromas but no other peripheral manifestations.

Diagnosis

NF2 is distinguished from sporadic acoustic neuromas because the latter are unilateral, occur in the over 40 age group with no family history and no excess of other tumours.

Consensus criteria for NF2 are met if the patient has:
(a) Eighth nerve masses on MRI or CT brain scan
plus
(b) A first degree relative with NF2 and either unilateral VII nerve mass or having two of the following:

- Neurofibroma.
- Meningioma.
- Glioma.
- Schwannoma.
- Juvenile posterior subcapsular cataract.

Tuberous sclerosis (epiloia)

This is an important cause of childhood onset epilepsy and learning disability. It is an uncommon (prevalence 1:30 000) dominantly transmitted disorder with two genotypes at chromosome 9q.34 (TFC1) and 16p.13 (TFC2). These are tumour suppressor genes coding for proteins designated hamartin and tuberin respectively.

Clinical manifestations

The clinical expression is highly variable.

1. Nervous system. Seizures occur in 80%, usually from the first year or life. Learning disability occurs in 50% and almost all these have early onset seizures. Brain hamartomas (tubers) are seen as calcified subependymal nodules on cerebral imaging in the majority. Malignant brain tumours (sub-ependymal giant cell astrocytomas) occasionally develop.

2. Cutaneous
- Adenoma sebaceum are skin hamartomas (angiokeratomas) over the nose and cheeks.
- Periungual fibromas occur in the nail folds and beneath the nails of the hands and feet.
- Shagreen patch is a fibrous plaque usually over the lumbar region.
- Depigmentation in the shape of a mountain ash leaf visible under ultraviolet (Wood's) light.

3. Others. Renal involvement occurs in 60%, including angiomyolipomas in 50% and simple renal cysts in 30%. Cysts also occur in the liver and spleen; cardiac rhabdomyomas are rare. Lung involvement is rare and usually in adult women.

Von Hippel–Lindau syndrome

This is an autosomal dominant multisystem disorder mapping to a tumour suppressor gene on chromosome 3p.

Neurological manifestations include haemangioblastomas of the cerebellum, retina, spinal cord or elsewhere in the brain. Somatic manifestations include renal, hepatic and pancreatic cysts and, more rarely, hypernephroma or phaeochromocytoma. Although a neurocutaneous syndrome, haemangioblastomas of the skin are rare.

Screening of unaffected relatives and also patients with isolated cerebellar haemangioblastomas is required to identify occult renal and adrenal tumours.

Basal cell naevus (Gorlin's) syndrome

This condition presents with:
- Multiple basal cell naevi over the face, neck and upper trunk, often with malignant transformation to basal cell carcinomas.
- Palmar and plantar pits.
- macrocephaly and congenital communicating hydrocephalus.
- Increased incidence of other tumours, especially cerebellar medulloblastoma, meningioma, craniopharyngioma and sarcoma.

The condition is autosomal dominant and the gene lies on chromosome 9q.

Conclusion

Despite the advances in the understanding of the genetics of several of these conditions their management remains symptomatic. Specific treatments may be developed as cellular pathways involved in these disorders become better known.

Further reading

Corf BR. Neurocutaneous syndromes; neurofibromatosis 1, neurofibromatosis 2, and tuberous sclerosis. *Current Opinion in Neurology,* 1997; **10:** 131–6.

Mulvihill JJ, Parry DM, Sherman JL, *et al.* Neurofibromatosis 1 (Recklinghausen disease) and neurofibromatosis 2 (bilateral acoustic neurofibromatosis). *Annals of Internal Medicine,* 1990; **113:** 39–52.

National Institute of Health Consensus Development Conference: Neurofibromatosis. *Archives of Neurology,* 1988; **45:** 575–8.

Pollack IF, Mulvihill JJ. Neurofibromatosis 1 and 2. *Brain Pathology,* 1997; **7:** 823–36.

Related topics of interest

Epilepsy management in adults (p. 78)
Respiratory neurology (p. 251)
Tumours of the central nervous system (benign) (p. 291)

NEUROGENIC BLADDER

Urinary incontinence is associated with many neurological disorders, notably multiple sclerosis, spina bifida, spinal cord compression or injury, stroke, multiple system atrophy and communicating hydrocephalus.

Bladder physiology

The normal bladder must spend 99% of its time in storage mode, and 1% in voiding mode. The balance between voiding (parasympathetic control) and storage (sympathetic) is maintained by cortical and pontine efferents in the spinal cord. Most spinal cord and some brain disorders will interfere with normal bladder control.

Muscles
- The detrusor (bladder smooth muscle) fibres funnel into, and are continuous with, the longitudinal fibres of the urethra. The detrusor can stretch to contain 500 ml without a significant increase in intravesical pressure. Detrusor contraction elevates bladder pressure, shortens the urethra and opens the bladder neck.
- The external urethral sphincter, a striated muscle, is the major guard against incontinence.
- The internal urethral sphincter is found only in males. Its contraction at ejaculation prevents retrograde seminal flow and failure may lead to dry ejaculation or seminuria.

Motor nerve supply
1. *Upper motor neurone*
- Cortical upper motor neurones in the medial frontal lobes project to the pons.
- Pontine micturition centre in the dorsal pontine tegmentum provides supranuclear control of the motor nerves.

2. *Lower motor neurone*
- Parasympathetic supply arises from preganglionic neurons in the intermediolateral region of the sacral cord and travels via the pelvic nerves providing the major excitatory bladder input. It stimulates detrusor and inhibits sphincters and so allows bladder voiding.
- Sympathetic supply (lumbosacral sympathetic chain and inferior mesenteric ganglia) travels via the hypogastric nerves and inhibits detrusor whilst

stimulating the sphincters, i.e. allows bladder filling.
- Somatic supply (Onuf's nucleus in the lateral ventral horn of the sacral cord at S2,3,4) travels via the pudendal nerve to the external urethral sphincter providing voluntary bladder control.

Sensory nerve supply Most bladder afferents travel in the pelvic nerves via the sacral cord to the pontine micturition centre. Proprioceptive afferents run in the pudendal nerve. Low level afferent activity during normal bladder filling ensures a predominant sympathetic tone; high level activity on bladder filling excites parasympathetic tone.

Cortical bladder

Medial frontal lobe damage, e.g. by communicating hydrocephalus, may result in disinhibition of the pontine micturition centre with loss of normal voiding reflexes and incontinence.

Flaccid (lower motor neurone) bladder

Lesions of the sacral cord, pelvic plexus or nerves, e.g. spina bifida, impair parasympathetic efferent supply to the bladder, leading to detrusor under activity, 'flaccid bladder' and chronic urinary retention. If sensation is retained the patient will feel the need to strain to pass urine. Movement may cause incontinence. Residual urine allows infection to occur.

Acute cord lesions initially leave the bladder flaccid and areflexic. Over weeks, unless the sacral nuclei were completely destroyed, reflex mechanisms become active and the bladder develops uncoordinated and poorly controlled contractions (see below).

'Spastic' (upper motor neurone) bladder

Interruption of the spinal descending efferents from the pontine micturition centre, e.g. in multiple sclerosis or spinal injury, leads to:
- A 'spastic' bladder (detrusor hyper-reflexia): limited bladder capacity and sudden rises of intravesical pressure lead to frequency, nocturia, urgency and urge incontinence. A 'spastic' bladder without known neurological cause is known as 'detrusor instability', a relatively common problem.
- Detrusor/sphincter dyssynergia when voiding. Spasticity of both the detrusor and the external urinary sphincter results in poorly sustained and abnormal detrusor voiding contractions out of step with sphincter relaxation. Thus the bladder contracts against a closed outlet, elevating intravesical pressure and leading to detrusor hypertrophy with poor bladder compliance.

Secondary factors

Factors exacerbating bladder dysfunction include:
- High post-micturition residual volumes (>100 ml) place the 'spastic bladder' on the steep part of its pressure-volume curve, ensuring that even small increases in volume provoke further detrusor contraction; the result is urinary frequency and urge incontinence.
- Chronic urinary tract infection (usually from chronic retention) commonly accompanies long-standing bladder symptoms.
- Interruption of bladder afferents in spinal cord disease may exacerbate urinary retention.
- Impaired mobility from any cause may worsen the handicap from bladder symptoms.
- Impaired cognitive function may lead to bladder symptoms.

Investigations

It is essential to exclude infection, urinary calculus or bladder tumour and to estimate residual volume following micturition.

Urine characteristics Dipstick urinary testing for protein and blood is easy. Identifying pyuria microscopically (white cell count exceeding $8/mm^3$) indicates infection. Microscopic bacteruria is occasionally apparent.

Bladder ultrasound This is an extremely important investigation used to:

- Estimate residual volume following voiding.
- Exclude hydroureter and hydronephrosis from chronic urinary retention.
- Identify bladder stones.

Urodynamics Urine flow is measured on micturition, post micturition residual volume is measured and detrusor pressure (intravesical pressure minus intra-abdominal pressure measured by rectal probe) is measured during slow bladder filling and during subsequent voiding.

Abnormalities in 'spastic bladder' include:

- A sudden rise in intravesical pressure after 100–200 ml indicating impaired bladder compliance, usually from bladder hyper-reflexia.
- Frequent rises in pressure during filling indicate detrusor instability, e.g. multiple sclerosis.

Management

The treatment strategy depends upon the bladder abnormality. Help from a continence adviser is recommended.

Residual volume <100 ml The drugs of choice for unstable bladder symptoms are anticholinergics which block the parasympathetic supply to the detrusor, e.g. oxybutynin 2.5 mg twice daily, or imipramine 75 mg twice daily. Side-effects, including dry mouth, visual disturbance and constipation may limit their use.

Residual volume >100 ml Intermittent self catheterization (ISC), often combined with anticholinergic treatment, is indicated. ISC is clean but non-sterile, with reusable catheters. The main limitation to its use is patient non-acceptance or impaired manual dexterity.

Other drug treatments Desmopressin may be useful for nocturnal enuresis. Calcium channel blockers or intravesical capsaicin have a limited role in neurogenic bladder.

Surgery Augmentation cystoplasty to enlarge the bladder, or anterior sacral root stimulation to induce bladder voiding, may be useful. The use of ileal reservoir or clam cystoplasty have fallen from favour owing to long term complications. Artificial urinary sphincters are being developed.

Catheters or sheaths A permanent in-dwelling catheter may be appropriate for some patients but is contraindicated if there is uncontrolled detrusor instability owing to subsequent pain and urinary bypassing. Supra-pubic catheter is useful for long-term drainage; because the bladder never fills, there is no need to close the ureter.
 An external sheath may be appropriate for some men.

Further reading

Fowler C, Julian P, Shah R. Urinary incontinence in adult men. *Prescribers' Journal,* 1994; **34:** 171–7.
Malone-Lee J. The management of urinary incontinence. In: Goodwill CJ, Chamberlain MA, Evans CD, eds. *Rehabilitation of the Physically Disabled Adult.* Cheltenham: Stanley Thornes Ltd, 1997; 491–508.

Related topics of interest

Autonomic disorders (p. 12)
Multiple sclerosis (p. 164)
Spinal cord injury (p. 263)

NEUROGENIC PAIN

Pain types
- Nocioceptive pain results from tissue damage and is opiate responsive.
- Neurogenic pain results from centrally mediated factors and is unresponsive to conventional analgesia including opiates.

Synonyms

Neurogenic pain is also described as neuropathic, causalgic (= burning pain), central deafferented or sympathetic-dependent.

Characteristics
- A burning, stabbing 'ice burn' or 'paradoxical burning' pain.
- Allodynia, pain evoked by non noxious stimuli, is characteristic.
- Hyperalgia: a lowered pain threshold to noxious stimulus with enhanced pain perception.
- Hyperpathia: severe pain provoked by noxious stimulus.
- Autonomic instability, including abnormal sweating and abnormal blood flow autoregulation with hyper or hypothermia.
- Altered perception threshold for warmth, cold and pinprick (except trigeminal neuralgia).

Neurogenic pain syndromes

Trigeminal neuralgia

Trigeminal neuralgia, or tic douloureux, is a severely painful, easily diagnosed condition typically arising in healthy middle aged people.

1. Clinical features
- Brief stabbing or pain clusters.
- Unilateral facial pain restricted to the distribution of one trigeminal nerve division, usually maxillary.
- Trigger areas on the face provoking pain when stimulated, e.g. by eating, shaving, brushing teeth.
- Pain episodes with long symptom-free intervals.
- No neurological signs including no facial numbness (except after ablative surgery).
- Anxiety during the physical examination.

2. Aetiology

- Vascular compression of the trigeminal nerve root, usually by the superior cerebellar artery, is usual. Focal demyelination at the compression site promotes ephaptic transmission and renders the nerve hyperexcitable to light mechanical stimulation.
- Multiple sclerosis may present with typical trigeminal neuralgia, from trigeminal nerve root focal demyelination.
- Trigeminal neuralgia from other structural lesions is surprisingly rare.

3. Management

(a) Medical: most are adequately controlled by aggressive medical management including a trial of carbamazepine using potentially toxic levels if necessary. Patients intolerant of carbamazepine might try lamotrigine, gabapentin, oxcarbazepine, phenytoin or baclofen.

(b) Surgical: since the disorder may remit spontaneously, surgery must not be embarked upon too readily.

- The trigeminal nerve may be damaged by radiofrequency rhizotomy, by glycerol injection or by balloon compression. Although effective, recurrence is likely; anaesthesia dolorosa, a continuous recalcitrant pain in the numbed area, occasionally follows.
- Microvascular decompression of the trigeminal nerve is becoming the surgical procedure of first choice. The compressing vessel is separated or cushioned from the nerve root, often with immediate and long-lived symptom relief. Operative risks include facial paresis, cranial haematoma, CSF leaks and infection.

Glossopharyngeal neuralgia

Recurrent neuralgic discomfort in the throat and neck (occasionally bilateral) occur. It is often associated with swallow syncope, where a bradyarrhythmia occurs as a reflex response to swallowing.

Reflex sympathetic dystrophy (complex regional pain syndrome)

This progressive illness is seen particularly in adults where localized pain usually follows relatively minor trauma with damage to a nerve, plexus or soft tissue.

1. Pain which is often more severe than expected following an injury. It develops into an intense burning with allodynia, usually over the distal and dorsal aspect of the limb and not confined to a dermatome or nerve distribution. Relief may be found by tight binding or ice. Sleep disruption and depression are common. The pain worsens and spreads with time occasionally moving to other limbs.

2. Autonomic dysfunction. The limb is usually cool but hyperhydrotic, cyanosed, sometimes with livedo reticularis. The initial pain appears sympathetically mediated, though eventually becomes independent of sympathetic processes.

3. Oedema. There may be mild tissue oedema giving the skin a shiny appearance.

4. Motor disturbances. The pain may lead to difficulty initiating movements with apparent weakness, tremor, involuntary movements and increased reflexes in the affected limb.

5. Trophic changes. The skin may appear wrinkled as the oedema subsides. There may be increased growth of hair (darker and thicker) and nails. Immobility promotes bone demineralization with subchondral erosions.

Central pain

1. Brain lesions. Central post stroke pain (thalamic syndrome) is characterized by:
- Pain developing gradually.
- Damage confined to the central nervous system.
- Associated sensory deficit, e.g. hemisensory loss.
- Allodynia.
- The skin temperature is lowered over the affected area.
- Pain exacerbated by temperature change or stress.
- Resistance to analgesia.

2. Spinal cord lesions. Pain commonly accompanies intrinsic and inflammatory cord lesions, e.g. multiple sclerosis.

3. Mechanism of central pain. The division between central and peripheral pain is blurred since peripheral mechanisms can induce central change, e.g. in post herpetic neuralgia. Pain may be caused by:

- Irritation of thalamus or spinothalamic pathways.
- Damage to central sympathetic pathways.
- Deafferentation. Degeneration of pre-synaptic terminals allows sprouting and reinnervation by other axons, unmasking previously ineffective synapses with excitation, super sensitivity and spreading of pain to neighbouring areas.

Post-herpetic neuralgia

The incidence of herpes zoster is 2 per 1000 in young adults, increasing to 10 per 1000 in those over 80 years. The pain is usually severe but transient though in 10% it persists beyond one month (especially elderly) and in 30% beyond one year. A total of 90% have allodynia. The pain occasionally spreads to neighbouring dermatomes. Conventional analgesia is ineffective. Acute treatment with acyclovir alone or with prednisolone does not reduce the risk of post herpetic neuralgia.

Brachial neuritis (neuralgic amyotrophy)

This is a (usually sporadic) condition of unknown cause which typically presents as severe unilateral pain in the shoulder, neck and arm associated with weakness, reflex loss and rapid onset of wasting particularly in the C5, 6 myotomes, e.g. periscapular muscles, deltoid, biceps, brachioradialis. Sensory loss may limited to a small area over the lateral upper arm. In more widespread cases there may be scapular winging, hemidiaphragmatic involvement, hand weakness and even bilateral involvement. Treatment is symptomatic with emphasis on pain relief and keeping the shoulder mobile to prevent capsulitis.

Hereditary painful neuropathies

Painful neuropathies are almost all acquired (e.g. diabetes, alcohol, malnutrition). Two rare hereditary neuropathies have pain as a major feature. These are the hereditary motor and sensory neuropathy type V (HMSN V) and X-linked recessive Fabry's disease.

Management of neurogenic pain

Ideally, management is multimodal and multidisciplinary.

Non-pharmacological   Explanation and appropriate reassurance, psychological interventions and physiotherapy are important. Physical treatments, including transcutaneous nerve stimulators, acupuncture and occasional use of dorsal column stimulators.

Pharmacological   Local treatments are preferred where practical since systemic treatments are often poorly effective. Injections of local anaesthetic, sometimes combined with steroid, into scars or localized painful areas may have a longer term action than expected, perhaps through resetting of pain receptors. Topical applications, e.g. for post herpetic neuralgia, include local anaesthetic cream, capsaicin (desensitizing afferent 'C' fibres) and aspirin combined with ether. Local anaesthetic sympathetic blocks are used for complex regional pain syndrome, particularly if sympathetic function is abnormal.

Systemic: neurogenic pain is unresponsive to conventional analgesia. Antiepileptics such as carbamazepine and antidepressants (either tricyclics or SSRIs) can be effective. NMDA antagonists, e.g. dextromethorphan, may be helpful.

Further reading

Bowsher D. Neurogenic pain syndromes and their management. *British Medical Bulletin,* 1991; **47:** 644–66.
Charlton E. Neuropathic pain. *Prescribers' Journal,* 1993; **33** (6): 244–9.
Fields HL. Treatment of trigeminal neuralgia. *New England Journal of Medicine,* 1996; **334:** 1125–26.
Schwartzman RJ. Reflex sympathetic dystrophy. *Current Opinion in Neurology and Neurosurgery,* 1993; **6:** 531–6.

Related topics of interest

NEUROMUSCULAR JUNCTION DISORDERS

Myasthenia gravis

In this autoimmune condition, circulating antibody to acetylcholine receptors (AChR) damages the motor end plates, impairing neuromuscular junction transmission.

Clinical features

The incidence is 4 per million and prevalence is 40 per million. The male to female ratio is 1:2. The mean ages of onset are 26 years (female) and 31 years (male). A thymoma occurs in 15% of myasthenic patients overall (but 35% of men); 30% of thymomas show local invasion.

Myasthenia presents with variable weakness of the extraocular, facial and bulbar musculature. Limb weakness may be relatively mild. Tendon reflexes are retained. Mild forms may show weakness only of extraocular muscles (pure ocular form). Occasional cases are induced by d-penicillamine when used for rheumatoid arthritis (but not for Wilson's disease owing to differing HLA susceptibility). Penicillamine-associated myasthenia is usually AChR antibody-positive and associated with HLA DR1; the disease often but not always remits following penicillamine withdrawal.

Investigations

1. Demonstration of myasthenia
- Tensilon® test: following 10 mg intravenously of edrophonium (Tensilon®), temporary improvement in muscle strength occurs (95% in generalized and 85% in ocular myasthenia).
- AChR Antibody is present in 90% of generalized, but only 65% of the pure ocular myasthenia. It is almost 100% specific for myasthenia gravis. The highest titres occur with associated thymoma. It is found in penicillamine-induced myasthenia but not in myasthenic syndromes (see below).
- Neurophysiology: during 3 seconds of 3 Hz repetitive stimulation the motor action potential amplitude decrements by >10% (75% of generalized but only 35% of pure ocular myasthenia). Single fibre electromyography shows increased 'jitter' owing to latency variability between excitation of

two of more single muscle fibres in the same motor unit. This occurs in all neuromuscular junction disorders and not specifically myasthenia gravis.

2. *Identifying associated conditions*
- Thymoma. CT scan of the thorax is indicated in all newly diagnosed myasthenia patients. Anti-striated muscle antibody occurs in 85% of those with thymoma.
- Thyroid function. There is an increased risk of thyroid and other autoimmune disorders in myasthenia gravis.
- CT brain scan may be indicated where there is solely ocular involvement with negative antibody to exclude a cavernous sinus lesion mimicking myasthenia.

3. *Breathing and swallowing*
- Vital capacity best reflects ventilatory function in neuromuscular disease. A mask replaces the mouthpiece if there is significant facial weakness.
- Maximum inspiratory static mouth pressure more directly measures inspiratory muscle strength and is useful in repeated assessments in an individual.
- A timed water swallowing test is important in assessing swallowing ability.

Management

1. *Acetylcholinesterase inhibitors (anticholinesterases).* Pyridostigmine can control mild symptoms. Associated cholinergic effects, including salivation, diarrhoea, cramps and asthma exacerbation, limit higher doses. Additional anticholinergics, e.g. propantheline, may help.

2. *Steroids.* These are indicated in moderate or severe myasthenia or those unresponsive to anticholinesterases alone. Prednisolone alone may suffice in purely ocular myasthenia. Steroids are introduced cautiously as sudden increases may acutely worsen muscle strength. The dose is increased slowly to a maximum of 1.0 to 1.5 mg/kg/day. When stable, steroids are slowly withdrawn to a maintenance of 20–40 mg on alternate days.

3. *Other immunosuppression.* Azathioprine (2.5 mg/kg/day) may be used as a steroid sparer although

taking 6 to 8 months for clinical effect. Cyclosporin is also effective; intravenous pooled immunoglobulin are occasionally used.

4. Thymectomy
- This is indicated for thymoma, although its removal does not benefit the myasthenia. Adjuvant radiotherapy is often required.
    Thymectomy is also indicated in myasthenia patients with all of the following:
    Generalized symptoms (not pure ocular).
    Positive AChR antibody.
    Disease onset before age 45 years.
    Thymectomy for this group gives full recovery in 30%, improvement in 45% and no change in 25%. A trans-sternal thymectomy ensures complete clearance. Plasma exchange and high dose steroids may be required in the peri operative period.

Myasthenic crisis

This is caused either by the myasthenia itself or by anticholinesterases excess ('cholinergic crisis' characterized by miosis, fasciculation and cramps). The two are distinguished by a Tensilon® test although a precise diagnosis should not delay emergency treatment. Plasma exchange and assisted ventilation may be needed and high dose steroids used unless there is septicaemia, thyrotoxicosis or definite cholinergic crisis.

Prognosis

Thirty to forty per cent of patients gain complete remission, the disease being most severe in the first 3 years. Most have obtained a steady clinical state after seven years. Patients with thymoma generally fare worse.

Neonatal myasthenia

Transient myasthenia in the newborn follows placental transfer of maternal AChR antibody.

Myasthenic syndromes

Lambert–Eaton myasthenic syndrome (LEMS)

1. Clinical features. A rare disorder presenting as variable weakness affecting predominantly the proximal limb muscles. There may be partial ptosis but extraocular muscle involvement is rare. Limb reflexes are depressed but may be facilitated following voluntary sustained contraction. Associated autonomic involvement gives dry mouth and constipation. Myopathy with 'dry mouth' is characteristic.

2. *Mechanism.* An immune-mediated pre-synaptic disorder of peripheral cholinergic neurotransmission where calcium-mediated release of acetylcholine from the motor nerve terminals is impaired. Younger patients have an idiopathic autoimmune form but older patients with a smoking history usually have underlying small cell lung carcinoma (SCLC) initiating the autoantibody response. LEMS is seen in 2% of neurologically examined SCLC patients. Neurological manifestations may precede overt cancer by up to 5 years.

3. *Electromyography*
- Reduced amplitude motor action potential facilitated following voluntary muscle contraction.
- Force increment during rapid repetitive stimulation (50 Hz).

4. *Associated antibody.* Voltage-gated calcium channel antibody is present in 90%.

5. *Treatment.* Steroids and plasma exchange are helpful. Motor and autonomic symptoms are improved by 3:4 diaminopyridine. The symptoms may also improve following removal of the underlying SCLC.

Congenital myasthenia

This heterogeneous group of non-immune disorders represents only 1% of neuromuscular disorders. They present at birth with feeding difficulty and apnoeic attacks and in early childhood with fatiguable ocular, bulbar, facial, trunk and limb weakness. Often there is a family history and consanguinity. They are non-progressive, often improving in adolescence.

1. *Types*
- Pre-synaptic: familial infantile myasthenia (recessive).
- Post-synaptic: congenital end plate acetylcholinesterase deficiency or neuromuscular junction acetylcholine receptor deficiency (both recessive).
- Others: slow channel myasthenic syndrome (dominant).

2. Treatment
- Some respond to anticholinesterases. 3–4 diaminopyridine is used for the pre-synaptic forms.

Drug, toxin and metabolic induced

These include:

- Snake envenoming.
- Organophosphorous poisoning.
- Pesticides, including sheep dip.
- Chemical warfare.
- Hypermagnsaemia.
- Botulism.

Botulism
(botulus (Latin) = sausage)

1. Pathogenesis. Botulism follows consumption of the tasteless, odourless toxin of the anaerobic spore-forming Gram-positive bacillus *Clostridium botulinum*, a ubiquitous organism present in 90% of soil samples. The spores are heat and drying resistant and lie inert for years. Botulinum toxins A to G bind to and enter the motor nerve terminal, blocking acetylcholine receptors. Bottled food is a typical source. Occasionally the source is a chronic wound, e.g. nasal sepsis in cocaine abusers or an infected needle in intravenous drug abusers. In babies a blind bowel loop may promote anaerobe growth producing the toxin.

2. Clinical features. An acute symmetrical descending paralysis with autonomic involvement, giving the classical combination of flaccid paralysis with fixed pupils. Babies aged 1–6 months with chronic bowel infection may present with constipation, poor suckling, facial weakness and have a positive stool culture.

3. Investigations. Electromyography: as in LEMS there are small amplitude compound muscle action potentials with post-exercise facilitation and physiological increment at 50 Hz repetitive stimulation.

Further reading

Drachman DB. Myasthenia gravis. *New England Journal of Medicine,* 1994; **330:** 1797–810.

Pourmand R. Myasthenia gravis. *Disease Monthly,* 1997; **43:** 65–109.
Wittbrodt ET. Drugs and myasthenia gravis. *Archives of Internal Medicine,* 1997; **157:** 399–408.

Related topics of interest

Paraneoplastic neurological syndromes (p. 215)
Respiratory neurology (p. 251)

NON-ORGANIC NEUROLOGY

Spectrum of disorders

- Anxiety. Normal reactive anxiety is extremely common in neurological patients and may give symptoms difficult to distinguish from organic neurology. An anxiety reaction with hyperventilation may start a vicious cycle provoking apparent neurological symptoms and further anxiety.
- Panic disorder. Discrete panic episodes are associated with apprehension and fear. Symptoms are intermittent, of sudden onset and without obvious provoking factors.
- Conversion. One or more sensory or motor symptoms not explained by a general or medical condition.
- Somatization. Multiple unexplained physical complaints with onset of symptoms before the age of 30 years.
- Other somatiform disorders, e.g. chronic fatigue syndrome, fibromyalgia.

Manifestations

Manner

Amusement or giggling on demonstrating neurological deficit is clearly inappropriate and raises the suspicion of non-organic disease.

Accessories

Patients using accessories, e.g. cervical collar, back brace, or seemingly unnecessary crutches, sticks, or wheelchair, raise suspicions of non-organic disease. Such 'jewellery' should bear evidence of frequent use – sometimes they are used only to visit the doctor.

Hyperventilation

This common anxiety manifestation is important as it may itself provoke neurological symptoms, leading to still more anxiety and diagnostic confusion.

The symptoms are usually intermittent and accompany other anxiety symptoms. Patients are usually unaware of the hyperventilation, although may acknowledge:

- Breathlessness and sighing without exertion.
- Sensations of incomplete lung filling.
- Needing fresh air.
- Tingling around the face and peripheries, particularly left sided.
- Blurred vision and lightheadedness.

- Throat and chest tightness.

Examination often reveals tachypnoea and sighing. Voluntary breath holding time is often markedly decreased. Forced hyperventilation may reproduce symptoms (helpful for patient understanding) but must be interpreted with caution as symptoms can also be provoked in non-habitual hyperventilators.

Sensory

1. Numbness. Hemisensory loss (usually left sided), is a well-recognized non-organic finding closely linked to hyperventilation. Superficial reflexes over apparently numb areas, e.g. superficial abdominals, plantar and corneal response, are preserved. Non-organic sensory loss is 'non-anatomical', e.g. facial sensory loss not limited by the trigeminal dermatome.

2. Visual disorders. A discrepancy between ability to carry out daily tasks and results of objective testing might suggest non-organic visual loss. Preservation of optokinetic nystagmus despite reported blindness might help.
   Visual field constriction is a common non-organic finding; it differs from organic constriction in that the deficit size remains unchanged whether the target is close or distant (tubular vision).

Motor

1. Weakness. 'Functional' weakness is common in neurological practice and suggested by:

- Weakness despite normal muscle bulk, tone and reflexes.
- Variability and improvement with encouragement; patients are asked to look at the limb and to try very hard, encouraged in a firm voice by the examiner.
- 'Give way' weakness where resistance is initially normal but suddenly fails.
- Simultaneous contraction of agonists and antagonists.
- Absent contralateral limb stabilization, e.g. the left heel should press down on attempted elevation of the right leg (a hand beneath the opposite heel is helpful).

2. Gait. 'Bizarre' gaits may accompany non-organic motor symptoms. Leg dragging without other hemiparetic features, odd limb posturing or a tendency to topple towards the examiner without falling, are usual features.

3. Muscle twitching. Myokymia, especially around the eye, is a common anxiety-related symptom, common among medical students.

Seizures

Psychogenic non-epileptic attacks fall into two main groups: panic and conversion disorder. In general, non-epileptic attacks from anxiety are common in patients with pre-existing epilepsy whereas conversion disorder patients often have never had epilepsy.

1. Panic disorder. Panic episodes commonly cause diagnostic confusion with complex partial seizures for three reasons:

- Panic symptoms resemble seizures, e.g. epigastric sensations, light-headedness, distant feelings and even loss of consciousness from hyperventilation. Panic symptoms generally are of gradual onset with increasing anxiety whereas complex partial seizures are of abrupt onset.
- Panic symptoms exacerbate epilepsy. Hyperventilation lowers the seizure threshold, hence hyperventilation is used in EEGs to bring out epileptiform activity. Disrupted sleep pattern from anxiety may worsen epilepsy.
- Panic disorder may be caused by epilepsy. Epilepsy is very frightening and itself provokes anxiety and sometimes panic. If anxiety symptoms resemble seizures, a vicious cycle of apparently worsening epilepsy results.

2. Conversion disorder. Attacks are generally convulsive, frequent, often with flailing, thrashing and back arching. Patients may fight and need to be held down during attacks. Pseudostatus epilepticus accounts for about half of hospital admissions labelled status epilepticus. Conversion disorder patients often are female (8:1 F:M) and may have:

- A history of apparently resistant epilepsy beginning aged >10 years.
- Previous episodes of apparent status epilepticus.

	- Previous multiple hospital admissions, e.g. asthma, irritable bowel, abdominal or chest pain.
	- Previous abnormal illness behaviour or self-harm.
	- A history of childhood sexual and/or physical abuse.
Higher function	- Memory loss reported by anxious patients is often attributable to poor concentration. Generally, patients reporting their own memory loss have poor concentration and anxiety rather than dementia; unconcerned patients whose carers report the problem, have true dementia.
	- Dysphasia. Anxious patients commonly experience difficulty saying clearly what they want to say and a distinction from mild dysphasia may be difficult.
	- Pseudocoma can quickly be distinguished from true coma by caloric testing: iced water into an ear induces vertigo, nystagmus and vomiting in alert patients.
Differential diagnosis	Finding non-organic signs never excludes a serious underlying disorder.
	In any apparent non-organic disorder it is important to consider 'functional elaboration' of an underlying disorder where patients subconsciously 'help' the doctor by exaggerating certain signs.
	The following are examples of conditions frequently mistaken for non-organic disease.
Episodic disorders	Disorders characterized by recurrent attacks without problems between, are particularly liable to misdiagnosis.
	(a) Epilepsy
	- Complex partial seizures may closely resemble anxiety symptoms and are particularly confusing as the two conditions may occur together.
	- Frontal lobe seizures are often misdiagnosed as non-organic since their presentation may be with bizarre behaviour or posturing, retained consciousness despite generalized movements, very frequent but brief attacks, resistance to medication. The EEG is often normal between and even during attacks (because a medial frontal lobe focus may be undetectable on the surface).

(b) Dystonia. Common patterns, e.g. blepharospasm, spasmodic torticollis, are easily recognized but others, e.g. occupational dystonia, may suggest non-organic disease. Paroxysmal dystonia may be particularly difficult to recognize.

(c) Hypoglycaemia. It is essential to consider hypoglycaemia in any condition presenting as altered consciousness or behaviour.

(d) Porphyria. Because symptoms occur in acute relapses and may be associated with psychiatric complications, this is commonly initially labelled as hysteria.

(e) Others. Patients with periodic ataxia, paroxysmal symptoms of multiple sclerosis, periodic paralysis, hyperekplexia, and cataplexy all risk being labelled as functional.

Weakness

In the early stages of conditions such as Guillain–Barré syndrome, myasthenia gravis or myasthenic syndromes, the apparently healthy and well-muscled but anxious individual reporting weakness is easily misdiagnosed.

Frontal lobe syndromes

- Infarction from anterior cerebral artery disease, e.g. anterior communicating aneurysm, may present as acute-onset behavioural change, leg weakness and somnolence without obvious cause.
- Tumour, e.g. frontal meningioma may present as an indolent behavioural problem, enlarging unnoticed over many years.
- Frontal lobe dementia is particularly difficult to diagnose since the abnormal behaviour may not be matched by changes on routine mental testing. Rapid onset frontal dementia, e.g. CJD, is especially likely to be initially mislabelled in its early stage.

Position sense loss

Loss of position sense, e.g. high cervical cord lesions, dorsal root ganglionitis, may be compounded by apparent 'give-way' weakness owing to impaired sensory feedback. Recognition of a contralateral parietal lobe lesion may be further hindered by sensory inattention.

Further reading

Hawkes CH. Diagnosing functional neurological disease. *British Journal of Hospital Medicine,* 1997; **57:** 373–7.

O'Brien MD. Medically unexplained neurological symptoms. *British Medical Journal,* 1998; **316**: 564–5.

Related topic of interest

Fatigue syndromes (p. 106)

NYSTAGMUS

Nystagmus is a rhythmic oscillation of the eyes, with each phase of equal amplitude. The oscillation is usually either jerk or pendular.

- Jerk nystagmus. The commonest form in which an initial slow phase (pathological drift from target) is followed by a fast phase (corrective); it is labelled right or left on the direction of the fast phase.
- Pendular nystagmus. The rarer form with opposite phases of the same velocity and no fast phase. It is usually congenital. Acquired cases are associated with white matter disease and internuclear ophthalmoplegia, e.g. multiple sclerosis or leucodystrophy.

Physiological nystagmus

1. End point. A few irregular jerks are common in normal people on eye movement, especially at extremes of lateral gaze. The nystagmus has a fast phase in the direction of gaze and amplitude greatest in the abducting eye.

2. Optokinetic. Jerk nystagmus elicited by moving a repetitive stimulus, e.g. stripes in a Barany drum. The slow phase is in the direction of the stripe; the fast phase corrective. With stripes moving right to left, the left parieto-occipital area controls the slow phase and the left frontal lobe controls the recovery phase. Thus, lesions affecting the fronto-midbrain or occipito-midbrain pathways affect their respective phases.

3. Vestibular. Following self-induced spinning, e.g. on a roundabout, a horizontal jerk nystagmus occurs; the slow phase determined by the vestibular nuclei and fast phase by the frontal lobe.

4. Sensory deprivation. In blindness or following prolonged dark exposure, nystagmus develops which is pendular and dampened by convergence. Latent nystagmus in an amblyopic eye may be unmasked by occluding the seeing eye.

5. Voluntary. By converging and looking down, some individuals are able to induce bursts of horizontal nystagmus.

Pathological nystagmus

1. Vestibular. Common causes include Ménière's disease, acute labyrinthitis or benign positional vertigo.

- It is a horizontal jerk nystagmus with a torsion component.

- The fast phase is towards the normal side. Following damage to one inner ear the normal labyrinth still 'pushes' the eyes towards the opposite side (slow phase), the corrective (fast) phase being towards the normal side.
- Vertigo is almost invariable.

2. Cerebellar. Cerebellar disease leads to abnormal amplitude of eye movement with a tendency to overshoot or undershoot. Cerebellar nystagmus

- Is gaze evoked.
- Is usually horizontal.
- Often shows 'rebound', i.e. initially with fast phase in the direction of gaze but after a few seconds the direction of nystagmus reverses. This fatigues on sustained fixation. On returning to the primary position, nystagmus occurs in the direction opposite to the initial gaze.

3. Congenital. Although present from birth, congenital nystagmus may be first recognized in adults. It is a common cause of unnecessary investigation. Perhaps surprisingly, oscillopsia (oscillating vision) is rare. Features include:

- The nystagmus is either pendular or jerk.
- Usually horizontal.
- Improvement on convergence.
- Latent nystagmus, a feature only of congenital and sensory deprivation nystagmus, becomes apparent with one eye covered. Thus ophthalmoscopy, by covering an eye, may unmask congenital nystagmus.
- A 'null point', the eye position where nystagmus is minimized.
- Involuntary head turning is common to optimize vision if the null point is not at the primary position.
- Head nodding, particularly in children.

4. Upbeat. Vertical nystagmus in the primary position or on upgaze usually denotes brainstem or cerebellar disease (especially anterior vermis and lower brain stem). It is often associated with impaired up gaze. Common causes include drug toxicity, multiple sclerosis and Wernicke's encephalopathy.

5. Downbeat. When present in the primary position, and often associated with impaired down gaze, this localizes to the craniovertebral junction. Common causes include Chiari malformation, multiple sclerosis, cerebellar disease, hydrocephalus and drugs.

6. *Convergence-retraction.* All the extra-ocular muscles contract abnormally on looking up; the medial muscles are stronger, and so the eyes converge. Vertical gaze is often impaired. It occurs as part of Parinaud's peri-aqueductal syndrome caused by lesions in the posterior third ventricle.

7. *See-saw.* Here, one eyeball rises and intorts whilst the other falls and extorts. It suggests a disturbance of the connections to the interstitial nucleus of Cajal. Usual causes include a third ventricular tumour, syringobulbia or as part of congenital nystagmus.

8. *Periodic alternating 'windmill'.* This rare horizontal nystagmus manifests as periodic reversal of the direction of the fast phase every few minutes. It is usually congenital but may occur in craniovertebral junction disorders, cerebellar disease, multiple sclerosis, blindness or following anticonvulsant toxicity. It is highly sensitive to baclofen, also clearing the oscillopsia.

Conditions mimicking nystagmus

1. *Saccadic disorders.* Saccades (rapid eye movements) are normally well controlled and have a brief intersaccadic interval.

- Square wave jerks, where the eyes repetitively briefly move off target, are an exaggeration of physiological changes.
- Opsoclonus, with chaotic movements in all directions of gaze without intersaccadic interval, is associated with neuroblastoma in children and breast or visceral malignancy in adults.
- Ocular flutter, describes opsoclonus confined to horizontal gaze.

2. *Superior oblique myokymia.* This is a benign condition presenting with unilateral torsional oscillopsia, which usually responds to carbamazepine but sometimes requires superior oblique surgery.

3. Spasmus nutans. This is a condition of the first year of life and has usually cleared by the age of 8 years. There are small amplitude rapid jerks associated with head nodding or torticollis in an otherwise neurologically normal child. The jerks are improved with sleep. It is benign with an excellent prognosis.

4. Ocular bobbing. Here there is conjugate repetitive vertical eye movement with fast descent and slow ascent. It is almost always accompanied by impaired consciousness. It indicates a serious intrinsic pontine lesion, such as haemorrhage, metabolic disturbance or toxic effects of drugs, and carries a poor prognosis.

5. Oculo-palatal myoclonus. Myoclonic jerks in the first branchial arch muscles (palate, tongue and face) may follow diffuse anoxic cerebral damage. There may be associated clicking tinnitus. It is totally unresponsive to medication.

6. Ping-pong gaze. The horizontal eye movements make it appear the patient is watching tennis. It indicates a posterior fossa lesion, usually haemorrhage, with a poor prognosis.

7. Oculo-masticatory myorhythmia. This is very rare, combining involuntary eyeball convergence with chewing and is pathognomonic of cerebral Whipple's disease.

Further reading

Slamovits TL, Hedges TR III, Kupersmith MJ, *et al. Neuro-ophthalmology. Basic and Clinical Science Course, Section 5.* San Francisco: American Academy of Ophthalmology, 1994.

Related topics of interest

OPTIC NERVE DISORDERS

Papilloedema

This is where optic disc swelling is attributable to raised intracranial pressure (ICP). It occurs following obstruction of optic nerve axoplasmic transport at the level of the lamina cribrosa.

Fundoscopy
- Disc margin obscured by peripapillary nerve fibre layer swelling.
- Pink disc with dilated surface capillaries.
- Dilated veins with loss of venous pulsation.
- Flame haemorrhages at disc margin.
- Disc elevation.

Visual acuity

This is normal unless:

- The macula is involved by haemorrhage or oedema.
- There is superimposed anterior ischaemic optic neuropathy.

Visual fields

These show:

- Blind spot enlargement.
- Visual field constriction in chronic papilloedema.

Associated visual symptoms of raised ICP
- Diplopia from VI nerve palsy.
- Transient visual obscurations.

Investigations

Papilloedema requires urgent investigation including:

- Blood pressure.
- Brain imaging (CT or MRI).
- If brain imaging is normal lumbar puncture may be indicated.

Papillitis

This describes optic disc swelling with visual loss. It occurs in:

- Anterior ischaemic optic neuropathy (*vide infra*).
- Optic nerve infiltration by tumour (leukaemia, lymphoma, myeloma, metastatic carcinoma) or other inflammation (sarcoidosis, tuberculosis, *Cryptococcus*).

Optic neuritis

This condition presents aged 15–45 years and is closely linked with multiple sclerosis.

Symptoms
- Subacute (over one week) unilateral visual loss.
- Pain on eye movement.
- Photophobia.
- Bright dots (phosphenes) on eye movement.
- Uthoff's symptom of transiently reduced vision following exercise or elevated body temperature.

Signs
- Reduced visual acuity.
- Reduced colour perception.
- Central scotoma.
- Afferent pupillary defect.
- The optic fundus appears normal but later may show optic atrophy.

Investigations
- Visual evoked potentials show prolonged latency.
- MRI brain scan may show swelling and high signal in an optic nerve; multiple plaques in the cerebral white matter suggests multiple sclerosis.

Prognosis
Optic neuritis recurs in either eye in 20% of cases. 60% of cases eventually develop multiple sclerosis. The large majority of MS cases have evidence of previous optic neuritis (often subclinical).

Treatment
If visual acuity is worse than 6/12, high dose methylprednisolone offers the best chance of improving speed and completeness of recovery. In children bilateral optic neuritis may occur as a post viral phenomenon associated with meningoencephalitis.

Optic atrophy

This describes the long-term result of various optic nerve insults. The fundus appearance is of marked optic disc pallor.

Causes
- Inflammatory optic neuritis.
- Ischaemic (AION).
- Tumour, e.g. optic sheath meningioma.

- Nutritional: thiamine or B_{12} deficiency (tobacco and alcohol amblyopia may also be nutritional).
- Drugs: chloramphenicol or chloroquine, ethambutol.
- Toxins: methanol, lead.
- Hereditary optic neuropathy, e.g. Leber's (*vide infra*).

Anterior ischaemic optic neuropathy (AION)

Optic nerve head infarction through occlusion of the short posterior ciliary arteries, either arteritic or non-arteritic.

Arteritic AION

Most are due to giant cell arteritis, though rare involvement may occur with SLE, rheumatoid arthritis, Behçet's disease, relapsing polychondritis.

Giant cell arteritis

Patients with giant cell arteritis typically are elderly with a short history of unilateral headache with scalp tenderness, malaise and weight loss, and have a tender, non-pulsatile temporal artery on examination. ESR is very elevated (but normal in 10%) and temporal artery biopsy shows an inflammatory reaction with giant cells in most cases but may be normal owing to patchy involvement. Urgent treatment with prednisolone 60–80 mg daily can prevent blindness.

If visual loss occurs, it is usually complete and irreversible. Following unilateral arteritic AION, 65% develop sequential involvement of the unaffected eye.

Non-arteritic AION

This comprises the majority of AION. Patients are usually elderly, aged 50–75 years and present with sudden and painless unilateral visual loss, which may be incomplete, e.g. involving only the lower visual field or inferior nasal quadrant. Predisposing factors include a small cup to disc ratio (present in most cases), hypertension (40%) and diabetes (20%).

The optic disc initially shows acute papillitis (swollen disc with nerve fibre layer haemorrhages) and later optic atrophy develops. There is usually no recovery of vision and the second eye becomes involved in 20–40% of cases.

Other causes of non-arteritic AION include herpes zoster, syphilis, acute blood loss, favism and staphylococcal cavernous sinus thrombosis.

Management	If giant cell arteritis or other arteritis is excluded, there is no treatment.
	Aspirin prophylaxis appears sensible but without any firm evidence base.

Optic nerve glioma

This grade I pilocytic astrocytoma presents in childhood. The tumour may stop growing after childhood though sometimes involves the chiasm and the contralateral nerve. About 50% have neurofibromatosis type 1 (NF1); 15% of NF1 cases have optic nerve glioma. Patients present with:

- Visual loss.
- Strabismus and nystagmus secondary to visual loss.
- Afferent pupillary defect.
- Swollen and pale optic disc.
- Endocrine dysfunction from hypothalamic involvement.

Brain imaging shows fusiform swelling of the optic nerve. Surgery is sometimes done to prevent spread to the other nerve but is controversial since it involves removing the affected nerve.

Optic nerve meningioma

This comprises only 1% of meningiomas. It occurs particularly in adult females and presents with progressive painless unilateral visual loss. Physical signs are:

- Unilateral visual impairment.
- Proptosis.
- Disc oedema or optic atrophy.
- Optociliary shunt veins on the optic disc.

Optic nerve meningiomas are usually managed conservatively since surgery inevitably is associated with visual loss.

Leber's hereditary optic neuropathy

This is a mitochondrial disorder transmitted by females but manifesting mainly in males (M:F = 5:1). Patients present in their late teens or early 20s with sequential loss of vision in both eyes over days to weeks. No treatment is available.

Female carriers may develop multiple sclerosis with prominent visual impairment (Harding's syndrome).

Further reading

Slamovits TL, Hedges TR III, Kupersmith MJ, *et al. Neuro-ophthalmology. Basic and Clinical Science Course, Section 5*. San Francisco: American Academy of Ophthalmology, 1994.

Related topics of interest

PARANEOPLASTIC NEUROLOGICAL SYNDROMES

Paraneoplastic syndromes occur as a remote effect of cancer. Most non-neurological paraneoplastic syndromes are caused by inappropriate hormonal secretion; neurological syndromes are caused by production of anti-tumour antibodies or by virus reactivation.

Paraneoplastic syndromes are important because they may be an early presenting feature of a treatable tumour and the symptoms are themselves potentially treatable.

Brain

Encephalomyelitis

This progressive disorder, sometimes termed 'paraneoplastic encephalomyelitis with sensory neuropathy' or 'anti-Hu syndrome', affects the nervous system at multiple levels:

- Limbic encephalitis presents with profound loss of short-term memory, a rapidly evolving dementia and occasionally with temporal lobe epilepsy.
- Brainstem encephalitis presents with progressive truncal ataxia, eye movement disorder and drowsiness.
- Spinal cord and peripheral nerve (see below). Myelitis, subacute sensory neuropathy ('ganglionitis'), or a motor neurone disease like syndrome may occur as part of the paraneoplastic encephalomyelitis syndrome.

1. Investigations. The brain MRI may show patchy abnormal temporal lobe signal; cerebrospinal fluid shows elevated protein, variable pleocytosis and occasionally positive oligoclonal bands.

2. Pathology. Lesions containing perivascular cuffing, neuronal loss and gliosis are seen at multiple levels of the central nervous system.

3. Associated malignancies. Small cell lung carcinoma (SCLC) is usual but occasionally associated are thymoma, seminoma, cancer of the bladder, colon or kidney, and Hodgkin's disease.

4. Associated antibodies. Anti-neuronal nuclear antibody type 1 (ANNA1 known as anti-Hu).

Opsoclonus-myoclonus syndrome

1. Clinical manifestations. Opsoclonus is caused by loss of inhibitory control over ocular saccades, the rapid eye movements necessary to fix an object on the fovea. It presents as non-stereotyped chaotic eye movements occurring at rest and on eye movement leading to troublesome oscillopsia and vertigo. It may be associated with ataxia and with involuntary jerking of the limbs, trunk, head, diaphragm or palate (opsoclonus-myoclonus or 'dancing eyes and dancing feet').

2. Associated malignancies. Breast, neuroblastoma and lung.

3. Associated antibodies. Anti-neuronal nuclear antibody type 2 (ANNA2 known as anti-Ri).

Subacute cerebellar degeneration

1. Clinical manifestations. Cerebellar dysfunction progressing over weeks or months, resulting in severe disability and sometimes preceding the cancer presentation by up to 3 years. Progressive and relentless truncal ataxia with dysarthria but with little nystagmus is usual.

2. Pathology. Profound loss of Purkinje cells with degeneration of those that remain.

3. Associated malignancies. Ovary, breast, SCLC.

4. Associated antibodies. Anti-Purkinje cell antibody (APCA known as anti-Yo) are seen mainly in women with gynaecological malignancy.

Progressive multifocal leucoencephalopathy (PML)

1. Clinical features. Although seen most often in immunocompromised patients, PML can occur as a complication of lymphoma. It presents with lethargy, nausea, headache, behavioural change and may progress to hemiparesis, hemianopia, dysphasia, involuntary movements, fits and coma. MRI shows diffuse white matter lesions especially posteriorly. There is no definite treatment.

2. Pathology. There are multiple foci of brain demyelination; immunocytochemistry may demonstrate evidence of the JC virus (not to be confused with CJD) which damages oligodendroglia causing demyelination.

3. Associated malignancies. Lymphoma and chronic lymphatic leukaemia.

Isolated cranial angiitis

This condition presents with headache and focal neurological signs; there are no systemic features of vasculitis. Brain and meningeal biopsy demonstrates vasculitis. It is usually sporadic but may occur in association with lymphoma, even arising outside the CNS.

Cancer-associated retinopathy

1. Clinical features. This presents with blurred vision, scotomata, impaired colour vision and rapidly progressive painless visual loss. Electroretinography is abnormal.

2. Pathology. There is loss of rods and cones with immunoglobulin deposits in the retinal ganglion layer.

3. Associated malignancies. SCLC.

4. Associated antibodies. Antibody against recoverin, a photoreceptor cell protein.

Spinal cord

Myelitis

Cord involvement is rare, representing only 10% of neurological paraneoplastic disease. A patchy, multifocal necrosis throughout the cord, especially the white matter, sometimes with massive necrosis of the thoracic cord (necrotizing myelitis). It is occasionally temporarily steroid responsive.

Subacute sensory neuropathy ('ganglionitis')

1. Clinical. This presents with sensory ataxia (owing to profound loss of position sense) and areflexia. Its appearance may precede the tumour diagnosis sometimes by years.

2. Pathology. The dorsal root ganglia are infiltrated by lymphocytes and macrophages giving secondary degeneration of the dorsal columns and peripheral nerves.

3. Associated malignancies. SCLC, lymphoma.

4. Associated antibodies. ANNA1 (Anti-Hu).

Peripheral neuropathy

Non-inflammatory peripheral neuropathy

Clinical evidence of axonal or demyelinating peripheral neuropathy is seen in 1–2% of cancer patients, especially those with recent weight loss; subclinical peripheral nerve disease is apparent electrophysiologically in <30%.

Inflammatory peripheral neuropathy

Chronic inflammatory neuropathy may be seen in lymphoma or seminoma.

Peripheral neuropathy is seen in 10% of Waldenström's macroglobulinaemia and in myeloma.

Patients with monoclonal IgM, especially elderly men, show a slowly progressive sensorimotor neuropathy with associated anti-myelin-associated glycoprotein (anti-MAG).

Mononeuritis multiplex

Involvement of multiple individual peripheral nerves is seen in many cancers, but especially lymphoma. Pathology shows a vasculitis of the *vasa vasorum* of unknown cause.

Autonomic neuropathy

Pseudo-obstruction in cancer patients may be due to infiltration of the myenteric plexus with mononuclear cells, especially in patients with SCLC and pancreatic carcinoma.

Similar autonomic dysfunction may accompany the Lambert–Eaton syndrome.

Neuromuscular junction

See also Neuromuscular junction disorders.

Lambert–Eaton myasthenic syndrome

1. Clinical. This disorder presents with progressive proximal limb muscle weakness augmented by maximal effort, autonomic features including dry mouth and constipation. Limb reflexes are reduced or absent but can be enhanced by voluntary muscle contraction.

2. Associated malignancy. Small cell lung carcinoma.

3. Associated antibody. Voltage-gated calcium channel antibody.

4. Treatment. Removal of underlying tumour. Steroids and plasma exchange can help. Symptomatic relief is gained from 3:4 diaminopyridine.

Myasthenia gravis (MG)	Although not traditionally regarded as a paraneoplastic syndrome, 10% of MG patients have an underlying thymoma, 30% of thymoma patients have MG and 90% of patients with MG and thymoma have acetylcholine receptor antibodies. The diagnosis of MG almost always precedes the diagnosis of thymoma. Tumour resection has no effect upon the myasthenia. MG with thymoma is more aggressive than MG without thymoma.

Muscle

Dermatomyositis	This is associated with malignancy in 15% of cases. There is no such association with polymyositis. Patients over 40 years with dermatomyositis should undergo a rectal and pelvic examination, chest radiograph and search for faecal occult bloods.
Acute necrotizing myopathy	This rare and aggressive condition is associated with carcinomas of the lung, gastrointestinal tract or breast.
Acquired neuromyotonia (Isaac's syndrome)	This syndrome of generalized stiffness, difficulty relaxing following forceful contraction, and excessive sweating is usually idiopathic but occasionally seen in association with thymoma.

Further reading

Dalmau J, Posner JB. Neurological paraneoplastic syndromes. *Springer Seminal Immunopathology,* 1996; **18:** 85–95.
Dropcho EJ. Neurologic paraneoplastic syndromes. *Journal of the Neurological Sciences,* 1998; **153:** 264–78.
Posner JB. Paraneoplastic syndromes. In: *Neurologic Complications of Cancer.* Philadelphia: F.A. Davis, 1995; 353–85.

Related topics of interest

PARKINSONIAN (AKINETIC RIGID) SYNDROMES

The differential diagnosis of Parkinson's disease includes a large variety of conditions affecting basal ganglia function.

Atypical Parkinson's disease

Parkinson's disease is described in detail in the next topic. Occasional cases of pathologically confirmed Parkinson's disease show unusual features, e.g. young onset (1:20 present before the age of 40 years), symmetrical onset, early falls, early dementia, prominent autonomic dysfunction, pyramidal signs or poor L-dopa responsiveness.

Multiple system atrophy (MSA)

This heterogeneous group of degenerative disorders comprises 10% of parkinsonism. It presents with:

- Adult-onset parkinsonism (especially bradykinesia and rigidity without prominent tremor).
- Poor L-dopa responsiveness.
- Occasional cerebellar features.
- Absence of dementia.

These combine to give three MSA syndromes along a triangular spectrum.

Striatonigral degeneration	This lies at the motor end of the spectrum manifesting as prominent parkinsonism sometimes with disproportionate antecollis, reduced deep tendon reflexes, absence of dementia and no significant autonomic or cerebellar features.
Shy-Drager syndrome	Here there is prominent autonomic involvement giving erectile failure, orthostatic hypotension with pre-syncope, laryngeal stridor and dysphonia, and urinary incontinence. Sphincter electromyography may be helpful in the diagnosis. Parkinsonism is mild at onset and without dementia.
Sporadic olivo-ponto-cerebellar atrophy	This lies at the ataxic end of the spectrum where patients present with progressive ataxia, occasional pyramidal signs and features of parkinsonism.

Other degenerative disorders

Progressive supranuclear palsy (Steele–Richardson–Olszewski syndrome)

This is an elderly onset condition presenting as progressive dementia, supranuclear gaze palsy, particularly for downgaze, and early onset falls, particularly backwards and often with injury. Response to L-dopa is partial and often short lived. The substantia nigra shows neuronal depletion and basophilic globose (spool like) neurofibrillary tangles in the surviving nigral cells.

Corticobasal degeneration

This elderly onset progressive, extrapyramidal syndrome is characterized by apraxia (alien hand syndrome) where involuntary unilateral hand movements occur which appear voluntary, and by progressive dementia. Asymmetrical degeneration of the *substantia nigra* occurs with achromasia of the residual nerve cells which appear swollen and chromatolized with eccentric nuclei.

Alzheimer's disease

Mild parkinsonian features, including shuffling gait, flexed posture and postural instability develop in about 30% of advanced Alzheimer's disease patients.

Juvenile Huntington's disease (Westphal variant)

The young onset form of Huntington's disease is more severe and runs a shorter course (and is associated with larger numbers of triplet repeats usually inherited paternally) and manifests as an akinetic rigid syndrome. The diagnosis may be obvious if there is a family history but doubtful paternity may explain sporadic cases.

Dentato-rubro-pallido-luysian atrophy

This autosomal dominant condition first described in Japanese families presents with progressive myoclonic ataxia, often with choreoathetosis, dementia and seizures. It is a triplet repeat disorder and with the recognition of the gene a much broader phenotype is now being recognized. It may present like, and be confused with, Huntington's disease.

Guam motor neurone disease

In this variant of MND confined to the South Pacific island Guam, there is the combination of dementia, parkinsonism and motor neurone disease.

Miscellaneous disorders

Arteriosclerotic vascular disease

Although this used to be considered a common cause of parkinsonism, a true parkinsonian syndrome due to vascular disease without Lewy body pathology has not been described. The combination of pyramidal dysfunction with pseudobulbar palsy and dementia is a rare manifestation of advanced diffuse cerebrovascular disease.

Communicating hydrocephalus

The triad of gait dyspraxia, dementia and incontinence is usual but prominent gait dysfunction with unsteadiness, shuffling and tendency to fall may lead to a mistaken diagnosis of Parkinson's disease (see Dementia).

Post-encephalitic parkinsonism

Acute parkinsonism may follow encephalitis, especially from Mycoplasma and fungal infections.

Encephalitis lethargica followed influenza pandemics between 1918 and 1926 but is now extremely rare. Parkinsonism followed the encephalitic illness with gradual onset of lethargy, sleep disorder and eye signs including oculogyric crisis. The condition responds, often dramatically, to L-dopa. Oligoclonal bands were found in the CSF.

Head trauma

Repeated minor trauma such as following boxing may lead to the combination of dementia, pyramidal and cerebellar signs together with a parkinsonian syndrome (dementia pugilistica). Neurofibrillary tangles are found in the brain stem nigral neurones.

Neoplasms

Tumours involving the upper brain stem, especially lymphoma, or tumours in the para-sagittal area or those leading to obstructive hydrocephalus, may each lead to features of parkinsonism with gait disturbance, rigidity, urinary incontinence and dementia.

Drugs and poisons

Chemical (reversible) change in nigral neurones following exposure to drugs (phenothiazines, reserpine, sodium valproate, calcium antagonists and sertrolene) may lead to parkinsonism. It is usually symmetrical and with little tremor; it may take several months to resolve.

Toxic (irreversible) damage to nigral neurones may follow exposure poisoning with carbon monoxide, manganese, benzene or other solvents. Poisoning with MPTP (1-methyl, 4-phenyl, 1,2,3,6-tetrahydropyridine), is a condition confined to drug addicts in Maryland and California who inadvertently self-administered a contaminated pethidine analogue and developed an acute onset irreversible parkinsonian syndrome. It resembles encephalitis lethargica and responds to L-dopa, but with prominent early drug induced dyskinesia.

Creutzfeldt–Jakob disease

A rapidly progressive dementia may be associated with prominent rigidity which can give confusion with acute parkinsonism syndromes.

Leucodystrophies

- Metachromatic leucodystrophy is an autosomal recessive lysosomal storage disease characterized by central and peripheral nervous system demyelination attributable to sulfatide accumulation. Patients present with gait disturbance, behavioural problems and dementia.
- Adrenoleukodystrophy is an X-linked (Xq28) demyelinating disorder associated with elevated levels of very long chain fatty acids. Boys with the disorder present with progressive gait deterioration, spasticity and seizures. A few have Addison's disease from adrenal involvement. Lorenzo's oil is advocated but of little proven benefit.
- Pelizaeus–Merzbacher disease is an X-linked recessive leukodystrophy resulting from mutations in the proteolipid protein gene. It presents in young children with developmental delay, nystagmus, ataxia and spasticity.

Hallevorden–Spatz disease

This autosomal recessive disorder of early adolescence shows a gradual progression of combined pyramidal and extrapyramidal signs with intellectual decline and sometimes ataxia and myoclonus. CT scan shows hypodense areas in the lenticular nuclei (eye of the tiger) and neuropathologically there is intense brown pigmentation of the globus pallidus and substantia nigra owing to iron deposition. Response to L-dopa is poor.

Further reading

Pearce J. *Parkinson's Disease and its Management.* Oxford: Oxford Medical Publications, 1992.

Riley DE, Lang AE. Non-parkinson akinetic-rigid syndromes. *Current Opinion in Neurology,* 1996; **9:** 321–26.

Related topics of interest

PARKINSON'S DISEASE

History

The shaking palsy (paralysis agitans), was described by James Parkinson (1755–1824) in 1817 and further defined by Charcot in 1877.

Epidemiology

The prevalence of Parkinson's disease (PD) is 1.5 in 1000 overall but rises steeply to 1.5 in 100 over 70 years. Males are more often affected than females. The prevalence in black and Chinese populations is lower.

Pathogenesis

The cause is unknown. Solvents exposure may be relevant. Paradoxically, a smoking history appears protective against developing PD. About 15% of cases are familial and one large family was linked to the PD-1 locus on chromosome 4q21-23 (α-synuclein gene) although this accounts for only a minority of familial PD.

The dopa-secreting pigmented neurones of the midbrain's substantia nigra are depleted to <20% of normal.

Functional imaging (e.g. PET scanning) demonstrates reduced dopa activity in the thalamic projections of the substantia nigra.

Lewy bodies (rounded, eosinophilic, hyaline, ubiquitin-positive inclusions) occur in the nigral neurones of all PD patients. They are the pathological hallmark of the disease; 15% of autopsied patients with a clinical diagnosis of PD have no Lewy bodies and an alternative diagnosis is made. Lewy bodies in cortical neurones, best seen using ubiquitin immunocytochemistry, also occur in all PD patients, especially abundant in those with Lewy body dementia.

Clinical features

Tremor

Although the characteristic symptom of PD, it is not invariably present at the onset and is not as disabling or as treatment responsive as bradykinesia and rigidity. Two types of tremor are seen in PD.

1. Rest tremor. A tremor present at rest occurs with the following characteristics:
- 4–6 Hz.
- Abolished by posture or voluntary movement.

- Predominantly in the upper limbs and occasionally the chin and lower lip.
- 'Pill rolling' or 'bread crumbling' between index finger and thumb.
- Unilateral at the onset.
- Initially intermittent.
- Disappears in sleep.
- Worse with anxiety.

2. Postural tremor. A 6–8 Hz tremor, present when maintaining a posture (e.g. outstretched arms) and worsened by anxiety, may be superimposed on the rest tremor and is responsible for cogwheel rigidity.

Rigidity

Rigidity is present in 97% of PD patients at diagnosis.

1. Symptoms
- Diffuse shoulder and back pain.
- Increased effort to move a limb.
- Limbs feel heavy and weak, though without true weakness.

2. Signs. Limb rigidity is enhanced during examination by voluntary distracting movements of another limb, e.g. 'Raise and lower your other arm.' PD rigidity has the following characteristics:

- 'Lead pipe' rigidity is increased tone unchanged by speed or range of limb movement.
- 'Cogwheel' rigidity is lead pipe rigidity with superimposed postural tremor.
- Asymmetrical at onset.
- Arms, neck and shoulders more involved than legs.
- Worse on arousal or exertion.
- 'Wilson's sign' of poor arm swing on passive shoulder rotation.

Bradykinesia

This is the major disabling feature of PD, and essential for the diagnosis. It is bilateral, though often worse on one side, and slows all movements. Particularly affected are:

- Facial expression giving infrequent blinking and positive glabellar tap.
- Hand and finger dexterity which is reduced with dysdiadochokinesis and micrographia.

- Gait is slowed with flexed posture, small steps and diminished arm swing.
- Speech which becomes quiet.

Postural instability

1. Gait. The gait of PD is more than just slow, there is instability and liability to topple. Assessment of righting reflexes is an important part of the clinical assessment of PD. Standing the patient with feet together while the examiner pulls the shoulders backwards may induce multiple small backward steps with risk of falling.

2. Eye movements. Upgaze and convergence may be become restricted. Voluntary rapid eye movements (saccades) are slowed and pursuit eye movements fragmented.

Lewy body dementia

A 'subcortical' dementia develops in about 20% of PD patients, especially elderly, showing the following characteristics:

- Forgetfulness.
- Slowing of thought (bradyphrenia).
- Confusion which is variable day to day.
- Associated affective disorder, especially depression.
- Visual hallucinations, characteristically seeing animals or people in the absence of altered consciousness and exacerbated by poor vision.

Lewy body dementia is the second commonest senile dementia after Alzheimer's disease in those over 80 years, being more common in this group than multiple infarct dementia. Elderly patients present with dementia as the predominant symptom, with only minimal motor symptoms. They are especially vulnerable to the extrapyramidal side effects of neuroleptic agents.

Depression

Depression is common in Parkinson's disease and may contribute to apparent memory problems. The combination of antidepressant medication and eldepryl should be avoided owing to reports of the 'serotonin syndrome' of coma, rigidity and seizures.

Autonomic dysfunction

Smooth muscle dysfunction is common in PD, and may lead to:

- Constipation and bladder symptoms exacerbated by anticholinergic drugs.
- Postural hypotension, often exaggerated by L-dopa preparations.
- Sexual dysfunction, especially in males, exacerbated by depression or medication.
- Hoarseness and dysphagia.
- Excessive sweating (seborrhoea).

Hyposmia

Reduced sense of smell is present in 70–90% of PD cases. Lewy bodies are identified in the olfactory bulbs of affected cases. Olfactory involvement suggests the possible olfactory pathway CNS entry of an environmental toxin as the cause of PD.

L-dopa responsiveness

The majority of PD patients show improvement in bradykinesia and rigidity on L-dopa preparations. Partial responsiveness is seen in other akinetic rigid syndromes. Re-examination of a patient 45–150 minutes after a 500 mg trial oral dose of L-dopa provides a useful clinical test; a 25% improvement suggests an expected improvement on regular treatment. Dystonic side effects following long term use of L-dopa are, in practice, seen only in Parkinson's disease.

Drug treatment

PD was the first neurodegenerative disease amenable to specific treatment. Central dopamine levels may be increased or enhanced by:

- L-dopa supplements, prescribed with peripheral decarboxylase inhibitors to enhance the central effect. Slow release preparations can provide more stable symptom control.
- L-dopa agonists, enhancing the effect of endogenous L-dopa, are generally less effective but carry less risk of dystonic side effects.
- Inhibition of the dopamine degrading enzymes:
    Monoamine oxidase (MAO) inhibitors such as eldepryl.
    Catechol-O-methyl transferase (COMT) inhibitors such as tolcapone.
- Apomorphine, by subcutaneous injection following anti-emetic treatment, may provide a rapid response in selected patients.

Symptomatic benefit
- Anticholinergics, e.g. benzhexol, may relieve tremor but are limited by their side effects and their theoretical potential to worsen the dementia.

	• Propranolol to control postural tremor.
Principles	• Treatment may not be required upon diagnosis.
	• A balance must be struck between providing benefit and potential side-effects.
	• Owing to the risk of long term dystonic side effects of L-dopa preparations, there are grounds for delaying the introduction of this treatment.

Prognosis

The average time from diagnosis to severe disability is 14 years. The time course in relation to progression is shown in Table 1.

Table 1. Time course of Parkinson's disease in relation to progression

'Hoen and Yahr' stage	Mean time from diagnosis
1 Unilateral only	3 years
2 Bilateral mild	6 years
3 Bilateral and postural	7 years
4 Severe, needing help	9 years
5 Chair or bed bound	14 years

Differential diagnosis

- Tremor: distinguishing PD from benign essential or familial tremor may be difficult, especially as postural tremor commonly accompanies PD. Typically, it involves all four limbs, head ('no-no'), tongue and voice; it is worsened by anxiety and often relieved by alcohol. Although it may gradually worsen with time, the overall prognosis is good.
- Rigidity and bradykinesia: see Parkinsonian (akinetic rigid) syndromes.
- In PD dementia, consider:
  Depression.
  Polypharmacy.
  Unrecognized cerebrovascular disease.

Further reading

Pearce J. *Parkinson's Disease and its Management.* Oxford: Oxford Medical Publications, 1992.

Related topic of interest

Parkinsonian (akinetic rigid) syndromes (p. 220)

PERIPHERAL NEUROPATHY (ACQUIRED)

Chronic inflammatory demyelinating polyradiculoneuropathy (CIDP)

Clinical features

CIDP presents with progressive (over >8 weeks) asymmetrical motor and sensory involvement of the distal and proximal limbs, with weakness, numbness and areflexia. A postural tremor occasionally occurs. CIDP relapses despite treatment in 40%.

Investigations

- CSF protein is elevated in 50% with normal white cell count.
- Nerve conduction studies show slowed conduction and variable degrees of conduction block.
- Biopsy of nerve roots or peripheral myelinated nerves show inflammatory demyelination; sural biopsy sometimes shows only axonal change from Wallerian degeneration.

Management

- Steroids (e.g. prednisolone 60 mg daily, reduced after 2 weeks) are usually effective.
- Azathioprine or cyclosporin are sometimes needed.
- Intravenous immunoglobulin 0.4 g/kg/day for 5 days is effective, but expensive, invasive and with concerns for its long term safety. Immunoglobulins or plasma exchange are useful in severe disease, the elderly (slower steroid response) and poorly steroid responsive patients.

Clinical variants

- Multifocal motor neuropathy with conduction block is a treatable condition presenting like motor neurone disease. It predominates in males, and affects mainly the upper limbs. 40% have GM1 ganglioside antibodies. Patients may deteriorate on steroids but 80% respond dramatically to intravenous immunoglobulins.
- Sensory ataxic CIDP is dominated by sensory ataxia without weakness. Steroids are usually effective.
- Pure motor CIDP gives symmetric motor involvement (markedly slow nerve conduction) predominantly in the legs and without sensory symptoms.

Distinction from hereditary neuropathy	Clinically, CIDP (treatable) may resemble HMSN type 1 (untreatable). A positive genetic test may settle this but distinguishing clinical features of CIDP include:

- Ability to date the symptoms onset.
- Asymmetrical clinical and electrophysiological findings.
- Positive sensory symptoms, e.g. tingling.
- Palpable nerve thickening, e.g. greater auricular nerve.
- No pes cavus.
- Proximal and distal weakness.
- Raised CSF protein.

Chronic demyelinating neuropathy with paraproteinaemia

Demyelinating peripheral neuropathy in middle or old age is occasionally associated with a monoclonal gammopathy of uncertain significance (MGUS).

Clinical features	It presents indolently, involving mainly the legs. Sensory features predominate and altered position sense leads to sensory ataxia.
Underlying conditions	Although MGUS is usually benign, checks are needed to detect development of significant haemopoetic conditions, e.g. myeloma, Waldenström's macroglobulinaemia or POEMS syndrome (**P**eripheral neuropathy, **O**rganomegaly, **E**ndocrinopathy, **M**onoclonal paraproteinaemia, **S**kin lesions).
Management	It is usually mild, stable and treated conservatively. Most treatments are unhelpful but a trial of steroids or immunoglobulins is justified for rapid progression.

Chronic axonal peripheral neuropathy (CAPN)

This is the best-known and commonest form of peripheral neuropathy but unfortunately is the least treatable unless an underlying cause is identified.

Clinical features	It is an indolent, symmetrical, predominantly sensory condition. 40% are purely sensory, 50% involve only the legs. There is a stocking sensory change, especially

for pain and temperature, together with distal wasting (e.g. of extensor digitorum brevis in the foot) and weakness (e.g. of toe dorsiflexion). It progresses slowly, rarely with significant disability at 5 years.

Nerve conduction show chronic axonal damage: low amplitude sensory and motor action potentials but normal conduction velocity.

Differential diagnosis

- Idiopathic: half of axonal peripheral neuropathy cases remain undiagnosed.
- Diabetes mellitus is the commonest cause and must be excluded.
- Medications: a drug history is essential. Major culprits are cytotoxics, amiodarone, perhexiline and gold.
- Toxins. Alcohol, though frequently implicated, is an uncommon cause of symptomatic neuropathy, e.g. 15% of alcoholics. Industrial toxins and organophosphorous agents certainly cause neuropathy but it is difficult to attribute certain blame.
- Deficiencies of vitamin B_{12}, thiamine and nicotinic acid present a readily treatable neuropathy.
- Vasculitis: uncommonly presents as a CAPN but must be considered if the neuropathy is asymmetrical or rapidly progressing.
- Hereditary motor and sensory neuropathy accounts for some apparently idiopathic forms. Particular types include HMSN IIa (older, foot deformity, predominantly motor), IIb (younger, foot ulcers, preserved ankle jerks) and IIc (rare, severe respiratory muscle involvement in middle age).
- CIDP: secondary axonal changes may predominate, giving a potentially treatable form of apparent CAPN.
- Paraneoplastic: often suspected but rare.
- Ageing itself is not a cause of significant neuropathy; most elderly do have preserved ankle jerks and vibration sense.

Management

Treatment is supportive with attention to the underlying condition if known.

Vasculitic neuropathy

Vasa nervorum (50–300 μm diameter) vasculitic involvement of peripheral nerves causes ischaemia and infarction.

Clinical features

- Rapid onset over several weeks.
- Pain: deep, aching and neuropathic.
- Symptoms of vasculitic disease.

The distribution depends upon the size and extent of the nerves involved:

- Large nerve infarction (50%): multiple mono-neuropathy (mononeuritis multiplex).
- Smaller nerve infarction: asymmetric sensorimotor neuropathy.
- Nerve ischaemia: distal symmetric sensorimotor neuropathy.

Associated conditions

Vasculitic neuropathy occurs in the following (% frequency):

1. Primary vasculitis
- Churg–Strauss syndrome (70%): asthma, eosinophilia, vasculitic rash, glomerulonephritis and positive anti-neutrophil cytoplasmic antibody (ANCA) in 60–70%.
- Microscopic polyangiitis (30%): systemic vasculitis with renal involvement.
- Wegener's granulomatosis (15%): upper and lower respiratory tract involvement, glomerulonephritis, ANCA in 90%.

2. Vasculitis with systemic autoimmune disease
- Rheumatoid arthritis (10%) also develop non-vasculitic neuropathy, e.g. carpal tunnel syndrome or axonal peripheral neuropathy from the disease itself and medication.
- Systemic lupus erythematosus (10%).
- Sjögren's syndrome (10%).

3. Others
- Cryoglobulinaemia (50%), especially mixed (often hepatitis C positive).
- HIV (2%).

Investigations	Nerve conduction studies confirm a multiple mononeuropathy or diffuse axonal changes.
Pathology	A nerve biopsy is essential as a basis for long-term immunosuppression. 90% are positive in vasculitis if the nerve is neurophysiologically abnormal. An additional muscle biopsy increases the diagnostic yield.
Management	Steroids alone are sufficient for mild or moderate cases. More severe forms, or with systemic features, require steroids with cyclophosphamide. Cyclophosphamide drawbacks include opportunistic infection, gonadal failure and bladder carcinoma (in 15%).

Diabetes mellitus

Symmetric chronic axonal peripheral neuropathy	This is very common in diabetes and increasingly so with long duration or poorly controlled disease.
Diabetic proximal neuropathy (diabetic amyotrophy)	This presents as an acute, painful, asymmetric proximal leg weakness with particular involvement of the L2,3,4 sensorimotor distribution (hip flexion, knee extension, lost knee jerk and anterior thigh and leg numbness). It occurs early and may be the presenting complaint. Weight loss is usual. Nerve biopsy shows inflammatory change. Treatment is symptomatic though steroids have been used in severe cases despite the diabetes. Recovery over 12–18 months is expected.
Multiple mononeuropathy	Diabetic damage renders nerves vulnerable to injury. Diabetes itself may involve the vasa nervorum. Management is to control the underlying condition, protect pressure areas from further trauma, and await improvement.
Autonomic neuropathy	Mild degrees are common in diabetes; severe forms are troublesome with nocturnal diarrhoea, postural hypotension and syncope.

Infections

Leprosy (Hansen's disease)   This is endemic in the tropics and subtropics. It usually presents with a chronic, hypopigmented, non-itchy rash with altered sensation and sometimes with widespread nodules. Peripheral nerves are thickened and foot ulcers present. Associated features are acute uveitis, erythema nodosum, epistaxis, nasal discharge, hoarseness, arthritis.

Microscopy of skin smears or nasal discharge show acid fast bacilli.

Management includes specific multiple chemotherapy (rifampicin, dapsone, and sometimes clofazimine), protection of anaesthetic areas and patient education.

Lyme disease   This tick-borne infection manifests as a characteristic rash (erythema chronicum migrans), and subacute onset painful patchy neuritis associated with CSF pleocytosis. Treatment is with tetracycline.

HIV disease   See HIV neurology.

Further reading

Dyck PJ, Prineas J, Pollard J. Chronic inflammatory demyelinating polyradiculoneuropathy. In: *Peripheral Neuropathy*, 3rd edn. Philadelphia: WB Saunders, 1993.

Fathers E, Fuller GN. Vasculitic neuropathy. *British Journal of Hospital Medicine,* 1996; **55:** 643–47.

Related topics of interest

Autonomic disorders (p. 12)
HIV neurology (p. 136)
Motor neurone diseases (p. 158)
Peripheral neuropathy (hereditary) (p. 236)
Vasculitis of the central nervous system (p. 301)

PERIPHERAL NEUROPATHY (HEREDITARY)

Hereditary motor and sensory neuropathy (HMSN)

The familial and slowly progressive condition formerly known as Charcot–Marie–Tooth disease, or peroneal muscular atrophy, comprises several hereditary motor and sensory neuropathies (HMSNs) with overlapping clinical and electrophysiological characteristics. Recent years have seen major advances in the understanding of the genetics of HMSN and it is logical now to classify inherited peripheral neuropathy according to their genetic basis.

Disorders of the peripheral myelin protein 22 (PMP 22) gene: HMSN type Ia

Clinical features	This condition shows a wide variation of clinical involvement even within families. There is a progressive, predominantly distal muscle wasting and weakness from childhood, involving mainly the lower limbs and often with accompanying pes cavus and sometimes scoliosis. Severe cases show 'inverted champagne bottle' shaped legs with atrophy of the peroneal muscles and calves but with relative sparing of the quadriceps muscles. Sensory involvement is slight and positive sensory symptoms such as tingling or pain are not expected. Autonomic function is preserved. The deep tendon reflexes are absent. Thickened nerves may be palpable; severe childhood cases with marked nerve thickening used to be distinguished as Dejerine–Sottas disease (or HMSN III). Upper limb tremor may be present and when prominent is known as Roussy–Lévy syndrome (see Ataxia).
Electrophysiology	The key feature is evidence of peripheral demyelination with severe slowing of peripheral motor conduction velocity (usually to considerably less than 38 m/s in the median nerve).
Pathology	Nerve biopsy typically demonstrates fibre loss with demyelination and remyelination in surviving fibres.

The characteristic finding beyond adolescence is 'onion bulbs' comprising concentrically proliferated Schwann cells surrounding the surviving myelinated fibres.

Genetics	There is a duplication or, rarely, a point mutation at 17p 11.2, the gene coding for PMP 22, a Schwann cell adhesion molecule. This genotype comprises the majority of HMSN 1 cases.

Hereditary neuropathy with liability to pressure palsies (HNLPP)

Clinical features	This autosomal dominant condition is characterized by recurrent pressure palsies sometimes with a generalized polyneuropathy. Typically it presents with a common peroneal or an ulnar neuropathy following minor trauma and which resolves only slowly and often incompletely. It is important to consider it in the differential diagnosis of multiple mononeuropathy.
Genetics	There is a deletion or sometimes a point mutation at 17p 11.2.
Pathology	Nerve biopsy shows fibre loss with demyelination and remyelination with characteristic sausage shaped enlargement of the myelin sheath (tomacula).

Disorders of the myelin protein zero (P_0) gene: HMSN Ib

This rarer condition is clinically identical to HMSN 1a but has a different genetic basis. There is a mutation at chromosome 1q22-q23, the gene coding for P_0, a large and abundant structural myelin protein.

Disorders of the connexin 32 gene: X-linked HMSN

Rare cases affecting males, clinically similar to HMSN 1, are caused by point mutations of Xq13.1, the gene for connexin 32, a gap junction protein.

HMSN with unknown genetic basis

Demyelinating neuropathies   *1. Autosomal dominant.* HMSN I non-a non-b is the term applied to the disease in families where linkage to chromosomes 17 and 1 have been excluded; their genotypes await identification.

2. Autosomal recessive. Autosomal recessive HMSN 1 is a rare, severe and early onset disorder mapping to chromosome 8q. Some forms have focally folded myelin sheaths on nerve biopsy.

Axonal neuropathies   *1. HMSN II.* This is distinguished from HMSN I by:

- Autosomal recessive inheritance.
- Axonopathy rather than demyelination.
- Median motor conduction velocity > 38 m/s.
- Sparse demyelination and no onion bulbs on nerve biopsy.
- The responsible genes have not been identified.

2. Complex HMSN. Other categories of HMSN with associated features have yet to be fully characterized. Some have pyramidal features (retained reflexes and extensor plantar responses), optic atrophy, deafness or pigmentary retinal degeneration.

Syndromic hereditary peripheral neuropathies

Refsum's disease   This is an autosomal recessive disorder associated with demyelination resulting from abnormal storage of phytanic acid. It is due to a defect in alpha-oxidation of beta-methylated fatty acids. Patients present in the first or second decade with night blindness (retinitis pigmentosa) and polyneuropathy; cerebellar ataxia and cardiac abnormalities are late features. Cochlear hearing loss occurs in 80% of cases. Treatment with a low phytanate diet is rarely very successful.

Fabry's disease   This is a rare (incidence 1 per 40 000) X-linked (Xq22) disorder of glycolipid catabolism associated with defective lysosomal alpha-galactosidase. Trihexosylceramide accumulates in various tissues of affected males aged 10–30 years. The main neurological manifestation is a painful neuropathy affecting hands and feet, with pain crises in the palms and soles. Manifestations elsewhere include involvement of the skin (angiokeratomata with lipid inclusions on microscopy), eye (corneal opacities in 80%), kidney (renal failure and birefringent lipid on microscopy) and heart (arrhythmias). Treatment is symptomatic, the pain usually responding to carbamazepine.

Porphyria

This is a group of autosomal dominant impairments of porphyrin metabolism in which exacerbations are usually triggered by medications. Neuropsychiatric manifestations are seen in acute intermittent and variegate porphyria. The peripheral neuropathy is predominantly motor and may present like Guillain–Barré syndrome or multiple mononeuropathy; its relapsing course together with the associated psychiatric symptoms may lead to a misdiagnosis of hysteria. The urine turns red-brown on standing. Treatment is supportive and symptomatic with strict avoidance of offending medications, the most important of which are female sex hormones, benzodiazepines and anticonvulsants. Other family members must be considered for testing.

Familial amyloid polyneuropathy

This is a heterogeneous group of autosomal dominant disorders first described in Portuguese people. Amyloid is deposited in the extracellular space. The clinical manifestations are those of a small fibre neuropathy (pain, spinothalamic peripheral sensory loss) together with autonomic dysfunction, cardiomyopathy and occasional vitreous and renal involvement. Nerve biopsy is diagnostic.

The condition is classified according to the constituent amyloidogenic proteins and their underlying mutations. The commonest fibrillar proteins deposited as amyloid are transthyretin apolipoprotein A-1 and gelsolin. For transthyretin alone there are 40 amyloidogenic point mutations (chromosome 18q).

Treatment is largely symptomatic but liver

transplantation in young adults (transthyretin is produced in the liver) can halt the progression of this subtype.

Management

There is still no specific treatment for HMSN and the emphasis is on symptomatic management. As with any genetic disorder, genetic advice to the patient and the family is of paramount importance.

Further reading

Reilly MM. Genetically determined neuropathies. *Journal of Neurology,* 1998; **245:** 6–13.

Thomas PK, King RHM, Small JR, Robertson AM. Review. The pathology of Charcot–Marie–Tooth disease and related disorders. *Neuropathology and Applied Neurobiology,* 1996; **22:** 269–84.

Thomas PK, Marques W, Davis MB, *et al.* The phenotypic manifestations of chromosome 17p11.2 duplication. *Brain,* 1997; **120:** 465–78.

Related topics of interest

Neurogenic pain (p. 189)
Peripheral neuropathy (acquired) (p. 230)

PREGNANCY AND NEUROLOGY

Eclampsia

Eclampsia is unique to pregnancy. It occurs particularly in poorly nourished, young primigravidas or elderly multigravidas. It follows pre-eclampsia (hypertension and proteinuria) and manifests as headache, visual hallucinations (eclampsia: Greek 'to shine forth') and epileptic seizures.

The marked hypertension exceeds the limit of cerebral perfusion autoregulation, leading to cerebral oedema and cortical petechial haemorrhages. MRI brain scan shows marked cortical and white matter (especially occipital) high signal abnormalities.

Management is to terminate the pregnancy and treat urgently with antihypertensives, anticonvulsants and steroids. Magnesium sulphate, used since 1902, remains the best treatment for eclamptic seizures. The prognosis with rapid intervention is excellent.

Cerebrovascular disease

Haemorrhage

1. Aneurysm. Ten per cent of maternal deaths follow intracranial haemorrhage. Cerebral artery aneurysms are increasingly likely to rupture with each trimester, probably from arterial wall elasticity changes. Aneurysmal haemorrhage is treated by surgical clipping in pregnancy (unless rupture occurs during parturition) and delivery by Caesarean section.

2. Arteriovenous malformation. These bleed more frequently during pregnancy, particularly in the second trimester and during delivery itself.

Spinal cord arteriovenous malformations may become symptomatic (claudication and paraparesis) during pregnancy owing to hormonal effects on the arteriovenous shunt.

3. Other arterial bleeding. This may be caused by vasculitis (SLE being exacerbated by pregnancy), metastatic choriocarcinoma (usually in the months following childbirth), eclampsia, cerebral venous thrombosis, diffuse intravascular coagulation or anticoagulant therapy.

Infarction

The risk, although still small, is increased four times by pregnancy, particularly in the 6 weeks post partum. If anticoagulating, e.g. for atrial fibrillation, heparin is preferable to warfarin as it does not cross the placenta.

In addition to premature atheroma, ischaemic stroke in pregnancy may be caused by:

- Arterial dissection during labour.
- Paradoxical emboli (Valsalva manoeuvre during delivery).
- Puerperal exacerbation of SLE.
- Infective endocarditis with pre-existing rheumatic disease.
- Post partum cardiomyopathy.
- Amniotic fluid embolism.

Venous thrombosis

This may involve the venous sinuses, the cortical veins, or both.

1. Superior sagittal sinus thrombosis. This usually occurs in the first week post partum and presents as:

- Intracranial hypertension due to impaired CSF reabsorption.
- Paraparesis by oedema and venous haemorrhagic infarct in the medial motor cortex.
- Simple partial (Jacksonian) seizures alternating right and left sides.

2. Cortical vein thrombosis. This may result from spread of sagittal sinus thrombosis or arise *de novo*. Patients present with headache, transient neurological disturbance, e.g. dysphasia, weakness or numbness, followed by seizures and altered consciousness.

Investigations demonstrate neutrophilia, raised CSF pressure and CSF red cell/white cell count. MRI brain scan and angiography demonstrate the site and extent of thrombosis. Thrombophilia screen may demonstrate an underlying thrombotic tendency (see Stroke in young adults).

Treatment is with heparin anticoagulation, anticonvulsants and steroids; in life-threatening situations, clot lysis can be done by direct injection of a thrombolytic agent into the sinus.

For the patient who survives the initial illness the prognosis is excellent.

Migraine

Overall, migraine tends to improve in pregnancy. In a few cases, however, it begins first in pregnancy. Frequent auras without headache (migraine equivalents) may appear in pregnancy.

Epilepsy

Effect of pregnancy on epilepsy

The outcome of pregnancy is little affected by seizures unless there are recurrent major convulsions, e.g. status epilepticus.

Effect of epilepsy on pregnancy

- Vomiting in early pregnancy may give inconsistent antiepileptic levels.
- Changes in anticonvulsant metabolism include increased clearance of some anticonvulsants (maternal liver hydroxylation), changes in plasma volume distribution and plasma protein binding.
- Loss of sleep by nocturnal symptoms in pregnancy or by baby care post-partum lowers seizure threshold.
- Risk to the new-born of maternal seizures during baby care.
- Breast feeding, although transmitting low levels of anticonvulsant to the baby, is not contra-indicated.
- Teratogenicity: a major concern. The risk is highest with the older drugs used in combination. Valproate and carbamazepine are each associated with increased risk of spina bifida. The risk may be lowered by taking folate 5 mg daily for the 3 months before a planned pregnancy. New antiepileptic drugs await assessment in pregnancy.

Neuropathy

Non-traumatic

- Bell's palsy is commoner in late pregnancy and early post partum.
- Carpal tunnel syndrome is well known to present first in pregnancy.
- Meralgia paraesthetica (meros = thigh; algos = pain), often bilateral, may occur in the second and third trimesters. Abdominal expansion and exaggerated lumbar lordosis stretch the lateral cutaneous nerve of

the thigh, rendering it vulnerable to injury. Treatment is symptomatic.
- Generalized neuropathy: exacerbations of acute intermittent porphyria and chronic inflammatory polyradiculoneuropathy (CIDP) are more likely in pregnancy. Thiamine deficiency neuropathy is now rare.

Traumatic

- Unilateral foot drop: the lumbosacral trunk (L4/5), may be compressed by the infant's brow (occipito-anterior presentation) on the posterior rim of the true pelvis.
- Proximal lower limb mononeuropathy (femoral neuropathy) follows pelvic nerve trunk trauma by the fetus or instrumentation.
- Obturator neuropathy: compression of the obturator nerve (L3/4) on the anterior pelvic rim causes thigh adduction weakness.

Neuromuscular disease

- Benign muscle cramps occur in 30% of pregnancies and restless legs in 10%, especially in the third trimester. Folate supplementation and avoiding caffeine is helpful.
- Myasthenia gravis is unpredictable in pregnancy: 30% improve, 30% worsen and 40% are unchanged. Neonatal myasthenia, transient weakness in up to 20% of neonates of mothers with myasthenia gravis, presents as a transiently floppy baby with poor feeding and feeble cry.
- Myotonic dystrophy: the pregnancy itself is unaffected but general anaesthetic complications may follow Caesarean section. Congenital myotonic dystrophy is a severe and permanent form in the new-born due to gross expansion of the maternally transmitted abnormal triplet repeat (see Muscle disorders (inherited)).

Multiple sclerosis

In the pregnancy year, there is no overall adverse effect. The relapse rate is, however, lowered in late pregnancy and increased in the 3 months post partum.

Tumours

Although the incidence is unchanged, several tumours progress more rapidly in the second half of pregnancy and shrink a little post partum, e.g. meningiomas, cerebellar haemangioblastomas. Pituitary macroadenomas may progress and require bromocriptine during pregnancy.

Choriocarcinoma, a trophoblastic malignant tumour, may present several weeks after delivery. Haemorrhagic cerebral metastases presenting as strokes are relatively common. Serum HCG is very elevated. If treated with radiotherapy and chemotherapy the prognosis is now reasonably good.

Benign intracranial hypertension

The more severe forms seen in obese women in early pregnancy can seriously threaten vision. Sinus thrombosis must be excluded in cases arising in pregnancy.

Movement disorders

Chorea gravidarum (usually a history of rheumatic fever with Sydenham's chorea) is now rare. No specific treatment is needed and it remits spontaneously but recurs in subsequent pregnancies.

Wernicke's encephalopathy

This was described first as a complication of hyperemesis gravidarum, but is now rare in pregnancy.

Sheehan's syndrome (post-partum hypopituitarism)

Pituitary gland enlargement in pregnancy renders it vulnerable to ischaemia if there is hypotension during delivery. It usually presents as indolent onset loss of secondary sexual characteristics and amenorrhoea.

Further reading

Bodis L, Szupera Z, Pierantozzi M, *et al.* Neurological complications of pregnancy. *Journal of the Neurological Sciences,* 1998; **153:** 279–93.

Donaldson, JO. *Neurology of Pregnancy*, 2nd edn. London: WB Saunders, 1989.

Kittner SJ, Stern BJ, Feeser ER, *et al.* Pregnancy and the risk of stroke. *New England Journal of Medicine,* 1996; **335:** 768–74.

Neilson JP. Magnesium sulphate: the drug of choice in eclampsia. *British Medical Journal,* 1995; **311:** 702–3.

Sawle GV, Ramsay MM. The neurology of pregnancy. *Journal of Neurology, Neurosurgery and Psychiatry,* 1998; **64:** 717–25.

Related topics of interest

PRION DISEASES

The transmissible spongiform encephalopathies in animals and man have aroused intense interest in the past decade with the emergence of a new disease in cattle and the alarming evidence of infectivity across the species barrier to humans. The diseases are both infectious and genetic.

Pathogenesis

Prion protein

Prion protein (PrP^c) is a membrane-anchored glycoprotein present in cell types of most organs. Its biological function is unknown but its phylogenetic conservation and its similarities to a protein modulating acetylcholine receptors suggest essential 'housekeeping' functions. A neuronal accumulation of **pro**teinaceous **in**fectious particles (**prions**) results from a change in shape of the cells' normal prion protein. The abnormally shaped and proteinase-resistant prion protein (PrP^{sc}) is the transmissible agent. Its amino acid sequence is identical to PrP^c but the tertiary structure differs. PrP^c is predominantly alpha-helix whereas PrP^{sc} molecules polymerize into beta-pleated amyloid sheets causing disease.

PrP^{sc} first arises in the brain in several ways:

- Somatic mutation: a rare event leading to sporadic Creutzfeldt–Jakob disease (CJD) (see below).
- Genetic abnormality on chromosome 20p (amyloid precursor protein gene) leading to genetic CJD.
- From infected human tissue leading to iatrogenic CJD.
- From infected animal tissue leading to new variant CJD.

Once in the brain, PrP^{sc} acts as a template (or 'seed molecule') converting PrP^c to the PrP^{sc} isoform in a chain reaction.

Codon 129

Conversion of PrP^c to PrP^{sc} occurs more readily if there is homozygosity at codon 129 (methionine or valine) of the prion protein gene; only 50% of the general population is homozygous at this site. Heterozygosity at codon 129 is unusual in CJD. Familial cases homozygous at 129 present earlier; iatrogenic cases with 129 homozygosity have a shorter incubation period.

Prion disease in animals

Animal prion diseases include scrapie in sheep and goats, transmissible mink encephalopathy, chronic wasting disease of mule deer and elk and bovine spongiform encephalopathy (BSE) in cattle. BSE can be transmitted via contaminated foodstuffs to cats (feline spongiform encephalopathy), or to zoo animals such as nyala, gemsbock or cheetahs (exotic ungulate encephalopathy).

Prion disease in humans

These are sporadic, acquired or genetic.

Sporadic

Creutzfeldt–Jakob disease (CJD)
- *Clinical.* A rare condition, 1 per million per year, with average age of onset 60–65 years. It presents as rapidly progressive dementia with myoclonus (involuntarily jerking and startle) progressing to akinetic mutism and death within 3–12 months.

  Clinical sub-groups include those presenting with cerebellar ataxia (Brownell–Oppenheimer variant), cortical blindness (Heidenhain variant), extrapyramidal and pyramidal signs and, rarely, motor neurone disease.
- *Investigations.* The EEG shows slowing of normal background rhythms and pseudoperiodic sharp wave complexes. Brain scan and cerebrospinal fluid are normal but electrophoretic detection of CSF marker proteins (e.g. 14-3-3 protein) may give diagnostic support. Tissue diagnosis is essential but is usually obtained only at autopsy. The classical pathological triad is spongiform vacuolation, astrocytic proliferation and neuronal loss.

Transmitted

1. Kuru
- This condition, confined to the Fore linguistic group in the eastern highlands of Papua New Guinea, was transmitted by cannibalistic rituals (now ceased) in which the women and children ate deceased

relatives' brains. There is no evidence of genetic or vertical transmission.

- *Clinical*: after an incubation period 2–30 years, the illness begins with headache and joint pain, followed after 6–12 weeks by difficulty walking, progressive cerebellar signs and later dementia with death at 1–2 years.

2. Iatrogenic CJD
- Accidental transmission of prion disease to humans has followed use of cadaveric pituitary-derived growth hormone, dura mater or corneal grafts.
- *Clinical*: the clinical course resembles Kuru in that, following an incubation period of 4–30 years (the shortest incubation periods follow intracerebral grafts and in those homozygous at codon 129), most present with cerebellar syndromes progressing over 6–18 months, occasionally with dementia in the terminal stages.

3. New variant CJD. This new illness affects a younger population (<45 years), almost exclusively in the UK, presenting with a Kuru-like disorder.

Behavioural and psychiatric disturbances and dysaesthesiae are followed by cerebellar ataxia. It follows a more prolonged course than sporadic CJD and without typical EEG changes. Pathology shows extensive prion protein staining plaques. Immunostaining of lymphoreticular tissue, e.g. tonsil biopsy may offer an early diagnostic test. Strong evidence for a link with dietary exposure to bovine spongiform encephalopathy comes from transgenic mice possessing human PrP. Their incubation periods and PrP strain types (ratio of glycosylated fragments following proteinase treatment) are almost identical following intracerebral inoculation with BSE or nvCJD and quite different from those following exposure to sporadic CJD. Relatively few cases have so far occurred but comparisons to Kuru and passage across the species barrier suggest potentially very long incubation periods.

Inherited

Familial CJD arises through two genetic mechanisms:

- Point mutations.
- Octapeptide repeat insertion.

1. Point mutations. These occur at one of several codon sites of the 253 codon PrP amyloid precursor gene, e.g. 102, 117, 178, 198, 200, 217, the altered amino acid sequence of the encoded protein producing a familial prion disease.

(a) Familial CJD (codon 200). Lysine replacing glutamate at codon 200 gives a mis-sense mutation.

The mean age of onset is 56 years but otherwise the condition is indistinguishable from sporadic CJD. However, phenotypes with progressive supranuclear palsy or peripheral neuropathy have been described. With a gene penetrance of only 0.56 (because only half the carriers are homozygous at codon 129), apparently unaffected carriers and 'generation skipping' examples occur.

A Slavic or Sephardic Jew ethnic origin can usually be identified. The 30 times excess of CJD among Libyan Jews, previously attributed to their diet including lightly cooked sheep's eyeballs, is actually due to codon 200 familial CJD.

(b) Familial CJD (codon 178). This severe condition has 100% penetrance and therefore a classical autosomal dominant inheritance (i.e. irrespective of the haplotype at codon 129). There is an early age of onset in early 40s but with a prolonged illness over 1–2 years. Typical EEG periodic activity is absent.

Familial fatal insomnia is an extraordinary variant of codon 178 CJD, manifesting as progressive insomnia with dementia and dysautonomia with pathology in selected thalamic nuclei; it occurs only when there is methionine homozygosity at codon 129.

(c) Gerstmann–Sträussler–Scheinker disease. This is an exceedingly rare autosomal dominant disorder caused by one of several point mutations at codon 102 (ataxic type), 117 (telencephalic type), 198 or 217 (Alzheimer type with neurofibrillary tangles).

A chronic progressive ataxia culminates in terminal dementia., The differences from familial CJD are the longer time course (2–10 years) and the presence of prominent amyloid ('Kuru') plaques at autopsy.

2. Octapeptide repeat insertions. The normal region of five octapeptide repeats between codons 51 and 91 on the prion protein gene may show insert mutations of 2–9 extra repeats giving a familial CJD picture.

Further reading

Haywood AM. Transmissible spongiform encephalopathies. *New England Journal of Medicine,* 1997; **337:** 1821–8.

Prusiner SB. Prion diseases in humans and animals. *Journal of the Royal College of Physicians,* 1994; **28** (2)(Suppl): 1–30.

Will RG, Ironside JW, Zeidler M, *et al.* A new variant of Creutzfeldt–Jakob disease in the UK. *Lancet,* 1996; **347:** 921–25.

Related topics of interest

RESPIRATORY NEUROLOGY

The lungs are rarely involved directly in primarily neurological conditions. However, severe respiratory problems arise indirectly either from respiratory muscle weakness or from disordered ventilatory control. Respiratory infection is the terminal event of many neurological conditions particularly those with bulbar involvement. Pulmonary thromboembolism threatens any patient with acute paralysis.

Respiratory disorder in neurological disease

Thoracic pump disorders

Spinal cord injuries

Ventilatory muscle involvement accompanies various sites of cord damage. The spinal root innervation of the respiratory musculature is: accessories C1–8, diaphragm C3–5, intercostals T1–11 and abdominals T2–L1.

- Lesions above C3 lead to diaphragm paralysis with fatal apnoea unless ventilated immediately.
- Lesions at C3–5 lead to diaphragmatic weakness and immediate onset of life-threatening hypoventilation, particularly if nursed supine.
- Lesions below C5 spare the diaphragm, but affect the accessories and intercostals leading to respiratory muscle fatigue at about 24 hours, often needing assisted ventilation.
- Lesions in the thoracic cord have little direct effect upon ventilation.

Respiratory muscle weakness

This results from involvement of:
- Anterior horn cells, e.g. motor neurone disease.
- Spinal nerve roots, e.g. Guillain–Barré syndrome.
- Peripheral nerves, e.g. hereditary motor and sensory neuropathy type IIc.
- Neuromuscular junction, e.g. myasthenia gravis.
- The muscles themselves, e.g. muscular dystrophy, acid maltase deficiency and nemaline myopathy.

1. Acute weakness. The problems of acute ventilatory muscle weakness differ slightly from chronic weakness (see over):

- Thoracic mechanics are normal, still operating on the steep part of the pressure-volume curve, allowing normal tidal breathing to continue with little effort so long as the vital capacity exceeds the normal tidal volume (c. 0.4 l).
- Patients with acute respiratory weakness may not experience breathlessness until dangerously late (curarized subjects can double their breath-holding time).
- The thromboembolism risk is greatly increased.

Thus, in acute and progressive ventilatory muscle weakness, e.g. Guillain–Barré syndrome or myasthenia gravis, monitoring (of vital capacity) and prevention are key objectives.

- If the vital capacity falls below 1.0 l, patients should be managed on intensive care.
- Prophylaxis against thromboembolism is essential.

2. *Chronic weakness.* The complications of chronic ventilatory muscle weakness are often more disabling than the weakness itself:

- Scoliosis: this occurs in patients with respiratory muscle weakness from childhood and seriously influences respiratory morbidity.
- Obesity is a common yet preventable additional burden to skeletal and respiratory muscle function.
- Inability to cough occurs through the combination of expiratory muscle weakness and low lung volume predisposing to respiratory tract infection.
- Ventilation-perfusion mismatch results from inability to change posture and to take occasional deep breaths.
- Poor compliance of the chest wall and lungs result from chronic hypoventilation and adds to the work of already over-burdened muscles.
- Disordered ventilatory control accompanies occasional neuromuscular conditions, e.g. myotonic dystrophy or mitochondrial cytopathy.
- Pulmonary thromboembolism is a problem in acute limb muscle weakness, but surprisingly rare in established disease.

3. *Diaphragm weakness.* The extent of diaphragm weakness is the major determinant of respiratory

morbidity in patients with muscle weakness. Patients report dyspnoea on exertion and lying flat; there is paradoxical (inward) epigastric movement on inspiration.

Early diaphragm involvement is seen in acid maltase deficiency, nemaline myopathy and motor neurone disease.

4. Assessment. Apparently acute events in neuromuscular disease are usually predictable and preventable by regular assessments. The analogy with an engine running out of fuel demonstrates how a potentially disastrous outcome could be avoided by making measurements.

- Vital capacity (VC) gives the best overall picture of ventilatory impairment. A well fitting face mask overcomes measurement problems in patients with facial weakness, e.g. Guillain–Barré syndrome. VC upright and supine gives a rapid indication of diaphragm weakness.

  In diaphragmatic palsy, VC halves when supine because the abdominal contents push the passive diaphragm into the thorax.

  In a C5 cord lesion, sparing the accessories and intercostals, the VC is better lying flat. The abdominal contents' weight on lying flat optimizes the domed shape of the diaphragm; when upright, the diaphragm is low, flat and mechanically disadvantaged.
- Maximum static mouth pressures (inspiratory and expiratory) provide a more direct assessment of ventilatory muscle strength. Bedside measurement can be made using a pressure gauge (the apparatus contains a small leak to prevent closure of the glottis during the manoeuvre).
- Cough peak flow (coughing into a hand-held peak flow meter) gives a useful bedside assessment of coughing ability.
- Blood gas tensions when awake are often deceptively reassuring in neuromuscular disease, particularly in the acute situation, e.g. Guillain–Barré syndrome, and must be interpreted with caution.
- Swallowing and bulbar weakness can be life threatening through pulmonary aspiration. Important symptoms of aspiration include coughing on fluid

and food, night-time cough, and nasal regurgitation. Physical signs include slow swallowing on a timed water drinking test. Palatal examination is poorly sensitive to bulbar involvement. Conditions presenting with swallowing disorder as a major symptom include myasthenia gravis, motor neurone disease, polymyositis, multiple system atrophy.

Central ventilatory control disorders

Medullary brainstem aggregates comprising the respiratory centre are influenced by:
- Supranuclear disorders, e.g. apnoea during an epileptic seizure.
- Nuclear disorders, e.g. acquired brainstem disease such as encephalitis, stroke, tumour, multiple sclerosis or multiple system atrophy. These typically present as hypoventilation and central sleep apnoea.

Ventilatory patterns

Specific ventilatory patterns occasionally accompany cerebral disease. Their localizing value is limited because the cerebral oedema and systemic metabolic disturbance accompanying most brainstem disorders themselves influence the breathing pattern.

1. Ataxic breathing. This is the commonest abnormal breathing pattern in cerebral disease, manifesting as breathing irregular in timing and depth. It does not help in localizing the lesion.

2. Cheyne–Stokes ventilation. This regular waxing and waning of tidal volume with brief apnoea between, results from:
- Bilateral interruption of descending cortical pathways.
- Chronic hypercapnia.
- Left ventricular failure.

3. Hyperventilation
- Behavioural: involuntary hyperventilation accompanying anxiety states is a common involuntary accompaniment of anxiety and often associated with non-specific neurological symptoms, e.g. light headedness, tingling, blurred vision and syncope.
- Neurological: Central neurogenic hyperventilation may complicate any acute cerebral disease, including those associated with neurogenic pulmonary oedema.

- Syndromal: Hyperventilation and breath holding may accompany certain neurological syndromes, e.g. Rett syndrome.

4. Sleep apnoea
- Central sleep apnoea due to disordered central ventilatory control is uncommon in isolation and is associated with brainstem disease (Ondine's curse).
- Obstructive sleep apnoea is common and sometimes serious. It is associated with obesity and is exacerbated by alcohol. Recurrent pharyngeal collapse leads to upper airway occlusion and apnoea

  The resulting recurrent arousals provoke sleep fragmentation, impair sleep quality and lead to daytime somnolence and morning headache. The symptoms respond often dramatically to continuous positive airways pressure (CPAP) via nasal mask.

Respiratory and neurological co-morbidity

Neurocutaneous syndromes Several have direct lung involvement:

- Neurofibromatosis type 1: Interstitial pulmonary fibrosis occurs in 20–30% of adult patients although usually with minimal symptoms. The chest radiograph shows bilateral basal reticular nodular shadowing, sometimes with bilateral upper lobe bullae; histologically, it is indistinguishable from fibrosing alveolitis.
- Tuberose sclerosis: Pulmonary involvement is rare (1%) but severe. It presents in adult female patients with progressive exertional dyspnoea, recurrent pneumothoraces and haemoptysis. The changes include lymphangioleiomyomatosis with cystic honeycombing and chylous pleural effusions. Chest radiograph shows diffuse or basal linear densities.
- Ataxia telangiectasia: the immunodeficiency accompanying this disorder leads to repeated sino-pulmonary infections which in 30% are followed by severe progressive lung disease, especially pseudomonas, staphylococcal or viral pneumonia.

Lymphomatoid granulomatosis This condition presents with subacute onset of neurological disease similar to cranial angiitis.

	Pulmonary and skin involvement with granulomas are common.
Malignancy	Small cell lung cancer is the commonest malignancy to have remote CNS effects and can present variety of neurological paraneoplastic syndromes (see Paraneoplastic disorders).

Further reading

Culebras A. Sleep and neuromuscular disorders. *Neurologic Clinics,* 1996; **14:** 791–805.

Teener JW, Raps EC. Evaluation and treatment of respiratory failure in neuromuscular disease. *Rheumatic Diseases Clinics of North America,* 1997; **23:** 277–92.

Related topics of interest

SLEEP DISORDERS

Insomnia

This common symptom, often explained by anxiety or medications, becomes increasingly prevalent with normal ageing. Usual causes are:

- Poor 'sleep hygiene' is often responsible and amenable to treatment.
- Irregular bedtime and rising hours.
- Daytime napping.
- Drugs including caffeine and alcohol.
- Exercise near bedtime.
- Negative associations near bedtime, e.g. television, reading.

Hypersomnia

Non-specific causes

Hypersomnia is often associated with vivid dreams and restless sleep. Common explanations are:

- Drugs, especially alcohol and ergot.
- Viral illness.
- Depression.
- Elderly onset dementia.

Sleep disordered breathing

This is a common, treatable and under-recognized condition. Broadly there are two categories:

Obstructive sleep apnoea

Sleep-related upper airway collapse with obstruction leads to frequent apnoeas and resulting sleep fragmentation, poor sleep quality and consequent excessive daytime somnolence. The predisposing factors are:

- Obesity, particularly a large neck circumference.
- Alcohol and other sedatives.
- Structural upper airway narrowing include nasal deformity or upper airway congestion.
- Ventilatory muscle weakness. During sleep, especially rapid eye movement (REM) sleep, muscle tone is lowered and upper airway resistance

increased; this leaves the weakened diaphragm unable to overcome upper airway resistance.

Central sleep apnoea Disordered control of breathing during sleep may be seen in disorders affecting brainstem ventilatory control and resulting in apnoea during sleep ('Ondine's curse').

Narcolepsy

Narcolepsy, the intrusion of REM sleep into wakefulness, is an uncommon but frequently overdiagnosed condition.

Clinical features It is a clinical diagnosis based upon the presence of cataplexy and excessive daytime somnolence, sometimes with other clinical features.

1. Excessive daytime somnolence. Patients fall asleep easily and in inappropriate circumstances, e.g. during meals or conversation.

2. Cataplexy. An essential component of the narcolepsy syndrome. It is a transient laughter-induced axial and facial atonia (with dysarthria or mutism), sometimes with facial jerking. It is the equivalent of REM sleep in wakefulness. It is not an epileptic phenomenon and there is no altered consciousness.

3. Sleep paralysis. This is a symptom of transient inability to move usually upon wakening (hypnapomic).

It is a rare event in 40–50% of normal people, especially likely after sleep deprivation or antidepressant treatments, and is not specific to narcolepsy. Occasional familial cases occur, commoner in black persons, usually without cataplexy, and responsive to 5HT re-uptake antagonists.

4. Hypnagogic hallucinations. These are vivid hallucinations present just before falling asleep and often associated with sleep paralysis. They are effectively dreams in wakefulness.

5. Insomnia and sleep fragmentation. Night time sleep is often surprisingly restless in narcoleptic patients.

6. Multiple parasomnias. These include kicking and teeth grinding.

Investigations	The diagnosis is essentially clinical. Investigations may include sleep EEG demonstrating short REM sleep latency, often within seconds. This is non-specific and may also occur in depression or with certain drugs. Human lymphocyte antigen (HLA) analysis to demonstrate DR2 status present in 99% of cases.
Management	Hypersomnia usually responds to amphetamines. Cataplexy is treated with tricyclic agents such as clomipramine.

Secondary narcolepsy

Narcolepsy resulting from underlying neurological disease is rare, often atypical and not associated with cataplexy. Predisposing conditions are:

- Multiple sclerosis. Half of patients with multiple sclerosis are HLA DR2 and so are more liable to develop the narcolepsy syndrome. Structural brainstem lesions may occasionally disrupt sleep control processes.
- Head injury.

Narcolepsy may occasionally be feigned to obtain amphetamines.

Other causes

Delayed sleep phase syndrome	This condition, commonest in adolescent males, results from the sleep/wake cycle being 6–8 hours out of phase. Almost all cases have some psychiatric disturbance and the condition is considered predominantly psychological.
Kleine–Levin syndrome	This condition presents with episodes of prolonged sleep of up to a week interspersed with periods of voracious appetite and sometimes hypersexuality. The cause is unknown, but occasional cases are caused by hypothalamic tumour. Depression is common. There is no effective treatment.
Prader–Willi syndrome	This condition occurs in 1 in 14 000 births. There is a deletion of chromosome 15q11-13, arising by inheritance of two chromosomes 15 from the mother and none from the father (uniparental maternal disomy).

It manifests as hypothalamic hypoplasia with short stature, mental retardation, sexual infantilism, excessive daytime sleepiness, obesity and diabetes.

Myotonic dystrophy

This is associated with hypersomnia resulting from:

- Primary central hypersomnia possibly due to brainstem neuronal impairment.
- Sleep apnoea of both central and obstructive types.

Encephalitis lethargica

An unknown viral infectious illness resulting in lesions around the III ventricle, aqueduct, midbrain and anterior hypothalamus.

Möbius syndrome

This is associated with failed midbrain development. It manifests as partial facial agenesis, eye movement disorder and a syndrome similar to narcolepsy, sometimes with cataplexy.

Parasomnias

Clinical features

These non-epileptic phenomena are seen especially in children, are often familial and are enhanced by emotional and physical stress. Examples include:

- Nightmares.
- Hypnic jerks.
- Somnambulism.
- Night terrors.
- Bruxism.
- Head banging.
- Bed wetting.

Related conditions

Periodic limb movements in sleep

This familial condition, associated with the awake symptom of restless legs syndrome, manifests as repeated myoclonic twitches in sleep preceding extensor movements of the ankles and hallux.

REM sleep behavioural disorder

This rare condition occurs when the association between REM sleep and axial atonia is lost allowing the patient to 'act out' dreams. It is rare, usually seen in elderly patients with a long history of thrashing in sleep, and may result in self injury. Often there is underlying brainstem disease such as multiple sclerosis or multiple system degeneration. Clonazepam is effective.

Tourette syndrome

This condition of multiple tics with utterances and coprolalia is frequently associated with parasomnias including:

- Frequent somnambulism.
- Enuresis.
- Awakenings from sleep.

Neurological conditions altered by sleep

Epilepsy

Sleep is well known to influence the manifestations of epilepsy. Seizures often present in sleep or upon wakening. Sleep deprivation may provoke seizures, especially in idiopathic epilepsies. Obstructive sleep apnoea, with its resulting sleep deprivation, may present a treatable cause of epilepsy exacerbation. Autosomal dominant nocturnal frontal lobe epilepsy is a syndrome previously known as paroxysmal nocturnal dystonia, which presents as frequent sleep-related simple partial and secondarily generalized seizures beginning around the age of 8 years and persisting lifelong. Bizarre symptomatology and dystonic posturing may lead to suspicion of non-epileptic seizures. The condition maps to chromosome 20. Carbamazepine or clonazepam are usually effective (see Epilepsy classification and syndromes).

Migraine

1. Cluster headache. Typical severe unilateral headaches with autonomic accompaniments occur from REM sleep (see Headache (migraine and cluster headache)).

2. 'Intracranial bumps in the night'. Older patients may describe being woken from sleep with sudden noises or pains in the head. The symptoms frequently recur and are considered to be a benign migraine variant.

Further reading

El-Ad B, Korczyn AD. Disorders of excessive daytime sleepiness – an update. *Journal of the Neurological Sciences,* 1998; **153:** 192–202.

Parkes JD. *Sleep and its Disorders.* London: WB Saunders, 1985.

Strollo PJ, Rogers RM. Obstructive sleep apnea. *New England Journal of Medicine,* 1996; **334:** 99–104.

Related topics of interest

Coma and disorders of consciousness (p. 37)
Delirium (acute confusional states) (p. 53)
Epilepsy classification and syndromes (p. 73)
Headache (migraine and cluster headache) (p. 115)
Syncope (p. 286)

SPINAL CORD INJURY

Acute injury

Site

The cervical and lumbar regions are the commonest sites of cord injury.

1. Cervical. The most flexible part of the spine and so most vulnerable to cord injury.

2. Lumbar. The junction of the rigid thoracic spine and the more flexible lumbar spine, i.e. L1–2, is the second commonest site.

Emergency management

The major aim is prevention of further neurological damage.

Immobilization

A rigid cervical collar and 'log rolling' on to a rigid transportation board are essential in situations where cord injury is suggested:

- Severe trauma (5% have unstable cervical spines).
- Spinal pain.
- Sensory or motor disturbance.

ABC

1. Airway and breathing. Acute cord injury gives major risk of hypoventilation and aspiration. Oxygen supplementation and oximeter monitoring are necessary; occasionally intubation and ventilation.

2. Cardiovascular. Abrupt loss of sympathetic vasomotor tone following cord injury above T5 gives vasodilatation, hypotension and a paradoxically low heart rate (distinguishing this condition from shock). Any bleeding or dehydration can lower blood pressure further. Management is fluid replacement with pulmonary wedge pressure monitoring as the autonomic responses to hypervolaemia are also affected; occasionally sympathomimetic drugs are needed.

Other injuries

- Thoraco-abdominal trauma accompanying a cord lesion may be masked by the sensory deficit and requires a high index of suspicion.

- Head injury accompanies <50% of serious spinal injuries.

Other measures

- Medication: intravenous methylprednisolone within 8 hours of spinal trauma can improve the long-term neurological outcome.
- Urinary catheter: patients require catheterization with monitoring of fluid balance.
- Nasogastric intubation may be necessary, but is contraindicated in significant facial injury.
- H$_2$ antagonist to prevent gastric stress ulcer.
- Deep venous thrombosis prevention: pneumatic boots are useful. In acute complete paraplegia, full anticoagulation should be considered until tone returns to the legs.

Neurological assessment

1. Motor. Muscle strength must be quantified as a baseline for subsequent assessments.

2. Sensory. Sensory level documentation is important (the most caudal dermatome with normal sensation is the sensory level).

3. Sphincter. Bladder function must be assessed (a flaccid bladder is usual immediately after injury). Also consider:

- Perineal sensation, since sacral sparing reflects an incomplete lesion with a better prognosis.
- Anal tone by digital rectal examination.
- Anal cutaneous reflex (stroking perineal skin provoking anal sphincter contraction).
- Bulbocavernous reflex (anal sphincter contraction in response to pinching of the penile shaft).

4. Respiratory
- Complete lesions above C3 give immediate apnoea and, if not immediately intubated, death.
- Lesions between C3 and C5 lead to diaphragmatic paresis and immediate onset of respiratory problems.
- Lesions below C5 spare the diaphragm but lead to accessories and intercostal weakness, provoking respiratory muscle fatigue and hypo-ventilation, microatelectases and possibly aspiration at about 24 hours.
- Lesions in the thoracic spine have little direct effect on respiratory function.

Traumatic syndromes

Spinal (neurogenic) shock

Lesions at T6 and above give flaccid paralysis with areflexia, loss of sensation, flaccid bladder, lax sphincter, bradycardia and hypotension. If still complete at 24 hours, recovery is unlikely.

Central cord syndrome

Acute cervical hyper-extension (usually older patients with spinal stenosis) gives:

- Weakness, especially of arms and intrinsic hand muscles.
- Variable sensory and sphincter involvement.
- Relatively good prognosis.
- Cord contusion or haematoma on MRI scan.

Spinal cord injury without bony injury

This occurs particularly in children, as spinal elasticity allows deformity without fracture; MRI scan confirms cord injury.

Brown–Séquard syndrome

A unilateral cord lesion usually follows penetrating rather than blunt injuries, giving:

- Ipsilateral motor and position sense loss.
- Contralateral pain and temperature loss.

Cauda equina syndrome

An L1 lesion may lead to acute cauda equina compression which, even if complete at onset, may improve with time.

Investigations

Plain cervical radiographs

- Lateral views will demonstrate cervical fractures or dislocation (vertebral bodies, spinous processes or odontoid) but must include the whole of the cervical spine, including cranio-cervical and thoraco-cervical junctions.
- Antero-posterior views are needed to see fractures of the pedicles and facets, and also lateral masses.
- Open-mouthed views are best to view odontoid fractures.

CT scan	This is indicated if:

- There is fracture or subluxation on plain films.
- There is neurological deficit without apparent fracture.
- There is severe unexplained neck pain.
- The cervical spine is obscured on plain radiology by soft tissue swelling.

MRI scan	This has less to offer as bones are not demonstrated; however, damage within the cord, e.g. haemorrhage, contusion, compression, is seen.

Chronic injury

Following the initial traumatic event, rehabilitation is hampered in several problem areas.

Respiratory	This is the commonest source of morbidity following spinal lesions, attributable mainly to weakness of intercostals and sometimes diaphragm, ineffective cough and retained secretions owing to abdominal muscle weakness. Treatment is with deep breathing exercises, assisted coughing and sometimes mini-tracheostomy for clearance of secretions and intermittent positive pressure ventilation if appropriate.

Autonomic	Lesions above T5 affect cardiac autonomic supply. Below the spinal level of the lesion there is:

- Impairment of baroreceptor reflexes giving postural hypotension.
- Peripheral vasodilatation, increased vascular permeability and venous stasis leading to oedema.
- Impaired thermogenesis owing to both vasodilatation and inability to shiver below the level of the lesion.

Autonomic dysreflexia	This only follows lesions above T5. When afferent autonomic pathways are activated, e.g. by acute urinary retention or other acute viscous dilatation, the resulting autonomic discharges are uncoordinated and abnormal resulting in:

- Vasoconstriction.
- Hypertension.

- Bradycardia.
- Cold limbs.

Patients develop episodes of throbbing headaches, sweating, pallor below the level of the lesions and flushing of the face and neck.

- Management:
    Remove the provoking cause, e.g. bladder drainage.
    Control hypertension by acute vasodilatation, e.g. glyceryl trinitrate.

Sphincters

In the acute spinal shock stage the bladder is flaccid with retention and over-flow of urine requiring drainage treatment. With the gradual return of tone there are reflex contractions and detrusor and sometimes detrusor sphincter dyssynergia.

Management at this stage is with intermittent self-catheterization to avoid incontinence and protect against a residual volume. Suprapubic catheterization is sometimes needed.

Metabolic

Immobility promotes hypercalcaemia and renal stone formation. Osteoporosis is common in the longer term.

Spasms

As muscle tone returns, especially in incomplete lesions, spasms may occur either spontaneously or provoked by neurogenic irritation, e.g. bladder fullness, infection or calculi, loaded bowel, pressure sores.

- Management:
    Remove provoking causes if identified.
    Antispasmodics, e.g. baclofen, dantrolene or tizanidine.

Sensory

Besides obvious difficulty with numbness below the lesion level, sensory loss may give difficulty in sitting balance, neuropathic pain and promote pressure sore formation.

Pressure sores

Traumatic paraplegia seriously threatens tissue viability over bony prominences owing to immobility, lost sensation and impaired vasomotor control.

Post-traumatic syrinx   This is a late complication of previous cord trauma, sometimes from many years before. Patients present with neuropathic pain, numbness and motor deficit ascending above the site of the original lesion. Prompt recognition and surgery can halt progression but not reverse the deficit.

Psychosocial   Paraparesis has wider implications than the medical deficit alone. Psychosocial and financial problems affect the individual, the partner, the family and society.

Further reading

Chiles BW III, Cooper PR. Acute spinal injury. *New England Journal of Medicine,* 1996; **334:** 514–20.

El Masry WS. Paraplegia and tetraplegia. In: Goodwill CJ, Chamberlain MA, Evans CD, eds. *Rehabilitation of the Physically Disabled Adult.* Cheltenham: Stanley Thornes Ltd, 1997; 372–93.

Related topics of interest

Head injury (p. 126)
Neurogenic bladder (p. 184)
Neurogenic pain (p. 189)
Respiratory neurology (p. 251)

STROKE

Definitions
- A stroke is a focal neurological deficit of abrupt onset lasting for more than 24 hours, of non-traumatic presumed vascular origin.
- A transient ischaemic attack (TIA) is qualitatively identical but lasts for less than 24 hours.

Epidemiology

The incidence of stroke (40–80 years) is 400 per 100 000, but with marked age-related increases (incidence aged 85+ is 2000 per 100 000).

Pathogenesis

1. Ischaemic. Ischaemic stroke comprises thrombotic and embolic disease and accounts for 80% of stroke and <100% of TIA. Mechanisms of ischaemic events are:

- Athero-thrombo-embolism of large and medium sized arteries (50%).
- Intracranial small vessel disease (25%).
- Cardiac embolism (20%).

2. Haemorrhagic. Primary haemorrhagic stroke is the mechanism in 20% of stroke.

Physical examination

Cardiovascular examination (identifying risk factors) is actually more important than neurological examination (documenting the signs) in stroke.

Blood pressure is especially important. Measurement in each arm may identify subclavian steal syndrome, a surgically remedial cause of posterior circulation stroke.

Carotid bruit is poorly sensitive to carotid stenosis but if present gives a clue to aetiology.

Stroke syndromes

The clinical manifestations correlate well with the site and extent of the lesion and also reflects the prognosis.

Total anterior cerebral syndrome (TACS)

The triad of hemiparesis, hemianopia and cortical dysfunction (dysphasia or visuospatial dysfunction) implies a complete carotid artery territory infarction, usually from vessel occlusion by embolism (haemorrhage in 25%). The prognosis is poor.

| **Partial anterior cerebral syndrome (PACS)** | The incomplete form of TACS, comprises two of the three deficits (hemiparesis, hemianopia and cortical dysfunction). Embolism is the usual cause. It carries an intermediate prognosis. |

Posterior cerebral syndromes (POCS)

A heterogeneous group including brainstem stroke. Most are thrombotic rather than embolic.

A calcarine (visual) cortex infarct presents as a visual field defect with macular sparing.

Brainstem infarcts are small but sometimes devastating. Although predictable from brainstem anatomy, classical syndromes are rarely pure since arterial anatomy is variable.

- Lateral medullary (Wallenberg's) syndrome, the classical brainstem syndrome, from infarction in the posterior inferior cerebellar artery territory, usually from vertebral artery occlusion, e.g. dissection. Sudden vertigo, vomiting, unsteadiness, dysphagia are accompanied by ipsilateral cerebellar signs and dissociated sensory loss (face: ipsilateral spinothalamic; limbs: ipsilateral dorsal column but contralateral spinothalamic).
- Other eponymous syndromes: contralateral hemiparesis with III palsy (Weber's), with VI palsy (Raymond's) or with VI and VII (Millard–Gubler); III and contralateral ataxia (Benedikt's); ipsilateral gaze palsy, V, VII, VIII and Horner's (Foville's).
- Basilar artery thrombosis may present as a progressive brainstem lesion.
- Locked-in syndrome: bibasal pontine infarction.

Lacunar syndromes (LACS)

These follow thrombotic occlusion of single perforating arteries (not embolic) giving small, deep infarcts, usually in the basal ganglia or pons. Most are clinically silent.

- Internal capsule lacunes present as pure motor or sensory stroke without dysphasia, field defect, altered consciousness or visuospatial symptoms.
- A basal pontine lesion gives ataxic hemiparesis (contralateral hemiparesis and ataxia).

Diffuse cerebrovascular disease

- Multiple small strokes throughout both hemispheres may give progressive dementia, pseudo-parkinsonism and pseudobulbar palsy.

- Cerebral autosomal dominant arteriopathy with subcortical infarcts and leucoencephalopathy (CADASIL) is a familial disorder (chromosome 19q12) characterized by migraine, depression and progressive diffuse cerebrovascular disease.
- 'Binswanger's disease' (leucoaraiosis), is the non-specific radiological appearance of arteriosclerotic encephalopathy from any cause, e.g. CADASIL.

Boundary zone infarction

Profound hypotension, e.g. asystole, causes bilateral infarction at the boundary zones between supply territories of the three major arteries (anterior, middle and posterior cerebral). This causes:

- Posteriorly: cortical blindness, agnosia and amnesia.
- Anteriorly: weakness, sensory loss (leg > arm) and aphasia.

Spinal cord stroke

This presents as paraparesis, initially flaccid, with dissociated sensory loss and sensory level at T10.

Differential diagnosis

Points to note are:

- Stroke usually gives negative not positive features, e.g. numbness, weakness, loss of vision, rather than tingling, jerking, flashing lights.
- Altered consciousness is rare in TIA and accompanies only serious stroke or subarachnoid haemorrhage. It implies brainstem or thalamic ischaemia, either directly (brainstem stroke) or indirectly (hemisphere swelling and tentorial pressure cone).

Causes of transient cerebral ischaemia other than atheroembolism and haemorrhage are:

- Tumour, subdural haematoma, or hydrocephalus.
- Migraine, the commonest TIA in those under 40 years, presents a slower evolution of positive symptoms, usually (not invariably) with headache, photophobia or systemic upset.
- Seizures have positive symptoms (tingling, jerking) and altered consciousness; seizures are unusual in

acute stroke (5%) though common with venous infarction.

- Hypotension (e.g. arrhythmia) with arteriosclerosis may give lateralized symptoms localized to the hemisphere with more critical circulation.
- Hypoglycaemia occasionally gives lateralized symptoms though is usually easily recognized; hyponatraemia is also rarely confused with stroke.

Investigations

Investigations detail depends upon the patient's age and general state. Young stroke merits detailed investigation to exclude rare but treatable causes (see Stroke in young adults).

1. Blood. Glucose, ESR, full blood count (FBC) and electrolytes are essential.

2. *Imaging*
(a) Brain scan. Its main importance is exclusion of haemorrhagic stroke since haemorrhage cannot reliably be distinguished from ischaemia on clinical grounds.
   Exclusion of other causes, e.g. tumour, abscess, and assessment of the extent of present and previous infarction are important.
(b) Carotid Doppler. In ischaemic stroke, significant internal carotid stenosis may demonstrate a surgical option in stroke prevention.
(c) Angiography. Magnetic resonance angiography is becoming a non-invasive alternative to intra-arterial angiography for imaging the carotid when planning surgery.

Management

Recent large randomized clinical trials have made a major impact on stroke management.

1. Acute. Despite advances in thrombolysis and neuroprotection (glutamate antagonists etc.) acute stroke still lacks a specific treatment. The reduced disability following acute thrombolysis treatment is offset by an increased death rate. Aspirin may be administered acutely but haemorrhage should ideally first be excluded.

Heparin has been advocated to prevent deep venous thrombosis and limit stroke extension; its advantages, however, are counterbalanced by haemorrhagic effects and therefore is not indicated. Its benefit in 'stroke in evolution' is not proven.

In acute embolic stroke with atrial fibrillation (AF), the risk of further embolus must be weighed against that of worsening haemorrhagic stroke with anticoagulation. Embolic strokes commonly are haemorrhagic because, as embolus breaks up, the soft infarct is reperfused at arterial pressure. For all AF embolic stroke (unless very large), anticoagulation is started immediately.

Management on a stroke unit gives better overall outcomes compared to a general ward.

2. Secondary prevention. Stroke management is mainly about preventing the next one – little can be done for the stroke that has already happened.

(a) Cerebrovascular risk factors
- Age is the strongest risk factor for TIA and ischaemic stroke.
- Hypertension has a strong linear relationship with all stroke types.
- Smoking 1.5× risk.
- Diabetes 2× risk.
- Cholesterol and lipids: statins are effective in stroke prevention.
- Family history.
- Male sex.

(b) Drugs
- Anti-platelet medication.
  Aspirin is effective in secondary stroke prevention. Almost all patients at risk of stroke should receive aspirin, some needing additional medication for dyspepsia. The major trials have used 300 mg daily doses, but 75 mg may be as effective. Other anti-platelet medications are proving useful for those intolerant of aspirin.
- Anticoagulants.

The main indications for warfarin in stroke prevention are:

AF (rheumatic or non-rheumatic).

Mitral stenosis with or without AF.

Prosthetic heart valves.

There is no clear evidence of its stroke prophylaxis benefit in other situations, e.g. carotid stenosis.

(c) Surgery. Carotid endarterectomy (plus aspirin) is justified with ipsilateral internal carotid stenosis of > 70%.

Angioplasty: a balloon inflated within the stenosed area cracks the atheromatous plaque, enlarging the lumen. Its place in stroke prevention has yet to be established.

Further reading

Warlow CP, Dennis, MS, van Gijn J *et al*. Unusual causes of ischaemic stroke and transient ischaemic attacks. In: *Stroke: A Practical Guide to Management*. Oxford: Blackwell Science, 1996; 258–86.

Related topics of interest

STROKE IN YOUNG ADULTS

Atheromatous stenosis of the extra- and intracranial arteries is an uncommon cause of stroke in patients under 40 years unless there are significant risk factors for premature arteriosclerosis e.g. hypertension, diabetes or hypercholesterolaemia.

Young patients with stroke need to be investigated in depth as the proportion of unusual and treatable causes in this group is increased.

Dissection

Arterial dissection is the commonest cause of young stroke. The carotid artery may be injured in the neck either by direct penetrating injury or blunt trauma, sometimes quite trivial, e.g. whiplash injury. Spontaneous dissection may occur in Marfan's syndrome, Ehlers–Danlos disease and pseudoxanthoma elasticum. Intimal tears promote mural thrombosis and subsequent embolism. More serious dissection involves blood entering and splitting the arterial wall, occluding and propagating thrombus in the lumen. Vertebral artery dissection is the commonest cause of posterior inferior cerebellar artery syndrome.

Clinical features   Dissections characteristically are painful, carotid dissections giving ipsilateral pain in the face, eye, neck and head and vertebral dissections giving neck pain. An ipsilateral Horner's syndrome (sympathetic plexus around the internal carotid artery), self audible bruit (dissection spreading to the skull base) or unilateral lower cranial nerve palsies, e.g. hypoglossal (expanded blood vessel at the skull base) may each occur in carotid dissection.

Investigations   Carotid dissection may be visible on MRI brain scan, but angiography (MR or standard) is often needed; it must be done within a few days as dissections frequently resolve spontaneously.

Migraine

This is an important cause of young stroke, particularly in females, although its exact incidence is difficult to gauge. Occasional patients presenting with typical migraine aura may be left with some focal neurological deficit, most typically homonymous hemianopia. Anecdotally patients on the oral contraceptive pill who have prominent auras, are at greater risk of stroke. Prominent aura is a relative contraindication to ergotamine preparations and beta blockers must also be used with caution in this situation.

Inflammatory

An inflammatory reaction in the arterial or venous wall may lead to vessel occlusion (cell proliferation necrosis and fibrosis), haemorrhage (aneurysmal rupture) or intracranial venous thrombosis. Clinical clues to a vasculitic aetiology include weight loss, fever, facial rash, livedo reticularis, arthropathy, renal involvement and headache. Angiographic appearances of 'beading' of the intracerebral vessels is non specific.

Antiphospholipid syndrome There is usually a history of recurrent miscarriages, arterial and venous thrombosis of any sized vessel, livedo reticularis, heart valve vegetations, migraine type headaches, thrombocytopenia and false positive syphilis serology. For a confident diagnosis, the anti-cardiolipin antibody must be significantly raised on more than one occasion since anti-cardiolipin antibodies are also found in asymptomatic individuals, SLE, malignancy, HIV disease and induced by various drugs.

Systemic lupus erythematosus A generalized subacute encephalopathy is the usual central nervous system presentation; focal ischaemic episodes may occur, occasionally through embolism from diseased heart valves (Libman–Sacks endocarditis).

Systemic necrotizing vasculitis A spectrum of disorders affecting the small and medium sized arteries presenting as ischaemic or haemorrhagic disease in the brain, spinal cord and eye includes polyarteritis nodosa, Wegener's granulomatosis and Churg-Strauss syndrome. Eosinophilia, positive ANCA and renal involvement suggest the diagnosis. Sjögren's syndrome, Behçet's disease and sarcoidosis may also present with small artery involvement and focal neurology; Behçet's disease typically presents with intracranial venous thombosis.

Isolated cranial angiitis This is a rare cause of subacute encephalopathy with stroke like episodes, often with surprisingly few systemic features but with elevated CSF protein and pleocytosis.

Takayasu's (pulseless) disease This affects predominantly young Oriental women and shows involvement of large vessels, pathologically identical to giant cell arteritis and with similar systemic features, including weight loss, raised ESR and anaemia.

Structural arterial disease

Fibromuscular dysplasia
Here there is stenosis of small and medium sized arteries. It affects predominantly women and may be familial. The commonest presentation is with renal involvement and hypertension (and hence increased stroke risk) but it may directly involve the carotid artery and be associated with intracranial aneurysms.

Moyamoya disease
This is a radiological description of numerous small dilated lenticulo-striate arteries appearing like a 'puff of smoke' ('moyamoya' in Japanese). It is a non specific appearance caused variously by fibromuscular dysplasia, infection, radiation and trauma.

Others
Hyperplastic carotid arteries or internal carotid artery loops may be sufficiently severe to provoke cerebrovascular events. Neck irradiation may lead to localized stenosis or moyamoya disease many months or years later.

Thrombophilia

The following conditions increase the risk of spontaneous venous (but not arterial) thrombosis: deficiencies of anti-thrombin III, protein S and protein C, activated protein C resistance (factor V Leiden) and plasminogen deficiency. Unless there is a suspicion of paradoxical embolism, their measurement is unlikely to be informative, particularly as many patients with these deficiencies are asymptomatic. Acute stroke may itself reduce levels of the coagulation factors and so thrombophilia testing is delayed for 2 months after the stroke. A positive diagnosis has implications for other family members.

Cardiac

Acute myocardial infarction is rare in young people but may be associated with stroke through hypertension or mural thrombotic embolism. Embolism from prosthetic valves, rheumatic heart disease, cardiomyopathy, infective endocarditis or atrial myxoma must be considered. Paradoxical embolism is occasionally suspected; patent foramen ovale may be identified by transoesophageal echocardiography in up to 10% of normals and so is relatively non-specific.

Infection

Prior to antibiotics, bacterial meningitis was a commoner cause of cortical venous thrombosis than malignancy or pregnancy. Arterial thrombosis may result from chronic meningitis such as tuberculosis, fungal or, occasionally, bacterial meningitis. Internal carotid artery involvement from pharyngitis and tonsillitis may rarely cause stroke in children. Herpes zoster may give sufficient peri-arterial inflammation to provoke ipsilateral stroke a few weeks after the skin lesion has healed. HIV disease is associated with an increased stroke incidence mainly through meningitis and when associated with protein S deficiency.

Haematological

Many haematological conditions increase the likelihood of venous and arterial occlusion, notably polycythaemia (primary or secondary) and essential thrombocytosis. Leukaemia is associated with increased risk of intracerebral haemorrhage and intravascular lymphoma may present as stroke. Sickle cell homozygotes can present with ischaemic or haemorrhagic stroke and paroxysmal nocturnal haemoglobinuria with intracerebral venous thrombosis.

Contraceptive pill and pregnancy

The oral contraceptive pill appears to increase the risk of ischaemic stroke by two to three times with some persisting risk even on low dose oestrogen pills. The absolute stroke risk however remains small unless there are additional risk factors, such as hypertension and smoking. Stroke in pregnancy is rare in the developed countries (1–2 per 10 000 deliveries), the main causes being venous thrombosis in the puerperium, paradoxical embolism from the legs or pelvis and arterial dissection during labour.

Mitochondrial disease

The MELAS phenotype includes stroke-like episodes in young people.

Undetermined

The cause of young stroke is usually identified following appropriate detailed investigation. If the cause remains undetermined, misdiagnosis must be considered since transient symptoms of migraine, seizures or multiple sclerosis may mimic stroke.

Migraine aura is commonly confused with transient ischaemic attacks in young people especially when presenting with transient monocular blindness.

Further reading

Warlow CP, Dennis, MS, van Gijn J *et al*. Unusual causes of ischaemic stroke and transient ischaemic attacks. In: *Stroke: A Practical Guide to Management.* Oxford: Blackwell Science, 1996; 258–86.

Adams HP, Kappelle, LJ, Biller J *et al*. Ischemic stroke in young adults. *Archives of Neurology,* 1995; **52**: 491–5.

Bousser M-G, Ross Russell R. *Cerebral Venous Thrombosis. Major Problems in Neurology,* Vol. 33. London: WB Saunders, 1997.

Related topics of interest

SUBARACHNOID HAEMORRHAGE

Bleeding into the subarachnoid space commonly accompanies any intracranial haemorrhage, e.g. following trauma. The term subarachnoid haemorrhage (SAH) generally applies to spontaneous haemorrhage from intracranial aneurysms (85%) or from arteriovenous malformations (15%).

Aneurysmal subarachnoid haemorrhage

Epidemiology

The incidence is 1 per 10 000 per year (median age 50 years). Mortality from aneurysmal SAH is considerable: 30% die before reaching surgery, 30% within one month of surgery and 30% of survivors have persisting major neurological deficit.

The prevalence of aneurysms is higher than expected, with 2–5% of adults having intracranial aneurysms at autopsy.

Pathogenesis

Intracranial vessels lack an external elastic lamina and have an attenuated tunica media and so aneurysms form more readily than on extracranial vessels. Associated conditions include polycystic kidney disease, Ehlers–Danlos Type IV, neurofibromatosis type I and Marfan's syndrome.

Site of aneurysms

About 80% of aneurysms occur on the anterior cerebral circulation (especially the internal carotid/posterior cerebral artery junction, anterior communicating artery and trifurcation of middle cerebral artery) and 20% occur on the posterior circulation (especially bifurcation of basilar and origin of posterior inferior cerebellar artery). A total of 25% of SAH patients have multiple aneurysms.

Risk factors

- Cigarette smoking gives a tenfold risk of aneurysm formation, increasing with accumulation of pack years.
- Hypertension is an independent risk factor.
- Heavy alcohol consumption is weakly associated with increased aneurysm risk.
- Oestrogens, including hormone replacement therapy (HRT), may protect against aneurysm formation.

Clinical features

- A family history of aneurysm rupture is fairly common; up to 2% of aneurysmal SAH patients having a first degree relative with SAH. Overall, first degree relatives, especially siblings, have a four times greater risk than the general population of SAH. A positive family history is associated with earlier age of SAH and rupture of smaller aneurysms.

Aneurysms are clinically silent until rupture. Aneurysmal haemorrhage can occur at any time but is more likely during stress and exercise. It presents as an abrupt onset, uniquely severe headache with nausea, vomiting and sometimes loss of consciousness. 30% describe a preceding 'warning leak' days or weeks beforehand, presumably from leaking into the aneurysm wall or minor SAH. Blood seeping down to the lumbar spine may give severe radicular leg pain after 12 hours.

Neck stiffness occurs only after several hours. Intraocular (subhyaloid) haemorrhage occurs in 25% of cases and are of venous origin, developing between the retina and vitreous membrane. Focal signs such as third nerve palsy, brain stem dysfunction or lateralizing signs are due to:

- Mass effect of intracerebral haematoma.
- Ischaemia from arterial spasm (see below), embolus from intra-aneurysmal thrombus or vessel dissection.

Prognosis

The prognosis strongly correlates with the clinical state on admission. The clinical grade is determined by the level of consciousness and the extent of motor deficit (*Table 1*).

Table 1. Clinical grading (I–V) of subarachnoid haemorrhage

Grade	Glasgow Coma Scale	Motor deficit
I	15	Absent
II	13–14	Absent
III	13–14	Present
IV	7–12	Absent or present
V	3–6	Absent or present

Investigations

1. Subarachnoid blood detection
- CT brain scan is preferable to MRI for detecting subarachnoid blood, 95% showing blood within 24 hours, 80% within 3 days and 30% within 2 weeks of the bleed. Intracerebral blood and hydrocephalus can also be demonstrated.
- Lumbar puncture is essential if SAH is clinically likely but CT scan is negative. Uniform blood staining with xanthochromia (yellow supernatant) is diagnostic but may not appear until 12 hours following bleeding. Spectrophotometry can demonstrate xanthochromia between 12 hours and 2 weeks following bleeding in all cases. Examination for blood in three consecutive CSF tubes does not definitively distinguish bloody tap from SAH and so is unnecessary.

2. Aneurysm location. Conventional angiography remains superior to non-invasive angiography using MRI or spiral CT. Only conventional angiography gives sufficient resolution for surgical planning, enabling detection of aneurysms <3 mm diameter. Conventional angiography carries a mortality of 0.1% and morbidity of 1%, higher in older patients with widespread atheroma, and in Ehlers–Danlos syndrome.

Screening

One per cent of the population has an asymptomatic aneurysm aged 50 years; the risk of bleeding from a previously unruptured aneurysm is 1% per year. The cost-benefit of aneurysm screening suggests a need for MRI or catheter angiography if two or more first degree relatives have had aneurysmal SAH (incidental aneurysm risk 30%). With only one family member affected, screening is not indicated since the four times risk in first degree relatives still represents a bleeding risk of only 1% aged 50 years and 2% risk aged 70 years.

Patient with autosomal dominant polycystic kidney disease must be screened since they carry a 5–10% risk of intracranial aneurysm and a 20–25% risk if they have both polycystic kidney disease and a family history of intracranial aneurysm. Re-screening after an interval, e.g. 5 years, is needed in high risk cases.

Complications

1. *Hydrocephalus*
- Obstructive. Distortion of the aqueduct or fourth ventricle may provoke acute hydrocephalus.
- Communicating. Subarachnoid blood may impair CSF absorption leading to generalized ventricular enlargement after about 10 days. Communicating hydrocephalus may also develop as a late complication of SAH, sometimes years later.

2. *Vasospasm.* About 25% of SAH patients manifest cerebral ischaemia from vasospasm, 4–12 days after the bleed. The exact mechanism of vasospasm following SAH is not understood, though it appears to be a true hyperplastic vasculopathy rather than actual vasospasm. The more blood is visible on CT scanning, the greater the risk of spasm.

Management

Aneurysmal SAH presents a potentially curable lesion with a potentially devastating mortality and morbidity. Prompt diagnosis is essential. Recent advances in surgical technique and medical care can potentially improve the morbidity but the overall mortality and morbidity remains distressingly high.

1. *Medical*
- Fluid balance. Electrolyte disturbance in SAH results from increased salt and water excretion (cerebral salt wasting), presumably from the action of naturetic hormone. Treatment is with salt and fluid replacement (with central venous pressure measurement) rather than fluid restriction as was previously thought.
- Prevention of spasm. The calcium channel blocker nimodipine can reduce the incidence of ischaemic deficit following SAH though does not reduce the incidence of angiographic vasospasm. Early surgery may be beneficial in preventing vasospasm and allows aggressive fluid replacement to maintain cerebral circulation despite arterial narrowing.

2. *Surgery.* Surgery aims to exclude the aneurysm sac from the circulation whilst preserving the parent artery.

- Aneurysm clipping. A clip is placed across the aneurysm neck. The timing of surgery remains controversial. Early surgery at 48–72 hours is beneficial in abolishing the high risk of re-bleed at this time, and allows aggressive treatment of arterial spasm. However, early surgery is more challenging owing to oedema and clot around the aneurysm. In general early surgery is indicated for patients grade I or II at 48 hours.

- Endovascular surgery. Coil embolization techniques are suitable for some aneurysms. Insertion and attachment of soft metallic coils into the lumen, which thrombose, obliterate the aneurysmal sac. This is useful if the aneurysmal neck is narrow. It can be performed early and may serve temporarily to reduce the risk of re-bleed.

Non-aneurysmal SAH

Perimesencephalic haemorrhage

About 10% of patients with SAH and two-thirds of SAH with normal angiogram show extravasated blood around the midbrain, particularly the interpeduncular fossa (peri-mesencephalic haemorrhage), presumably from a venous or capillary source rather than aneurysmal rupture.

Arteriovenous malformations

These are a common cause of devastating intracerebral haemorrhage in young normotensive individuals, the bleeding commonly extending into the subarachnoid space. The mortality following bleeding is much lower (c. 10%) than in aneurysmal SAH.

Cavernous haemangiomas (cavernomas) are a common incidental finding on cerebral imaging; bleeding occasionally occurs but is seldom life threatening.

Further reading

Schievink WI. Intracranial aneurysms. *New England Journal of Medicine,* 1997; **336:** 28–40.
van Gijn J. Subarachnoid haemorrhage. *Lancet,* 1992; **339:** 653–5.
Warlow CP, Dennis, MS, van Gijn J *et al.* Unusual causes of ischaemic stroke and transient ischaemic attacks. In*: Stroke: A Practical Guide to Management.* Oxford: Blackwell Science, 1996; 258–86.

Related topics of interest

SYNCOPE

Syncope (*synkoptein*, *Gk.* 'to cut off') is a loss of consciousness, usually from a sudden decrease in cerebral blood flow. There are several aetiological types.

Neurally-mediated

Reflex (vasovagal) syncope This is the commonest form affecting mainly young adults. It is caused by active mechanisms and requires an intact autonomic system.

1. Clinical features
- Triggers: precipitating factors include prolonged standing, rising from lying, emotional trauma, venepuncture or seeing blood.
- Prodrome: the symptom onset is gradual; pre-syncopal symptoms include light headedness, nausea, sweating, palpitation and greying or blacking of vision.
- During the episode, patients are pale, sweaty and cold with flaccid muscle tone and occasionally a few uncoordinated clonic jerks. Incontinence is unusual and lateral tongue biting rare.
- Recovery is rapid with no confusion.

2. Mechanisms
- Diminished venous return results from venous pooling in the legs (prolonged standing) or in the splancnic circulation, e.g. from a vagal surge, such as the sight of blood.

   Cardiac output falls, but blood pressure is initially maintained by sympathetically induced peripheral vasoconstriction allowing a gradual build up of pre-syncopal symptoms over about a minute.

   Vigorous cardiac contraction stimulates ventricular wall mechanoreceptors transmitted to the brainstem via 5HT-mediated vagal brainstem afferents, falsely indicating that the heart is overfilled rather than underfilled.

   Vagal stimulation and withdrawal of sympathetic tone result, leading to bradycardia and a fall in peripheral resistance in a vicious cycle with circulatory collapse.

Cerebral vasoconstriction may precede the major haemodynamic changes, so accounting for pre-syncope occurring prior to any fall in blood pressure.

Orthostatic (postural) syncope

See Autonomic disorders.

Whereas in reflex syncope there is activation of vasodilatation and bradycardia leading to syncope, here autonomic dysfunction leads to a failure to vasoconstrict in response to a postural blood pressure fall. It results from autonomic nervous system disease, e.g. age-related, diabetes, alcohol or medications).

Investigations

Where there is diagnostic doubt or unusual features, further investigations are needed.

- A fall in blood pressure from lying to standing together with a rise in pulse rate, is sometimes found in severe cases but is poorly sensitive.
- Bloods to exclude anaemia or hyponatraemia.
- Electrocardiogram (ECG) for arrhythmias, short PR, prolonged QT etc.
- A tilt table test (60 degree tilt for 45 minutes) is highly sensitive (<90%) and specific (70%). Measures to induce syncope, e.g. isoprenaline, increase sensitivity but lower specificity argues against its usefulness.

Management

1. General measures
- An explanation with reassurance and advice on posture (head down or lie flat at symptom onset; rise slowly from lying and intermittent leg crossing when standing) is often sufficient. The experience of a typical but controlled induced syncope on a tilt table is itself often helpful in its prevention.
- Withdraw provoking medications.
- Systematic desensitization, for example to the sight of blood, may be appropriate for vasovagal syncope.

2. Drugs. The wide choice of available drugs demonstrates that none is ideal.

- Fludrocortisone, through salt and water retention, reduces the ventricular underfilling, limiting inappropriately vigorous ventricular contractions.
- Beta blockers control the ventricular contractions limiting the vagally-mediated brainstem stimulation.

- Selective serotonin re-uptake inhibitors (SSRIs), e.g. fluoxetine, inhibit the centrally mediated vagal messages, so limit the subsequent vagal efferent tone.

3. Pacemaker. This is considered for malignant vasovagal syncope and carotid sinus hypersensitivity: it does not prevent the blood pressure fall or necessarily stop the syncope, but by maintaining heart rate it allows a warning of impending syncope which otherwise would be absent.

Cardiac

Clinical features

- Exercise-induced syncope should be investigated urgently for possible cardiac causes. Healthy athletes commonly feel faint after finishing exercise and this is normal. A variant of vasovagal syncope may also present as exercise induced syncope but structural causes must first be excluded.
- Cardiac syncope may occur from any posture and is common whilst in bed. There is often a history of palpitation or of pre-syncopal symptoms both during attacks and at other times. The overall mortality from cardiac syncope is up to 30% in the first year; correct diagnosis and appropriate management is a priority.
- Cardiac syncope may be misdiagnosed as epilepsy with potentially fatal consequences. Patients with recurrent syncope or those with a significant family history of syncope should undergo an ECG. It is possible that some cases of sudden unexplained death in epilepsy are missed cardiac syncope.
- Cardiac output is reduced by problems with the heart's electrical circuit (arrhythmias) or plumbing circuit (structural causes).

Arrhythmias

- Tachyarrhythmias (e.g. Wolff-Parkinson-White, prolonged QT syndrome).
- Bradyarrhythmias (e.g. sick sinus syndrome, complete heart block).

Prolonged QT disorders

The QT interval on ECG is measured from the peak of the Q wave to the end of the R wave. The normal value (corrected for heart rate, QT_C = QT interval divided by the root of R-R interval) is <0.46 in males and <0.47 in females.

Prolonged QT syndromes have congenitally wide variations in refractoriness between adjacent myofibrils allowing 'micro-re-entry' phenomena. Ultimately, this causes an arrhythmia called torsades de pointes where the QRS axis repeatedly rotates through 360 degrees giving recurrent presyncope and syncope and sometimes ventricular fibrillation and sudden death. This is most likely to occur after rising and on exercise when there is further paradoxical prolongation of QT interval. Children presenting with loss of consciousness following exertion should raise suspicion of cardiac syncope from a prolonged QT syndrome.

There are several prolonged QT disorder genotypes. The major phenotypes include

- Romano–Ward syndrome (autosomal dominant).
- Jervell and Lange–Nielsen syndrome (recessive) associated with deafness.

Any cardiac disease, particularly ischaemic, may manifest as prolonged QT with associated vulnerability to arrhythmias. Drugs include class 1 and 3 anti-arrhythmics, the anti-histamine terfenadine (particularly combined with erythromycin, anti-fungals or grapefruit juice).

Structural causes

- Left ventricular outflow tract obstruction (aortic stenosis, hypertrophic obstructive cardiomyopathy (HOCM)). Syncope occurs through reduced stroke volume and increased vagal tone following vigorous ventricular contractions.
- Impaired ventricular filling (atrial myxoma, pulmonary hypertension). Again, vigorous contractions contribute to syncope.
- Arrhythmogenic right ventricular dysplasia. This autosomal dominant condition may present as sudden death. The ECG shows inverted T waves in V2-4 but is normal in 30%. The right ventricular wall shows fibrosis.

Respiratory

- Vigorous coughing (especially in elderly males) or performing the Valsalva manoeuvre (e.g. trumpet playing) may elevate intrathoracic pressure sufficiently above venous pressure to impair adequate venous return.
- Breath holding in young children can be provoked by emotion and cause collapse, cyanosis and brief twitching.
- Hyperventilation from anxiety contributes to syncope through cerebral vasoconstriction.

Central nervous system

- Brainstem ischaemia from arterial disease, e.g. congenital, arteritis or steal phenomena.
- Migraine syncope is uncommon, presumably resulting from brainstem arterial spasm.
- Raised intracranial pressure occurring intermittently from obstructive hydrocephalus, e.g. from third ventricular colloid cyst or Chiari malformation; may potentially cause sudden death.
- Panic disorder with anxiety episodes may culminate in syncope from hyperventilation-induced cerebral vasoconstriction.
- Swallow syncope, often with glossopharyngeal neuralgia, is rare; bradycardia occurs as a reflex response to swallowing.
- Cataplexy mimics syncope but consciousness is retained.

Further reading

Ben-David J, Zipes DP. Torsades de pointes and proarrhythmia. *Lancet*, 1993; **341:** 1578–82.

Braden DS, Gaymes CH. The diagnosis and management of syncope in children and adolescents. *Pediatric Annals,* 1997; **26:** 422–6.

Lizner M, Yang EH, Estes NA III, Wang P, Voperian VR, Kapoor WN. Diagnosing syncope pt 2. Unexplained syncope. *Annals of Internal Medicine,* 1997; **127:** 76–86.

van Lieshout JJ, ten Harkel ADJ, Wieling W. Physical manoeuvres for combating orthostatic dizziness in autonomic failure. *Lancet*, 1992; **339:** 897–8.

Related topics of interest

TUMOURS OF THE CENTRAL NERVOUS SYSTEM (BENIGN)

Meningioma

Origin and site

These arise from the arachnoid lining (meningothelial) cells. They are usually of adult onset, predominantly in females (ratio 2:1). They arise in relation to the falx, olfactory groove, optic foramen, sphenoid ridge, posterior fossa, lateral ventricle or spinal canal.

Presentation

Meningiomas comprise 10–15% of brain tumours. They present as gradual onset space occupying lesions with a broad range of manifestations depending upon their site. Convexity tumours present as progressive hemiparesis and epilepsy; parasagittal tumours may present with an asymmetrical paraparesis.

Radiologically they are densely enhancing, smooth outlined lesions adjacent to the dura, often with oedema and sometimes with bony reaction (destruction or osteoblastic) and dural vein infiltration.

Pathology

The tumour is encapsulated and shows characteristic histology:

- Uniform sized nuclei.
- A 'syncytial' cytoplasm pattern apparently without cell borders (the cells are interdigitated on electron microscopy).
- Whorls, psammoma bodies and calcification.

There is a broad range of other less common histological types: 11 variants are listed in the WHO classification, including psammomatous, angiomatous, secretory and clear cell. Occasionally there are atypical features (grade 2) or local erosion through bone or even skin (grade 3). Many menigiomas show a chromosome 22 deletion.

Management and prognosis Complete surgical excision is undertaken if possible and is usually preceded by angiography to define the blood supply. Radiotherapy is not used for the common benign forms. The prognosis for most forms, if amenable to resection, is good.

Schwannoma

Origin and site

These arise from Schwann cells on cranial nerves and spinal nerve roots. They form predominantly on sensory nerves at the junction between central myelination by oligodendroglial cells and peripheral myelination by Schwann cells.

The commonest form is acoustic Schwannoma (vestibular neurilemmoma) arising on the vestibular division of the VIII cranial nerve.

Presentation

Schwannomas comprise 8% of adult primary intracranial tumours and present aged 20–50 years. Acoustic Schwannomas present as ipsilateral deafness and tinnitus; later there may be ipsilateral facial weakness, numbness and ataxia. An important early physical sign is ipsilateral loss of the corneal reflex.

In the spine they develop on dorsal roots and present as a radiculopathy, sometimes with cord compression.

Bilateral acoustic Schwannomas are the hallmark of neurofibromatosis type 2 (NF2).

Radiologically they are best seen on MRI with gadolinium contrast.

Pathology

Schwannomas are encapsulated. Microscopically, they comprise two appearances, representing ends of a spectrum, different tumours showing different proportions of each:

- Antoni A, of compact, spindle-shaped cells.
- Antoni B, which is looser with cells separated by matrix.

Occasionally there are haemorrhages, lipid cells and lymphocyte infiltration. S100 immunostaining is positive.

Management and prognosis Complete excision is ideal if possible. Malignant transformation almost never occurs and so the prognosis depends upon the resectability of the tumour. In NF2, however, further tumours are very likely.

Neurofibroma

Site and presentation   Neurofibromas comprise Schwann cells, fibroblasts and axons and occur sporadically as solitary tumours (90%) or, when part of neurofibromatosis type 1 (NF1), as multiple lesions. Solitary neurofibromas usually develop on peripheral cutaneous nerves. Neurofibromas on spinal nerve roots may present as a radiculopathy, sometimes with cord compression.

Pathology   Neurofibromas are non-encapsulated and often form plexiform tumours. Microscopically, they comprise spindle cells forming a 'wavy' pattern with bands of collagen with axons passing through.

Management and prognosis   Surgical excision is usually possible with excellent prognosis. Transformation to neurofibrosarcoma, however, occurs in about 4% of NF1 cases, though almost never in isolated neurofibroma.

Pituitary adenoma

These arise from the cells of the adenohypophysis and clinically present with the effects of:

- Abnormal secretion, e.g. hyperprolactinaemia, acromegaly.
- Compression, e.g. bitemporal hemianopia (the earliest sign is bitemporal upper quadrantanopia to red) and headache.

Microscopically, there is a monotonous cell sheet within a fine vascular framework, occasionally with a sinusoidal pattern. Sometimes they calcify. Immunostaining for hormones, e.g. prolactin, may be appropriate.

Craniopharyngioma

- These derive from developmental epithelial inclusions and present with the effects of local compression, e.g. bitemporal hemianopia (initially a bitemporal lower quadrantanopia) or extension into the third ventricle leading to hydrocephalus.
- Histologically they show an 'adamantinomatous' pattern with circular enclosures of basal epithelial cells surrounded by loose material, sometimes containing cholesterol crystals and haemosiderin.

Haemangioblastoma

- These tumours arise particularly in the cerebellum and may be associated with von Hippel–Lindau disease. Occasional cord tumours present as syringomyelia.
- Radiologically they present a cystic lesion with an enhancing nodule at one edge.
- Histologically there is a mass of empty capillary channels and some lipid containing cells; occasional atypical nuclei occur but are still consistent with a benign course.
- Management is with surgery, aiming for complete removal without radiotherapy.
- The prognosis with successful resection is excellent.

Neurocytoma

This is a recently recognized benign tumour, histologically resembling oligodendroglioma, but showing neuronal cell markers, e.g. for synaptophysin. Prognosis is excellent following surgical removal.

Tumours presenting as epilepsy

Tumours are a major cause of epilepsy in adults. In general, tumours presenting with epilepsy are slower growing and have a better prognosis than those with other presentations. Some relatively benign tumours are visible only on MRI scanning, making this essential in patients with focal epilepsy, especially if their seizures are difficult to control.

Two such low grade tumours are:

- Dysembryoplastic neuroepithelial tumour (DNET), a hamartomatous intracortical lesion composed of neuronal and oligodendroglial elements. It presents with young-onset, long duration seizures with minimal neurological defects and stability of the lesion over time.
- Ganglioglioma are rare, usually childhood, tumours, almost always presenting with treatment-resistant seizures. Pathologically they are composed of malformed (heterotopic) neurons and glial cells. They are indolent and may cause epilepsy for decades before their discovery and resection.

Epilepsy from these low grade tumours may be very resistant to medical treatment; epilepsy from more malignant tumours is often easier to control but the tumour itself is clearly more serious.

Further reading

Franks AJ. *Diagnostic Manual of Tumours of the Central Nervous System.* Edinburgh: Churchill Livingstone, 1988.

Brada M, Thomas GT. Tumours of the brain and spinal cord in adults. In: Peckham M, Pinedo H, Veronesi U, eds. *Oxford Textbook of Oncology*. Vol. 2. Oxford: Oxford University Press, 1995; 2063–94.

Related topics of interest

Neurocutaneous syndromes (p. 179)
Paraneoplastic neurological syndromes (p. 215)
Tumours of the central nervous system (malignant) (p. 296)

TUMOURS OF THE CENTRAL NERVOUS SYSTEM (MALIGNANT)

The majority of CNS tumours are malignant. The commonest overall is metastatic spread from elsewhere.

Gliomas

These neuroepithelial tumours comprise astrocytomas, oligodendrogliomas and ependymomas.

Astrocytomas

These are the commonest primary malignant brain tumours.

1. Clinical. The presentation varies with the tumour location and speed of growth.

- The adult forms are generally more malignant and develop in the hemispheres with rapidly progressing symptoms (over weeks) of pressure type headache, localizing symptoms and sometimes seizures.
- The classical childhood (cerebellar) form is relatively benign.

Radiologically they are inhomogeneous, irregularly enhancing lesions with surrounding oedema and shift. The radiological appearance does not reliably predict histological grade of tumour.

2. Grading
- Grading reflects the histological appearance.
- The most malignant area in the section gives the grade.
- Sampling error often results from histological heterogeneity.
- Glial fibrillary acidic protein (GFAP) immuno-staining is usually positive in astrocytomas.
- (a) Grade 1. Pilocytic (juvenile cerebellar) astrocytoma is at the benign end of a spectrum and presents with ataxia and hydrocephalus. Histologically the cells are regular without mitoses and show characteristic Rosenthal fibres, comprising collections of GFAP. The prognosis is excellent and cure following complete surgical excision is expected.

(b) Grade 2. These slightly more malignant tumours comprise three histological types: fibrillary, protoplasmic and gemistocytic. There is cellular irregularity and occasional mitoses. They are usually amenable to resection and have a 50% 5-year survival.

(c) Grade 3 (Anaplastic or malignant astrocytoma) and grade 4 (glioblastoma multiforme) represent the malignant and more common end of the glioma spectrum. The histological features of malignancy are variation in cell and nuclear size (pleomorphism), mitotic figures, endothelial proliferation, and necrosis. Grade 4 tumours show all of these characteristics. The tumours occasionally seed within the neuraxis but only rarely metastasize outside the CNS. They are poorly responsive to treatment and carry a grave prognosis despite optimal treatment (grade 4: 10% 1-year survival).

3. Management
- Steroids. All patients are considered for high dose steroids, e.g. dexamethasone 16 mg daily for short term symptom relief.
- Surgery. Practice varies widely with interventions tailored to the patient's age, general condition and tumour site. Most undergo either biopsy (for diagnostic certainty) or tumour debulking.
- Radiotherapy is usually reserved for grade 3 and 4 tumours.
- Chemotherapy for gliomas is controversial.

4. Prognosis
- Factors suggesting better prognosis include young age, good general health, low histological grade, long history, presentation with seizures, extensive surgical resection.

5. Differential diagnosis
- Subependymal giant cell astrocytoma is a relatively benign variant almost exclusively confined to tuberose sclerosis.
- Pleomorphic xantho-astrocytoma may be confused with glioblastoma histologically owing to bizarre shaped and giant cells but is distinguished by the presence of lipidized cells and has a good prognosis.

Oligodendroglioma

1. Clinical. This hemisphere tumour arises from myelin-forming cells and presents as a space occupying lesion in middle age with a slow history over several years. CT brain scan shows a mass containing calcification.

2. Pathology
The histological characteristics are best remembered by:

- 'Chicken wire' reticulated vascular framework.
- 'Poached egg' cell appearance owing to a consistent artefact around cells.
- 'Egg shell' patches of calcification.
- 'Egg nests' (satellitosis) at the tumour edge from oligodendroglial cells congregating around neurones.

GFAP is negative except when very malignant.

3. Management and prognosis. Most are amenable to subtotal removal but radiotherapy may have only a marginal benefit. Prognosis is reasonable with 50% 10-year survival.

4. Differential diagnosis. An important but rare differential diagnosis is neurocytoma (see Tumours of the central nervous system (benign)).

Ependymoma

These arise from ventricular lining cells.

- In children they usually arise in the fourth ventricle, presenting as hydrocephalus with cerebellar signs.
- In adults they often arise in the spinal canal and particularly present as a conus lesion (myxopapillary ependymoma).

Histologically they are highly cellular, forming perivascular pseudo-rosettes where tumour cells encircle blood vessels but separated from them by their GFAP-positive astroglial fibrils.

Surgical resection is usually possible and radiotherapy helpful. The prognosis is intermediate with 30–50% 5-year survival.

Primitive neuro-ectodermal tumours (PNETs)

Medulloblastoma is the commonest, presenting in children aged 5–15 years as a posterior fossa tumour with hydrocephalus with cerebellar signs. It is highly malignant and metastasizes within the neuraxis. Histologically it is very cellular with frequent mitoses;

true rosettes occur in 30% (cells encircling blood vessels). Immunocytochemistry demonstrates neuronal markers, e.g. synaptophysin, S100 and neurofilaments.

The main histological differential diagnosis is ependymoma.

Surgical resection is followed by whole neuraxis radiotherapy irrespective of clinical or radiological spread at diagnosis.

Lymphoma

Primary cerebral lymphomas:

- Present predominantly as mass lesions.
- Show marked and uniform enhancement on brain imaging.
- Are almost always B cell type.

Secondary CNS lymphomas:

- More commonly present with diffuse meningeal involvement rather than as discrete deposits (though secondary cord lymphoma is usually a compressive mass).
- Are usually T cell type.

Histologically, as in lymphoma anywhere, there are pleomorphic neoplastic lymphoid cells with perivascular cuffing. B and T lymphoid cells can be distinguished immunocytochemically.

CNS lymphoma classification is very detailed but management and prognosis are similar for all types. Lymphoma often initially responds dramatically to steroid and radiotherapy, though rapidly recur with an overall prognosis as poor as glioblastoma multiforme.

Brain metastases

These present as:

- Multiple lesions.
- Solitary lesions.
- Meningeal infiltration.

Tumours most likely to metastasize to brain are: small cell lung carcinoma, acute lymphatic leukaemia, lymphoma, breast, and non-small cell carcinoma. Melanoma typically seeds in the posterior fossa. Haemorrhagic metastases suggest melanoma or chorionic carcinoma.

The clinical presentation is similar to any malignant tumour. Brain imaging usually shows multiple enhancing masses.

Management is palliative with corticosteroids and occasional whole brain radiotherapy.

Further reading

Franks AJ. *Diagnostic Manual of Tumours of the Central Nervous System*. Edinburgh: Churchill Livingstone, 1988.

Brada M, Thomas GT. Tumours of the brain and spinal cord in adults. In: Peckham M, Pinedo H, Veronesi U, eds. *Oxford Textbook of Oncology,* Vol. 2. Oxford: Oxford University Press, 1995; 2063–94.

Related topics of interest

Neurocutaneous syndromes (p. 179)
Paraneoplastic neurological syndromes (p. 215)
Tumours of the central nervous system (benign) (p. 291)

VASCULITIS OF THE CENTRAL NERVOUS SYSTEM

Vasculitis affects either the central or peripheral nervous system, occurring in isolation or with systemic vasculitis. CNS vasculitis is a serious but uncommon condition which is difficult to recognize, diagnose and manage. Nevertheless, it is a potentially treatable cause of otherwise progressive disease.

Mechanisms

Vasculitis occurs when white blood cells adhere to and penetrate vessel walls, releasing cytotoxins and promoting inflammation and necrosis. Causes include:

- Antibody reaction to circulating antigens, e.g. immune complexes, trapped on the vessel wall.
- Damage by anti-neutrophil cytoplasmic antibodies (ANCA).
- Damage by activated T lymphocytes.
- CNS damage by anti-neuronal antibodies.

Presentation

This depends upon the cause and the location of vasculitis. Vasculitis with systemic disorders present systemic symptoms; vasculitis confined to the CNS has no systemic features or specific symptoms and signs and is harder to diagnose.

Common patterns are:

- Headache, the most frequent symptom, occurring in half of patients.
- Acute or sub-acute encephalopathy with mental symptoms, intellectual loss, personality affect and changes, and altered conscious level.
- A multiple sclerosis ('MS-plus') type picture.
- Focal signs mimicking a space-occupying lesion, e.g. hemiparesis or aphasia sometimes progressing rapidly.

Types

1. *Primary.* Isolated cranial (granulomatous) angiitis is confined to the CNS. The cause is usually unknown. Occasionally it accompanies Hodgkin's lymphoma or herpes zoster infection.

Inflammation occurs in very small vessels (<200 mm diameter) mainly in the leptomeninges.

2. *Secondary.* More commonly, CNS vasculitis complicates systemic vasculitis.

ANCA-associated necrotizing vasculitis

- Wegener's granulomatosis involves upper and lower respiratory tracts, kidney and nervous system. Glomerulonephritis predicts a poor prognosis. Cytoplasmic ANCA (c-ANCA) occurs in most cases, aiding diagnosis and partially reflecting disease activity.
- Microscopic polyangiitis, a multisystem vasculitis including glomerulonephritis, resembles Wegener's granulomatosis but without respiratory involvement (apart from alveolar haemorrhage). The ANCA titre reflects disease activity.
- Churg–Strauss syndrome is a multi-organ disorder characterized by asthma, pulmonary infiltrates and eosinophilia. Peripheral nervous system involvement with multiple mononeuropathy is commoner than CNS vasculitis. Perinuclear ANCA (p-ANCA) is usual.

Non-ANCA-associated necrotizing vasculitis

Giant cell arteritis
This elderly-onset condition affects large extracranial and posterior ciliary arteries (see Optic nerve disorders). CNS involvement occasionally occurs, e.g. vertebral artery angiitis causing brain stem disease.

Lymphomatoid granulomatosis
This principally involves the skin, lungs and nervous system. Pulmonary involvement predominates with cough, dyspnoea, sputum and sometimes bilateral pulmonary nodules; patients describe fever and malaise. Pathology demonstrates vessel necrosis, granulomata and atypical plasma cell infiltration. A few progress to lymphoma. It responds poorly to steroids.

Vasculitis in connective tissue disease
- Systemic lupus erythematosus (SLE): cerebral vasculitis is rare in SLE (see below).
- Sjögren's syndrome: CNS involvement accompanies <25% of cases, usually aseptic meningitis or progressive dementia. It is notoriously difficult to diagnose unless there are systemic manifestations.
- Behçet's disease is a chronic multi-system vasculitic disorder, typically with genital and oral aphthous lesions with uveitis. Neurological manifestations result from thrombophlebitis (e.g. dural sinus thrombosis), arterial damage with thrombosis and aneurysm (with a poor prognosis) and, less commonly, CNS vasculitis.

Other vasculitides

- Infection with many viruses (especially herpes zoster) bacteria and mycobacteria, fungi or spirochaetes (especially syphilis) can provoke CNS vasculitis. HIV gives vasculitis from the infection itself, opportunistic infection or lymphoma.
- Lymphoproliferative disease such as lymphoma may cause CNS vasculitis.
- Drug abuse.

Investigation

The diagnosis is essentially clinical but several tests can help:

- Ophthalmological examination using low-dose fluorescein angiography with slit-lamp video microscopy of the anterior segment is frequently abnormal in cerebral vasculitis, reflecting associated retinal vasculitis.
- Serum ANCA is important in recognizing and monitoring some systemic vasculitides (see above).
- Brain imaging shows non-specific white matter changes.
- CSF protein, white cell count and pressure are typically elevated but glucose is normal. Oligoclonal bands are occasionally positive.
- EEG shows generalized non specific slowing.
- Indium-labelled white cell cerebral imaging is only rarely helpful.
- Angiography shows segmental narrowing ('beading') in 50% but often affected small vessels cannot be distinguished.
- Leptomeningeal and brain biopsy, the specific investigation, carries its own morbidity. Biopsy may show haemorrhagic or ischaemic infarction associated with meningeal and cerebral small blood vessel occlusion by granuloma or thrombosis.

Management

Initial management is with steroids to which about 60–70% of CNS vasculitis respond; isolated cranial angiitis is usually the most steroid responsive. Pulsed cyclophosphamide is usually well tolerated and successful in the ANCA-associated vasculitides. Other immunosuppression includes cyclosporin, plasma exchange and immunoglobulins.

Related conditions

Cerebral lupus

Although advanced SLE commonly is associated with neurological problems, SLE presenting with CNS involvement (cerebral lupus) is rare (<10%). Neuropsychiatric involvement in SLE is more often due to associated conditions than to cerebral lupus.

- Infection: SLE patients are at risk of infection, particularly encapsulated bacterial organisms, even when not immunosuppressed.
- Hypertension may lead to small vessel cerebral disease.
- Embolic stroke from SLE endocarditis.
- Steroid treatment may have psychiatric consequences.

1. Manifestations
- Psychosis, depression, confusion and cognitive impairment.
- Epilepsy, particularly tonic-clonic seizures.
- Stroke-like episodes.
- Cranial nerve palsies.
- Multiple mononeuropathy.
- Chorea.

2. Mechanisms
- Micro-infarction causes focal disease, e.g. strokes or cranial nerve palsies. There is non inflammatory fibrinoid necrosis of small blood vessels with intimal thickening and luminal thrombosis. Venous and arterial thrombosis is likely with anticardiolipin antibody, present in 45%.
- Venous sinus thrombosis is relatively common in SLE, again with anticardiolipin antibody.
- Antineuronal antibodies cause diffuse symptoms, e.g. psychiatric disorder. These antibodies target several neuronal antigens (neurofilament, glycolipids, glycoproteins, endothelial surface antigens) and occur in 90% of SLE patients with (and only 30% of those without) CNS involvement. They probably result from local CNS synthesis giving CSF oligoclonal bands.
- CNS vasculitis is surprisingly rare in SLE.

3. Diagnosis

- Anti-nuclear antibody, anti-double stranded DNA antibody and low complement (C3 and C4) levels are almost invariable in SLE with secondary cerebral involvement; they may be absent in isolated cerebral lupus making diagnosis difficult.
- CSF protein and white cell count are elevated, occasionally with lowered glucose. Oligoclonal bands occur in 10–20%; CSF anti-neuronal antibodies occur in <90% making this an important test.
- Cerebral imaging is non specific (white matter changes) but help to exclude other disorders.
- EEG often shows non specific abnormalities.

4. Management

- Immunosuppression: treatment is initially with methyl-prednisolone and low dose maintenance steroids, together with pulsed cyclophosphamide.
- Anticoagulation: patients with a history of SLE-related cerebral venous thrombosis require long term anticoagulation.

Intravascular lymphoma

Intravascular lymphoma (neoplastic angioendotheliomatosis), is uncommon but important as a mimic of CNS vasculitis. Systemic symptoms include fever, lethargy and fatigue. Non-neurological manifestations include skin (red-purple nodules), and involvement of the heart, lung, kidney and adrenals.

Brain involvement manifests as progressive dementia or focal deficits, e.g. aphasia, apraxia. Cord involvement can produce an ascending spinal syndrome.

Biopsy of meninges, brain or cord shows atypical mononuclear cells within the lumen and infiltrating small blood vessel walls. CT brain scan shows low densities, CSF shows elevated protein and white cells and EEG rhythms are generally slow. It often responds temporarily to steroids.

Further reading

Bluestein HG. The central nervous system in systemic lupus erythematosus. In: Lahita RG, ed. *Systemic Lupus Erythematosus*, 2nd edn. New York: Churchill Livingstone, 1992; 639–56.

Fieschi C, Rasura M, Anzini A, Beccia M. Central nervous system vasculitis. *Journal of the Neurological Sciences,* 1998; **153:** 159–71.

Scolding NJ, Jayne DR, Zajicek JP, Meyer PA, Wraight EP, Lockwood CM. Cerebral vasculitis – recognition, diagnosis and management. *Quarterly Journal of Medicine,* 1997; **90:** 61–73.

Related topics of interest

VERTIGO

The sensation of spinning or movement, either of oneself or of the surroundings, is usually associated with nausea, imbalance and nystagmus.

It is essential in the history to distinguish vertigo from light-headedness. Vertigo implies a lesion in the inner ear or its central connections; light-headedness is less specific, often implying postural hypotension, hyperventilation or general medical conditions.

Labyrinthine causes   The bony labyrinth is the convoluted space within the temporal bone (comprising cochlea, vestibule and semicircular canals). It contains the membranous labyrinth (cochlear duct, saccule and utricle, and membranous semicircular ducts containing endolymph) and surrounded by perilymph. Collectively, these represent 'the labyrinth'.

Acute viral labyrinthitis

Acute labyrinthine inflammation in association with a viral infection is the classical inner ear disorder. Symptoms are vertigo (often severe) with vomiting and ataxia, occasionally sweating, pallor, nausea, vomiting, diarrhoea and even syncope.

Benign paroxysmal positioning vertigo (BPPV)

This is the commonest form of episodic vertigo in adults.

Clinical features   Brief attacks of intense vertigo are provoked by sudden posture changes or by certain postures, e.g. head down to the affected side, and accompanied by nystagmus beating towards the downmost side. Characteristically, patients avoid the provoking postures. Hearing is preserved.

The Dix–Hallpike manoeuvre involves lying the patient flat with the head laterally rotated to one side and the head extended over the top of the bed. Typical features in BPPV are:

- A latent interval of up to 10 seconds.
- Vertigo with torsion nystagmus, fast phase towards the downward ear.
- Settling of the vertigo and nystagmus after 10–20 seconds.

- Further vertigo on sitting up with the direction of nystagmus reversed.
- Reduced response (fatigue) with repeated testing.

Mechanisms

Two mechanisms operate in BPPV.

1. Canalolithiasis. Particulate debris is free-floating within the (usually posterior) semi-circular canal fluid. On head movement, the debris sinks to the lowermost part of the canal; the resulting endolymph drag distorts the canal's ampullary organ, inducing vertigo and nystagmus.

2. Cupulolithiasis. Debris adherent to the cupula (dome-shaped membrane covering the ampullary nerve endings) in the posterior semicircular canal increases the cupula's weight, causing its abnormal distortion with gravity on head movement. In this form, because there is no settling of particles, the vertigo and nystagmus persist in the provoking posture.

Anatomy

1. Posterior semicircular canal BPPV. This is the common and typical form with clinical features outlined above.

2. Horizontal semicircular canal BPPV. In this uncommon form, vertigo and nystagmus occur with the head to either side when supine, though usually worse to the affected side. It may therefore mimic a CNS lesion.

Management

The high success rate of repositioning manoeuvres has led to a major change from the traditional conservative management of BPPV.

Physical treatments

1. Repositioning manoeuvres. These aim to float debris round the posterior semicircular canal and into the utricle where it can no longer cause vertigo. The modified Epley manoeuvre is the most popular. After being positioned in the provoking Dix–Hallpike position (see above) for 3 minutes, the patient's extended head is turned slowly to the opposite (non-provoking) side over 3–5 minutes, and then, by lying prone, turned another 90° to look downwards for 3 minutes. The patient then sits up and remains upright for 24–48 hours. It is 70–80% successful in posterior canal canalolithiasis. Non-responding cases may have cupulolithiasis rather than canalolithiasis (see above) and so need more vigorous and abrupt head movements during the manoeuvre (sometimes with a mastoid vibrator) to shift the debris from the cupula.

2. *Exercises.* Patients with persistent symptoms may be helped by the more traditional positional exercises. The patient deliberately assumes the provoking posture several times daily, aiming to habituate to the asymmetrical labyrinthine output.

Drug treatment

This is of limited benefit; cinnarizine probably being the most effective.

Post-traumatic vertigo

Positioning vertigo commonly follows head injury, sometimes several weeks later. It is usually caused by perilymph leak by direct trauma, e.g. with fracture in the petrous temporal bone; some cases may be caused by material dislodged from the wall of the membranous labyrinth.

Ménière's disease

Clinical features

This well-known condition is frequently diagnosed, though is actually rather uncommon. Most patients carrying the diagnosis probably have BPPV.

It usually affects people aged 30–50 years and is rare in the elderly. It is a syndrome probably with multiple aetiologies. Although the pathology of endolymphatic hydrops ('labyrinthine glaucoma') is always present, no cause is known and no specific diagnostic test exists. It remains a clinical diagnosis and characterized by the classical triad:

- Episodes of vertigo, each lasting up to one day (classically 24 minutes to 24 hours), sometimes with nausea, vomiting, pallor and sweating.
- Tinnitus, usually unilateral.
- Progressive unilateral sensorineural deafness, initially low-tone deafness but later high tone as well. Although fluctuating, there is gradual progression.

Additional symptoms include an aura of fullness or pressure in the affected ear for minutes or hours and exacerbation of deafness and tinnitus during the attack. The symptoms are only rarely bilateral. Pre-existing ear disease may predispose to Ménière's.

Management

1. Acute attacks. Treated with orally absorbed prochlorperazine.

2. Preventative treatment. Dietary salt restriction and diuretics may perhaps help. Betahistidine is the current favoured treatment; it is harmless and sometimes helpful. Long term prochlorperazine must be avoided.

3. Surgery
• Saccus decompression is a logical treatment but lacks a firm evidence base.
• Destructive procedures include operations that preserve hearing, e.g. aminoglycosides into the middle ear space, vestibular nerve section, or, as a final resort, labyrinthectomy.

Other labyrinthine causes

Other structural inner ear lesions, e.g. chronic mastoiditis or cholesteatoma may first present with vertigo. Aminoglycoside toxicity may lead to chronic vertigo.

VIII Nerve: acoustic Schwannoma

See Tumours of the central nervous system (benign). Although rare it is important to consider this possibility in every case of vertigo, deafness or tinnitus, since early intervention may prevent progressive morbidity. Characteristically a Schwannoma forms on the vestibular branch of the eighth nerve causing progressive compression of structures in the cerebello-pontine angle. Bilateral acoustic Schwannomas are characteristic of NF2.

CNS causes

1. Brainstem pathology. Brainstem involvement with multiple sclerosis, encephalitis, stroke (e.g. posterior inferior cerebellar artery thrombosis), tumour (e.g. pontine glioma) or Chiari malformation may present with vertigo. A brainstem stroke in the elderly may easily be misdiagnosed as labyrinthitis.

2. Benign vertigo of childhood. See Headache (migraine and cluster headache).

3. Basilar artery migraine. Basilar artery migraine and variants of familial hemiplegic migraine may present in young adults with recurrent vertigo.

4. Paroxysmal cerebellar ataxia. This autosomal dominant calcium channel disorder (chromosome 19p), presents as episodic vertigo and ataxia. There is overlap with familial hemiplegic migraine. Acetazolamide is often effective.

Cervical spondylosis
This is a much over-rated cause of recurrent vertigo. Although the vertebral artery may be kinked by severe cervical spondylosis, (and lead to stroke as a single devastating event), it is unlikely to cause recurrent vertigo. One must resist accepting a label of 'vertebrobasilar insufficiency' as an explanation for dizziness in the elderly.

Further reading

Anderson DT, Yolton RL, Reinke AR, Kohl P, Lundy-Ekman L. The dizzy patient: a review of etiology, differential diagnosis and management. *Journal of the American Optometric Association,* 1995; **66:** 545–8.

Baloh RW. Vestibular and auditory disorders. *Current Opinion in Neurology,* 1996; **9:** 32–6.

Epley JM. Positional vertigo related to semicircular canalolithiasis. *Otolaryngology – Head and Neck Surgery,* 1995; **112:** 154–61.

Furman JM, Jacob RG. Psychiatric dizziness. *Neurology,* 1997; **48:** 1161–6.

Saeed AR. Diagnosis and management of Ménière's disease. *British Medical Journal,* 1998; **316:** 368–72.

Related topics of interest

INDEX

Bold type indicates the main reference.

C000318682

contents

" Look out in this issue for quotations from Tennyson's
poems and Edith Wharton, *The House of Mirth*. "

Freedom of the Universe

Guest Editor Frances Macmillan

World Book Day (2nd March) 2006 saw the launch of a major new UK initiative to win reluctant readers back to books. In response to statistics such as 'seven million adults in the UK have serious problems with reading' and '33% of the population never buys a book', publishers and booksellers have come together to produce the *Quick Reads* series. Written by best-selling writers, these short, fast-paced new books will be accessible, fun and easy to read, and are specifically aimed at those with reading difficulties.

A primary aim of the *Quick Reads* series is to put pleasure back into reading and it is hoped the titles will appeal to those who are non-readers by choice, as well as those who are improving their basic reading skills. It's a worthy and important project, but no-one dares suggest we should read for anything other than pleasure. For many non-readers, the concept of reading for enjoyment is foreign enough. They have struggled through the prescribed, oppressive teaching of literature in schools, eventually turning away from books with disgust and relief. Who has told them that there is more to be found in books than 'major themes' or sentences which are useful for the 'assessment objectives'?

Jonathan Rose's *The Intellectual Life of the British Working Classes* tells the stories of many nineteenth-century 'self-educators': miners, factory workers and tradesmen who met – before the days of free schooling – to teach themselves to read. They did this partly so that they might enjoy the great works of literature. A cowman's son says:

> Here were wonderful things to know… Knowledge of this sort could make all times, all places, your own. You could be anybody, and everybody, and still be yourself all the time… Here in books was a limitless world that I could have for my own. It was like coming up from the bottom of the sea and seeing the universe for the first time.

The sense of the collective discovery of a new world, 'the freedom of the universe', as one potter puts it, runs through Rose's history. There

are many accounts of these new and voracious readers stumbling across the classics, ancient or modern, almost by mistake. Deborah Smith, a weaver and the daughter of poor, illiterate parents, found 'a wider view of life' in Tennyson, while a fourteen-year-old Durham collier hungrily consumed Walter Scott and George Eliot. That adventurous and motivating spirit is almost entirely absent from the teaching of literacy and literature today.

In *On Learning to Read*, child psychologist Bruno Bettelheim wrote about the danger of teaching reading as a skill, an end in itself:

> Mastering a technical skill such as decoding might be likened to the ability to open a door: whether one will actually open the door depends on what one believes to lie behind it. When one has received the impression that behind the door are more or less the same disagreeable things one experienced while gaining the skill to open it, there is no motivation to go on.

Behind the door is the world of books, the 'freedom of the universe', but if children are never taught that reading is the key to a kind of adventure, they will never really want to know. Some will not learn to read at all, while others learn it as a mechanical, purely necessary skill of decoding. Meanwhile, in English Literature classes, students are taught about the structure of the text they must read, how to refer to audience and language, and those remorseless 'assessment objectives' – a dissection which takes all the joy out of reading. Some pupils and teachers blame the books themselves, demanding that dusty old classics are replaced with something modern and engaging: 'Shakespeare isn't relevant; the language is too difficult; why not teach something fun?' The classics are duly prescribed like bad-tasting medicine – good for you, but extremely unpleasant to swallow. This unfortunately often backfires, resulting in the pupil developing immunity against these books, or indeed any book, for life. Judging the results instead of scrutinising the method, many will conclude that Shakespeare and the literary canon is the property of the intellectual elite, with nothing relevant, valuable or enjoyable to offer to the rest of us.

Literacy and literature have been separated in our age; we no longer improve the one in order to enjoy the other. 'Literate' now means able to read and write but until quite recently the word meant 'well-read'. This qualification of the term isn't a particularly bad thing in itself – the idea of a scale or spectrum of reading ability is more true to life – as long as the fundamental value of any level of literacy is understood.

> What is required for a child to be eager to learn to read
> is not knowledge about reading's practical usefulness, but
> a fervent belief that being able to read will open to him
> a world of wonderful experience... [for] it is faith that
> kindles one's imagination and gives one the strength to
> undertake the most difficult tasks.

Bruno Bettelheim talks about 'faith' – nowadays a loaded and dis-
comfiting word that is rarely mentioned in the teaching of literature
or literacy. But once upon a time reading was a matter of faith:
people learnt to read with the Bible because they believed being able
to read it was necessary to their salvation. The Bible was for many,
'their storybook, their treasury of words and sayings, and... their
one book of poetry' (Flora Thompson). There are numerous reasons
why the Bible is not and was not suitable as a reading aid or primer.
But the idea of reading for life's sake is vitally necessary if reading is
to be re-established as a meaningful activity. The *Quick Reads* cam-
paign has a lot to accomplish.

But the campaign can take inspiration from a Reader project
already in existence. About the same time the initiative was
announced in October 2005, participants of the Get Into Reading
(GIR) project were celebrating its first birthday, and the receipt of
a £100,000 grant from the Paul Hamlyn Foundation which would
allow the programme to continue for a further two years. Devised
and set up by The Reader, the original aim of the project was at
once modest and impressively bold: to set up 13 reading groups in
Wirral's most deprived communities, and to improve people's lives
with books. The achievements of Get Into Reading's pilot year are
too localised to show up on any government surveys, but they are
unquestionably convincing, heartening and real.

Take the case of Pauline (not her real name), who joined the
Book at Breakfast group on Merseyside's Woodchurch estate:

> I had a really bad time with books. I'd never have both-
> ered with Shakespeare after leaving school. Our teacher
> thought we were 'thickos' and he never bothered to
> explain the plays, so I thought they were rubbish. Now
> we're reading *The Winter's Tale*, next month it's *Bleak
> House*. This is what I've been waiting for.

Pauline's group includes young mothers like herself, but also octo-
genarians and nurses on their way home from the night shift. Some
members come for companionship, others for respite – an hour or
two 'off', while some come simply to listen. The group is, in Pauline's

words, 'for everyone'. There are very few cultural activities (watching sport is another one) where professionals and beginners, readers and non-readers are all in the same position, starting from the same place, experiencing the same activity. The books are always central to the discussion, and there are no time-constraints, no exams or tests, no right or wrong way of responding. 'Difficult' texts are tackled seriously and with pleasure, and reading is no longer a meaningless chore. Even the absolutely non-literate can participate as the books are read aloud and all you have to do to join in the discussion is listen.

Or take the case of Sally (not her real name), who had in the past experienced terrible problems at school – she suffers with dyslexia. However, Sally had two small children and felt that in not being able to read to them she was missing something important. Sally met a GIR staff member for one-to-one sessions once a week for nearly a year. At each meeting the project worker would read a poem or short story out loud while Sally followed, pausing now and then to talk over what they had read. Over the course of the year Sally became involved with reading for her own sake, not just for the sake of her children. In her own words, she has 'discovered the world of books'.

Sally and Pauline are only two individuals, but there are over 100 like them as a result of Get Into Reading's pilot year, and over 600 one-off beneficiaries. A total of 20 reading groups were established, in libraries and community centres; their members include YMCA residents, recovering drug abusers, isolated mums and carers. As one group member wonderingly put it, 'You need it, but you don't know you need it'.

The support provided by Get Into Reading groups goes beyond reading aid. Because a lot of what is being read is 'great literature' – demanding, complicated, truthful – the books can be seen to provide a language through which reading group members can encounter personal problems and challenges. It is an indirect, 'safe' way of tackling experiences that would otherwise seem overwhelming, looking at them from distance, but face on. For many group members, it is a new experience to *recognise* in a work of literature the same intricate emotional world they live in from day to day. Even more of a surprise when the book's age or use of language should mean it is entirely alien. It is a liberating experience, breaking down many different sorts of barriers – time-travelling from a library in North Birkenhead to 'all times, all places'.

Ruskin's Organic Vision

Alan Davis

Drawing is a risky pastime. John Ruskin discovered its dangers while trying to draw an aspen at Fontainebleau in 1842, and he recalled the incident in his old age:

> Languidly, but not idly, I began to draw; and as I drew, the languor passed away: the beautiful lines insisted on being traced, – without weariness. More and more beautiful they became, as each rose out of the rest, and took its place in the air. With wonder increasing every instant, I saw that they 'composed' themselves, by finer laws than any known of men. At last the tree was there, and everything that I had thought before about trees, nowhere.

This experience changed Ruskin profoundly, and we can see its effect by looking at two of Ruskin's drawings. He drew the first one – *Watendlath Tarn* – when he was nineteen, a few years before the Fontainebleau moment. It's a very neat and tidy piece of work – a safely conventional and respectable article that can be admired for its craftsmanship and polish. The second drawing is a *Tree Study*, from 1845. It doesn't seem to have been made by the same artist. Its pencilled lines are strangely wild; the grey washes are brushed in expressively but roughly, with no attempt at neatness. The whole picture looks unfinished and imperfect, and the mysteries of its shadows are unsettling. There are loose ends everywhere. It looks as if the lid has come off something beautiful but dangerous. Many years later, Ruskin chose a special word to describe this quality – so evidently present in the *Tree Study*, and so absent in *Watendlath Tarn*. He called it 'savageness'.

There are some other differences worth looking at. Going back to *Watendlath Tarn*, we can't help but notice that the pencilled marks, however skilfully done, are repetitive and formulaic. Everywhere, Ruskin has used a particular type of mark for suggesting foliage; and another, always, for rocks; and another, similarly, for water. But the marks in the *Tree Study* are quite different. They're fluid, non-repetitive, and experimental. Leaves in one part of the drawing are not handled in the same way as leaves in another part.

The mark-making is richly various; unpredictable. Ruskin chose a special word for this quality too. He called it 'changefulness'.

Watendlath Tarn reproduced by permission of the Ruskin Foundation (Ruskin Library, University of Lancaster)

   In *Watendlath Tarn*, Ruskin approaches the landscape with a series of conventional notions about nature and beauty, and he adjusts its features to suit his preconceptions. The lines he draws are imposed on the landscape, not abstracted from it. The *Tree Study* is essentially different: the movement of his pencil is inspired by the natural grace of the organic forms, and his lines owe their beauty to the curves and relationships that he perceives among the stems and branches. Ruskin would later call this quality 'naturalism'.

   These three concepts – savageness, changefulness and naturalism – are fundamental to Ruskin's vision of nature and art, although it took him ten years after the Fontainebleau experience to identify them. What he'd seen at Fontainebleau transformed his whole notion of what drawing was and could be: from something safe, known and predictable, to something risky, searching and limitless. After Fontainebleau, his drawings became more like the recordings of experiments in perception than exercises in picture-making, as he sought to discover more about the underlying rhythms of the natural world that he'd perceived while drawing the aspen. Paul Walton's description of this

Tree Study reproduced by permission of the Ruskin Foundation (Ruskin Library, University of Lancaster)

quest, in his book on Ruskin's drawings, is the best I know. Ruskin interpreted these rhythms, Walton writes, 'as visible signs of an impulse that moves everywhere, in accordance with the divine law':

> Ruskin now saw this vital current widespread, so that to his eyes, nature was no longer a more or less haphazard collection of forms, waiting to be transformed by the artist into images of ideal harmony, but a living organism shaped from within by forces that imposed a common harmonious visual rhythm on rock, and cloud, and wave. From now on this rhythm was to be, for Ruskin, the essence of beauty, and at the same time, the essential truth of nature.

Ruskin's drawings were made not for their own sake, but for the enhanced perceptions that accompanied their making – perceptions of something behind or beyond the obvious material facts. In the 1870s, with the experience of three decades of intensive drawing to support him, he recommended the practice to his Oxford students – not to acquire a polite accomplishment, but to gain the kind of insight that has mystical implications:

> Having learned to represent actual appearances faithfully, if you have any human faculty of your own, visionary appearances will take place to you which will be nobler and more true than any actual or material appearances; and the realization of these is the function of every fine art, which is founded absolutely, therefore, in truth, and consists absolutely in imagination.

Ruskin recorded different aspects of his perceptual travels in his diaries and sketchbooks, and the nature of these personal, private drawings is often surprising. Sometimes they are almost abstract, abandoning surface detail in order to probe more deeply into the essence of things. His drawings can seem as organic as the objects that he studies, taking on an inner life of their own. One of his most accessible books, *The Elements of Drawing* (1857), gives some insight into why this is so:

> Try always, whenever you look at a form, to see the lines in it which have had power over its past fate and will have power over its futurity. Those are its *awful* lines; see that you seize on those, whatever else you miss.

Elements is a very autobiographical guide to drawing. Ruskin invites his reader to tread a path very similar to the one he followed himself,

and he doesn't hesitate to point out the profound nature of some of the discoveries that can be made. He writes, for example, of three aspects of the natural world that should be discerned by anyone hoping to make a good landscape drawing. There is

> first, the organic unity; the law ... which rules the masses of herbs and trees, of rocks, and clouds, and waves; secondly, the individual liberty of the members subjected to these laws of unity; and lastly, the mystery under which the separate character of each is more or less concealed.

All three must be perceived and expressed if the drawing is to be successful.

Ruskin's study of nature was conducted alongside his study of Gothic architecture, and sometimes in his diaries it isn't obvious how to distinguish the two. Drawings of trefoil Gothic arches are found intermingled with plant studies. In one example, he sketches a trefoil arch loosely around the structure of a growing plant, but it isn't clear whether the form of the arch inspired the plant drawing within, or whether the structure of the plant inspired the sketching of the arch around it. In drawings like these, Ruskin was working towards some of his deepest insights concerning art and nature. They were to find expression in what William Morris would describe as 'one of the very few necessary and inevitable utterances of the century': 'The Nature of Gothic'.

It's here, in this central chapter of *The Stones of Venice*, that Ruskin formally identifies those three fundamental qualities or characteristics that were so useful in discussing the differences between *Watendlath Tarn* and the *Tree Study*. (He identifies six altogether, but the first three are by far the most important.) Curiously, he didn't coin these terms in relation to the art of drawing, but to Gothic architecture. 'Savageness', he explains, arises from the necessary imperfections that will be found in any great work of art, and these imperfections arise from two causes. First, Ruskin's great artist will always stretch his art to its limits because his art is growing: 'no great man ever stops working till he has reached his point of failure'. But also, imperfection will inevitably arise because it

> is in some sort essential to all we know of life. It is the sign of life in a mortal body, that is to say, of a state of progress and change.

Savageness is an essential quality of life and, therefore, of art. The demand for perfection, Ruskin observes, 'is always a sign of a mis-

understanding of the ends of art'. When he wrote this, he'd come a long way from *Watendlath Tarn*.

'Changefulness' is the antithesis of repetition or order. Do not let us suppose, Ruskin writes, 'that love of order is love of art'. Great art 'does *not* say the same thing over and over again'. There is no formula. It isn't repeatable. And 'Naturalism' is the quality possessed by work that has involved 'the loving and attentive examination of every natural fact which came within its range'. It isn't the imitation of natural detail that makes great art; what counts is an awareness of the underlying essence – of the abstracted, organic forms. We may find ourselves admiring a work of art because 'its lines are nobly arranged, and of noble character', even though we 'may not have the slightest idea for what the forms are intended, whether they are of man or beast, of vegetation or drapery'.

Part of Ruskin's tragedy is that in pursuit of the implications of his organic vision of the world, he was led into a labyrinth that was inescapable. By 1860 he had reached an understanding that art and the natural world and the workings of an ideal society were each subject to the same laws, with the only true value being life itself – but his vision had become overwhelming in its complexity. If you try to link everything to everything else – as Ruskin did in the fifth and final volume of *Modern Painters* – you're heading for trouble, because the process is endless. Some years later, in a letter to his friend Charles Eliot Norton, Ruskin tried to explain how the nature of his task had defeated him. In bringing *Modern Painters* to a close, he had attempted to demonstrate the multiple layers of relation and meaning in J.M.W. Turner's series of engravings called the *Liber Studiorum*. He observed how

> every touch in these plates is related to every other, and has no permission of withdrawn, monastic virtue, but is only good in its connection with the rest, and in that connection infinitely and inimitably good; – and the showing how each of the designs is connected by all manner of strange intellectual chords and nerves with the pathos and history of this old English country of ours; and on the other side, with the history of the European mind from earliest mythology down to modern rationalism and ir-rationalism – all this showing – which was what I meant to try for in my closing work – I felt, long before that closing, to be impossible; and the mystery of it all – the God's making of the great mind, and the martyrdom of it, and the uselessness of it all for ever, as far as human eyes can see or thoughts travel. All these things it is of no use talking about.

But there is no need to allow Ruskin's personal despair to devalue the importance of his organic vision. As Robert Hewison once wisely put it: to learn from Ruskin we need to follow him into the labyrinth, but we have to find our own way out; and in 'The Nature of Gothic', Ruskin has left us a kind of toolkit which can help us do that. The concepts of savageness, changefulness, and naturalism possess a significance that even Ruskin himself may not have fully recognised. They are archetypal in nature – fundamental to art, and to its relationship with the natural world. With Ruskin's organic toolkit at our disposal, we can enrich and illuminate our personal experience of a wide variety of art forms in ways that Ruskin could never have contemplated.

Bernard Leach, for example, was the most influential studio potter of the twentieth century. To look at a Leach pot with Ruskin's concepts of savageness, changefulness and naturalism in mind is to see it with deepened understanding; and the concepts are implicit, if not named, in some of Leach's writings about his art. 'It is the uniformity of perfection that kills', he states – and in so doing succeeds in getting the ideas of changefulness and savageness into a single sentence. Unlike the modern industrial process that aims to make every plate of a dinner service identical, the Leach approach is to begin each pot as though it were the first of its kind. No two 'leaping salmon' vases by Leach are the same. The slashing brushstrokes that define the 'salmon' shapes are rough, like living things, and ever changeful. The shapes formed by the brush are virtually abstract, yet they capture the essence of the salmon's leap. Leach recalled how, when first trying to produce decorative motifs for his pots with his friend the Japanese potter Tomimoto, they would

> go out to nature looking for simple forms in birds, clouds, leaves or flowers which could be seized upon with a few swift lines conceived as brushwork, inlay, slip-trail, or sgraffito. What we sought to capture from nature was some small but significant portion of the beauty we had seen; but only when it no longer imitated the external object and acquired an irreducible related form of its own did either of us feel that we had begun to discover a way towards making living patterns.

This is Ruskinian naturalism; it can be recognised in the decoration of almost any Leach pot.

Abstract art has been with us for nearly a century, though it can still arouse deep suspicion. The abstract work even of a highly respected Royal Academician like Sandra Blow can seem unap-

proachable to many, for whom it seems to resemble nothing in nature; there may seem to be no way of grasping it; no way of relating it to anything recognisable. As far as I'm aware, Ruskin's thought has had no influence on her art at all, yet to deduce that there is no connection with Ruskin's ideas would be fundamentally wrong.

A picture by Sandra Blow often employs a mixture of media, including collage elements, and it's enlightening to discover how this comes about. In the course of developing a work, the artist is in search of what she calls a 'startling rightness' – a composition in which all parts of the picture work together in a dynamic and coherent way. (She speaks of this interdependence as being almost biological; Ruskin would call it 'The Law of Help'.) The moment this condition of rightness is reached, the picture is finished. It may be that at this stage the work contains alarmingly rough elements: a torn piece of hessian, carefully placed; or an experimental smudge of charcoal. No matter: once the 'rightness' is achieved, the hessian, or the smudge, must stay. There's nothing to gain and everything to lose by tidying up those loose ends, because this is Ruskinian savageness. It's here that we meet the difference between true and false finish in art, as Ruskin identifies it. This is the kind of imperfection that is 'the sign of life', which is 'a state of progress and change', and to smooth it away, to neaten it, will result in less truth, not more. In art, Ruskin observes, we should 'never imagine there is reason to be proud of anything that may be accomplished by patience and sand-paper'.

Blow's abstract art, then, is savage. It's also changeful. Every new picture is treated by the artist as a new exploration. There are recurring themes in Blow's art, and developments of them, but there's no trace of formula; there's no predictability. This is an artist who has spoken passionately of

> that extraordinary sense of shedding everything, of leaving all the known tracks. And then just looking for something that could be my own, of interpreting the actual structure of painting which seemed to connect with abstract art – structure and space – and finding my own language in it.

So here, at the heart of the work of one of Britain's finest abstract painters, we find two of Ruskin's archetypal concepts. What about naturalism?

Sandra Blow acknowledges two fundamental sources of inspiration. One is art; the other is nature. She delights in the beauty and construction of leaves and flowers, and in places where she can

enjoy great sweeping, undulating lines of moorland scenery. But place as we experience it, she explained in an interview,

> is not something that is entirely visible. In a way, place is made up of a combination of the visible and the invisible. I chose to make visible the hidden principles of nature.

She paints what she describes as the 'push and pull' of the natural world; the counterpoised forces that hold things together. Her pictures are not imitations of nature, but they are constructed from principles that she discovers in nature. The pleasure we take in them has been described by the critic Mel Gooding as the same kind of pleasure that we enjoy when we marvel at a dry stone wall, or a balancing act.

Such art has Ruskinian naturalism embedded at its core. It is rooted so deeply in the natural world that it becomes almost an extension of it. Blow's perceptions of 'the hidden principles of nature' are the very reasons why Ruskin would have us draw: 'visionary appearances will take place to you which will be nobler and more true than any actual or material appearances', he promises. The sense of rightness we get from Blow's strokes of paint or strips of collage is fundamentally Ruskinian because her use of them is based on a lifelong awareness of the forms and rhythms of the natural world. Her compositions are 'nobly arranged, and of noble character' even though we do not have 'the slightest idea for what the forms are intended'.

Sandra Blow and Bernard Leach are not special cases. I've just finished arranging an exhibition at the Ruskin Library in Lancaster, to demonstrate how an understanding of Ruskin's organic vision can illuminate a wide variety of art forms. The structure of the Ruskin Library is perfect for the job. It has two long public galleries joined in the middle by a short corridor. The first gallery tells the story of Ruskin's organic quest, through his books, drawings, diaries, and sketchbooks. Then, armed with the key components of the Ruskin toolkit, visitors can move into the second gallery, which offers a diverse display of ancient Chinese ceramics, British studio pottery, abstract works by Sandra Blow, Terry Frost, Wilhelmina Barns-Graham and S.W. Hayter – and there's even a cabinet devoted to the performance art of Bob Dylan. It was a risky enterprise, but the response of most visitors has been one of surprisingly ready acceptance. If you hold those archetypal qualities of savageness, changefulness and naturalism firmly in your mind, and then surround yourself by unfamiliar works of art that manifestly exhibit them to a generous degree, it seems that all kinds of perceptual barriers can dissolve almost immediately.

The 'ancient world' that Ruskin inhabits isn't something to be indulgently nostalgic about, or to leave to the scholarly discourse of academics. Nothing could be more misleading than the outward appearance of those old, dull, olive-green volumes of Ruskin that lie in dusty neglect on the shelves of secondhand bookshops. If you want a quiet life you'd better not risk opening one, because reading Ruskin puts us in contact with a living force that releases the past, pulsing and vibrant, into the present. And speaking of the present – I was in the Ruskin Library this afternoon, showing a group of people around the exhibition (which is still on display as I write this). After they'd gone, I stood in the second gallery, surrounded by more than a thousand years of art, ranging from a terracotta horse of the Tang dynasty to an abstract collage made last year by Sandra Blow. I looked around, tingling with the sense of the rich complexity of it. It could so easily be overwhelming, and it very nearly is; but with Ruskin's help we can become aware of the tough, deep roots that link all of it together, nourished from a common source – savage, changeful, and very much alive.

A Poem by
Carol Rumens

Second Heart
(for Isabella Patston)

I grope back;
Tearing through the web of sixty years –

My webbed, sixty-years-old, beginning-to-tear hand –

Past the spinning figures
Of the nearly-young, who jump away
To the trembling edges, afraid,
A little afraid they might see themselves inside it.

But my hand's not clawed, its feelers are pianissimo,

Scaling the shyness of a broken chord,
Light as shed skin-cells,
Till it meets, swimming along the Milky Way,
A fist that splashes, spangles,

Shows its span of miniature iris-bloom nails,
Polished by barely sixty dawns – and not a single crime
Under the faintly-inscribed, articulate,
Sea-clean, shrimp-shell fingers.

New Hand doesn't fear Old Hand,
But seizes it and smothers it – as much of it as she can –
In a bone-gummed, lippy slobber
Until it almost melts,
Melts into mouth, into baby –

Little Oblomov,
The doing-years done, wrapped up,

Painter of eyes, grasper of nettles, money-masseuse,
Reviser of stories – my hand

Folded away in the dream-time,
Practising dunes and tunnels, branchy sleep-forms –
A webby, double-chambered, pulsing, sci-fi organ

That thrills awake to what pulls
Against it, the fat sea
At the slip-down shore, the sea-anemone

That's almost solid tongue – my hand, licked clean,
New-born, with a small second heart.

Phantom Pain

David Constantine

Yes, she said, I'm the last. That's why it's only neighbours coming to fetch me, I've got no relatives, I'm the last.

Mother didn't seem to want to drink any more so I took the plastic beaker out of her right hand and set it down on the tray. The hand remained on the bedspread, the fingers still enclosing the space vacated by the beaker. I believe I noticed that. Then I forgot.

Your mother doesn't say much, does she, said the woman in the next bed. No, not now, I answered. She used to though. She used to be a great talker. Well she's a very nice lady, the talkative woman said. I can tell you that. She was sitting up straight on the bed, not in it, and watching down the corridor for the neighbours coming to take her home. I don't belong here, she said. I belong in Salford. I was on holiday, would you believe it.

I was holding my mother's left hand in my left hand and stroking it with my right. I was looking into her face and wishing she would look at me but she had her eyes on the corridor where there was the usual coming and going. At least she is paying attention, I said to myself, and her eyes look almost the same as they always did, very beautiful, but sunk in under the bone of the sockets now, sunk deep in, far back under the bony hood, and from back there still watching. And I was supposing that none of it made much sense to her, neither the WRVS trolley arriving with tea and snacks, nor the trolley with the prone white figure on, shoving away at speed.

Yes, said the Salford woman, you get a good view from here and it's a lovely day by the looks of it. The old volcanoes, the yellow gorse, a child could draw you little hills like that, the sky so blue. A few weeks ago there was a sort of mist of bluebells in a skirt or apron around each hill, a sort of vapour that became substantial, a substantial blue, the nearer you approached. There's a castle up there, I said. You see that tower? That belongs to it, the ruins are in the place between the hills. I know, said the woman, I came here once. I was going there again last week when I took bad.

I was impressed by the old woman in the next bed, sitting so upright and holding forth. She looked rather like a watch-tower still

more or less intact, her face was big and broad with a bad complexion, quite ugly really, but you couldn't help admiring it. The two other women in the ward were fast asleep, sunk right down below the level of their bed-ends and invisible to me. Opposite the Salford woman the bed was empty. That was Mrs Williams, she said. Poor soul. So if the woman from Salford hadn't been so talkative we should have been very quiet in there, which I might have preferred, since my mother wasn't listening to her but looking at the comings and goings on the corridor. But I was listening, though I kept my eyes on my mother's face.

Yes, said the talkative woman, I'm eighty-seven and nobody left. My husband died seven years ago and he was the last. So there's only neighbours fetching me and I hope they remember to call at the B&B and collect my slacks or I'll have to leave here in my nightie with my bag of pills. You're well off for pills, I said, glancing her way. I am that, she said, and tipped them all out in her lap. These are for my thyroid, these are on account of my pacemaker... One by one she put them back in the plastic bag, each with a little rattle. Some I don't know what they're for. But they keep me going, I suppose.

I raised my left hand into my mother's line of vision. She contemplated it. I wanted her to look at me and not be watching what was going on by the nurses' desk and along the corridor all the time. And her eyes did come my way, looked into mine, and her look for a moment hesitated sadly. Then she smiled.

You'll be her son, said the talkative woman. I can see the likeness. Yes, I said, I am her son. And my wife will be along in a minute. She's gone to buy some fruit. And was that your brother and his wife come visiting yesterday? Yes, it was, I said. That would be them. She knows who you are still, I suppose? I disliked the woman from Salford when she asked me that. I saw in her face that she thought the answer must be no. So, Yes, I said, she knows who we are all right. And the day before yesterday, was that your daughter and her husband and their little boy? I can see the likeness now. Mother, son, his daughter and her son. That would be them, I said. There's no mistaking them. And I touched my mother's face so that she must look at me and listen when I said: Sam was here on Saturday, wasn't he? You remember Sam, don't you, mother? I felt the woman from Salford watching us, to be proved right that my mother did not know who we were. But her voice when she interjected was a gentle thing, woman to woman or mother to little girl, at any rate all kindness. He sang you a song, your Sam did, didn't he? He sang her a song. Stood by the bed and looked her in the eyes, she looked at him, she listened,

she watched him, there can be no doubt, he sang his song for her, two verses, concentrating, and smiled, well pleased with himself, when he was done. Enjoyed it, didn't you? the woman from Salford said. I saw her face light up. Beyond any shadow of a doubt. Her face lit up and she raised her hands, to clap. Didn't he, mother? Didn't he stand over there on your right side and look you full in the face and sing his song? She shook her head so very slightly I took the sign to be wonderment, not a negative. Wonderment. Wondering. Was it only she was wondering what on earth I meant? Or wondering was it truly as I said it was? And her hesitation, that wrings my heart, was that the passing over into the wonder of it, the wonder that he stood there by her bed and sang his song and earned her quiet applause? Again I vowed there would be no more interrogatives in my speaking with my mother, no more asking her could she remember it. From now on only the steady assertion: it happened, you were there. Fact upon fact, such a multitude I could tip out for you and fill your lap to over-flowing, all our doings together on this earth, a multitude of stories and every one of them is true. Cupping your hands in mine, you will believe me. Slightly, very slightly, she shook her head.

Yes, said the woman from Salford still waiting for her neigh-bours to come and take her home, he was a lovely boy, your little visitor, six next birthday, so they told me when I asked. He reminded me of our Michael at that age, the same clear skin and his eyes were that same dark blue. Rising six, and all we had of him was the same small number of years again.

But at that moment, distracting me from what the talkative woman had begun to broach, my mother did a very strange thing. She had looked away again to the comings and goings on the cor-ridor and I continued in my contemplation of her face, pleased by its attentiveness, saddened by its disregarding me, when suddenly all her attention lapsed, the will for it died in her, a small shudder passed through her or perhaps she shook herself very slightly as though to be rid of something, and the vacancy in her look filled up with sadness. I was about to speak, ignoring the Salford woman's broached remembrance, when my mother herself seemed to remem-ber something. Again the small shudder. And very slowly she lifted her right hand, still shaped around the absent beaker, very slowly and carefully as though she must not spill what it contained, she raised the phantom glass to her lips. It was an exact reproduction, as a silent actor might have mimed it. Then her lips felt for the rim, her hand performed the necessary tilting, and only then, as though the liquid shocked her by its palpable absence, did she halt, startled,

and seemed to wake and looked to me for an explanation and then shamefacedly she smiled.

Twice we went up there, the Salford woman continued. She was looking through the window at the two gorse hills between which, invisibly, the ruins of the castle stood. We came here for two holidays, you see. The first was after his little sister died, as soon as I was fit to travel again, my husband brought us on a holiday here, me and our Michael, the three of us, so we might begin to get over it, as he said. And the second was seven years after that, when we were as over it as we'd ever be, and we came again to the seaside here and for an outing one day climbed up again to where we had been before, between those hills. Michael was twelve then and a famous climber of rocks and other difficult places and no sooner were we in among the ruins and I was getting my breath back and getting the bit of a picnic out than Michael vanished and the next we saw of him he was up there on that hill, the near one, do you see, above the castle and far above our heads. And Father and I stood in the ruins underneath and he stood up there in the sunshine in his red shirt waving down to us and shouting, Mam! Dad! I can see them big mountains! And I was fearful and begged him to be careful and to find an easy way down and come and eat the picnic I had made. But I needn't have been fearful, he was as nimble as a monkey, and down he came in no time and hugged us, both of us, and said he'd climb all the Himalayas when he was a man. And seven days later he was dead, and it wasn't his climbing rocks and mountains I should have been fearful of.

I'm sorry, I said.

My mother's hands were lying together on the bed disconsolately. They had fallen open like a broken bowl and she was looking down at them as though they were a mystery to her. As though, if they were hers, she had no idea on earth what she might have done with them.

And now I'm the last, said the woman waiting to be taken home, and soon I'll be done with thinking about it or trying not to think about it. Our Elaine was bad, I thought she would break my heart, but she didn't, because we still had Michael, I suppose, and when we didn't have him to love for both of them then it was worse and worse. And my only comfort since it happened has been that nothing worse could ever happen. Because twelve years is a lot of life to remember, there's a deal of a lot of things will keep coming back to you as sharp as needles when you've got twelve years of a life to keep on mulling over. That picnic for one thing, up there in the ruins between them little hills, you might spend a day over

that, remembering and thinking. I used to wonder how a thing that wasn't there could hurt so much.

I'm very sorry, I said.

I mean the things he did but also the things he never did but might have done. With our Elaine, of course, there was nothing to go on, she never began, but Michael was already taking shape. He'd have been as old as you are now, I guess, you won't mind me saying so, and who knows what he might have done with the years, one friend of his became a doctor and another's an inspector in the police. I could stop myself dead on the street only suddenly thinking what he might have been. A famous mountaineer at the very least.

Then my wife arrived. She came in with the neighbours who would take the Salford woman home. No, they hadn't collected her slacks from the B&B, she would have to go out in her nightie with her stick and her pills. But you see worse sights than that in the sunshine nowadays. They sat one either side her bed, all nattering. The man said he fancied a stroll along the prom.

My wife had brought some raspberries, which she washed at the sink. Mother seemed to have forgotten her hands, she was watching my wife at the tap under the window, for her coming back. I went and borrowed a saucer from the WRVS and we put a good few raspberries in it and laid them down like that, in a soft mound, on the resting place of my mother's open hands. And from there we fed her and ourselves. They were wonderfully sharp, an acute sweetness. Her mouth received them at intervals, one by one, and between-times I suppose she forgot what the taste was like. So she smiled and widened her eyes whenever it came again.

I set the empty saucer on the tray and took my mother's empty hands in mine. Listen, I said. At home the raspberries were behind the rustic where the roses grew. You gave us a bowl and sent us to pick them for an afters when Dad came home for tea. The bowl was an ordinary white one that you used for baking. I remember pulling them off the stalk with three closed fingers and the thumb, I remember the feel of that, and how white the little stub was when the raspberry came off. We ate a lot, of course. We looked into the heart first to see if any grubs were there, and on the outside for any greenfly. And if they were clean we put them in the bowl, or ate them, as we liked. Little brother can't remember, I've asked him, but I was old enough to remember and I do.

Because that day I'm thinking of I squashed some raspberries in the palm of my left hand and with this finger on my right hand I painted a line across his throat from ear to ear, as though it had been

slit. Quite realistic, so it seemed to me. And then I slobbered his face and my own hands with juice and told him to lie across my lap and act like he was murdered. You and Dad were on the lawn by now, on the other side of the rustic, I could see you through the roses. He had just come home, he had his arm around your shoulders, and you were looking our way into the raspberries, smiling and any minute you'd be sure to come and find us. I remember that best of all, being on the very point of being found by you and what a fright you'd have and when you saw it was all a joke how you would laugh. It gave me a funny feeling between my legs.

The talk around the Salford woman's bed had stopped.

Then you and Dad came close and I stood up red-handed with my little brother in my arms all slobbered with raspberry blood and with his eyes shut tight like he was dead.

That's how it was, I said, on that occasion, mother. And the look of you went through me like a spear.

You say so, she replied. So I believe you.

Three Poems by
Richard Meier

Canute explains

What narked me, watching England
dwindle from the boat
that first time I'd invaded,
wasn't so much being forced
to retreat (humiliation
I felt quite at home with)
but that it meant missing
the looks on the faces
of those who would arrive
victorious at that shoreline
only to find their brothers
bloodied and sobbing on
the sand, scattered around them,
like the leftovers from
some outrageous banquet,
ear lobes, noses, hands.

Three years later, and king now,
I got married. Odd
how we clicked, Emma and I,
she being the old king's widow;
but she liked me, liked
teaching me what she'd learnt
about the country (she
was a foreigner too).
To my amazement, and hers,
I got into all things
English. *Even the food.*

How many hundreds, thousands,
must have been praying peacetime

would suit me too? And when
it palled – anathema
to rage – this deep, dear fund
of rage – I found myself
conquering Norway and chunks
of Sweden till there I was,
aged thirty, with the vastest
empire ever, immeasurably
unhappy.

          Hard,
isn't it, to say where
or when they start, our changes
of heart, these softenings?

Much later though, in Rome –
what a place! *Warm* for one thing
(the Pope himself had asked
me there) – and some way through
not so much a conversion,
more a kind of *becoming*,
I wrote a letter home
'To The English People'
apologising for all
the wars and shortages,
the maiming and the rape,
for the galaxy of taxes.
Everyone loved me then.

Only that made things worse.

Back home, Emma would find me
some nights in the rain
and I would try to tell her
how good it felt, standing there
for those simple, limpid
minutes rinsed of that weight
of who I was, or might be,
the whole lot washed away…
O, the humility,
the ecstasy of it!

But how to make that last?

Just once I managed to:
that notorious morning
throned there on the beach,
as if to show those toadying
nobles I was human,
or else how I was sure
the tide would stop, that I,
Canute, could command the world…

when all I wanted was
this: to prove myself
alive – to feel, in front
of witnesses, the water
rise, to embrace its cold,
to be above nothing,
level with the sea –

and for days, hours, it worked.

The Feeder

In what seemed something of a departure, you bought
me this lovely if quite demanding gift
for Christmas. After lunch I held it aloft
by various trees and fence-posts till we thought
we'd found its ideal spot, so we could watch.
Or one of us could since you'd left me by
the time, an untouched fortnight later, I
first noticed that the seed level had dropped.
Bit by bit, much like the temperature,
it then fell daily and, since one tense wren
was all I'd glimpsed come near the thing, I began
to see, topping it up, how lightly there
you'd always been and how it could sustain
me, failing love, your presence here alone.

Winter morning

Shyly coated in greys, blacks, browns –
to keep us out of sight of the cold –
we weren't expecting *this* this morning: sun

and shadows, like a summer's evening, like summer
teasing. And not quite under the shelter on
the southbound platform, an old man, the sun

behind him, just his crown ablaze; and heading
northbound, a woman inching ever nearer
the platform edge, the light a tear

across her midriff, ribcage, shoulders, closer
and closer that dearest thing, completeness,
all her darkness light at the one time.

Isaiah and Ezekiel, But What About Charley?

An Essay on 'Wanting to Believe'

Philip Davis

The Prophets Isaiah and Ezekiel dined with me, and I asked them how they dared so roundly to assert that God spake to them; and whether they did not think at the time, that they would be misunderstood, & so be the cause of imposition.

Isaiah answered: I saw no God, nor heard any, in a finite organical perception; but my senses discover'd the infinite in every thing, and as I was then perswaded & remain confirm'd that the voice of honest indignation is the voice of God, I cared not for consequences but wrote.

Then I asked: does a firm perswasion that a thing is so, make it so?

He replied: All poets believe that it does, & in ages of imagination this firm perswasion removed mountains; but many are not capable of a firm perswasion of any thing.

(*The Marriage of Heaven and Hell*)

This is William Blake, speaking in what he wills to be his own age of imagination – an age in which you could naturally *believe* in what you imagined, and not think that you *only* imagined it. But the satiric voice of the logical, rational sceptic that is also in Blake may indeed ask: 'does a firm perswasion that a thing *is* so, *make* it so?' In our emphatically post-Romantic fashion, most of us would agree that the truth of a thought is not to be measured by the subjective intensity with which it is held or asserted. The poet in Blake is able to find a freer place in his own world where, as he again puts it in *The Marriage of Heaven and Hell*, 'every thing possible to be believ'd is an image of truth' – that is to say, where everything possible to be believed holds some truth somewhere and in some way. But these days we are supicious of fundamentalism, though also worried about meaninglessness. Even if we suppose that it *is* good to have a belief, it seems

harder to do so whilst still being intelligent, tolerant and certain. As John Stuart Mill said, of his own nervous breakdown, 'To know that a feeling would make me happy if I had it, did not give me the feeling.'

You are told that 'firm perswasion' can move mountains. But – say the prophets – many are not capable of that firm persuasion. What do you do if you are not Isaiah or Ezekiel, but one of those many? It is not simply that you disbelieve: you believe in belief, its power, its confidence, but you don't seem to *have* any. How do you go about *getting* belief? And is it a belief, if you have to try to get it?

In order to be clear, I am going to call these reluctant non-believers, these sensitive, sincere and vulnerable agnostics, *Charley*, for reasons I will speak of later.

Now let's put Charley where actually he or she most belongs – not in Blake's 1790s but in George Eliot's 1850s. And now imagine Charley having to hear this, from Feuerbach's *Essence of Christianity* which George Eliot translated as Marian Evans:

> That which the unreligious man holds in his head merely, the religious man places out of and above himself as an object, and hence recognises in himself the relation of a formal subordination. The religious man has an aim. Only activity with a purpose, which is the union of theo-retic and practical activity, gives man a moral basis and support, *i.e.*, character. Every man, therefore, must place before himself a God, *i.e.*, an aim, a purpose. He who has an aim has a law over him; he does not merely guide himself; he is guided. He who has no aim, has no home, no sanctuary; aimlessness is the greatest unhappiness. An aim sets limits; but limits are the mentors of virtue. He who has an aim has a religion.

This is of course a broad and liberal version of what is a religion, of what is a God. Here with Feuerbach any aim, potentially, can be the object of belief – not just religion, but politics, money, love, private life. It seems as though you could choose your ground. But even so the pressure on Charley is severe. If you do not believe in anything, you are not a real person, your life hasn't a purpose, and you must be fundamentally unhappy. So, Charley, what do *you* believe in and what is *your* ultimate aim? No wonder our Charley believes in the importance of belief. Under such social and historical pressure, what is remarkable is not so much that Charley does not know if he has anything matching up to that belief, but that he dare admit that he may have none. What is more, these Charleys are intelligent people, not least because their intelligence is relatively free of any allegiance.

What they see is that what *unreligious* people know they have made up inside their heads, *religious* people unconsciously place outside themselves, as though to make those meanings somehow more real. We do not want to guide ourselves; we want to feel guided. That is why all our religions, all our beliefs may really be subjective fictional meanings we do not want to discover to be unconsciously fictional and subjective. We do not want to think we have made them up rather than received them as given.

There is an easy way out beckoning here, as I am sure you can see. We could say: this is the trouble with the Victorian age, this is its historical dilemma in the transition towards a more full-blown secularisation: namely, that by a vicious circle, the more the conditions for belief became unpropitious, the more the pressure to retain some version of belief symptomatically increased. The greater the fear of no-belief, the greater the pressure to produce that fiction of belief. And the greater that pressure to believe, the less chance of believing – in particular amongst those, like Charley, who wanted most sincerely to do so. For they conscientiously wanted their faith to come from within when all the pressure was from without, and had to fight against what outside forces were demanding, even as they wanted the same thing – belief – inside. Charleys want their beliefs to be neither an unconscious form of coerced and dutiful social conformity nor a fiction projected out of their own individual psychological neediness.

Was not this to set the bar too high? As Henry Scott Holland puts it, in *Lux Mundi*, looking back at his century from 1889:

> Now faith, under rapid and stormy challenges, is apt to fall into panic. For this, surely, is the very meaning of panic – a fear that feeds upon itself. Men in a panic are frightened at finding themselves afraid. So now with faith: it is terrified at its own alarm… If our faith were real faith (we say), would it ever lose its confidence? To be frightened is to confess itself false: for faith is confidence in God, Who can never fail. How can faith allow of doubt or hesitation?

And so, says Scott Holland, a whole generation has talked itself into distrusting and then abandoning faith not just because of a crisis of confidence, but more because they thought they shouldn't be having any such crisis if they were true believers. Under the pressure of over-high demands, these Charleys believed that the very fact of *having* a crisis of confidence was incompatible with belief, was already a sign of the inner failure of not believing.

I concede that it is historically true that these Victorian Charleys were placed in the intolerable position of – as Lewis Carroll might put

it – having to try to believe three impossible things before breakfast. In this I speak as someone who has tried to write a literary history of the Victorians which is also, necessarily, a history of feeling in that period. Some of my critics have said that they are not sure that I actually believe in history. And now I have to say that, in a sense, they are right. I don't believe in writing off the Victorian predicament as though it were merely historical – a post-Romantic religious hangover *en route* to the later haven of secular modernity and post-modernity. Let us not make it easy for ourselves by putting in a safe historical distance and remaining outside these concerns. To make the thought harder, to get closer to a genuine experience of the mid-century predicament, let's just suppose, instead, that for all this counter-productive pressure to believe, what the Victorian pressure was signalling might not *necessarily* be false: in other words, that not to have any belief, if that is possible, is indeed a potential disaster. This is like saying: they may have been paranoid, but they also did have real enemies at the same time. The best Victorian novels think *both* these things.

I am arguing that we should take seriously the phenomenon of 'wanting to believe' – as a position characteristically 'stuck' in between believing and not believing. What is clear is that wanting-to-believe is a secondary or second-order condition and one, moreover, which belongs not to an age of imagination so much as to an age of self-consciousness. So Carlyle writes in his great essay 'Characteristics' (1831), 'The healthy know not of their health, but only the sick'. That is to say, the sign of health is unconsciousness, a certain primary spontaneity of being and of doing. Ages of action and of heroism and of belief are not ages of moral philosophy, says Carlyle. As soon as something has ceased to be an involuntary part of a whole way of being, has had to become separately aware of itself, and has to be argued, then, says Carlyle, it is already in decline. Thus self-consciousness comes afterwards, comes second and is secondary, and is itself the sign of disease, even whilst still seeking for its own cure. Wanting-to-believe is of just that fallen condition because there would not be this want-as-desire were there not the want-as-lack.

'The healthy know not of their health, but only the sick.'

It is this second-order condition that is occupied above all in the Victorian period by Arthur Hugh Clough, aka Claude of 'Amours de Voyage'. In one of the poem's drafts, Eustace writes to his friend Claude that Claude's doubt is all too much the product of inaction, of living always in the scrupulous beforehand: 'Action involves belief,' writes Eustace, 'Act and all will be clear'. But in the final version of the poem Claude himself writes:

> *Action will furnish belief*, – but will that belief be the true
> one?
> That is the point, you know. However, it doesn't much
> matter.
> What one wants, I suppose, is to predetermine
> the action,
> So as to make it entail, not a chance-belief, but the true
> one.

It is the same here as it is in Clough's *Dipsychus* – both warn that the mid-Victorian stress on the priority on action, on the cold shower of practical duty, may have degenerated into a version of the anti-intellectual PE master of Rugby School. For what Dipsychus says is that action might be a form of giving up and selling out; that action might itself be a fear of hesitation and a flight from waiting; and thus, above all, that action ironically might be a form not of belief but of despair, sacrificing a larger hope you cannot seem to realise to a smaller practical gain you immediately can. Get on with it, throw yourself into it. But all too automatically, action *will* furnish belief and you become what you have done, not out of first principles or true belief but chance-belief and knock-on effects. The sheer autonomous rational *intelligence* of Clough is characterised by its no longer being, as it were, in time with time: intelligence is what steps out of the temporal sequence, and by the sheer force of extraordinary intellect turns time round to get at what lies behind it:

> *Action will furnish belief*, – but will that belief be the true
> one?

– and thus the intelligent one tries, even by secondary reflection upon what one *might* do, to produce what one *should* do:

> What one wants, I suppose, is to predetermine
> the action
> So as to make it entail, not a chance-belief, but the true
> one.

It is an attempt to re-create within this realm of the secondary the lost world of truth's priority, from back to front. That is to say: that if you know in advance, as a result of what has happened before in the past, that x stimulus will almost automatically produce in you y response, and you find yourself in a situation where y is what you truly know you need to offer, then this time you artificially use x stimulus to get y out of yourself.

Thus, for example, the early eighteenth-century Anglican divine

William Law advocated the use of set and external habits of devotion rather than waiting till the spirit spontaneously moved him to prayer: if we could not always get into the right religious spirit from inside-out, because of our fallen infirmities, we would have to get into it more regularly from outside-in. This was the right way for Law because he was first of all sure that that believing spirit was the true and necessary one – howsoever we fallen creatures by secondary means could get ourselves into it. But Clough was not so sure, was scared of 'factitiously' creating in himself what he might not otherwise accept. In a notebook of 1849, written partly in Rome and partly in Liverpool, Clough commented upon what he called the wrong doctrine of habits: such that by doing acts *like* those of love, we shall indeed come to love. To Clough this was mechanical habituation – getting soldiers into the way of marching by means of music, schoolboys into the way of thinking by learning off by heart, husbands into the way of loving by giving their wives flowers. The establishment of a virtuous 'hexis' or disposition, by acts of repetitive habit, was the way classically prescribed by Aristotle – but to Clough it increasingly seemed a form of what he called Victorian virtue-manufacture. For Clough was a covert Platonist, a would-be idealist who wanted to re-call, re-create and re-discover in himself in the second place only what he was certain he secretly or half-forgottenly already believed in, in the first. Yet the first did not seem to be there. He does not even love God second-hand, complains a young woman in *Wilfrid Cumbermede*, a novel of 1872 written by that great, uneven and still-neglected genius, George MacDonald. He does not even love God second-hand. To which another character replies, 'Perhaps because he is very anxious to love him first-hand.'

The person they are talking about is called Charley, Charley Osborne. And Charley is the son of a stern, remorseless evangelical. Let's not simply talk of the pressure to believe created by 'Victorian Society' – that's too easy; let's talk more intimately of the emotionally confusing form in which that goes on, the form of the parent–child relationship. As Wilfrid Cumbermede says of his friend's father:

> A good man I do not doubt he was; but he did the hard parts of his duty to the neglect of his genial parts, and therefore was not a man to help others to be good. His own son revived the moment he took his leave of us – began to open up as the little red flower called the Shepherd's Hour-Glass opens when the cloud withdraws. It is a terrible thing when the father is the cloud, and not the sun, of his child's life.

That is why there is no first base for such children, even as they grow. The father that remains in Charley *wants* to believe, as a fallen derivative of faith; but the son part of Charley cannot simply believe, and cannot even trust the wanting to, in all its mere secondariness. It is easier if you simply dish the religion with the father, but what if the father is only a confusingly *wrong* version, the twisted personal form, of what may still be *right*? 'From his father,' says Cumbermede, Charley 'had inherited a conscience of abnormal sensibility; but he could not inherit the religious dogmas by means of which his father had partly deadened, had partly distorted his.' Let's look these Victorian challenges in the face: if you don't believe in anything, if you had a poor relationship with your parents, not only do those two go together but together they mean you may be a lost person.

At any rate, Charley finally says to his friend: 'If there *were* a God – that is, if I were sure there was a God, Wilfrid!'

> I could not answer. How could I? *I* had never seen God, as the old story says Moses did on the clouded mountain. All I could return was,
> 'I suppose there should be a God, Charley! – Mightn't there be a God!'
> 'I don't know,' he returned. 'How should *I* know whether there *might* be a God?'
> 'But *may* there not be a *might be*?' I rejoined. . .
> I do not mean this was exactly what he or I said. Unable to recall the words themselves, I put the sense of the thing in as clear a shape as I can.

'*May* there not be a *might be*?' Is that *always* an easy indulgence or is it not, on the contrary, sometimes a great risk? Charley says that the worst of all possible miseries would be to believe in a lovely thing and then find that, after all, it was not true.

> 'You might never find it out, though,' I said. 'You might be able to comfort yourself with it all your life.'
> 'I was wrong,' he cried fiercely, 'Never to find it out would be the hell of all hells.'

Even while you thought it was heaven. This is Charley's impossible thought – refusing a delusion which you would not know if you had it. It is the other side of the position Clough himself for once achieved by the end of his 'Hymnos ahymnos', saying to God:

> Be thou but there, in soul and heart,
> I will not ask to feel thou art.

There are the two thoughts: I don't feel God is there but he is; I think God is there but he is not. And both of them are beyond the limits of thought, are double thoughts we cannot really think, nor wholly avoid, and need literature even to imagine. In his respect for a God he cannot believe in but will not falsify, how can it be that this Charley, potentially the most religious of persons, could not be religious at all? Is there something wrong with him or something wrong with what religion is taken to be? What do you call Charley's refusal of a comforting fiction which you might never find out to be a fiction? It is all like some preparation for something that may never happen – as if *that* might be what life itself *is* for such people whose intelligence leaves them still, scrupulously, in the realm of possibility, without decision or action.

Even in his intelligence, even in his resistance to a practical narrowing down, I call Charley still the son of his father, and I think that his honourable refusal of easy belief is almost as much a product of that father in him as his signing up for evangelicalism would be. We like to talk of Keats's 'negative capability' but I am not sure that we can or should long hold positions of sustained neutrality. There is, I grant, a cruelty involved in forcing the premature taking of sides. But, equally, there is an abuse of intellectual freedom when all it serves is a refusal of what such freedom is for. Everything is a decision at some point. We are, biologically, feeling, believing and doing creatures, with all the risks involved. It is William James who takes on the Victorian heritage in these matters, when in 1895 he writes for a talk at Harvard on W. H. Mallock's book *Is Life Worth Living?* as follows – speaking of intelligence's neutrality as finally unsustainable:

> This is because, as the psychologists tell us, belief and doubt are living attitudes, and involve conduct on our part. Our only way, for example, of doubting, or refusing to believe, that a certain thing *is*, is continuing to act as if it were *not*... If I doubt that you are worthy of my confidence, I keep you uninformed of all my secrets just as if you were *un*worthy of the same. If I doubt the need of insuring my house, I leave it uninsured as much as if I believed there were no need. And so if I must not believe that the world is divine, I can only express that refusal by declining ever to act distinctively as if it were so, which can only mean acting on certain critical occasions as if it were *not* so, or in an irreligious way. There are, you see, inevitable occasions in life when inaction is a kind of action, and not to be for is to be practically against; and in all such cases strict and consistent neutrality is an unattainable thing.

What William James offers instead of a self-damaging scrupulosity held safe in the world of literary ambiguity is the venturing position of 'as if'. In lecture 3 of *The Varieties of Religious Experience* (1902) he writes of how 'we can act *as if* there were a God; feel *as if* we were free; consider Nature *as if* she were full of special designs; lay plans *as if* we were to be immortal; and we find then that these words do make a genuine difference in our mortal life.' I call this position a venture because it involves what James calls going with ideas upon which we can ride – ideas that seem to create a vitality in us and make for a greater possible movement into a future. They are called thoughts or ideas because their 'as if' dynamically frees them from the pressure of having to be static and certain beliefs. For let us be clear about the pragmatism of these *as ifs*: they are instrumental and provisional, essays in the very process of our making ourselves do more and be more and go further than we might dare in advance. 'I am well aware,' says James in 'What Pragmatism Is', 'how odd it must seem to some of you to hear me say that an idea is "true" so long as it is profitable to our lives ... Ought we ever not to believe what it is better for us to believe?' That is the bold proposition: if it makes things better, there must be truth in it. But is not this precisely what Clough would dismiss as truth turned into comfortable convenience, as the sustaining illusion of fiction or the self-deception of fantasy? I think not: James does not simply choose a belief because it is comfort-able. His point is rather this: that if it works, there must be something in it – something literally vital because 'belief and doubt are living attitudes'. And this is why pragmatism is a venture, a narrative that replaces 'thinking before' with 'following through', a testing out of a living future for an idea, because pragmatism is not only to do with results, but with a radical change in orientation. That is to say, prag-matism is: 'The attitude of looking away from first things, principles, "categories", supposed necessities; and of looking towards last things, fruits, consequences, facts' ('What Pragmatism Is'). Not going back to check where it has come from, but going on with where it may be going to. A route therefore in which one trusts first principles to come into play as part of their biological development rather than in the anterior abstract planning.

> '*Ought we ever not to believe what it is better for us to believe?*'

In James's life, this was about a son's fight against youthful depression. As a young man, on the verge of a breakdown, he had looked at the world and wondered whether he could believe in the life it seemed to offer. The world could look like a mere machine of

which we were no more than determined parts. But James himself, evaluating life, knew he was already an element in the equation he was trying to make out in advance. And the first act of freedom might be to risk believing in freedom itself. He is writing to his past, young self when he later writes in 'Is Life Worth Living?': 'Your mistrust of life has removed whatever worth your own enduring existence might have given it.' Think of a train robbery, he says in 'The Will to Believe': a whole train of passengers may be robbed by a few highwaymen simply because the highwaymen can count on one another, while each passenger fears that if he makes a movement of resistance he will be shot before anyone backs him up. 'There are, then, cases where a fact cannot come at all unless a preliminary faith exists in its coming... *where faith in a fact can create the fact*'. That is what is wrong with taking oneself out of the account in apparent neutrality. The subject – what you are and what you make of yourself – has also its part to play in the summing of the objective. It is a great moment, a great shift from mere defeated sadness, when suddenly you realise that gift of responsibility, that second gear you can find in yourself. The difference you feel you need, for life to be worthwhile, is already there as a nascent element in you. Define life but remember that our own reactions upon the world, small as they are in bulk, are *themselves* 'integral parts of the whole thing, and necessarily help to determine the definition'; 'Believe that life *is* worth living, and your belief will help create the fact' ('Is Life Worth Living?'). Above all then, this makes wanting-to-believe not merely secondary, wistful or untrustworthy: it makes wanting-to-believe itself a form of personally risked belief – through the route created by 'as if'. It expresses belief in human 'need' not as defeat but as aspiration.

Indeed, James goes so far as to say that this personal want may be how what we call 'God' works, with God coming into being in the world through our flawed personal belief in him. Charley thinks he needs an external or higher validation for a true sense of belief. It may be we only need the imagination of such a sanction. If that is so, we couldn't at once exercise that imagination *and* be conscious that that *was* what we were doing, without returning to Charley's fear that it was fiction. It may be that it doesn't matter. What we can do for ourselves, even if we have to call that God – even if it *is* God – we must do in whatever ways we find we have to. But I say again as to Charley: these aren't thoughts that, in our limitation, we can really think. That is why I pause briefly to urge upon you two theological works that are written precisely on that very boundary of human understanding: H.L. Mansel's *The Limits of Religious Thought*, the

Bampton lectures for 1858, and the book that he acknowledges lies behind it, Bishop Joseph Butler's *Analogy* (1736).

Both these works, for all their ostensibly austere rationality, are secret books, works consisting in two parts of which only the first part is written. For the first part, written on *this* side of our limits, is about the attempt to think and the inability to accomplish the attempt. The first part is an act of reason to show reason's own limitations. This first part thus speaks to the sense that our whole consciousness is compassed about with restrictions which we are ever striving to pass, and ever failing in the effort. But the first part is also clear that the very experience of this limitation implies something on the *other* side of itself, the very inadequacy of reason pointing to some higher truth, of which it indicates the existence but does not make known the substance. And the second part? The second part if written would be mystical but is not there. The second part is left secret, implied and unwritten on the other side of the first, with everything left in place there by remaining silent about it.

The secret book might say with James that God himself allows us to create him in our own way, that whatever we creatively believe in is, as with Blake, an image of truth, however distorted or mishandled. But to Feuerbach, of course, it was always we who did it, we who made the difference, even though we have to think it is God who is responsible. We *are* God, says Feuerbach; unconsciously we made him; the divine attributes are really the best of human ones, projected upon a fictive Other. Feuerbach says to Charley or to Claude: why can't we go on now, pointing the creativity of our previously religious gifts and values no longer out towards God but back to our own purely secular, human ends?

But I am saying that we should not be too sure of what is human and what is religious, or where our best things come from. You remember where we started – that deep sentence of Feuerbach's: 'That which the unreligious man holds in his head merely, the religious man places out of and above himself as an object'. To this, William James adds one crucial consideration with which I must end. And it is this: *our real thinking is that we do not make thoughts, but thoughts in some sense come to us* that the religious person may be right about our essential experience of thinking – that it does not just exist in our heads. Of course, thinking exists in our own heads if it is merely the putting of thoughts into ready-made names and categories. But James hates *that* kind of thinking which still, I fear, dominates even the study of literature: neat, tamed, uncreative and pigeon-holingly thematic or contextual.

He loves instead what he calls 'the unclassified residuum', a literary sort of thinking which in him can go on outside literature itself. To George MacDonald, for example, in his own struggle against Charley, when a new thought arises in the mind, a person is rather *being thought* than thinking. And the best thing that Nature did for Wordsworth, says MacDonald, and that Wordsworth does for us, is to put a human being into that mood or condition or space or shape in which thoughts come of themselves. That is what finding belief might be like. For to James, our real thinking is that we do not make thoughts, but thoughts in some sense come to us, not felt as originating in ourselves, but as if a demand or a gift or a necessity from somewhere else. And such thoughts exist in us precisely to refer us towards what they stand for outside us, blurring just that boundary between the person who has them and the things they themselves point to. It is as though we are the bar of iron James describes as follows:

> It is as if a bar of iron, without touch or sight, with no representative faculty whatever, might nevertheless be strongly endowed with an inner capacity for magnetic feeling; and as if, through the various arousals of its magnetism by magnets coming and going in its neighbourhood, it might be consciously determined to different attitudes and tendencies. Such a bar of iron could never give you an outward description of the agencies that had the power of stirring it so strongly; yet of their presence, and of their significance for its life, it would be intensely aware through every fibre of its being.
> (*The Varieties of Religious Experience*, lecture 3)

So there we are, like blind and dumb things, sensing a field of forces and energies around us in which we are involved. 'All we know is that there are dead feelings, dead ideas, and cold beliefs, and there are hot and live ones; and when one grows hot and alive within us, everything has to re-crystallize about it' (lecture 9).

When the thoughts that come light up the brain as if they were beliefs, then we are in the process of seeing how important they are, by seeing how far forward they can take us, how far they can work for the making of life, what they do for us in brain and affect. When Thomas Hardy read William James's vitalist dictum, 'Truth is what works', he wrote in his notebook that a worse abuse of language had never been perpetrated: truth to Hardy was all that did *not* work. Then indeed a belief might not make for life, might be reluctantly negative, in the name of a tough truth that goes against the grain of all our warmest feelings. It is all too possible to believe that life is fallen, and that, despite ourselves, life itself remains intrinsically disappointing. That

too was part of James' struggle against depression, to work within and struggle against such considerations, to see what if anything was still resiliently left in us when we tried to accept them. Therefore I do not discount such objections. Yet at some level, James implicitly believed that belief itself always, finally, has to be a faith in an ultimate good in the universe which the very belief helps exist. Reading James really does give you just that feeling of thoughts generating live excitement, energy, heat, change – whatever the pain or difficulty of their specific content. 'As if' those thoughts were a response to something which Doris Lessing in her *Canopus in Argos* series of space fictions calls Need – Need, which includes a sense not only of neediness but also of necessity. These thoughts feel called for: that's the wager.

It is, above all, writing that is the most genuine form of thinking in terms of trying out what works. And by that I mean writing, like James's own, which does not know in advance where it is quite going, where it is taking us. James's 'as if' and MacDonald's 'might be a may-be' are syntactical instruments for a dynamic form of writing not knowing in advance the way or shape it is trying out. As one of James's own disciples, John Dewey, put it:

> Different ideas have their different 'feels', their immediate qualitative aspect, just as much as anything else. One who is thinking his way through a complicated problem finds direction in his way by means of this property of ideas. Their qualities stop him when he enters the wrong path and send him ahead when he hits the right one. They are signs of an intellectual 'Stop and go'. If a thinker had to work out the meaning of such ideas discursively, he would be lost in a labyrinth that had no end and no centre.
> (John Dewey, *Philosophy and Civilization*)

Art teaches us how to think by and through writing, in the thick of biological-mental experience. We have such trusts and trials and economies deep inside those 'feels' of ours that writing works within. Let's not try to work it all out cerebrally in advance, if that is impossible, but, Charley, try instead to follow it all through.

> So many worlds, so much to do,
> So little done, so much to be.
> Tennyson, *In Memoriam*

Three Poems by
Gary Allen

Beneath the Skin

This old man is a prophet
collar studded down
a child's round face, clean shaven.

His strong hands have swung hammers
on rivets, and heads

have pulled down the stars
and placed them on his arms

created images from wood
made flesh his presence –

and he has heard the voice of God

telling him,
This is the last child
his large eyes know his own death.

And I am a magician too grandfather

making whistles from split grass stalks
as we walk across the fields

my blood turning to devour itself

and the knowledge trapped within –
that what will kill you soon after,
took my uncle within six months,

is with me forty years on.

Leaving

I no longer fear death –
seeing its hand in everything

it has grown familiar

has become no more than a mood
the closing of love

the beginning of a theme:

the endurance in these faces
has taught me to understand again

how natural it is to fail.

It's coming through these open doorways
of island houses

stooping under low stone lintels –
how little room it takes to contain us.

Is this existence?

Thrown together on this rock
dependent on the sea

and yet the pain of uprooting
leaving the island for the uncertain boundaries

of an immense world

the closed-in skies of a tenement
the slow dying of a way of life

until nothing is left
but these stone runnels

the barely discernible back alleys
rusted iron rings, hooks, pulleys

so it is for each of us –
the cryptic sweepings of a collective life.

Smallholding

This is where it went wrong
a poxy piece of land between bog and hill

and the wind –
inhuman, hard against the barn,
cold stars
that are no good on the table.

He has no understanding, nor opinion,
on monstrous birth,
has crude feeling only for the lost profit
of death:

and what kind of midwife is this,
a knotted rope and a firm foot –

the adult child in the barred room
playing with her dolls,

she has no equation of light or halflight
a moon face at the window
everything she discerns is shadow.

His wife moving about in the byre
her hand as hard as each hide rump she slaps
ambling down the line

and the oil-lamp burns low
over the straw covered gore

what good is this to him?
the wasted hours of waiting, the hardened sweat
yet God makes it all the harder
without giving breath

no matter, he'll open the soft earth
of the poorer field
and bury it with the earlier bones.

A Leaf from
the *Exeter Book*

Stephen Pollington

The Old English (OE) verse tradition straddles ancient and modern worlds: it features lost words, forgotten grammatical structures and fossilised ideas of time and event, and yet a large part of what we find in OE verse and prose is still with us today and, with a little help, even the genuinely ancient texts can be brought back to the surface for modern readers to discover.

Deor is a fine example of a living voice from an ancient world – the poet narrating his own tale as the closing comment to a longer narrative. The theme of the poem is 'misfortune endured' or 'bad luck turned to good', and the examples of misfortune require some background knowledge to be appreciated. For that reason we're going to look closely at only the closing section – the poet Deor's summing up – but I offer a translation of the whole poem and a summary of the tales which stand behind it so that interested readers can get a feel for the sound and pace of the Old English world.

The text of Deor is included in the Exeter Book, a miscellany of English verse compiled at the end of the tenth century and presented to the cathedral of Exeter by Bishop Leofric shortly before his death in 1072; it has been there ever since. It was described in an inventory as .i. mycel englisc boc be gehwilcum þingum on leoðwisan geworht 'one large English book concerning various matters expressed in verse'. (More on those unfamiliar characters þ and ð shortly.) The manuscript is written in a fine, neat hand and the scribe is known to have been responsible for at least one other surviving manuscript. The Exeter Book was not always accorded the honour such an ancient tome deserves: the book shows evidence of having been used as a beer-mat and a chopping-board at various points in its career. The first and last sections have suffered the greatest damage, and a whole middle section seems to be missing. I have stood in front of the locked cabinet where the great work resides, and experienced the thrill of examining it at first hand – the finest hair's breadth pen strokes are visible, the trace of a feather quill and oak-gall ink set down in a Wessex scriptorium some forty lifetimes ago.

Concerning the language, there is scope for misunderstanding. 'Old English' is not modern English dressed up in funny writing, or casually misspelt: 'Ye Olde Tea Shoppe'. It is a Germanic language, with close surviving relatives in Dutch and Frisian. From OE are derived both Modern English and *Lallans*, the language of lowland Scotland. (The works of Rabbie Burns are not composed in a dialect of English, but a sister-language.) The Germanic group of languages have a written history extending back to the first century AD, and by various arcane processes even earlier forms can be traced back to the language of the first farmers in Europe, some 6,000 years ago. From that ancient speech are derived the many early languages of Europe and Asia (Latin, Greek, Sanskrit, Iranian and Celtic among others) and their descendants.

The earliest records of the Germanic group are in various Latin authors – odd words recorded by Caesar and Tacitus – but there is a native written tradition in the script known as runes, which is probably based on a rustic form of Latin script acquired through trade or military contact with the Empire. The earliest English texts are simple runic formulae, mostly found in eastern England on items buried with their dead owners. Our main records of OE date from after the conversion to Christianity, a process begun in the early 600s and substantially complete by the end of that century. English began to be recorded in Roman script and a characteristic handwriting style developed in English scriptoria. The letter forms are not so very different from those we use today:

Ƿelunð him be ƿurman ƿræces cunnaðe, anhýðiȝ eorl earfoþa ðreaȝ,

Welund him be wurman wræces cunnade, anhydig eorl earfoþa dreag,

Some of the characters are taken over from runic script, such as Ƿ for 'w' and þ for the sounds we write 'th', also written ð. The ligature æ was used for the vowel in 'cat'.

Old English is so engaging because it is both Old and English. Quite a lot of it is very familiar – *he, we, me, us, him; in, on, under, hand, wrist, man* are all spelt now as they were a thousand years ago, and many other words are substantially unchanged: house (*hus*), mouse (*mus*), boat (*bat*), ship (*scip*), arm (*earm*), ear (*eare*), tongue (*tunge*), hair (*her*), bed (*bedd*), board (*bord*), drink (*drinc*), sleep (*slæp*), wake (*wac*), strong (*strang*), short (*sceort*). Other aspects of OE are probably known to users of the modern language who have learnt another

tongue – things like grammatical gender and case assignment. But here again we return to the notion of its antiquity – there are modes of expression bound up in Old English that are really ancient, which the language shares with its distant European cousins.

The poetry needs some introduction. The verse tradition of the early English was rather different from our mediaeval-to-modern inheritance. Verse was regarded as a particularly rigid and formal kind of speech, but not as fundamentally different from prose – indeed, there are early English writings which approach the verse tradition in the choice of words and in metrical patterning, but which are not as tightly constructed as formal verse; this is no doubt what an early English audience expected of highly polished diction. Verse was never written out with separate lines, punctuation or end-stops. Neat end-rhymed lines with constant rhythm do not feature at all – there is no tum-ti-tum-ti-tum-ti-tum to guide us through the text. OE verse is instead built around a line which consists of four stressed syllables and it is on these that the metrical constraints operate; unstressed syllables are generally not counted. (This is the tradition that G.M. Hopkins looked back to with his sprung rhythm – poetry for the ear rather than the eye: 'Thou mastering me / God! giver of breath and bread; / World's strand, sway of the sea'.) The distribution of the syllables gives the verse its rhythm and power, but this rhythm is derived from normal speech – and Old English was stressed very much as modern English is.

There were five permissible rhythmic patterns for the line, such as 'loud-soft-loud-soft' (e.g. 'Winston Churchill'), 'loud-soft-soft-loud' ('Baskerville Hall') and 'loud-loud-soft-soft' ('Jim Callaghan'). The 'soft' syllables could be up to four in number, and the loud (stressed) syllables had to be metrically heavy, but there are occasional exceptions to these rules.

The main binding element is not the rhythm of the lines – with such a loose allowance of unstressed, 'soft' syllables this would not be possible – but rather the alliteration, what Tolkien called 'head-rhyme'. The third stressed syllable must alliterate with one or both the previous two, but the fourth must not. An example alliterating on 'd' from our poem (stressed syllables underscored) would be _dryhtne dyre, me wæs Deor noma_. Think of Gandalf on the frozen mountain path answering Saruman's curse.

OE texts are usually written in West Saxon, the language standard associated with the court of Winchester. However some OE verse shows traces of a different dialect, the Mercian of the Midlands, which enjoyed some prestige as the language of choice for

poetic composition. Some texts show signs of having been composed in Mercian, then quietly but imperfectly corrected to the West Saxon standard in copying.

The poem known by the modern title *Deor* is unique in surviving OE verse in having a refrain at the end of each section or tale: 'That went by, so may this' (*þæs ofereode, þisses swa mæg*). Apart from its stoic beauty, the refrain has one other great value for the translator: it is possible to tell where the sections and sentences begin and end – often an impossibility in OE poems. I give below a fairly free translation of the major part of the poem, but for the final personal section I have used a more detailed approach to convey, I hope, some of the joys and problems of translation from Old to Modern English. The succession of tales the poet relays were known to the Anglo-Saxon audience of the poem – intimately, we must assume, as the allusions are all rather brief. Interestingly, the tales are not generally English, in the sense that they do not concern England, but rather they are drawn from the semi-legendary history of the English people, so that *Deor* is more than an accurate portrayal of the world; it is a conjuring of the poet's inner stock:

Deor

Welund him be wurman wræces cunnade,
anhydig eorl earfoþa dreag,
hæfde him to gesiþþe sorge ond longaþ,
wintercealde wræce; wean oft onfond,
siþþan hine Niðhad on nede legde,
swoncre seonobende on syllan monn.
þæs ofereode, þisses swa mæg!

Among snakes Wayland came to know exile,
The steadfast hero underwent miseries,
Had sorrow and longing as his companions,
winter-cold wretchedness – he often found woes
once Niðhad laid constraints on him
supple-sinew-bonds on the better man.
That went by, so may this.

Wayland the Smith, whose smithy, a Neolithic long-barrow, stands on the Berkshire Downs, was a figure of Germanic legend. In one tale, he was captured by King Niðhad, lamed and imprisoned on an island where he had to create great treasures for his new master. But things change. Wayland was 'the better man': he fashioned a pair of wings and flew away but only after exacting a terrible revenge

on his captor – as we learn in the next verse. But before going on, look at those long compound phrases: 'winter-cold wretchedness', 'supple-sinew-bonds', plain words hewn and tethered in a way that is characteristic of the OE style – bleakly, tersely telling.

> *Beadohilde ne wæs hyre broþra deaþ*
> *on sefan swa sar swa hyre sylfre þing,*
> *þæt heo gearolice ongieten hæfde*
> *þæt heo eacen wæs; æfre ne meahte*
> *þriste geþencan, hu ymb þæt sceolde.*
> *þæs ofereode, þisses swa mæg!*

> Her brothers' death was not to Beadohild
> So great a pain in the heart as her own matter
> Which she had readily understood,
> that she was with child – she could not ever
> reflect with hope how that should turn out.
> That went by, so may this.

Wayland's revenge was fearsome. The king's daughter, Beadohild, came to the smith with her small brothers to negotiate the making of a piece of jewellery, but Wayland drugged her, killed the boys and raped her. When she knew she was pregnant by the killer of her brothers – an intolerable situation in the story of feuding kinsfolk – she simply despaired. But things change. Her child, Widia, grew up to be one of the greatest heroes of the Germanic world.

> *We þæt Mæðhilde monge gefrugnon*
> *wurdon grundlease Geates frige,*
> *þæt hi seo sorglufu slæp ealle binom.*
> *þæs ofereode, þisses swa mæg!*

> We have heard that the complaints of Mæðhild
> were ceaseless; Geat's loved one
> So that sleep took away all that sorrowful love.
> That went by, so may this.

This tale refers to a maid, Mæðhild, who was foretold her own death at the hands of a water-demon; on her wedding day she was on a bridge which collapsed and she was thrown into the river and appeared dead or sleeping. But that changed, she was revived by the harping of her new husband, Geat.

> *Þeodric ahte þritig wintra*
> *Mæringa burg; þæt wæs monegum cuþ.*
> *þæs ofereode, þisses swa mæg!*

> For thirty years Þeodric had
> The stronghold of the Mærings; that was known to many.
> That went by, so may this.

Theodric was a young son of King Clovis of the Franks, who ruled at Rheims in the early sixth century. His rule was 'known' to many as a time of great hardship in which certain nobles were expelled into exile; but that changed: on his death these nobles returned to reclaim their inheritance.

> *We geascodan Eormanrices*
> *wylfenne geþoht; ahte wide folc*
> *Gotena rices. þæt wæs grim cyning.*
> *Sæt secg monig sorgum gebunden,*
> *wean on wenan, wyscte geneahhe*
> *þæt þæs cynerices ofercumen wære.*
> *þæs ofereode, þisses swa mæg!*

> We have heard of Eormanric's
> Wolfish mind, he had wide rule
> Of the Goths' kingdom – he was a grim king!
> Many a man sat bound with sorrows –
> Woes his expectation – often wished
> That the king's reign were overthrown.
> That went by, so may this.

Eormanric of the Goths was at first a great ruler who extended his domain across eastern Europe. But that changed, his grip on his folk grew ever tighter and he ceased to listen to his advisers, gaining a reputation for cruelty and greed. His power was destroyed by an attack of the Huns in 375 AD.

Now we reach the poet Deor's personal conclusion to the piece. To show the process of translation, I've included first a literal, grammatical transliteration of the OE, and then a more fluent modern-sounding version, with occasional notes to follow. Because it may be hard to follow, at the very end there's an uninterrupted reading text that puts the lines of the poem back together:

> *Siteð sorgcearig, sælum bidæled,*
> Sitteth sorrow-caring, [from] joys separated
> 'he sits, sorrowful at heart, bereft of joys'

Sorgcearig is 'sorrow – care-y', weighed down with sorrow. *Bidæled* is based on *dæl*, both 'deal' and 'dole', which was originally 'cut up and share out'; *bedæled* is therefore 'cut off from'.

on sefan sweorceð, sylfum þinceð
in mind darkeneth, [for] himself thinketh
'his mood darkens, (as) he considers about himself'

þæt sy endeleas earfoða dæl.
that may be endless [the] deal of troubles
'that his dole of troubles may be endless'

mæg þonne geþencan, þæt geond þas woruld
may then think that across this world
'he is then able to understand that, throughout this world'

þencan is 'to think'; the prefix *ge-* makes the sense perfective 'think as far as one may, reach a conclusion'

witig dryhten wendeþ geneahhe,
wise lord wendeth often
'the Lord in his wisdom often changes (things)'

Witig means 'having *wit*' or understanding, not quite the same as 'witty' today. 'Wend' means 'move, move on, go along' and so 'change'; its past tense is 'went' (as 'sent' to 'send') which has replaced the older word 'yede' as the past tense of 'go'.

eorle monegum are gesceawaþ,
[to] many [an] earl honour showeth
'shows honour to many a good man'

wislicne blæd, sumum weana dæl.
wise-seeming fame, [to] some of woes [a] dole
'fame for wise thought (but) to another (he shows) a deal of troubles'

þæt ic bi me sylfum secgan wille,
that I about myself to say will
'I wish to say this concerning myself'

þæt ic hwile wæs Heodeninga scop,
that I [for a] while was [the] Heodenings' poet
'that for a while I was the minstrel of the Heodenings'

The Heodenings are presumed to be a people of the Baltic region, although almost nothing more is known of them; like so many legends of old, their story is lost and barely any reference remains.

dryhtne dyre, me wæs Deor noma.
[to] lord dear, [to] me was Deor [the] name
'dear to my lord, my name was Deor'

The construction *me wæs* is unusual: it says 'to me was' but the sense is 'I had'. It is paralleled in some of the ancient languages such as Latin (*vae mihi* – woe to me) and dates from a time before the verb 'have' had been coined.

> *Ahte ic fela wintra folgað tilne,*
> had I many winters [a] following good
> 'for many years I had a good position'

Ahte is our word 'ought' in the sense 'owned, had possession of'. *Folgað* is really 'following', i.e. being a follower to some leader, and therefore a position of responsibility. *Tilne* is an inflected form of *til* meaning 'good' in the sense of 'gainful, profitable'; to make land productive it is necessary to 'till' it.

> *holdne hlaford, oþ þæt Heorrenda nu,*
> steadfast lord until Heorrenda now
> 'a true lord, until now (that) Heorrenda'

> *leoðcræftig monn londryht geþah,*
> song-strong man land-right received
> 'has received (my) estate, the verse-skilled man'

The *londryht* or land-right is the entitlement to hold an estate; this reverted to the king on the holder's death and had to be earnt anew by the successor. This system prevented too much power being concentrated in the hands of 'followers' without earning it through service to the king.

> *þæt me eorla hleo ær gesealde.*
> which [to] me earls' lee ere sold
> 'which the heroes' protector previously gave to me'

The heroes' protector is the lord or king, the person who places the military forces in such a way as to avoid unnecessary risk. Phrases of this kind are typical of OE verse: even when the topic is not military, leadership is expressed in martial imagery, as part of the ethos of that society. *Gesealde* is the ancestor of 'sold', although OE *sellan* has rather the notion of 'give, hand over' than 'exchange for money'.

> *þæs ofereode, þisses swa mæg!*
> That went by, so may this.

Putting it all together, here is the promised reading text:

> He sits, sorrowful at heart, bereft of joys
> his mood darkens, (as) he considers about himself

that his dole of troubles may be endless.
He is then able to understand that, throughout this world
the Lord in his wisdom often changes (things),
shows honour to many a good man
fame for wise thought (but) to another (he shows) a
                                      deal of troubles.
I wish to say this concerning myself
that for a while I was the minstrel of the Heodenings
for many years I had a good position
a true lord, until now (that) Heorrenda
has received (my) estate, the verse-skilled man
which the heroes' protector previously gave to me.
That went by, so may this.

There are some peculiarities in this last tale, both in the language and in the story itself. The first few lines refer to an unnamed individual – perhaps the poet or more likely an unspecified 'everyman' – who must sit with a sorrowful heart and can see no end to his troubles, reflecting that some people receive honour and joy and all that goes with them, while others are beset by one problem after another. Ar 'honour' was very much the positive quality in Old English thought. Their society was based on the polarity of approval: 'public honour' and 'public shame'. Only with the advent of Christianity did they learn of the internal, private polarity with guilt rather than shame as the negative value. The poet then turns to himself, his own troubles, and here we may detect a certain ironic bitterness in his words. The poet had to earn his right to the estates his family had held, but in this instance while his position had once seemed secure, it passed to a more skilful rival. As we might remark: that's show business!

The overall shape of the poem is clear: each of the tales shows an example of misfortune overcome, or endured, or turned to the good. Just how we should read 'that' and 'this' in the refrain is of course debateable, and much discussed. From the context 'this' must mean the plight of Deor, dispossessed of his land and out of favour at court. It may be that the poet, in performing the piece, set out enough clues for the audience to understand this and to apply the knowledge to the narrative. The poem, in this reading, is an extended riddle – a genre very familiar to the early English and apparently much loved by them.

Alternatively, one could take the view that all the tales recounted, including that of Deor, are to be understood as *exempla*, case studies, and therefore 'this' is the personal context of the person reading or hearing the poem. The audience thus constructed the meaning anew at each performance. If this seems too sophisticated an explanation for early mediaeval England, it should be mentioned that a large part

of OE verse is 'wisdom literature' of various kinds, and the hearer's personal involvement is implicit in many examples. *Deor* therefore would function as an example of 'consolation literature', a genre known in the early Middle Ages, if not generally very fruitful.

It would help us to define the message of *Deor* if we knew just how much background knowledge to assume in the audience: we don't really know whether the poem was intended to be read aloud as a performance piece, or was for private, silent study. The majority of the verse in the *Exeter Book* does seem to have been intended for public declamation but whether this was in the context of a king's court, a bishop's refectory or a warlord's beer-hall we cannot say. Perhaps such distinctions would not have been made a thousand years ago.

The verse tradition of Old English is one of the ancient voices which has never really gone away. As we have seen, many of Deor's words are still with us, both everyday ones such as 'me', 'is', 'so', 'may', 'this', 'that', 'self', 'say', 'will', 'grim', 'endless' and the rest, and the slightly more unusual usages such as 'ere' for 'before', 'witty' for 'wise', and so on. This aspect of Old English is probably the most fascinating: the way it combines the very familiar with the really strange, and the modern-mundane with the ancient-exotic.

But that changed, as Deor would have remarked. Within Leofric's lifetime, England suffered the twin invasions of 1066, and the Norman victory. A generation of soldiers and secular leaders was cut down or turned out; a generation of scholars found they had a new master and, as greedy as they were for English taxes and lands and men-at-arms, the Normans had no time for the traditions of the land they conquered and almost no English text was to be written for almost 150 years. During that period of linguistic suppression, the character of the language changed. New words entered English; not new words for new ideas, but new words which Normans could understand. The link with the Germanic past was weakened: 'table' came to compete with 'board', as 'chair' with 'stool' and 'chamber' with 'room'. Of course, in the end, English gained by making room for these new words, yet it lost something too. The cadences and subtleties of the traditional verse medium were lost within a few generations, and only careful scholarship over more than two centuries has enabled us to regain some small part of it. Indeed, the struggle to understand OE verse is not over: there is barely a text which is not argued over as to vocabulary and syntax and meaning. Let us hope that we can look forward to a change in this direction too.

Readers may be interested to learn that the *Exeter Book* is still available to view at Exeter Cathedral Library.

Two Poems by
Pamela Coren

finding my father

A strata line in a lump of slate recalls him,
precise, thin, wandering into crumb, shale,
a bronze thread in the stone, bitten off.

And the distant hill which may be a cloud
or it may be the one we're trying for
on the brown map gone thick with finding.

I remember the grief of a child, shock
that slithered and unwound its coils
into red eyes and saw broken things.

The dreams of coffins were unreal:
coffins do not fall out of pantries
or rear up gothic from broken slabs.

I do not know if it was his, or hers,
or where the child went: in the end
I slept. Having no hands but scales

I can't grasp much of a father, but
in the mirror familiar lines crumble,
child, woman, man, the same eyes

tensed on distant detail, things that are
exact and disappear like deer-tracks,
the mortise turn, exit, the no more of things.

Falling Through the Floor

You object to its trompery – a soft vinyl floor,
green, printed with the detail of old boards,
a jolly fake. But I like the way my gaze slips
into its deep grains and spaces
as into water: underfoot I'm in two places,
looking on green, watered by two streams.

This summer we sailed from Portsmouth to St Malo,
wallowing over a green sea of jellyfish and dolphins,
drove to a cottage built of cobbles and tree-trunks.
We loved its roughness, its wooden horse creaking,
broad planks with a scar and scatter of nails,
splinters, scratches. Knot-holes flared in morning light,
dry earth, chaff and mothscale stuffed the cracks.
Scrubbed with age, the cottage waved
in the Normandy sun, poplars applauded,
stone and wood bulged with light.

But here's an English town, and underfoot
vinyl; machined and tough, made in Manchester.
It seals the room clean to the edges,
soft and warm under bare feet.
You, certain of what's real, say fake –
but what's what, going down through print,
plastic, chipboard – the lost room
which lay such careworn detail down?
A print's an echo, and echoes reach,
like the sun's rays, to the cold limit.

My green floor's a trump of fitness,
firm stamp of all that basks and grows:
the trick's to keep colour and print in phase,
steadying a tremolo to find a hidden tune
ringing in the space between what is
and isn't stopped along our senses' string;
tumbling down the cracks to find the place
where rime slides off the eye and seeing starts.

Personal Eucharisting
From *Digging for Himmler*

Jonathan Meades

They are denouncing I am vampire.
Men are hooked on vampire. Newspaper says top soapstar divorces vampire movies actress Vadi Sadgrove because she refuse to wear false vampire teeth when she go loveplay gobbling.

Not true I am vampire. That is not nice to say. Vampire is drinking from blood of still living. I am not fulfilling strange vice habit. For thirty minutes poor Petr does not move. Nor I cannot move. Nor I cannot move him. This is beyond joke.

So I can tell straight off he is dead. My love is dead. The dove of life is flown dressed as crow. Then he is cold. Colder than ambient which is frankly muggy for time of year. No joke at all.

Absolute Discretion Assured is overlooking what kitten must do in total irreversible fatality circumstance.

His lips are blue like same blue as blue bits of blue cheese. Yeh? Drinking from blood of dead is not vampire. It is sacrament drinking. I make bond with my dead Lovelord. But not till I am wriggling out from under him inciting bruising to ribs and breasts which is professional no-no albeit not vocation threat.

Why?
I am asking why does he die.
I am not referring The Mycardial Infection.
It is fate question I demand answer to.

When I am having good luck why must bad luck be following straightaway like woodjaw after good old knees up night on town?

There is family jigsaw puzzle when I am living in Our Country. Difficult difficult puzzle because so much so white and I am child. Many months to complete.

When pieces are joined picture is showing faithful dog guarding body of Master perished in snow blizzard. Scene is so sad so many pathos. Beard of Master has icicles in him and eyebrows also. There is loyal tear in eyes of dog. There is same tear in my eyes too.

There is blood on dogteeth of dog, blood on snow. Dog is hungry. He drinks Master to survive himself. It is not same as me.

I am personal eucharisting tradition of Our Country where we are religious – just like Pope. It makes My Departed Love holy like Blessed Jesus Lamb Of God. I drink Jesus Lamb Of God every week. I drink so much him there should be nothing left! But Jesus not running dry like pub nor popular bar in happy hour. He is special case, Jesus.

Hunters from Grandmother village hunting The Savage Elk With Crown Of Infinity Tines find man living in rock cave inside Hook-nose Mountain of famous mists legend in Our Country. Mists are pale ghost wreaths dancing slowly.

Man is very old and very young. He is eating red white spot fungus mushrooms. He is saying I Am Blessed Jesus Lamb Of God. He is saying Saviour is returned to earth. In order to do Saving. Starting with hunters who are finding him. He makes miracles with tree resin and moss. With clouds and ice. He has hand palm marks. Strange strange voice. Sweet sweet breath. He knows to mend engine of tractor. Distributor head who is at fault.

He sits with hunters in tractor trailer. They forget The Savage Elk With Crown Of Infinity Tines. Blessed Jesus Lamb Of God shivers at mountain descent where forest begin to grow so all is dusk in road between dark high trees. But He brings light with His eyes and being. He shivers because He is victim thin from diet of fungus mushrooms and pine needle and lichen.

The hunters chain Him to floor at old pig sty house.

They feed Him milla grain, orchard fruits apple greengage pear plum, root of swede, duck eggs, hen eggs, goose eggs, potato pie, bruss, ass's curd, onion broth, fresh cheese, barley bread soup they make with woman breast milk for honoured guest.

Month after month Blessed Jesus Lamb Of God grow fat fat.

When he is fat enough so fat he cannot move they pull him from pig sty house. So fat they have to break pig sty house walls so they can move him on trolley.

They try crucify him on hill but he cannot climb hill.

They build new cross near river. But wood of cross snap break because Blessed Jesus Lamb Of God is obesity heavy like My Beloved Petr.

So instead they are silently cutting His throat at altar in historical monument church of Santa Hessel.

They eat Him because that is way to honour communion oneness with Him in Ultimate Eucharist in remembrance of Him.

He is so fat there is goodmouth morsel for everyone of grand-mother village.

They drink honey beer they sing they are joyous shouting dancing they free-feast Him every bit. Warm blood, strip flesh bones, colon, intestines coil (which are being wash and brushed up because Jesus Blessed Lamb Of God is constipated by eggs), kidneys, white kidneys, brain, liver.

My Mother is just a nipper when she partake Ultimate Eucharist.

She make joke when she come to Our Blighty Shore about God liver oil that she must feed me for my crumbly bones!

See then it is not because of body thirst I am drinking Petr. It is spirit thirst. It is souvenir mouthful of remembrance. Memory is rust taste of elite blood. I am never forgetting My Petr because of that taste.

Other souvenir is cash he is winning. GBP4,200. He cannot take them with him is he? I believe myself full entitlement.

But not credit/debit cards: Elysium Diamond, Odysseus, Lagoon, Orchid, Nimrod, Otter, Plantagenet, Aristocard, Pegasus, Zephyr, Ambrosia.

I am not stealing thief. They are all signed with Petr's manful signature.

I leave also passports. He has three passports from different countries – he is international consultant. No use for me: face is not fitting!

Bonus souvenir is in wardrobe where I look because Petr passing on orbits me in deepvein shock. There are boxes and many suitcases. There is strange strange smell. Not bad smell but smell like forest in autumn time, brown smell not box and suitcase smell. I am wondering. I open.

I never see so much toys. So much old toys from far-off time. Such beautiful toys. Owl with turning head is money box. Tin horses pulling carriage with driver and milady in high wig inside. Wooden theatre stage with curtains and rows of pirates and sailors and rigging ships and town tavern on olden days quay and cloud with lightning. Dogs. Wigwams. Kaleidoscopes. There are many many. Country farm with barn, cows, hayricks, milkmaids, nose-ring bull, gates who open, churns, farmer, cart, pigsty... Is so like real farm because so dirty. All beautiful old toys are so dirty. Why does no one look after them? It is like lovely ruined buildings. Why I ask myself. Why does everything have to be like us human folks and die? Many toys are rusty. I am thinking Petr has not done corrosion limitation! I do not know if Desna (9) will like them because they

are old and dirty. I take two suitcases of toys. So heavy I can hardly walk. I call taxi control. No available vehicular solution they say. I have to wait till one come along.

I mourn for Petr.

World is sad. Sun is hiding now. Sky needs wash and brush up. There is grime type dirt on rhododendrons. There is plastic bag litter tidemarking round roots. Pavement is dog toilet even in quality leaf suburb.

The taxi driver make improper suggestion. He is old, he is ugly. I repartee him he has to be joking matey.

I am wondering now: is it him grassing me up because I am scorning?

Next Saturday bright and early boys in blue come calling. They are not vice boys in blue. I gratify mutual benefit aplenty in working relationship with vice boys in blue.

No. Boys in blue who come calling are The Revenue. They are going rattattattatt on front door. Rattattattatt go their pick axes. They do that because they are wanting neighbours to hear for humiliating purpose at breakfast. They are asking question about Petr. They are rough men and bad voices.

Where are toys in suitcases? They are cruel joking me that I manslaughter Petr with energy sex. Where are toys in suitcases? They threaten. How do I like sound of prison? Where are toys in suitcases? How do I like sound of lesbo-butch electrodiesel screws rupturing with strapadictomy in piss stink cell? I am weeping. Where are toys in suitcases? My Mother is trying to enter room for comforting. They are saying she is obstructing in execution of duty. They are saying she is old whore. They are laughing saying she is worse: she is old whore trying to make comeback. My Petr is fat thieving vat-dodging bastard crim fraud. Why was he not connecting his landline? Where is his mobile? Where are toys in suitcases? I am heartless bitch. Do I know where toys in suitcases come from?

They come from graves of children.

In olden days there is more illness epidemic issues to name scarlet fever, yellow fever, mauve fever, grey fever, mallowrash, the Wailes, diphtheria, witherhives, Quartermaine's, typhus. In olden days children die often. In France, Germany and others they are burying precious sentiment toys with tragic tot.

They are saying My Petr with accomplice unknown possibly Swiss featuring eastern Mediterranean origins male (35) and accomplice unknown probably Turkish speaker German at Bavarian accent bald male (45–50) – do I know them? – are pretending to be cem-

etery workers so they are digging up kiddy graves for looting toys from coffin sometimes under cover of night at many far-off cemeteries such as Mulhouse, Metz, Sedan (France), Braunschweig, Verden, Luneburg (Germany) plus other places many more. They say me I am accomplice too of evil desecration trade. Me.

Upstairs I show them toys I give to Desna (9). I am innocent. If I am knowing do I give them to Desna? No – because of tetanus disease risk. My way of thinking is tragic tots are not playing with dirty rusty toys in heaven. Now they are angels with angel toys.

The Revenue are labelling toys each one to sterilise bag. It is slow work. They are yearning in their eyes to spit on me when they go but they do not. Instead they are promising they are going to throw books at me.

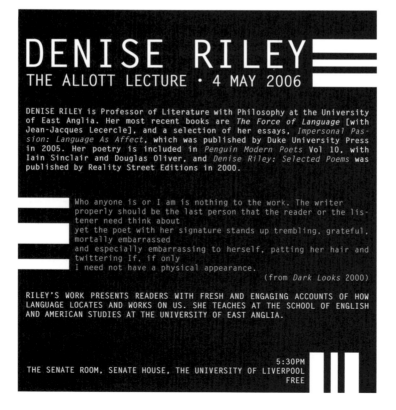

DENISE RILEY
THE ALLOTT LECTURE · 4 MAY 2006

DENISE RILEY is Professor of Literature with Philosophy at the University of East Anglia. Her most recent books are *The Force of Language* [with Jean-Jacques Lecercle], and a selection of her essays, *Impersonal Passion: Language As Affect*, which was published by Duke University Press in 2005. Her poetry is included in *Penguin Modern Poets* Vol 10, with Iain Sinclair and Douglas Oliver, and *Denise Riley: Selected Poems* was published by Reality Street Editions in 2000.

Who anyone is or I am is nothing to the work. The writer
properly should be the last person that the reader or the lis-
tener need think about
yet the poet with her signature stands up trembling, grateful,
mortally embarrassed
and especially embarrassing to herself, patting her hair and
twittering If, if only
I need not have a physical appearance.
(from *Dark Looks* 2000)

RILEY'S WORK PRESENTS READERS WITH FRESH AND ENGAGING ACCOUNTS OF HOW LANGUAGE LOCATES AND WORKS ON US. SHE TEACHES AT THE SCHOOL OF ENGLISH AND AMERICAN STUDIES AT THE UNIVERSITY OF EAST ANGLIA.

5:30PM
THE SENATE ROOM, SENATE HOUSE, THE UNIVERSITY OF LIVERPOOL
FREE

A Poem by
Sam Trainor

Hippocrene

I

a memory
seared the
retina /
: in
the tungsten filament /

that prances like a

from down to down

no charioteer could drive her up

no prong &

of soft, bright lime

and print this fountainhead

no type of pegasus could stamp a hoof

no great picasso (giant) with a calcite

wand

could chalk such

lines
flowing

II

"dynamic lines in space which act without intermediary upon the spirit linking it directly with spectres & phantoms before characters"

that speaks be-fore words / an old language /

nature and history, with

Gilles Deleuze

with gestures which develop before organised bodies with masks before faces, with

III

only to remember & remind / the usual need /

these still warm words

turning nothing up except

my lines with moving lips

& read

my own slow limbs you

the grooves your body leaves behind it with

sleep only finds me as I search the way your palms smooth out of the contours

a doodle on a rumpled dayglow post-it

The Practice of Poetry

Syntax and Old Style
in Basil Bunting's Seventh Ode

Adam Piette

Syntax is the grammatical structure of a sentence or phrase. In other words, it means the order and structure of a phrase or sentence. In a poem it signifies the architecture of its sense relations, the walls and foundations of its meanings. A reader of even a very straightforward poem will be parsing the significances being generated by the syntax quite unconsciously – as any normal language user does. But with slightly odd and formal and difficult poems, the syntactical experience can often be baffling, forcing readers to entertain rival possibilities and surmises, testing their knowledge base, sometimes at the cost of their patience. For a poet of ancient ways like Basil Bunting, learned as he was in the classics and in medieval Persian literature and at the same time anxious to translate those old styles into modernist idioms in the manner of Pound, the attempt to balance old formal syntax with 'make-it-new' idiolect was a strain, especially in the youth-obsessed culture of late modernity, beautiful, shiny, self-obsessed, ignorant. The difficulty of communicating lovingly with such an audience, so happy to abandon the classics and all vestiges of Graeco-Roman culture, is the secret subtext of Bunting's Seventh Ode, written in the 1960s when he felt like a very old man:

Ode 7

Ille mi par esse deo videtur

O, it is godlike to sit selfpossessed
when her chin rises and she turns to smile;
but my tongue thickens, my ears ring,
what I see is hazy.

I tremble. Walls sink in night, voices
unmeaning as wind. She only
a clear note, dazzle of light, fills
furlongs and hours

so that my limbs stir without will, lame,
I a ghost, powerless,
treading air, drowning, sucked
back into dark

unless, rafted on light or music,
drawn into her radiance, I dissolve
when her chin rises and she turns to smile.
O, it is godlike!

The poem opens conventionally enough on the theme of wracked, lovesick poet, with only a slight question mark hanging over the first sentence – the syntax does not make clear who it is who sits 'selfpossessed' and 'godlike' in the dazzle of his lady's smile. Unpicking the meaning of the first two lines entails quick acts of half-translation to test the sentence's potential, as in 'any man who has enough control over his own feelings to enjoy looking at her when she smiles at him (without cracking up like me) must feel like a god, must have superhuman powers of indifference'. Or, 'I know what it feels like to enjoy her smile, since I used to be able to gaze at her smiling face – but that was when I still had a strong sense of self – look at me now'. Or even, more jealously: 'that man over there whom she's just about to smile at (oh that chin!), I know how he feels because she smiled on me once – not any more, wreck that I am.' The hazy syntax allows for all three readings, 'it is godlike' as general axiom, self-descriptive or specific to a rival he.

But the confusion is as nothing to the floaty difficulties produced by the long, involved fourth sentence beginning 'She only'. The syntax meanders, drifts, unmoored, the thread of meaning set loose, rather like the lovelorn poet himself. To fix the meanings, again the reader must extrapolate, translate, make rapid trial inferences, as in: 'She alone has the clarity of a single musical note or sunbeam radiating out through space and time, making the universe beautiful, but making a slave of me, a mess of broken fragments in comparison to her. Her beauty makes me feel dead, as though I'd died already, my body broken; it's somehow robbed me of all my power or will to live. It's as if I'm drowning, being sucked into a dark place, I'm so unhappy. Maybe, just maybe, I'll feel like I felt before, godlike in the blaze of her smile. Maybe when I really do die, I'll see her on the

other side, I'll dissolve into her radiance like a particle into the sun, like a believer into his god.'

These kinds of test paraphrase are not articulated in this concrete way, of course – the mind makes meanings with electric speed, but relationally, associatively, creating clusters of potential stories along the line without ever quite breaking into actual words. This haze of inarticulate significances is developmental, a rapidly changing structure of fructifying deductions being generated by the mind as it processes the syntax of the poem.

That is why, incidentally, it hardly ever makes sense to demand that a poem be simple, accessible, uncomplicated. For the mind that reads performs such extraordinarily complex acts of making and creating of meanings, and a poem is nothing if not a loving form of address to the making mind of the reader. As such, to be true to that mind, subtleties of feeling and sense must be captured and released in the special, condensed language of poetry.

Or rather, this was once the way poets felt about their craft. One possible interpretation of 'Ode 7' would be to read it as a very heartfelt statement about the poet's ancient relationship with language and reader. Once upon a time, in the old world, poets loved their addressees with a religious passion, and went through hell and back for art and the 'thou' of mystical poetry. Poems were the product and also the mode of communication of that love. Now the world shines on others, prefers simple, direct, uncomplicated utterance, not this old-fashioned syntax of the passionate heart. The suspicion one might harbour that the poet's suffering is being artificially exaggerated in the ode is witness to modern incredulity. Loved one as sun goddess? Lover drowning in hell? We don't think so, chuckle the young iconoclasts.

With this reading in mind, the desperate tone of the poem gathers strange pace. There seems a reason now beyond the passionate for the broken nature of the syntax. The difficulty of communicating with a sceptical readership may be animating the breaks and stutters in the lines, like holes in the sinking walls of the syntactical structure. Difficulties of translation too, as though the loving mind might be sensing how hard it is to make sense of its own voice on its way, how hard it is to half-translate in the manner suggested above. One of the fundamental laws of syntax is anaphoric reference, a hard way of saying that a word in a text refers back to another, in particular pronouns back to persons. In the loose inflections of the ode's long sentence, the anaphoric reference is difficult to track, to say the least. Is she filling furlongs and hours like a clear

note or dazzle of light? Or does a clear note and dazzle of light fill
her for furlongs and hours? Such imprecisions threaten the cohesion
of the whole poem, so that we are led to ask whether the 'I' who is
a ghost is the same whose limbs stir without will? Is she turning to
smile at him in the end, or at another, or inwardly within herself?
If he is a ghost and dissolves at a smile then who is speaking this
poem, and can we trust such a weak voice?

   Another set of meanings emerges, however, another poem alto-
gether, if we attend to the most obvious difficulty on the page, the
Latin tag in italics, '*ille mi par esse deo videtur*'. In a poem so intri-
cately dependent on a reader's acts of translation and agility with
strange syntax, so structured by the opposition between a shining
young beauty and a heavily learned old age, the appropriateness
of translating that tag from an ancient dead language and culture
is intriguing. The tag is an ultimate form of anaphoric reference,
referring back through hundreds of years of text to another cultural
moment. The tag is the first line of Catullus' 51st ode *Ad Lesbiam*, as
the excellent website Peithô's Web shows (http://classicpersuasion.
org/pw/sappho/index.htm). Here is a translation (based partly on
Leonard Smithers' version): 'That man seems to me to be equal to a
god, / (even, if I dare say so, to surpass the gods) / who sitting oppo-
site you each night / can gaze on you, and listen to you // sweetly
laughing – that's what robs poor wretched me / of my very senses:
for the moment I look on you, Lesbia, nothing is left to me of … //
but my tongue is numbed, sharp flame / runs quick along my limbs,
sounds only I can hear / ringing in my ears, both my eyes / veiled
with dark night.'

   We see here how closely but loosely Bunting has followed Catul-
lus – the jealous triangle is preserved, the isolation of the poet in
suffering body, the obsession with gaze and smile. But what strikes
one straight away too is that gaping hole in the middle of the Catul-
lus: 'nothing is left to me of …' The version passed down to us does
not have the complement to Catullus' 'nihil est super mi …, though
most have speculated that the missing words must be something
like 'vocis in ore', or 'voice in my mouth' (in other words, he loses
his voice when gazing on her). The reason they can reconstitute the
gap is that Catullus is himself imitating another poet, is alluding by
anaphoric reference back in time outside Roman culture to Greece
and Sappho.

   The poem he is translating is her *Ode to Anactoria*, which
only survives in fragmentary form. I give it here in H.T. Wharton's
version: 'That man seems to me peer of gods, who sits in thy pres-

ence, and hears close to him thy sweet speech and lovely laughter; that indeed makes my heart flutter in my bosom. For when I see thee but a little, I have no utterance left, my tongue is broken down, and straightway a subtle fire has run under my skin, with my eyes I have no sight, my ears ring, sweat pours down, and a trembling seizes all my body; I am paler than grass, and seem in my madness little better than one dead. But I must dare all, since one so poor …'

It is instantly clear from this that Bunting is not only imitating Catullus but also taking his poem back to Catullus's source too, back to Sappho. Catullus imitates Sappho's metre.[1] Bunting doesn't attempt to do Sapphics, but the adonic sound does come back, strong and clear, in the final line, 'O, it is godlike!' But much more movingly to my mind, what he does imitate is the fragmentariness of both the Sappho ('since one so poor …') and the Catullus ('nothing is left to me of …') with its modernist counterpart – fragmentary, loose syntax, his lines bearing the wounds of the holes and gaps in its flow of utterance like tears in the text of ancient poetry. How fragile the voice is in its transmission through to future readers. Yet how tenacious too, the beat and stress of old passions resonating into those mysterious spaces and holes between words, between estranged lovers, between poet and reader.

Whether we know that Bunting's poem is a double imitation of both Roman and Greek poems may seem to be beside the point: what we need, surely, is simple appreciation of the passion in *his* words. But for Bunting the passion in his words is a thing made up of deep feeling about the ancient passions preserved in the poems he has so lovingly received and retransmitted to us from those lost other worlds. The odd triangle of Sappho-Catullus-Bunting generates another set of sweet meanings to the love triangle being attended to in the three poems. The 'she', the loved one, is first a lesbian, is then Lesbia, and ends as passionate-classical poetry itself. Bunting is addressing, partly, the loved ones of the classical age, the intensities of Graeco-Roman culture, a compound of Lesbia and Sappho, a vortex of sweet wild feeling which the old and withering West with its new amnesia is about to forgo and forget. But Bunting does not and will not, stays true to the core of that ancient tradition, unreasonable love for the loved one – in all her light and music and radiance.

1. Three eleven-syllable lines or hendecasyllabics, each line made up of two trochees either side of a dactyl (/- /- /-- /- /-) followed by a five-syllable line known as an adonic, dactyl plus trochee (/-- /-).

Two Translations by
Bill Milner

Anon: A Dog's Epitaph

Though I was born in Gaul, to honour my fine frame
the jewel from the rich seas' shell gave me my name.
Experienced and well-trained, I quartered, unafraid,
the forest's dangerous, impenetrable shade
and scoured the hills for game. I never had to wear
a rope or leash, nor did my pure white body bear
any chastisement. Baskets were not for me – instead
I shared my master's and my mistress's soft bed.
No dumb beast ever had so many ways to talk,
and I was careful not to frighten with my bark.
But Fate commanded that, by giving birth, I die,
so this small marble stone now shows you where I lie.

Latin *margarita*: a pearl
This poem is no. 308 in *The Oxford Book of Latin Verse*

The End
(After Propertius III/XXV)

I was the big joke at all gatherings,
every gossip-monger's party-piece –
yet managed to stay faithful for five years
to you. I bet you'll chew your fingernails
hoping for such faithfulness again!
But don't try tears on me – I fell for them before,
when every one was loaded with some lie.

Of course to lose you cost me a few tears,
but thinking of my wrong has soon dried them.
Your yoke was not an easy one to bear.

I hold no grudge against your tear-wet threshold
and, though provoked, I never raised a fist
against your door.
                            But you? I hope that age,
by ploughing up your face will show itself
no matter how much rouge you plaster on
until you want to tear out your grey hairs
urged on, from the mirror, by a crone,
and your turn comes to have some scoffing boy
slam the door – as you did, in my face.

I hope your deeds still fill you with regrets
in your old age – and you see through my lines
the shape your face will come to in the end.

Something Great

Mary Weston

The Get Into Reading project is one of The Reader's satellites: three project workers who set up and run reading groups, trying to reach people who wouldn't normally think of themselves as readers. We currently have fifteen groups, some put on for the clients of organisations such as Riverside Day Centre (a workplace for adults with learning disabilities), Phoenix House (a residential drug rehabilitation project), the YMCA Hostel for homeless men, or the Tranmere Community Project (for children excluded from school), while others are open to anyone interested, in libraries (St James, Ridgeway, Wallasey Central and Woodchurch) or other community centres.

Unlike many other reading groups, Get Into Reading (GIR) groups meet weekly, and instead of reading books at home and discussing them when we come together, we usually read the texts aloud in the sessions. This began as a way of making literature accessible to those who are not confident readers, but we soon found that even the most literate really enjoy *listening* to stories, novels and poetry. Responses to the text are more immediate, and competitiveness is defused: you can't spend the weeks before planning clever remarks! More than this, there is potential for profound shared experience in participating in stories, something that takes us back to times when literature had to be a communal experience, before it was 'privatised' by the written word. Steinbeck captures it in *The Grapes of Wrath*:

> And the people listened, and their faces were quiet with listening. The story tellers, gathering attention into their tales, spoke in great rhythms, spoke in great words because the tales were great, and the listeners became great through them.

I'm not sure that our funders will accept 'becoming great' as a key outcome, but something transformative does take place in our groups.

Before I joined the GIR team I worked as a counsellor, and when I try to analyse the processes that go on in individuals and groups, I tend to use therapeutic ideas and categories: it is natural to me to compare what is going on in my reading groups with

the things my clients used to experience in counselling or group therapy. To anchor myself in the literary here, I will conduct my analysis through the medium of one particular text, Mitch Albom's *The Five People You Meet in Heaven*. My colleagues and I have used this book in many of the settings I listed above, and have found that it really works for some of the most hard to reach and book-shy clients we encounter.

Five People 'begins at the end' with the death of its main character Eddie. A countdown of his last hour on earth, a death on a theme park ride: these catch the attention. Curiosity about what happens in the afterlife brings listeners back for a second session, and thereafter an ongoing stream of narrative twists and surprises, along with plenty of action (a powerful Second World War episode) help keep the audience hooked. Pace is particularly important for a target audience of non-readers: reading takes stamina, and reading aloud does slow things down further. With all that, the book touches into profound territory fairly swiftly, even through the medium of pace, the ticking clock:

> Thirty-four minutes to live, Eddie lifted the lap bar, gave each boy a sucking candy, retrieved his cane, then limped to the maintenance shop to cool down from the summer heat. Had he known his death was imminent, he might have gone somewhere else. Instead, he did what we all do. He went about his dull routine as if all the days of the world were still to come.

Groups whose primary task is therapeutic (I include the dreaded Personal Development group of counselling training in this category) often spend a lot of time in discussion and negotiation. 'What are we here for? What are our ground rules? What is it appropriate for me to reveal about myself, and how honestly can I respond to others' self-disclosure?' Other questions, such as 'Who are the powerful people in this group?' and 'If someone attacks me, will the facilitator come to my rescue?', may not be spoken aloud, but will be answered by what actually happens in the interactions and skirmishes between members. A frustrating business, but necessary to create a space in which it is safe to engage in therapeutic work.

The fact that the agreed task of a group is sharing literature does not make these questions go away. In my experience, they often surface when the group is first faced with a difficulty in interpretation, perhaps an ambiguous passage in the text, or a poem. Does the facilitator (or other powerful person in the group) get to impose

their meaning on everyone else, or are all views equally valued? How much difference can the group tolerate? How much conflict? Generally, GIR groups tend not to engage in the kind of robust debate that might characterise a Continuing Education class; it usually feels more important to hold the boundary that each individual's interpretation is right for them, and to celebrate the expansion of one's own understanding that can occur as a result of taking another person's point of view on board. But within the GIR model, groups vary in confidence and in ethos: some are more literary in purpose ('We're here to learn'), some more therapeutic ('We're here to help each other'), others mainly recreational ('We're here to have fun!').

In negotiating boundaries, we are essentially setting up a relationship between the inner world of each member and the shared social world. To offer an interpretation of or a reaction to the text is to make a part of the private world public. Even a judgement does this (for we are judged by our judgements, they give away the depth of our understanding, the limitations of our sympathies). But because the focus is on the object, the text, and not on the self, it doesn't feel like we are taking the same kind of risk we would be in telling a bit of our life story. The story becomes a kind of bridge between the inner world and the outer.

Counselling relies for its effect on interactions between the (painful or otherwise unsatisfactory) inner world of the client and the social world of the client–counsellor relationship. Take the example of a woman suffering from self-hatred. In a counselling session, she gets in touch with the inner world, the experiences of rejection that have led to her constructing such a negative self-concept. And yet in the outer world, she is receiving genuine respect and acceptance from the counsellor (at least, it is to be hoped that she is!). Flicking back and forth between these states, there is the possibility of a reparative experience that enables her to begin to change her feelings about herself. Counsellors want their clients to 'get in touch with their feelings' not because it is cathartic, but because it is only when the inner world is fully present that it can be transformed.

It isn't always easy to get in touch with feelings and, if someone has been abused, the prospect of revisiting painful experiences can be terrifying. Even the most courageous and determined can find an unwanted, immovable internal block in their way. The therapeutic process is held up, or terminated in despair.

But in a reading group, working with a book like *Five People* (which deals with abuse), there are possibilities for small-scale therapeutic effects. Take a passage like this one:

> All parents damage their children. It cannot be helped.
> Youth, like pristine glass, absorbs the prints of its handlers.
> Some parents smudge, others crack, a few shatter child-
> hoods completely into jagged little pieces, beyond repair.

It's interesting that, like *The Grapes of Wrath*, *The Five People You Meet in Heaven* has passages in which the narrator speaks generally, and risks big statements. Eddie is shown as one case, one man whose experiences are not essentially different from others, just as the Joads are more systematically foregrounded and then submerged into the big story of the migrant people (another kind of flicking between the inner and outer world?). The statement 'All parents...' pretty much obliges us to glance at our own childhood, and having a graduated scale of damage tempts us to assess our own condition, smudged, cracked or shattered, the way questionnaires do. Using scales ('On a scale of one to ten, how do you feel?') is a technique some counsellors use: it helps people who are not used to reflecting to focus on the inner world. Imagery is another powerful therapeutic tool, and here the two are combined. The narrator assures us that he sees our innocence, that as children we are pristine glass; he is non-judgemental, on our side, like an ideal counsellor. A 'social world' like that between counsellor and client is created, and perhaps hearing the story read aloud heightens the effect: there is a real person, a real storyteller saying this.

And so, in this safe space, we hear what happened to Eddie, how his father damaged him. It is not unbearably horrendous, but it is bad enough; moreover, it is typical: a man unable to express his softer emotions, given to venting his frustrations on his children, something that many can identify with.

Earlier I talked about the text acting as a bridge, allowing people to make the inner world public unselfconsciously, by providing a point of focus other than the self. Through a similar mechanism, it can also act as a bridge into one's own inner world, arching over the blockage of our defences. In contemplating the pain of the story, we can edge up to our own pain, almost without knowing it. If it gets too heavy, we can back away, focus on the text again. It's his story, not mine. But if a reading group member is able to make the connection, and feels safe (or brave) enough to share this, and if the group is able to respond to this gently and well, actual restorative work can take place. When things like this happen, a quality of intimacy develops in the group. Members know something great has happened, and they were part of it, and this makes them great.

Love, Actually

E.M. Forster, *Alexandria: A History and a Guide*
and *Pharos and Pharillon*
edited by Miriam Allott
volume 16 of the Abinger edition
Andre Deutsch, 2004, 407pp, £25

Peter J. Conradi

'One may as well begin with Helen's letters to her sister': with *Howards End*'s opening sentence E.M. Forster undid Victorian certainties quite as effectively as Strachey in *Eminent Victorians*. The sentence has a well-rehearsed casualness that is (and is meant to be) disarming: nonchalant, spinsterish, fey, sometimes confiding to the point of ingratiation, and then capable – as it later turns out – of sounding brisk, unexpected, waspish as well as exact. 'Small is beautiful' might have been Forster's motto. Smallness is anti-mandarin. And smallness, it turns out, is also durable.

When Peter Davison published his epic collection of Orwell's writings some reviewers at first asked whether Orwell's opus truly merited all of Davison's pains. Now Forster has been paid an analogous tribute with this Abinger edition. The achievement is quite as momentous as Davison's collected Orwell. Indeed, since each of the seventeen E.M. Forster volumes has a different editor, the effort of harmonisation is the more extraordinary. The Abinger edition of Forster has taken many years to produce, and such factors may quite undeservedly have diffused its impact. Forster's two works on Alexandria – the *Guide* from 1922, and the essays he collected in 1923 as *Pharos and Pharillon* – comprise together the sixteenth volume.

It was Cyril Connolly in *The Enemies of Promise* (1938) who first noted Forster's anti-mandarin voice. Forster's modesty, brevity and immediacy have marked twentieth-century prose style as much as did the voices of Hemingway, Orwell, or D.H. Lawrence, each of whom in his different way has proven to be a torch-bearer for a distinctively modern informality, for a voice that reads as if spoken and not written, or (which comes to the same thing) is cunningly written in order to sound spoken. Small wonder that Zadie Smith's

new novel echoes *Howards End*'s opening and in so doing pays
Forster loving homage.

Love: Forster is sometimes cited as a novelist concerned with
friendship, greatest of Bloomsbury topics. One thinks of how acutely
Margaret Schlegel is described when she fears that Mrs Wilcox
– dying, though Margaret doesn't yet know this – might be one of
those who 'flirt with friendship'. Such flirtation, Forster reminds us,
can wound as much as betrayal in love. Or of how moving Fielding
and Aziz's friendship is. And, when we speak of Forster as a writer
exploring friendship, this is opposed to the Lawrencian theme of
love. The embarrassment of the passage in *A Longest Journey* in
which Rickie sees a girlfriend in sexualised embrace is acute because
Forster himself shares Rickie's swooningly girlish and virginal excite-
ment, and scarcely knows it.

And yet his masterpiece *A Passage to India*, one wants to say,
concerns love too, in its metaphysical as much as its sensual dimen-
sions – its capacities to effect transfiguration, if not redemption.
What happened between 1910 and 1922 to effect Forster's matura-
tion as a man, and then as a writer too? The younger Forster had
been the poet of friendship, and of those troubles that accompany
friendship. Italy in the two pre-war Tuscan novels he opposed to
Sawston, an imaginary suburb exemplifying English stultification.
Italy – by contrast – meant southern spontaneity, absence of hypoc-
risy and notional sex. England is bad at love and Italy is good at it.
At least that is what Italy seems to mean for others, if not for Forster
himself. Italy for Forster stays exotic.

The present volume suggests that the most important thing to
have happened to him after *Howards End* was Alexandria, where he
arrived in 1915 as a Red Cross volunteer, already a celebrity from
Howards End and the Italian novels, but depressed and pessimistic
about what the Great War meant for the values he espoused. In Alex-
andria he himself found love. Here, in a South deeper than Tuscany,
Forster had, in his forties, his first love affair, with a young bus con-
ductor called Mohammed, poor, proud, clever and eloquent, and
dying young, as it happened, of TB. With Mohammed Forster had
his first experience of full sexual fulfilment. Mohammed's letters to
Forster are included in the present volume, and immensely moving
they are. It is marvellous that Miriam Allott has collected and made
them available to us.

Alexandria, after all, not for nothing the city of Cleopatra,
was a city of love as much as or more than Paris. Here Forster met
that greatest of love poets – as also of Alexandrian poets – Con-
stantin Cavafy and, in two essays, brought him to the attention of

English speakers for the first time. The poems Forster celebrates are not Cavafy's louche and erotic ones – Forster lacks that particular courage. It is Cavafy's love for the city, not his love for other men, that Forster is willing to write about. But in hymning Cavafy's Alexandria Forster is aware that he is honouring one of the places where love poetry began, with, among others, Theocritus. Like Cavafy, Forster is acutely aware of how the grand and now almost entirely invisible Hellenistic past haunts the wan present: such haunting of the modern by the ancient city is built into the very structure of Forster's remarkable guide. The experience of Alexandria, as Amos Elon has pointed out,[1] remains bookish to this day.

No guide to the city existed when Forster embarked on his pioneering study. It has an original structure: he furnishes a History in short bites, and at the end of each section page references point to appropriate objects described in the *Guide*; then the guide proper, which is done on conventional lines, with routes. It is mentioned admiringly in Evelyn Waugh's *Officers and Gentlemen*, where Julia Stitch offers it to Guy, describing it as both 'topping' and 'very scarce'. This legendary scarcity was the product of a perverse publishing history: among its perversities the fact that the first publishers claimed insurance money when they believed that fire had destroyed all copies, then discovering that the stock had unexpectedly survived, and retrospectively to prove their own veracity, burned every extant copy anyway.

Alexandria is many things to Forster: it was, as he put it in 1956, a mixture or bastardy, for nearly 2000 years – ever since it was founded by a Macedonian who believed in miscegenation and thought he was an Egyptian god. Mathematics, geography, astronomy and medicine all grew to maturity in this little spit of land, together with servility and snobbery. From here the Jewish philosopher Philo led a delegation to Rome vainly pleading with the emperor Caligula to put an end to Greek attacks. The emperor demanded to know why Alexandrians were not worshipping him as a god. Here, too, the Old Testament was translated into Greek on the orders of a Ptolemaic king by seventy Jewish sages working away simultaneously in their secluded cells: all seventy versions were said to be mysteriously identical and therefore proven to have been inspired by God.

Though the city had, in its time, like New York today, the largest Jewish population in the world, it was also cosmopolitan, and in it miscegenation was itself one aspect of a remarkable tolerance, one chronicled by Lawrence Durrell. In his famous *Quartet*, Durrell commemorated the city in the last days of its glory, before first an arrogant Anglo-French nationalism at the time of Suez, then an

answering Egyptian nationalism under General Nasser, destroyed the dream of brotherly love between the races for ever and resulted in the expulsion of many minorities.

I had never known that the prototype of the minaret or tower on every mosque from which the muezzin calls the faithful to prayer is none other than Alexandria's famous lighthouse; the Arabs conquered Alexandria in the seventh century. Forster makes mistakes: he locates Nicaea on the Black Sea and Actium on the Adriatic. Yet his picture of the city is one to which modern scholarship still broadly subscribes, with modifications from recent archaeological findings. And it is charmingly idiosyncratic and personal in tone, as one might expect, with brusque dismissals like 'Art: Unimportant'.

Miriam Allott is far too good a critic not to fear the contrast between Forster's economy and lightness of tone and the inevitable weightiness of an academic apparatus. This includes here her authoritative, comprehensive and always helpful preface to both Forster's Alexandrian books. She sorts out their complex and separate publishing histories, and dates them conclusively; and she notes Forster's unerring mastery of tone in each, which distinguishes the journalistic pieces in *Pharos and Pharillon* from the apparently easy scholarship of the *Guide*.

Besides her main preface, she also provides – perhaps confusingly – a second preface, devoted to *Pharos and Pharillon*. This re-emphasises the individual publishing history of the essays it contains and reminds us of Forster's journalistic articles on general themes, written for the *Egyptian Mail* and the *Egyptian Gazette* and recently gathered by P. N. Furbank in his own volume for the Abinger edition, *The Prince's Tale and Other Uncollected Writings* (1998). Unfortunately, a note intended to supply the title and date of Furbank's book (indicated by Allott's 'see below') has been lost in transcript. Forster frequently draws on the *Pharos and Pharillon* articles for his *Alexandria* and the notes throughout record changes made in substance and style so as to bring the material into keeping with its new context.

Allott has also included contemporary reviews as well as Forster's preface to the second edition of *Alexandria: A History and a Guide*, and a 1956 retrospective talk, and some notes Forster made in 1920. All this will help the student and scholar alike. I had never read Forster's Alexandrian books before and was both enchanted and grateful.

Allott met and has written on Forster, and indeed spent part of her own childhood, not so long after Forster's sojourn there, in an Egypt that must have closely resembled the one he knew. She writes with a judicious Forsterian agility about her subject. She is

scrupulous and illuminating, too, in demonstrating how hard-won was Forster's anti-racist rhetoric in *A Passage to India*: he had his own struggle with the demons he attacked and was capable of reflex prejudice. Some Egyptians seemed as determined to sour life for him as Mohammed was to sweeten it.

Alexandria was at once the most worldly and the most other-worldly of Mediterranean cities. And the book's high point – also the chapter Forster liked best – was 'The Spiritual City', summarising with typically lucid skill the very different efforts of Pagan, Jewish, Christian and Neoplatonic philosophers to reconcile divine love and human imperfection. Love, perhaps, as an Alexandrian might have put it, in two different aspects that are only apparently contradictory.

1. Amos Elon, 'The Ghost City', review of Michael Haag's *Alexandria: City of Memory* (Yale UP), *New York Review of Books*, 26 May 2005, pp. 44–46

Family Reading

Edward Lear, '*Over the Land and Over the Sea*':
Selected Nonsense and Travel Writings, ed. Peter Swaab
Carcanet, 2005

Brian Nellist

I should have known of course that to leave this highly desirable book on my table waiting for review would attract the covetous eyes of various relations dropping in. As a bargain for its loan I asked for brief reports from each on its return.

My second cousin, Reebok, aged 11 1/2:
Hi, kidz. Listen: this is poems. I know, SKOOL! But this is different, really wild stuff, rap for babes. There are these things called limericks and everything goes upside down in them. Old men behave really badly. They murder themselves with forks, cut off their thumbs, have beards so long that birds nest in them and an old nerd reading Homer at Cromer leaps from the cliffs in boredom. In Chester, CHESTER?!, the lads throw stones at a fatso which breaks most of his bones. And not an ASBO in sight. Just this once forget Play Stations One, Two and Three, Gameboy and Nintendo. The beat is strong, the words are

simple. Spread the news on the street; we can do these ourselves.

His sister, Nike, aged 15 3/4:
Oh but it's all so sad, sad and sexy. That poor Dong wandering in the night looking for his lost Jumbly girl. He ties a long wicker nose with a candle in it round his face to see where he's going. Not cool but weird. Owls and pussy cats get the hots for each other but which is the bride and which the groom? All very TRANSSEXUAL. Ducks go off on kangaroos' tails and nut-crackers pair up with sugar-tongs (how posh). It's all a bit Freudian, do you think? Everybody is trying to get to some enchanted place where they'll be happy but mainly they're not. Fantasy? Don't you believe it. It's all on the edge of doom and yet I couldn't stop laughing, funny and sad at the same time. Think of the Yonghy-Bonghy-Bo with a huge head and no body; not like your favourite hunk. Still he loves the Lady Jingly Jones. The only trouble is they're in Coromandel (wherever) and she has a husband back in England. Very colonial. But instead of falling into bed, he sails away and they're both broken-hearted:

> On that coast of Coromandel,
> In his jug without a handle,
>   Still she weeps and daily moans;
>   On that little heap of stones
>   To her Dorking hens she moans,
> For the Yonghy-Bonghy-Bo,
> For the Yonghy-Bonghy-Bo.

Silly I know and yet I really find that touching.

My Greek great-aunt, Anaglypta:
Well, Edward Lear, just fancy and I thought he was an artist. Your great- great-grandfather knew him, of course, somewhere in the Levant. We have one or two sketches, I believe, in the attics. But since I have been reading your book, his best pictures are in words, I think. Scenes are framed by the olive with 'its twisted branches and the veil-like glitter it throws around by its semi-transparent foliage'. I haven't felt so homesick in years. But then a painting can't move and Lear's best scenes change as he rides through them. In the moonlight on the way to Tirana he passes through a wood where he sees 'the giant aerial stems of abeles, with their white branches loaded with wild vine grouped together with the majestic oak and spreading beech'. He's short-sighted so he sees everything in colour and outline, good, but that also means he keeps hitting his head on those lovely trees: ha ha! I like the way the funny poet and the oh-so-romantic artist keep confusing each other.

Her son, Thrombosis, in import-export:
I've never thought much of these literary Johnnies myself, all dreams
and no do, but the ma persuaded me to have a go. Once you get past
all the nursery-rhyme drivel, actually he has something, old Lear.
Real guts he shows poking around in places that are still danger-
ous. The war-lords continue to flourish in the Balkans even if the
fleas don't and the brigands all run hotels these days. But then he's
not just swanning about either. He's earning a decent living by pro-
ducing a saleable product, pictures; 'Ten hours' riding is as much
as you can manage, if any sketching is to be secured.' This is no
bally limp-wristed aesthete, I can tell you, though thank God for
Henry Ford. He's very good at letting you see how remoter Europe,
Albania, Corsica, Calabria, has changed yet stayed the same. So I
tell you now I shall hang on to this book; a bit of solid, reliable fact
is worth more than all this fiction lark. My only grumble about Lear
is that he seems to like everyone he meets or finds them interesting;
the only unrealistic bit in the book.

Thank you, Bosie. Acutally, this is literary scholarship at its best,
immensely informative about the life and times but generously
enthusiastic about its subject. It includes poems not in the old Fred-
erick Warne omnibus and the wonderful Italian journals have never
been reprinted. I shall have to buy another copy but it's worth it to
get cousin Bosie actually reading something worthwhile.

Human Effort

John Kinsella, *The New Arcadia*
W.W. Norton, 2005
ISBN 0 393 06053

Aggie Shepherd

John Kinsella's *The New Arcadia* is a complex prospect; it's sharp-
energied, unsettling poetry about being at home: 'We're all as
connected / to this place, and all as uncomfortable / about how close
we feel' ('Reflectors: Drive 4'). On one level there are clear judge-
ments: ecological, historical, political; while on another, the lines are
open and anything that calls on the poet's attention is simply there

as if a camera had been left running: dead roos by the road, salt in the ruts, farmers, boat people, tiny movements of small birds, bees in the middle of pausing, the welcome felt by a whole community for a new pregnancy...

The first thing you notice is how energetic the lines are: meaning flies off sideways and you have simply to let yourself ride over any difficulties until you get the feel and pace of the verse. In fact, trying to make sense too soon might be the wrong approach. It's almost as if deflection were a necessary part of seizing attention – the way that Kinsella describes a hawk hunting: 'the vacuum drawing small birds / and their song into its attention' ('The Task: Distraction and Hawk'). There are lots of birds in *The New Arcadia* and it pays to watch out for them. Untroubled occupants (unlike the human dwellers), they are good guides to the land:

> Tacked down pat by heavy rain
> a twitching tail absorbs refrains
> of late season, and wheat ears
>
> filling out to flesh the fields
> bedraggled, purple flowers
> suppressed and crushed
>
> limply to their centres; but
> the puff of a tiny chest
> alert to pressure, switches
>
> and swivels surveillance,
> the sun behind the clouds
> mirrored in its actions,
>
> ungreyed by shelter,
> its quick reaction
> to imitation: we step out
>
> chilled by reservations,
> keen to shed our syllables, call
> its actions models of behaviour.
>   ('Willy Wagtail')

The wheat ears and the purple flowers lose shape in the rain, and the syntax crushes with it so that it's easy for a reader to lose track in the first two stanzas. Is 'flesh' noun or verb? It's the small bird's movements that orientate the world. The puff of the tiny chest turns attention on the whole panorama as if suddenly to notice creation, 'the sun behind the cloud / mirrored in its actions'. It's beautifully

rooted observation, and I like how what the poem registers first in the wagtail is acknowledged to be the bird's reaction to the larger change. Man can only catch up with the sense of belonging, and the human figures have got an Adam and Eve look of shocked new experience.

The book is arranged in Five Acts, each begun by a poem about driving the same road from the city to home, under Mount Blakewell in Western Australia. These poems are called 'Reflectors', which is a handy metaphor for poetry that avoids introspection: 'Reflectors with contact skew light / and illustrate unexpected places. / They catch nothing directly, / and, we suspect, produce something / like spells or divinations' ('Reflectors: Drive 2'). The setting is rendered by multiple partial views rather than than by one account centred in the poet, or owned by him. On one of the drives, there is a smell of burning:

> you decelerate
> and smell woodsmoke through a partially
> opened window, though it's so far off
> you might be imagining it. But not
> that far – there are no horizons,
> only light, darkness, the gaseous
> states in between.
> ('Reflectors: Drive 1')

It's wonderfully phrased: 'so far off / you might be imagining it. But not / that far', making a kind of vertigo in the expanse and then contraction of the senses. It's as though there were a shortfall, or a region found that is not governed entirely by either imagination or by realism: a questionable place. The new Arcadia is also Western Australia, a land familiar to the poet from his birth, and the overlay creates a Hardy-like density of place – at once rural and worka-day, remembered, symbolic, and alien. In 'Cleaning the Rainwater Tank During the Onset of an Electrical Storm' there are four dis-tinct pictures of the same occasion ('Scene', 'Summary', 'Ellipsis' and 'Description'). The storm remains witnessable 'by the night-vision / of recall' but yields accounts that cannot alone contain its meaning, as if sudden abundance were part of the mechanism:

> 'A summer's worth in minutes!'
> he yells as the forks turn to sheet
> and bathe the whole place in religious light.

In contrast with the richness of perspectives, the land itself is sparse and antagonistic to human aspiration, as in these lines from 'Quellington Road':

> the disc plough semi-abandoned
> in the right angle of fenceline, these architectures
> of a violent sublime where the awe is worn down [...]
> These are the best prayers for human effort I can manage,
> these dessicated lines to the road, to the deceptive
> light that surrounds –
>   so bright the shadows are burnt out,
> silhouettes wells struck where water won't flow,
> plant machinery touching off no memories.

Kinsella is angry – rightly – about modern farming methods (the crop duster pilot's ears will be burning) but there's respect too for the struggle of the farmer to hold onto a living. The 'disc plough semi-abandoned' commands a grand language if only to mark where sublimity and awe have faded. In the same way the plant machinery reminds him of no memories. It's striking that what he gets from this is not so much the failure of human things as a persistent quality of human effort.

At microscopic and miniature levels, the pastoral world is thriving, as with the pollen carried by a man walking across a field, and these superbly present bees:

> As dust to the cuffs of trousers,
> puff, atomise; black-cored planets
> launching yellow satellites,
> as trailing through uninhabited pasture:
> wild oats, daisies, Salvation Jane, lupin flowers.
> This body, a carry-all, a vehicle for reform [...]
> furiously bright in the spring sunshine,
> striking up discussions, confident as bees
> almost stalling, but breaking
> away – laden – just in time,
> our instinctive, driven
> representatives.
>   ('Pollen')

Kinsella's poetry shows that there is nothing – not even walking across a field – that happens without trace or consequence, and there's both contentment and a weight of responsibility in that thought.

> It was easy enough to despise the world, but decidedly difficult to find any other habitable region.
> Edith Wharton, *The House of Mirth*

Angry (but Controlled)

Richard Dawkins, *A Devil's Chaplain*
Phoenix, 2004

Simon Starkey

A Devil's Chaplain is a selection of unrelated articles, lectures, reflections and polemics, book reviews and forewords, tributes and other eulogies published over twenty-five years. Its editor, Latha Menor, describes the book as follows: 'largely good-humoured and passionate, often angry (but controlled!), it expresses the author's claim that science "is a source of living joy"'. It is divided into seven sections, each with a vigorously written introduction. Contrasts are strongly drawn; for instance, between the nature of science, its unique ability to seek out 'crystalline' truth, and the 'crystal balls' of New Age gurus. These last have a hard time of it, of course, as a source of truth. Sometimes the ways of the ordinary person in the pew or on the prayer mat get lumped together with the mumbo-jumbo. But I did not read the book as an all-out attack, rather as a lively critique of some more harmful features of religion. Dawkins distinguishes helpfully, if sharply, between 'data' and 'philosophy', and underlines a Darwinianism which 'is the minimal theory that evolution is guided in adaptively non-random directions by non-random survival of small random hereditary changes.' So it is difficult in places, but includes some fine quotations and warm memories of an African childhood, of inspiring teachers and departed friends. I certainly did not feel I had to choose between Darwinian evolution, Intelligent Design, or theistic evolution. I enjoyed the sense of wonder at the complexity of the world, and Dawkins' point blank prose invites interaction not antagonism.

On Reading Montaigne

Jane Shilling

I wish I could remember the circumstances in which I first read Montaigne's *Essays*, but I can't. He has been my companion and friend for so long that, like the books of childhood which one reads without clearly distinguishing the experience of reading from that of living, he has become not just a text, but a palpable presence in my life.

As a child, I shouldn't have been at all surprised to run into E. Nesbit's Would-be-goods playing in the park, or Noel Streatfeild's Pauline, Posy and Petrova Fossil at ballet class. Even now, though four centuries have passed since he published his great work, it seems to me entirely possible that one day I shall look up from my desk to see a shortish fellow with a bristling Gascon moustache and a curious, intelligent eye seated opposite me.

Michel de Montaigne was born in 1533, at the Château de Montaigne, in Bordeaux, which had been his family's home for three generations. The family wealth came from trade, though Montaigne's father, of whom he writes lovingly and at length in the *Essays*, was a soldier – a more suitable occupation for a nobleman than business. Pierre de Montaigne brought up his son to speak only Latin for the first six years of his life, and raised Michel with a gentleness and consideration that later became a guiding principle of Montaigne's philosophy.

Montaigne studied law, served as a magistrate and member of the Bordeaux Parlement, and was periodically involved in affairs of State. In 1568, however, his father died and Montaigne, inheriting his estates, resigned from public life. Three years later, at the age of 38, he had painted on the wall of his study a Latin inscription announcing his retirement to the bosom of the Muses, 'where in calm and freedom from all cares he will spend what little remains of his life now more than half run out'.

The early years of Montaigne's retirement were far from calm. At painfully short intervals he lost his father, his dearest friend, Étienne de la Boétie, dead of dysentery at 33, his younger brother, killed by a blow to the head from a tennis ball, and five of his six

daughters, of whom all but the second, Léonore, died as infants. Outside the walls of the Château de Montaigne, plague and the wars of religion raged. It is no wonder that (as he describes it in the *Essays*), he failed to find the peace he hoped retirement would bring, and instead found it necessary to settle the 'chimeras and fantastic monsters' of his troubled mind by writing them down.

What we know of Montaigne (and we know an astonishing amount) comes from himself. His subject in the *Essays* is philosophy, the grand abstractions of the good life, the good death; the nature of man and his relationship to the world. But his approach is anything but abstract. He writes about what he knows, and the thing that he knows best is himself.

If you find the intimacies of reality television brutal, prepare to be appalled by Montaigne. He spares his readers nothing. 'I am myself the matter of my book', he writes, and he means just that. He writes about how he likes to sleep (on a hard bed, without his wife but with plenty of blankets), and when he likes to get up (late, at about 7am). We learn about his diet (gamey meat, unsalted bread, watered wine, melons), when he prefers to open his bowels (straight after getting up in the morning) and what a huge and exquisitely painful kidney stone looked like when he eventually succeeded in passing it (like a phallus).

He tells us what he wears (black and white garments, with silk hose in summer and winter alike and a doublet padded with rabbit fur or vulture skin); how he walks (fast – though he prefers riding a horse to going on foot, as 'little men are liable to be jostled'); what his voice sounds like ('strong, booming'); how he prefers sexual intercourse (just before bedtime, and never standing up) and what he most dreads (bad smells and the loss of his wits – his memory, he laments, is terrible).

We know, because he describes it in loving detail, what his library looked like, in what sounds like a self-contained flat with a chapel, bedroom and dressing room in a tower at the Château de Montaigne, with its beams painted with Greek and Latin inscriptions, good views on three sides and five rows of shelves filled with books. We know what he considered to be the essentials of a good life: 'Our most great and glorious achievement is to live fittingly. Everything else – reigning, building, laying up treasure – are tiny props and small accessories.' And how he hoped to die: 'I want Death to find me planting my cabbages, worrying neither about it, nor about the unfinished gardening'.

Everything interests Montaigne, from the great conundrums of

moral philosophy, the nature of friendship and the education of chil-
dren, to farting, the construction of birds' nests, and the behaviour of
his cat ('How do I know that she is not playing with me, rather than I
with her?'). It is not just his self-revelation and the spontaneity of his
style that are shocking in their freshness, but his subject matter too. As
I write, it is 413 years to the month since his death, on 13 September
1592 – yet open the *Essays* at random and you turn up reflections
on all our most pressing modern concerns: education, binge drink-
ing, religious fanaticism, relations between the sexes, even cosmetic
surgery ('Who has not heard of that woman of Paris who had herself
flayed alive merely to acquire a fresh colour from a new skin').

Montaigne's biographer Donald M. Frame quotes Sainte-
Beuve, the nineteenth-century critic, who distilled the essence of
boredom into a single line: 'There is nothing on the other side of
the hedge'. For Montaigne, there is always something on the other
side of the hedge. He never, even in the grip of the fiercest agonies
of body or mind, loses his kindness, his independence of mind or
his marvellous curiosity. If the house were burning down, this is the
book I should snatch from the flames (and somewhere in the *Essays*,
I should be certain to find some wise and profane reflections on the
saving of worldly goods from house fires).

Dark Redemption

Michel Tournier, *The Erl King*
Collins, 1972
ISBN 0002212129

Jonathan Meades

Abel Tiffauges (his family name is that of Gilles de Rais's castle)
is a polymorphously perverse, gigantic garagiste in immedi-
ately pre-war Paris. He is an ogre (the title of the US translation,
which loses the allusion to Goethe's thrillingly morbid poem). He
is a literal paedophile: he adores children. Yet he does not molest
them. He is equally drawn to birds and animals. At the outbreak of
hostilities he is conscripted and tends messenger pigeons in eastern
France before he is taken prisoner. Thus begins one of the strang-
est journeys in modern literature. Tiffauges is a traitor. He works

on Goering's hunting estate where he becomes preoccupied with stags and their taxonomy. He subsequently works at an SS school, a Napola. In the closing hours of the war he redeems himself, mutating into a sort of St Christopher to rescue a Jewish child and dying in snowy mud. Tournier's writing has the absolute precision of a Christian Schad painting. The detail is massive. His imagination is immense. He is self-consciously creating a myth and peopling it with creatures whose properties are extra-human – which is perhaps the only way of fictively treating the immane enormities of the regime which Tiffauges has served.

The Song Belongs to the Hearers

Larry McMurtry, *Lonesome Dove*
Pocket Books, 1986
ISBN 0671623249

Ann Stapleton

> 'It's like I told you last night, son. The earth is mostly just a boneyard. But pretty in the sunlight,' he added.
>
> Augustus McCrae

If all this life boils down to bones and a few sunsets, and we are to know this from the start, it matters greatly where our country lies and who our countrymen might be. For novelist Larry McMurtry, Texas, with its 'isolating space' and its 'brutal light,' its 'aridity' and 'erosion,' is the context for this life, which is to say, the one place in the world that calls love (with all its dark little fortifications and all its gorgeous, sunlit ruins) into being. Even as his grandparents 'stopped at a point in the emptiness and made their start' in ranching, their grandson, in the same spirit of adventure and daring, sat down at a typewriter, fed in a blank sheet of paper, and began to write the West:

> In my teens, already a failed cowboy, I realized that – one way or another – my work was going to be with words, not

herds, though, of course, being a word-herder means that one has not entirely escaped the herding imperative. Didn't I just herd a few drifting strays into this paragraph?

Indeed, his bookplates are said to feature a miniature version of the McMurtry cattle brand.

A topnotch antiquarian bookseller who grew up in the once 'bookless' town of Archer City, Texas, McMurtry has established his own version of Hay-on-Wye there, a used bookstore containing hundreds of thousands of volumes, some quite rare, housed in four separate buildings around his hometown; only one has a cash register, and patrons are on the honor system to bring their selections from the other (often unlocked) buildings to the main one for purchasing. In a wonderful bit of irony, McMurtry's book enterprise (the dream of a Texas childhood in which the printed word was of little value, and boys like him who loved it, suspect) is now central to the economic survival of tiny Archer City, population 1848. The man who grew from the 'bookish and suspiciously observant youngster' who might 'in time disgrace the line' of cattle-herding McMurtrys may, in fact, have saved the whole town – in his spare time, that is, when he wasn't busy writing the best Western of all time, a strong contender for the Great American Novel, *Lonesome Dove*.

Though his father and uncles, cattlemen all, could only watch from the roof of his grandfather's ranch house as the last cattle drives passed by, it was McMurtry's loving act of attention, *Lonesome Dove*, that stopped the exodus in its tracks and committed the symbolic last drive to paper, where it can reasonably hope to run on forever. Yet this achievement is a problematic one for him – a student of Western history and a person of conscience, a man of his time: his mind surveys a broader map of the West than just the territory his own people recognize. To McMurtry, a supreme irony seems to be that a book he believes he intended as an indictment of an inglorious past, a negative comment on the violence and destruction that accompanied the settlement of the West, has been seen by most of its readers as a salute to its incomparable splendor, an eight-hundred-plus-page encomium to the Age of Heroes in its passing. In the range wars between the triumphalist view, which sees the settlement of the West as a flawed but amazing achievement, and the revisionist one, which sees it as something of a horror story, McMurtry the liberal thinker sides with the latter. But sometimes the heart's truths lie deeper down, and buried in *In a Narrow Grave*, McMurtry's early book of essays on Texas and the demise of the West, is this admission: 'The death [. . .] moves me – the way of life

that is dying had its value. Its appeal was simple, but genuine, and it called to it and is taking with it people whom one could not but love,' just such people as fill the pages of *Lonesome Dove*.

Hard-working former Texas Ranger Captain Woodrow F. Call, chasing down the ever-receding frontier to its furthest redoubt, hopes to catch a glimpse of the waving, green sea of northern grass 'before the bankers and lawyers get it.' His fellow Ranger and long-time partner, the fun-loving philosopher-king Augustus McCrae (a character described by actor Robert Duvall, who played the part in the beloved television mini-series, as 'at least as good as Hamlet'), is persuaded along by his dreams of a reunion with the strong-willed Clara ('I expect it was the major mistake of my life, letting her slip by'). Young Newt Dobbs, Call's unacknowledged son, searches for identity and kinship while trying to earn the respect of his father and the other cowboys ('He was a good boy, as gentle as the gray doves that came to peck for gravel on the flats behind the barn. He would try to do any task that was asked of him, and if he worried overmuch it was that he wasn't good enough at his work to please the Captain'). Joshua Deets, the black scout, peers ahead into the distance for them all, his own loneliness and misgiving ('We way up here and it ain't our country') subsumed by his mission always to guide them safely home. Jake Spoon pursues pleasure in the form of women or gambling or fine clothing, but has just enough residual restlessness in him to spur him ever onward toward some worsening trouble ('Jake just kind of drifts. Any wind can blow him'). Beautiful Lorena Wood, *Lonesome Dove*'s sole 'sportin' gal,' who has 'never lived in a place where it [is] cool,' has just 'one aim' in life: to get to San Francisco, to see for herself 'how blue the water [is] in the bay, and how the ships [come] in from everywhere.' July Johnson, a solemn young Arkansas sheriff, is brow-beaten into an ill-conceived mission to find and arrest Jake Spoon, whose stray shot accidentally killed Johnson's brother ('bad luck all around'). July's wife Elmira (Ellie), a former saloon girl, then embarks on her own journey to find Dee Boot, the gunfighter in whose coarse company 'she could belong to herself.' Roscoe Brown, the reluctant deputy, is sent after July, to deliver the bad news that his wife has decamped ('Traveling was even worse than Roscoe had supposed it would be, and he had supposed it would be pure hell'). In a kind of collective yearning, all roads lead west-northwest, and the reader follows willingly the crisscross trails left by inspiration or mania or just a weary ordinariness run dry of other options.

The American West was settled one person – one vision – at a time, in obduracy and tenderness, folly and courage, its inevitable

taming brought about as much by failure and obsession and recurrent bad luck as by any vision of a higher good. That McMurtry uses this undeniable-as-an-arrowhead-in-your-hand pointed fact as the basis for his story is what gives *Lonesome Dove* the right to be called an American epic. For the characters' personal wests, 'Wests-in-the-mind's-eye,' as McMurtry calls them, are the peculiar, animating forces that determine destination, whether where these pioneers end up is the place they dreamed of, or simply the spot of ground where they are standing when they can go no further. Many trails cross through the mud here – brand new starts and sudden peterings out that can signify a failure of nerve or a decision to stay, no matter the cost. You can never be wholly certain which is a beginning and which a conclusion, or how it is that one journey ends in the ground, while another, crossing a far hill in glorious light, at least for a time seems to enter the sky. And somehow all these deep and disappearing tracks, taken together, make up a country.

McMurtry knows that the human psyche must always have its point on the horizon for which to aim. The cattle drive is the perfect embodiment of this impulse, and a wonderful metaphor for the strange, maniacal ways in which we focus on attainment and arrival, when the way there, in all its lurches forward and loopings back, is all we really have. For the cowboy, the admirable performance of duty is life itself. But like life, the drive also admits of love and loss and terrible grief, and even in a man like Call, for whom work is everything, the possibility that one day you may pause in the saddle and take a good look around you at the broad horizon and feel a sudden, overwhelming fear that none of it is worth the trouble.

But there is Newt, the good boy, who, over the course of the drive, is changed forever by the passing landscape (even as he and the others change its contours by the force of their lives passing over it) to become that everyday, rare thing: a good man. And there is the incomparable Gus, ever the connoisseur of experience, who tells Newt, 'I can't think of nothing better than riding a fine horse into a new country. It's exactly what I was meant for, and Woodrow too.' Indeed, one of the deep pleasures of this novel is that McMurtry, while refusing to underplay the difficulty of human endeavor in all its clumsiness and partial realization, never shorts the joy of life. Even in desperate straits, Gus declaims, 'It's a fine world, though rich in hardships at times,' and McMurtry means to keep the main clause just where it is.

Crude, funny, and tender, forbearant and fearful, and often achingly young for the responsibilities he bears, the American cowboy

(look quickly now, before he disappears) is perfectly preserved in all his contradictions in *Lonesome Dove*. McMurtry comes from a long line of cattlemen, more at home and most themselves on a horse than anywhere else in the world, and resistant toward anything (often, even domestic life) that requires them to swing back down to earth. He captures the essence of what it is to exist 'a-horseback,' to herd living, breathing creatures with minds of their own, in rhythms both singular and collective, across an open, hazardous space toward an ending (even as time itself herds the cowboy along toward his own). He describes (with an insider's knowledge) the herd mentality of the cowboys themselves: a herd – of men – driving a herd – of beasts. With their (justifiable) fears of drowning, for example, it is as tenuous an enterprise to cross the men over the rivers on the way north as it is to cross the cattle. McMurtry depicts (with much humanity all around) the cowboys' in-town exuberances, yes, but also the poignancy of their shyness toward women, their humble gratefulness for any female presence, their tendency, as in Dish Boggett's unrequited feelings for Lorie, to fall deeply in love and to stay that way, and their loneliness for home: 'Even on a nice clear night the sad singing and the knowledge that there were no ladies was enough to make the men feel low. They ended up talking of their sisters, those that had them, most nights.' Po Campo, the cook, 'a strange man,' 'friendly and kind to everyone,' yet keeping apart, 'walking all day behind the wagon,' at night whiles away the time by whittling 'little wooden [women] about two inches high.' 'Soon each of the cowboys had been given one of the carvings. "To remind you of your sisters," Po said.'

Even as McMurtry has a true gift for helping us see – often in just a few brief sentences – far into the mystery of human relationship, with all its unaccountable choices and mixed results, he is a fine poet of solitude, giving voice to the regions of remoteness, the far ranges of the inaccessible and unshared, in each of us. Many a night, you suppose, he must have treated loneliness to the drink of its choice and whiled away a good long time just listening to its crazy tales: Dish Boggett guarding Lorena, deep in love and so close 'he could have crept up to the tent and heard her breathing,' yet knowing he will 'never be able to eliminate those [last] few yards'; forlorn Pea Eye Parker's stark naked trek, in the aftermath of an Indian attack, across the prickly snow-and-sunburn landscape, his bare feet 'swollen the size of a cow's bladder and cut to shreds'; Lorena Wood, captured by Blue Duck and his depraved henchmen, wondering 'if she could just learn to die'; July Johnson weeping in the Dodge City post office as he tries to compose a letter home, real-

izing that 'all he [has] to report [is] death and failure'; his wife Ellie's knowledge that the indifferent Dee Boot, when he hears of her quest to find him, will only laugh, as he always loved to, 'about the absurd things people [do] for bad reasons.'

The scout Joshua Deets, whose responsibility for the outfit's welfare is second only to Call's, is perhaps the loneliest of all the Hat Creek men. His intelligence and awareness particularly acute, he absorbs all that experience can teach him, but sometimes wishes he could have 'some schooling.' He is respected by the men, who over the years have become his people, but is set slightly apart from them by his dark skin. The hardest of hard men, riding point into the unknown, constantly scanning the dust for trouble's impress, making expert nooses for hangings, and working burial detail, Deets is nevertheless fascinated by the little woman Po gives him, the closest he will ever come to a female presence in his life. In Deets, McMurtry locates the precise point at which friendship stops and turns back and we are left alone again with just the moon to comfort us:

> They were friends, though, he and Newt. The boy was young and had all his hopes, while Deets was older and had fewer. Newt sometimes asked so many questions that Deets had to laugh – he was like a cistern, from which questions flowed instead of water. Some Deets answered and some he didn't. He didn't tell Newt all he knew. He didn't tell him that even when life seemed easy, it kept on getting harder. Deets liked his work, liked being part of the outfit and having his name on the sign; yet he often felt sad. His main happiness consisted of sitting with his back against the water trough at night, watching the sky and the changing moon. He had known several men who blew their heads off, and he had pondered it much. It seemed to him it was probably because they could not take enough happiness just from the sky and the moon to carry them over the low feelings that came to all men.

Though one of the severest limitations of the cowboy culture is that it debars women, McMurtry's own ethic is much more inclusive; part of the genius of *Lonesome Dove* is that, far from being another *High Noon* with a male figure standing alone in the street, its women sit as tall in the saddle as the men (sometimes taller). July Johnson's wife Ellie has never entertained a feeling anything like love for him, nor any motherly impulse toward her son Joe. But rather than ask us to judge her (the least complicated thing to do), McMurtry presents her as a relentless obsessive (so many settlers were, in one way or

another), as someone in the grip of a magnificent, in its degraded way, and very hazardous idea, one that will probably destroy her, but someone with a great deal of courage and a blind instinct for life. McMurtry turns you toward her as she slips by into history, but not before she becomes real:

> Soon the skies above the river got wider and wider as the river wound out of the trees and cut through the plains. The nights were cool, the mornings warming quickly, so that when Elmira woke the river behind her would be covered with a frosting of mist, and the boat would be lost in the mist completely, until the sun could break through. Several times ducks and geese, taking off in the mist, almost flew into her as she stood at the rear of the boat wrapped in the buffalo robe. When the mist was heavy the splash of birds or the jumping of fish startled her; once she was frightened by the heavy beat of wings as one of the huge gray cranes flew low over the boat. As the mist thinned she would see the cranes standing solemnly in the shallows, ignoring the strings of ducks that swam nearby. Pockets of mist would linger on the water for an hour or more after the sun had risen and the sky turned a clear blue.

This is a radical little passage, insisting, as it does, that here, in the perceptions of a filthy dirty, husband- and child-abandoning, pregnant ex-prostitute, the world exists, fully and vibrantly intact, completely independent of (even the most desperate) circumstance, and within the context of a singular (and perilous) inattention to male expectation. McMurtry gives Ellie a real life, replete with its own sights to see. Indeed, McMurtry's decision to have Ellie board the whiskey boat at all, with only rough buffalo hunters for companions, is to let the dangers of such an action be dwarfed by the presence of her Big Idea. In Ellie, McMurtry gives us a stunted, fixated female Odysseus wrapped in buffalo hide, scratching at countless fleas, and dreaming of a golden time that likely never existed, her dear Penelope a good-timing gunfighter who always found a reason to let her go. Thus she becomes a bizarre visionary of sorts, by virtue of McMurtry's close attention to the mystery of her presence in a world startling and beautiful in spite of itself. And perhaps *Lonesome Dove*'s readers are capable of entertaining a broader definition of the word 'heroic' than the author, in his aversion to the golden lighting of mythos, may imagine.

And herein lies one of the difficulties inherent in McMurtry's assertion that he's written a (woefully misunderstood) debunking

of Western mythology. If he gives us a West that is brutal and unas-
suageable, that guts our plans and tramples us flat (no one who
reads *Lonesome Dove* can possibly come away with the idea that
the West was just a cloud-lit canter over a green hill into a stunning
sunset), and if the characters, faced with such daily hardship, cleave
to their dreams, such as they are, and refuse to surrender, though
their obstinacy may (and often does) cost them their very lives, the
result must necessarily be an increased, not a diminished, respect
on the part of the reader for such pitiable, stubborn strivers. Ellie,
looking backwards from the boat with the birds for company, her
back to the men, represents an irreplaceable consciousness in all its
fierce hopes and its helplessness to be anything but mortal, gliding
across a day that will end. How many such strange souls, in the grip
of ideas perhaps too enormous for their power to carry them out,
of imaginings that at least to them looked a little bit like happiness,
must have perished ungreeted and unknown and unmourned on
the way west to the Pacific, like thousands of hatchling turtles, each
setting a solitary course across a treacherous stretch of sand toward
a sea they somehow had faith would be there when they arrived.
The miracle is that some actually made it. And in the context of
Lonesome Dove, it is, perhaps, worthwhile to consider that if such
intrepid lovers of the far horizon had a say in things, it might not be
the revisionists they'd choose to tell their stories.

The unforgettable character of Woodrow F. Call is based loosely
on that of the Old Man himself, Charles Goodnight, one of the most
successful and perhaps best known of all cattlemen, whose long
life (1836–1929) spanned the coming and going of the great cattle
drives and the so-called taming of the West. And the Indian fight in
which a sorely wounded Gus is left behind while Pea Eye attempts
to go for help is patterned after a similar incident that led to the
death of Goodnight's longtime partner and friend, Oliver Loving. It
may be true, as McMurtry has written, that the god (of that time)
is 'riding away fast and will soon be out of sight and out of hearing,'
perhaps is already, but it is the god McMurtry's people sacrifice to,
the god he rails against, the god that (even in his unbelief) he loves.
And it is the Old Man, Charles Goodnight (was there ever a more
magnificent, sadder true-life name for the embodiment of an era's
passing?), whom the Indians sometimes called Buenas Noches, who
haunts his dreams.

McMurtry has written that 'On the rims of the West – and
perhaps, in America, only there – one can still know for a moment
the frontier emotion, the loneliness and the excitement and the

sense of an openness so vast that it still challenges – in Gatsbian phrase – our capacity for wonder.' And yet, as the men of the Hat Creek company ride over the rim of their known world, we can't but see that they are waving goodbye, that they are riding away for good, and even for McMurtry the revisionist there is an undeniable sense of bereavement:

> In their youth, as I have said, my uncles sat on the barn and watched the last trail herds moving north – I sat on the self-same barn and saw only a few oil-field pickups and a couple of dairy trucks go by. That life died, and I am lucky to have found so satisfying a replacement as Don Quixote offered. And yet, that first life has not quite died in me – not quite. I missed it only by the width of a generation and, as I was growing up, heard the whistle of its departure. Not long after I entered the pastures of the empty page I realized that the place where all my stories start is the heart faced suddenly with the loss of its country, its customary and legendary range.

'No tears in the writer, no tears in the reader,' wrote Robert Frost, but the converse is equally true, and *Lonesome Dove* is wet with McMurtry's. Surely the reader, who retains his own love for his own lost lands, wherever they may be, cannot be faulted, as he watches a world ride out of sight, for shedding a few tears of his own. And once the story is told, once the song is sung, it ceases to matter much what the author, the singer, might think or feel about it, for the music has passed on into other lives, as it was meant to. As Po Campo says of the sad songs he sings to the cowboys around the evening campfire, 'The songs don't belong to me. [. . .] They belong to those who hear them. [. . .] If you hear them, they belong to you.' *Lonesome Dove* is not McMurtry's anymore, a fact he understands. History is personal, always; and love, a triumphalist, saying to Call, who'll half understand, in Gus's irritatingly loud voice, ' 'I god, Woodrow,' 'It ain't dying I'm talking about, it's living.'

> The woods decay, the woods decay and fall,
> The vapours weep their burthen to the ground,
> Man comes and tills the field and lies beneath,
> And after many a summer dies the swan.
>
> Tennyson, *Tithonus*

In Open Boats

The Orkneyinga Saga, or The History of the Earls of Orkney
Translated by Hermann Pálsson and Paul Edwards
Harmondsworth: Penguin, 1978

Christopher Routledge

What makes the *Orkneyinga Saga* so compelling? It certainly doesn't have the prizefighter glamour of *Beowulf*; its action is matter-of-fact and political, rather than the sweeping heroism of the lone warrior. But where *Beowulf* grips us with the bravery and glory of an individual, *Orkneyinga* impresses with the momentum of a whole dynasty. It tells the story of the Earls of Orkney, who ruled the islands from at least the time of the first Viking invasions of mainland Britain, around 780 AD. Compiled by an unknown Icelandic scribe from myths, legends, historical documents, and plain old conjecture, the saga was written some time after 1192, but probably before 1206 AD. At the time Orkney, Shetland, and the Outer Hebrides were all Norwegian territories and the saga has much to tell us about the lives of the people who lived in that time. But one of the many charms of *Orkneyinga* is its medieval view of what constitutes historical knowledge. More docudrama than rigorous historical description, for readers bothered by literary veracity the saga should come with a disclaimer: 'Mostly based on real events.'

Twenty-first-century Orkney consists of around 70 islands, of which 16 are inhabited. The largest, Mainland, is home to the vast majority of the 20,000 population. Its climate is mild, the soil fertile, and back in Viking times the sea was full of fish. In 2005 the sea is full of divers exploring the wrecks of Scapa Flow. At only two days' sail from Norway it is easy to see why eighth-century Norwegian migrants were attracted to the place. The saga explains how the Earldom came into being. King Harald Fine-Hair of Norway had set out to deal with Viking raiders who based themselves in Orkney, the Hebrides, and the Isle of Man, taking with him Earl Rognvald, whose son was killed in one of their many battles: 'On his way back to Norway King Harald gave Earl Rognvald Shetland and Orkney in compensation for his son, but Rognvald gave all the islands to

his brother Sigurd, the forecastleman on King Harald's ship. When the King sailed back east he gave Sigurd the title of earl and Sigurd stayed on the islands.'

What follows is an account of battles, occupations, alliances and treacheries, comings and goings, daring exploits, and heroic failures. There is a great deal of drinking and many feasts, which seem to have been especially bloodthirsty affairs, often ending in fighting and killings. Descriptive passages are few and if at times the telling seems relentless, the action and the movement are enough to keep us interested. These two things – an account of the past and skilful storytelling – are present in the best sagas and *Orkneyinga* is one of the best. What is attractive about it is not the language or the style – this translation does not have the brilliance of Seamus Heaney's *Beowulf* – but the sense of immediacy it brings to distant events. We hear about farming, fishing, but above all plundering, and wonder how men in open boats could travel as far afield as Russia and Byzantium.

For all its inaccuracies, inventions, and exaggerations, the *Orkneyinga Saga* is one of the closest things we have to a sustained historical account of the British Isles in the medieval period. It is also a swashbuckling story of heroism and valour across generations, a record of some of the most dramatic dinner parties in history, and a fascinating glimpse into ordinary life on a small island a very long time ago.

Stop Making Sense

Gertrude Stein, *Tender Buttons*, pub. 1914

Dana Cairns Watson

The words in the prose poetry of *Tender Buttons* turn toward each other, unfold, and ease outward to create a kaleidoscope of meaning. The same words appear over and over again, but at each appearance they fall in different directions toward significance. Meanings appear and spread rather than becoming focused, pinpointed. We cannot grab handfuls of *Tender Buttons* and shove them into our minds' categories – ones that have been pre-fabricated by other, normal, reading. Gertrude Stein's writing is different.

Stein does so many things at once that she's impossible to summarize, but I can say that *Tender Buttons* is almost always describing itself. Stein writes about rhetoric, she imitates the staccato noises of daily life, and she opens epistemological questions. *Tender Buttons* explores the psychology of reading. As someone who successfully completed all but a couple of classes of medical school, Stein may even be pondering human neuroanatomy, especially the way that the brain processes language. The book is a study in attention, including inattention, and it challenges the brain's knack of making sense of whatever inputs it receives. It explores and plays with the cooperation between the sights and sounds of words. It forces us to recognize and re-embrace our own unique visions and to recognize our own personal multiplicity. Parts of *Tender Buttons* are sensual, celebrating love or specifically lesbianism. Parts of it celebrate the visual or (as some readers have said) make writing a visual art form. I think she's exploring friendly conversation, too.

Readers can develop systems for understanding the book, but good readers will also notice when (not if) Stein disrupts these systems. We may become frustrated along the way but, as Stein writes here, 'What is the use of a violent kind of delightfulness if there is no pleasure in not getting tired of it.' We can enjoy *Tender Buttons* for the pleasure of the sounds and the feel of the words on the tongue, or for its amusing word play, or because it's fun to discover (even to help invent?) its coded meanings – but why not have it all? There is always more than we can account for – and 'more' is one of the words Stein uses most often here.

After all, nothing can be wholly known. More can be added to any understanding of anything. All we can do is collect words, let each addition alter our understanding, and recognize that we'll never wholly comprehend the thing we are trying to know. Stein writes, 'A single image is not splendor' and 'A sign of more in not mentioned.' The silence does not mean an ending; it signifies that there is much more to be said. If more were said, something very different would be known: 'A sudden slice changes the whole plate.' And Stein writes, 'Sugar is not a vegetable,' even though we know sugar is extracted from vegetables. That which we find a use for, that which we state overtly, certainly does not tell the whole story.

Stein writes, 'A white hunter is nearly crazy,' and I think of the many colors in white light and the impossibility of seeing all things. A standard single-goal-oriented hunter kills (meaning, or pheasants); a white-light-spectrum hunter doesn't kill, but goes crazy in attempting to see 'it all.' But what if, *at the same time*, Stein means the opposite? Maybe people just think this hunter's crazy? If the white hunter (the

white-skinned hunter, instead of someone hunting for whiteness) stands in for the dominating world-view, then Stein is suggesting that this dominant perspective is crazy. The confusion Stein causes makes readers think back to the roots of words, and here readers might start to see myriad small 'crazed' cracks appearing in the smooth surface of mainstream understanding. In short, a white hunter kills multiplicity (though signs of it remain in the crazed surface of its façade), and a different white hunter goes crazy trying not to.

Readers might feel ridiculous reading such a text, but I find the experience joyful, freeing, refreshing. One of Stein's sentences reads: 'Water astonishing and difficult altogether makes a meadow and a stroke.' The words themselves are lovely, and even funny, but also thought-provoking. Water contributes to meadows (all life, in fact) and swimming (bodies of water). But that's a very silly paraphrase, and even an ugly one. Appreciate the lovely mystery of her syntax 'Water astonishing and difficult altogether'; notice the multiple meanings of 'stroke'; see 'mead' and 'together' and 'all' and 'cult' and even imagine seeing 'stork'; hear 'doe' and 'swishing' and 'fishing'; and add all the meanings of those words to the mix. Sometimes the word puzzle can't be resolved, but more has been seen in the process of trying. And Stein describes these lucrative failures: 'A piece was not exchanged, not a bit of it, a piece was left over. The rest was mismanaged.' Think about that: notice, see, hear, exchange, imagine. This most unusual book, the most stylistically innovative of any of Stein's works, can be infinitely pleasing. 'And why complain of more, why complain of very much more.'

Stein reminds me that words are living beings, with a history of their own, and that true word-lovers can choose not to make words march in line to direct orders from their speakers or writers. She writes, 'It makes mercy and relaxation and even a strength to spread a table fuller,' and I imagine an author acting as a cheerful, welcoming host to her words. Stein has the courage to give up some authorial power, and she reminds us that even when we do try to make words mean something, they have a knack of breaking out of those sensible confines – expressing hidden meanings, causing laughter or just confusion, or even expressing ideas we didn't think until after we heard ourselves say the words.

Wanting to be efficient, to finish the book, will not help you read Stein, especially *Tender Buttons*. Instead, break away from your normal tendencies, start to envision difference, and welcome surprises. Stare at words, sound them out, turn the book's pages backward and forward as you notice repetitions and internal allusions, and look up definitions and etymologies for words you already

know. Stein prepares you for these new approaches to a familiar activity with her first poem, 'A carafe, that is a blind glass':

> A kind in glass and a cousin, a spectacle and nothing strange a single hurt color and an arrangement in a system to pointing. All this and not ordinary, not unordered in not resembling. The difference is spreading.

Life-and-Death Argument

Don DeLillo, *Underworld*
Picador, 1998

David Attwooll

He speaks in your voice, American, and there's a shine in his eye that's halfway hopeful.

The kid skipping school in these opening lines could be a latter-day, inner-city Huck Finn, but this is a different kind of Great American Novel, and he's not even a central character. The baseball he catches is, though. It becomes a touchstone in DeLillo's epic, refracting kaleidoscope of American myths and lives, times and places, covering the latter half of the twentieth century.

It's not just any baseball game he jumps the turnstiles into, as *Underworld* kicks off with its characteristic rhythmic and spiky prose:

> He picks up speed and seems to lose his gangliness, the slouchy funk of hormone and unbelonging and all the stammering things that seal his adolescence. He is just a running boy, a half-seen figure from the streets, but the way running reveals some clue to being, the way a runner bares himself to consciousness, this is how the dark-skinned kid seems to open to the world, how the bloodrush of a dozen strides brings him into eloquence.

It's the third of October 1951 and it's the famous New York World Series – a home derby between Giants and Dodgers, Bronx and Brooklyn. Among the many jump-cut narrative strands in the vast crowd, Frank

Sinatra sits next to J. Edgar Hoover, who is briefed during the game about the Soviet test explosion of an atom bomb. While everyone is cheering the improbable winning home run, Hoover is looking at a reproduction of Brueghel's *Triumph of Death* someone has torn from a magazine. That's the chapter title of this tremendously vital opening set piece. And the kid grabs the winning ball, which subsequently becomes a kind of Holy Grail of lost innocence.

The paperback edition my daughter gave me, published in 1999, has a ghostly cover picture of the World Trade Center towers, and there are odd premonitions of '9/11' – and perhaps how America got to where it is now. One character apprehensively watches the towers being built in 1974 ('Very terrible thing...'). Elsewhere, another says: 'You need the leaders of both sides to keep the cold war going. It's the one constant thing. It's honest, it's dependable. Because when the tension and rivalry come to an end, that's when your worst night-mares begin... other forces will come rushing in, demanding and challenging.'

The whole novel crackles and fizzes in the force field between polarities: the 1950s and the 1990s; New York and the Arizona desert; alienation and immediacy; loyalty and betrayal; paranoia and hope; clinical technological order and muddled human improvisation. But this makes it all sound very abstract and theoretical: these elements vibrate in a beguiling plot that centres on Nick Shay, who like the author was born and brought up in the Bronx, of Italian-American parents. He works for a waste disposal corporation in an antiseptic bronze tower in Phoenix; he has complicated relationships with his wife, family, friends and colleagues, a jokey gangster growl, and a guilty secret.

Underworld's secrets are public as well as private, and involve the FBI, secret nuclear testing, the Mob ('That particular life. Under the surface of ordinary things'), conspiracy theories, and burying hazard-ous waste. They act as a kind of ground bass to the novel. Many key scenes happen underground; rats and cockroaches crop up fairly reg-ularly. Yet if all this sounds too solemn, it's also illuminated by a subtle black humour. Some of the dialogue, for example, is funny in a way that Pinter can be, when played for laughs: a middle-aged couple half listening to each other, each unpacking their own domestic clutter at the end of a day; corporate colleagues drunkenly sparring in a night club. The effect is a sort of repetitive musical round or counterpoint.

Although another key character is a painter and installation artist, her name – Klara Sax – and the titles of several sections ('Long Tall Sally', 'Elegy for Left Hand Alone', 'Cocksucker Blues')

betray the musicality of the book. If it was a European novel it might be called symphonic in its scale and interweaving of themes, but I feel it has more in common with 'jazz that had the texture of life-and-death argument' (as DeLillo writes). Not only are there several scenes in jazz clubs, and references to Mingus and Parker, but the prose has the rhythm and 'sound of surprise' that jazz is famous for, in its unexpected choice of words and phrases, its bloody-minded individuality and immediacy. Klara the artist says:

> See, we're painting, hand-painting in some cases, putting our puny hands to great weapons systems, to systems that came out of the factories and assembly halls as near alike as possible, millions of components stamped out, repeated endlessly, and we're trying to unrepeat, to find an element of felt life, and maybe there's a sort of survival instinct here, a graffiti instinct – to trespass and declare ourselves, show who we are.

What I love about this big novel isn't in the end its grand themes, brilliantly though they're handled; it's the local pleasures of passages such as this, which lyrically articulate DeLillo's trump-card theme:

> And you can glance out the window for a moment, distracted by the sound of small kids playing a made-up game in a neighbor's yard… under the glimmerglass sky, and you look at the things in the room, offscreen, unwebbed, the tissued grain of the deskwood alive in light, the thick lived tenor of things, the argument of things to be seen and eaten, the apple core going sepia in the lunch tray, and the dense measures of experience in a random glance…

I read slowly for pleasure, since I read a lot of material rapidly for work. So I have a prejudice against long novels. Some people have a prejudice, given where we are today, against things that are American, large, and ambitious. This is a novel to overcome prejudices. Since reading it I started *War and Peace*…

> Why do we call our generous ideas illusions, and the mean ones truths?
>
> Edith Wharton, *The House of Mirth*

Looking for a Language
Christopher Fry,
One Thing More

Christopher Fry, 18 December 1907–30 June 2005

Sue Lloyd

In 1986, as he approached his eightieth year, Christopher Fry intended to give up writing. However, Jane Morgan, who had directed most of his plays for BBC Radio, along with her colleague Michael Bakewell, persuaded him to write one more play, to be performed in Chelmsford Cathedral and broadcast on Radio Four.[1]

The result was *One Thing More, or Caedmon Construed*. In this play, Fry was returning to the kind of religious drama with which he had begun his writing career. *Boy with a Cart*, the story of St Cuthman of Sussex, was written in 1938 for his local church. It led to a commission for the Tewkesbury Festival, *The Tower*, which was performed in 1939 but is unpublished. Fry continued to fulfil commissions for plays to be performed in places of worship: *Thor, with Angels* for the Canterbury Festival (1948), and *A Sleep of Prisoners* for the Festival of Britain committee, which was performed in churches all over England, beginning with the University Church at Oxford in April 1951.

That makes a gap of thirty-five years before Fry returned to religious drama with *One Thing More*, though all of his plays have a serious intent beneath the sparkling verse and gentle humour. His working life spans very different eras. In the fifties, theatre-goers revelled in his plays, in part as an escape from the difficult postwar years. When the reaction came, with kitchen-sink drama, Fry continued to work for the theatre, but he turned to translation as his confidence in his own work ebbed: Anouilh, Giraudoux, Rostand and Ibsen. Screenplays, television dramas and smaller-scale works were written too, including a family history for OUP in 1978, *Can You Find Me?*

After such a long and active writing life, perhaps it is not surprising that Fry considered retiring. But *One Thing More* gave him

one more opportunity to set out his philosophy of life in dramatic form. The play tells the story of Caedmon, a farmhand who is unable to communicate with his fellows. 'It's an advantage to start off with a fellow-feeling for your main character', Fry told an audience at Chichester in 2002.[2] Much like his tongue-tied Caedmon, Fry too had spent his life searching for a language with which to convey his intentions: 'How can we hope to find a tongue to match the mysteries within and about us?' He used to joke that he bought a donkey to encourage himself: at least he could write without the distress that a donkey seems to experience every time it brays.

The story of Caedmon was taken from Bede's *Ecclesiastical History*. Fry imagines Caedmon as a man burdened by guilt for having loved a girl of only sixteen. She died bearing their daughter. Unable to forgive himself, he becomes a soldier, seeking to deal out death as he feels he gave his lover death. Thirty years later, he returns home for news of his daughter to find she has joined the Abbey of Whitby as a novice. He goes there to listen to her singing and is taken on at the abbey as a farmhand. But although, in the words of the Overman, 'he seems to look as straight at things as the warp of the world will let him', he is unable to talk with his fellows. The crisis comes when he is unable to take his turn at singing at a special feast with the other farmhands.

That night he has a dream, in which a Person comes to him and tells him to sing. The key is that he is forced to confront his feelings of guilt and find forgiveness within himself. Then songs of praise pour from him. He is accepted as a monk, and sings in the abbey with his daughter.

> As though a harp had been put into his hand, he sought out words with the beat of the human pulse, trying to find, however awkwardly, the indwelling music that created us.

His capacity for song is innate and vital but still special conditions are needed to release it and that sense of direction in life is characteristic of Fry. He believed that life has meaning, that a purpose is working itself out in individual creatures and in humanity generally. As he says, in *Looking for a Language*, sometimes we have 'the sensation of overtaking what had always been waiting for us':

> To be content to write off the hanging-gardens of the universe and the pilgrim-progression of life, which stretch and break our comprehension, to an unpurposed chain of cause and accident is to me a failure of sensibility as irrational as a rain dance.

It's a fine and great vision in which the defeat of sensibility by apparent reality is felt to be irrational. Fry says we must trust our intuition that life has more meaning than can be perceived through our senses: 'Shall we live in mystery and yet conduct ourselves as though everything were known?' asks Moses in *The Firstborn*. It is this mystery that Fry tried to find a language to express in his plays. He chose to write in poetry because he felt its form, 'like a kind of coiled spring of energy', would better impart the sense of purpose underlying 'the silent order whose speech is all visible things'. Prose deals with surface reality, the individuality of living things; poetry can try to express true reality and the underlying unity of creation. So *One Thing More* is written in prose, except for the songs sung at the feast by the farmhands, and when Caedmon finds his voice, he sings the praises of God in verse.

There is humour in it, too, as one would expect from Fry, not so much in word-play (though his delight in words is still evident) as in the wry but sympathetic humour which pervades all his plays. It springs from his positive, joyous attitude to life. 'Whoever you are, this can't be made light of', says Caedmon of his guilt to the Person. 'More's the pity, since that may be the very aim of the dark mills', comes the reply. Caedmon has to forgive himself and put the past behind him, or he will be frustrating God's purpose for him.

All these themes run through Christopher Fry's work, and another keeps them company – a sense of wonder at the world and gratitude for the miracle of being alive. So it is fitting that, in his *One Word More*, he gives Caedmon this to say in his last moments:

> I've been shown such a universe! … Before I am lost and found in God's love I should like to make one thing more, a song or half-song or no song, but one thing more in thanksgiving for having seen and known and lived and died.

With typical modesty, Fry claimed only to have 'tried' to find a language. But he succeeded more than he knew.

---

[1] In fact, Fry was to write a further play, *A Ringing of Bells*, commissioned for the Millennium by his old school, Bedford Modern School, and performed at the National Theatre in 2001.

[2] Published as *Looking for a Language*, this was a revised version of a talk originally given at Leicester University in 1987, itself based on an article in *Adam International Review*, no. 428-30, 1980.

Good Books

Have you read any good books recently? Tell us – answers on a postcard – about your all time favourite book, a great book you've read recently or simply the book you're reading at the moment. Many thanks to Erica Bridges and Catherine Sheldon for this issue's contri- butions.

Susanna Clarke, *Jonathan Strange and Mr Norrell*
Catherine Sheldon

I'm only halfway through but totally absorbed! It's a wonderfully amusing early nineteenth-century pastiche with a rigmarole of partly amusing, partly thrilling, partly sinister magic thrown in.

Good Books,
The Reader,
19 Abercromby Square,
Liverpool,
L69 7ZG

David Mitchell, *Cloud Atlas* & Johanna Spyri, *Heidi*
Erica Bridges

My book club read at the moment (or not!) is David Mitchell's *Cloud Atlas*. A long and involved read. I had to finish even though others gave up. It has stayed in my thoughts. It is a massive book. I would like to know more about the characters and author.

I'd also like to recommend *Heidi*. This is the first book that made me cry; I couldn't put it down.

Good Books,
The Reader,
19 Abercromby Square,
Liverpool,
L69 7ZG

Newman's Notes

A Word for Jane Austen (2)

An occasional series in which good friend of The Reader *Stephen Newman posthumously shares unfailingly vivid insights on a wide range of subjects, both literary and otherwise.*

Stephen Newman

Misery seeping through the comedy is the essence of Jane Austen. The effect of these beautiful books is strangely akin to Keats's 'Ode on a Grecian Urn'. There is the same formal perfection, the same inconsolable absence: 'Bold lover, never, never, never canst thou kiss'. The art that serves, on the surface, a comic vision of fulfilment actually serves to freeze the will in an eternal winter of unfulfilment. Jane Austen learnt the superficies of her craft from the Augustans: wit, decorum, sense, reason; but the heart of her vision is Romantic. The love that irradiates these ravishing unravished brides of quietness is permanent and poetic, not historical. The very exclusiveness, artificiality, even, of her Sphinx-like structures tells of a Temple of Venus where only those who worship perfection may pray.

It is not a comfortable vision. It is indeed cruel in its exigence. It lacks the spacious liberation of tragedy – the taking on of the burden of failure and humanity and death. Something of that awareness haunts *Persuasion*, more doubting and tentative than the previous novels. It reminds you that behind every book, however complex, is a human being, and that behind the Romantic dream lies a face 'Faultily faultless, icily regular, splendidly null' like Tennyson's Maud. A writer has to hate as well as love. Whatever their limitations, the Augustans from Pope to Crabbe knew how to hate, and Jane Austen inherited this cold blast of candour. A famous *Scrutiny* essay by D. W. Harding is entitled 'Regulated Hatred in Jane Austen'. Everywhere – the Eltons, the Misses Bingley, John Dashwood ('a face of strong, natural, sterling insignificance') – life which a Victorian would

'understand' is hosed down with a verbal power-pump.

Well might D. H. Lawrence attack Jane Austen's 'sharp knowing in apartness'. In her regulated world all the little or big lies with which we oil the strains of civilisation are burnt clear away by a bunsen flame blue with amused fury. From one angle her world is full of piranha fish busily nipping off the balls of unfortunate swimmers. What Lawrence neglects to notice however is the comedy, which, as well as destroying, preserves. People we would flee from in real life are turned into enchanting gargoyles. The paradisal preposterousness is the pearl secreted by the imagination under the grit of experience.

'Reality' is an impossible term to apply to the novel. All we ask of a book is that it smells of life. Jane Austen's characters are as free as mountain winds. Whether she approves or disapproves is finally of no concern. Morally, Mrs Elton ought to be chastised. Imaginatively, she flourishes like an enormous magic beanstalk of vegetable luxuriance. It is this sense of a garden bursting with blooms from jasmine to deadly nightshade that makes you call her Shakespearean.

The question of evil remains. At first sight she ignores it. Mr Elliot is her only double-dyed villain, and he is a stick. But the deeper answer is that she excommunicates it, as categorically as the Pope. 'Let other pens dwell on guilt and misery. I quit such odious subjects as soon as I can.' In an England of violence and urban deprivation and depravity, this sounds pie-in-the-sky. But a Jane Austen novel is, properly read, an education. It is not that guilt and misery don't exist but that properly disciplined, they need not.

Rose-tinted spectacles? Perhaps. But which of us would dare enter her field of observation? We would be stopped dead like rabbits caught in a car's headlights. A word, a gesture, a haircut even, would betray us. It is not that Jane Austen's morality is too simple for the world but that the world is too simple for her morality. Not that she's too limited but that we're too lax.

> It was a meagre enough life on the grim edge of poverty, with scant margin for possibilities of sickness or mischance, but it had the frail, audacious permanence of a bird's nest built on the edge of a cliff – a mere wisp of leaves and straw, yet so put together that the lives entrusted to it may hang safely over the abyss.
>
> Edith Wharton, *The House of Mirth*

Our Spy in NY

Enid Stubin

'Make a party, everybody will come.' This pronouncement, dense with sarcasm, issues from Grandma Etka from Minsk, the addled dowager of Laura Shaine Cunningham's memoir *Sleeping Arrangements*. Etka sees the role of hostess as subservient to the pleasures of others and therefore beneath her ('I hate even the word,' she sneers. '*Baleboosteh*'). But I was delighted when the editor of *The Reader* asked me if it were 'possible' to have a reception to celebrate the magazine's distribution in the States. And could it be held in a small, independent bookstore? Sure thing, you bet.

Having perfected the medium of the wine and cheese party during graduate school, I spent more years than were academically advisable calculating portions per bottle, simmering industrial-sized batches of ratatouille, and stuffing cherry tomato halves with homemade pesto. I called on the manager of Shakespeare and Co., my local bookstore. She was leaving to settle in New Hampshire but referred me to the new managers, Jenna and Jonah, young people of such charm and enthusiasm that I couldn't believe my good fortune. They were eager to have the reception in the store, and it remained only to choose a date for the party and send out invitations. My correspondence with the staff of *The Reader* was intended to reveal a nonchalance born of ease and experience: this would be a labor of love.

Normal people understand the use of email to contact several hundred people expeditiously, but I had something less sensible in mind. *The Reader* folks had sent me two hundred postcards of the cover for Number 20, the Americans issue. After consultation with Solomon, manager of Kanter Press, a stationery store I consider my office, I found labels that could be printed with the particulars and, judiciously pruned, affixed to those gorgeous postcards. Everyone should have a friend like Rita, who spent a Sunday afternoon and evening helping me decide wording and typeface and figuring out how to photocopy my message onto three hundred mailing labels.

Designing the guest list posed a challenge: count on no more than 40 percent showing up, I was counseled. The invitees consisted of professional (that is to say political) and personal friends, with

some students and family thrown into the mix. I stuffed 130 mail-boxes in my school's English department and asked one of the aides to keep an eye out for discards. These were fished out of wastepa-per cans and redeployed at the library and administrative offices. If the expected flood of responses never surged in, the tactful silence that ensued prompted a little dust-up with a colleague who patiently 'explained' why no one in my department responds one way or the other to an RSVP ('We get so much junk in our mailboxes'). And it kindled my fury at being instructed in the niceties of collegial eti-quette. My tone in the following flurry of emails distinguished me as a sorehead of the Lady Hester Stanhope school. But my buddies and family, some of whom hadn't seen each other for more than a decade, came through.

Contemporary sensibility assesses invitation as demand; people apparently have too many social claims on their time, or they resist festivity in a misguided attempt to project gravitas. But just as we once preferred hot pink and turquoise to beige and taupe, parties used to promise glamour and fun rather than world-weary obligation. In Updike's *Couples*, Piet recognizes his craving for the company of his more sophisticated neighbors as a longing for the fun his childhood never provided. Somehow these apprehensions have resolved for me in the role of host, impresario, stage manager, and bosser. Imagining what people might like and then providing it – what could be more gratifying?

My naïveté was exposed as I waited for colleagues to respond, with the attendant declension of anxiety (What if they all show up?) to relief (Nobody yet) and then hurt (Nobody's coming). Reticent to tell the staff of Shakespeare and Co. that I'd invited over two hundred people, I was shy about approaching the people I saw in school four days a week. 'So what is this, a big deal or something?' 'Well, it will be if you show up, Tina.'

Indeterminacy has its own satisfactions, and the shopping for X number of guests released me from vexing limitations: British cheeses and American wines, French pâtés crafted in New Jersey, olives, and grapes. Nothing makes you feel as if you're a big shot like a case of wine delivered with your name on it. (*The Reader* may very well be the only literary journal with a consulting som-melier.) And rather than tidy up an apartment that looked as if three sixteen-year-old boys were leading lives of quiet desperation in it, I had a beautiful book-lined living room down the block as my base of operations. 'Don't worry,' Jenna assured me, 'I'll vacuum before anyone shows up.' My grand scheme for selling subscriptions

by pushing discounts and deals evaporated when I acknowledged the logistical problems before the ethical ones: how could I collect checks while schmoozing with guests and scooping scrunched-up cocktail napkins? Moreover, how could I invite people to a reception in order to sell them something? (Please, it's called fundraising, and it's done every day in NYC.) Then again, I was promoting a beautiful journal that publishes the likes of Seamus Heaney and Les Murray, four issues a year, perfect for holiday giving. No one ever went broke – or lonely – telling New Yorkers what to buy.

The murky gray warmth yielded to a monsoon, and rather than plan my toilette, which subsequent photos prove to have been a mistake, I *hondled* with the man selling fruit from a cart near Lexington Avenue and came away with a bonus pomegranate and six tangerines. Rinsing eight pounds of grapes at the sink in my kitchen, I thought of Pnin's preparations for his party and was suddenly seized by a comparable sense of well-being and anticipation. At Shakespeare and Co., everything came together: the jewel box of a store, the cunning little bags sent from Liverpool, introductions and hugs, and a table cleared to highlight an impressive display of nine years of *The Reader*. A bookstore, I saw, is the ideal venue for a party: there are no awkward corners, no disgruntled wallflowers. In the longueurs between conversations, anyone can lean up against a wall of shelving to choose a book and read, gossipers can gather and yak away, and there's always the opportunity to buy.

The rain might have posed a problem: warm but heavy, the kind of night that has one leaving some important piece of clothing behind – a much-loved scarf or favorite pair of gloves. Dan showed up from the office, drenched to the skin in office penitentials, but Ray, who had arrived earlier from coaching basketball at nearby Baruch College, had brought a towel. And despite the rotten weather, sixty hearty souls gave every sign of having a racketing good time. Was it the novelty of the locale? The Oregonian Pinot Noir? I think it was the occasion itself. Not a birthday ('She's what? Looks every day of it') or retirement or some conventional excuse for a gathering that reminds everyone of mortality and regret, but the launch in America of *The Reader*. And that, I can tell you, is cause for celebration.

Ask the Reader

Q I am always irritated by the references in English literature to the ancient gods and goddesses, not to mention the nymphs and shepherds that accompany them, by poets who obviously didn't believe in them but pretended that they did. Are they simply displaying the fruits of an elite education and is that why I feel excluded?

A You are not the first to complain. Thomas Carew praised the poetry of his contemporary Donne, because he had banished from his verse such Classical references, 'The goodly exiled train / Of gods and goddesses', though he knew they would return, as they did, in his own writing occasionally but with a vengeance in Milton's, flaunted in a minor way in the eighteenth-century novel and poetry and even putting in an appearance in Yeats and Eliot. But what you object to is not esoteric information from exploded cosmologies such as you find in Donne (and even Carew) but allusions to something certainly not exclusive, a series of stories. Learned handbooks to Classical mythology may have been around from say the twelfth century up to Graves and Kerényi but practising poets gathered the tales of the gods mainly in bits and pieces from their reading, as we do. Sharing a series of stories is common to all vital cultures whether they are orally transmitted, as with Maoris, Australian aborigines or native North Americans, or written down, as with literate Indians or Europeans. The Celtic nations of Britain have always had their own mythologies and tales and I'm told the story-teller still flourishes in Ireland.

But only a few years ago most people had in their minds a selection from the greatest gathering of such shared stories, the Bible. Apart from their religious value, they served the same purpose as proverbs and popular sayings, touchstones for familiar human situations and reactions. They were transmitted by word of mouth through teachers in week-day and Sunday schools as well as in numerous 'Tales from the Bible'. Alongside them, there flourished also that body of stories from the old European world which you dismiss as 'the ancient gods and goddesses'. One can never know enough stories, not this or that great novel, the product of an individual mind, but the stories known to us all, preferably from childhood. Stories predate conscious thought but knowing them

early gives ideas when we start thinking them something to work upon.

Europe has always benefited by having two such very different narrative sequences to think with. Every series of such traditional tales implies a point of view, assumptions that lie behind the sequence. Put crudely, in the stories of your despised gods and goddesses the world seems an arena of competing forces. If the events seem arbitrary, dictated by chance or rather the passions of some irresistible deity, the implications for a reading of human life may even today seem true, be confirmed by experience, command belief to that extent. Equally (if not more so) the Bible stories, with their sense of a hidden purpose determined by a single God progressively revealing Himself, imply a believable reading of collective life. Thinking in the presence of both traditions produces complex results. Hardy's novels, for example, often seem to be conceived in terms of the Bible's story of a secret purpose guiding human life only to reveal the arbitrary realm of the pagan gods.

Both sets of stories embody a vast range of emotions, situations and reactions, which is why the poets used them, and both involve also the sense of awe, fear of the numinous, reverence in the face of what we don't understand. If our only reply to such a sense of wonder is to dismiss it and think, 'It's all superstition; give it a few years and we *shall* understand and be able to use and control such powers', then that is actually the road to self-destruction. So give us back our stories. Bring back the gods and goddesses as well as Noah's ark, the burning bush and David, Bathsheba and Uriah.

Words We Had to Look Up

We had to pull down the dictionary to check the meaning of immane (p. 87, Jonathan Meades' recommendation of Michel Tournier, *The Erl King*).

immane *a. arch.* E17. [L. *immanis* monstrous, huge, savage, (earlier) wicked, cruel.] **1** Monstrous in size or strength. **2** Monstrous in character; inhumanly cruel.

subscribe

Make sure of your copy of *The Reader*
and enjoy big savings *
by taking out a **subscription**:

UK
p&p free

1 year	4 issues	**£24.00**
2 years	8 issues	**£38.00**
3 years	12 issues	**£57.00**

Abroad **
including p&p

1 year	4 issues	**£36.00 GBP**
2 years	8 issues	**£57.00 GBP**
3 years	12 issues	**£86.00 GBP**

Please make cheques payable to the
University of Liverpool and post to
**The Reader, 19 Abercromby Square,
University of Liverpool, L69 7ZG.**

Include your name and address and specify the
issue with which you would like your subscrip-
tion to begin.

* Save 20% on 2- and 3-year subscriptions
** The easiest way to take out a subscription abroad is by using Paypal
on our website: www.thereader.co.uk

In the first of an occasional series, The Times *advice columnist, Bel Mooney, answers life queries from characters in literature, and from some of their creators.*

If someone on your bookshelves has a problem which might benefit from Bel's thoughtful but down-to-earth advice please write to her c/o The Reader.

Problems in Life and Letters

Bel Mooney

Dear Bel,
I bet you don't get many letters from men and certainly not from men like me. I warn you that I'm not ready to hear your advice. Too much damned pride is my problem, apparently. Get round that one if you can. I'll fight you all the way. What could you say to help me in any case, in your light, safe world that I despise and envy?

Here it is. My father, a tyrant you will have found out about if your reading goes beyond the first few pages – I won't say his name – has exiled me, his one-time favourite son. I hear he has a new heir now but you can forget him. All you need to know is that my suffering in this hell-hole is humiliating. There's nothing here, not a single thing powerful or pure enough, to give me a moment's consolation for what I have lost. Do I have your sympathy?

So I find that anger is my protection from despair, and anger is a pretty useful rallying call for my fellow exiles who of course look to me for direction. Your complacent calm disgusts me, and your conspicuous consumption, and your unseeing, happy lives. I'm making bombs in my head. I bet you don't believe me. That's your worst mistake. Your first, your last, your worst.

Is it possible to escape torment, dear agony aunt?
The former L—

No doubt it will irritate you further to know that – yes – I truly pity you. I do receive many letters from men, but most (thankfully) are blessed with a good deal more self-knowledge than you display. Why have you written, if the terrible clanging of your Ego

will drown out any advice I have to give? Why should I bother, when you will mock my kindness, or any other good qualities? Yet still, there is a power in the way you write which touches me, indicative as it is of lost potential: an intelligence and strength of mind which has, through some fatal flaw, turned in upon itself. With no explanation of your exile, I have to assume you did wrong and deserve your punishment. You ask if it is possible to 'escape torment'. The simple answer is No. All of us have our torments, the crosses we must bear. Any hope of redemption (a good word) comes through how we bear them.

Much as you like to feel your suffering is unique, your tale of a fall from grace afflicts many people. The spouse supplanted, the experienced worker made redundant, the politician voted out, the once-popular singer no longer feted… all have to contend with near-fatal blows to pride, to self-esteem. You have lost your home and your sense of identity. Yet you could still use your good qualities (surely they still struggle within you?) to overcome these setbacks. Like that blues singer Robert Johnson, you are at the crossroads. Out of the bad things we can seek to create good, or we can take the opposite path. Sadly, I surmise that this is the one you are already on.

But first let me be optimistic and hope it is not too late. You need to think positively, and what better place to start than your immediate environment? You describe it as a 'hell-hole', but the most unprepossessing of homes can be made attractive by the application of some creative design touches. Think cool, neutral colours – and I recommend scented candles, and a little head of Buddha here and there, for their calming effects. Take a pride in making this new place your own.

You say you have some chums who were exiled at the same time as you. Invite them round to your transformed home, for a good debate about what to do next. I would like to think you could involve yourselves in good works and not dwell on the injuries you feel have been done to you by this rather harsh-sounding parent. Yet, re-reading your letter, I have a sense of foreboding. You are turning your rage against people like me, and yet what have we done to you? In sorrow rather than anger, I have to tell you frankly that your nasty, threatening tone does not frighten me – nor will it divert me from my task of trying to help people. I believe that kindness and forgiveness are ultimately more powerful than violence and rage. Still, I certainly believe you capable of great harm, but I hope and trust that something will stop you – that good will prevail. I urge you to start with the Buddha.

Dear Bel,
I am a woman in my mid-twenties, with soft brown hair and full
of unusual energy. I am married to a baronet and we live at his
country seat in the soulless coal-and-iron Midlands. My husband
was disabled in the war and he cannot father children. Mostly he
stays in his study listening to the radio and thinking about more
efficient ways to run the coalmines.
    Just recently I have become aware of a strange weary yearning,
a mad restlessness thrilling inside my body. I find myself rushing
into the woods and lying prone in the bracken in the middle of
the afternoon. Last week I was wandering about in the woods as
usual when I came across the gamekeeper's cottage and saw the
shirtless keeper washing himself. I hid behind a tree and watched,
overwhelmed by – what shall I call it? – a lambency, a warm, white
flame, a shock of vision in my womb. I came back to the house in
time for tea but I am beset by strange and terrible feelings. Should
I stay at home and take up crochet?
Yours, CC

I somehow suspect that, appropriate though such activities may be
to a woman of your station, neither crochet nor embroidery will
satisfactorily fill the long, lonely hours whilst your husband is in his
study. Nor would watercolours, although I can assure you that the
long, moist stroke of a brush can be deeply satisfying. I sympathise
with your loneliness, for it is clear that you need attention – ten-
derness even – which your husband fails to provide. His condition
is not his fault; his indifference is. But do you not think this is a
product of his class? Brought up to be reserved, upper-class men
turn away from emotion because they are trained to fear it. Your
husband is almost certainly as cut off from his workers as he is from
you; his disability is no excuse for his shortcomings as a man.
    Your restlessness has taken you into the woods, and so my first
suggestion is that you make use of the time you spend there. You
could begin by making a friend of the gamekeeper, and I urge you
not to be inhibited by awareness of class. In my experience, once
you get beyond the vowels and vocabulary, working-class men can
be full of vitality and enthusiasm, with much to offer. This man will
have a broad knowledge of the natural world, from pheasants to
wild flowers, and you may find it fascinating to share some of his
experience, to know what he knows. I am convinced that biology is
an under-rated science, which even ladies of your class would enjoy
were they only given access to its mysteries.
    The alternative course I would prescribe is – Mining Engineer-

ing. Like it or not, industrialisation is a force to be reckoned with, and you might find you quell your strange longings by involving yourself in your husband's business. There is no law that says women should not be as adept as men at running mines, and since your husband's life expectancy may prove short, you could soon find yourself in the enviable position of being a wealthy and powerful widow. However, from the tone of your note I suspect this pot of gold will not be at the end of your personal rainbow, and that the study of stamens will prove the more alluring option.

Dear Bel,
It has been nearly a year now since I received that terrible letter telling me that my best friend, Arthur, 'is no more'. As you can imagine, I just went to pieces after that and the terrible thing is that I can't seem to think of anything else. He was my north, my south, my east, my west. I have tried writing poetry to sort out my feelings but I just keep on going round in circles. I have tried praying, but there seems to be no answer and now I am beginning to doubt there ever will be. Do you think it would have been better never to have loved, rather than loved and lost?
Alf

The deep affection between men should not be underestimated; I am sure a friendship like yours with Arthur could sometimes feel like a marriage, and I suspect, therefore, that some people find it hard to understand the depth of your grief. Your question to me is an important one, and the short answer is a resounding 'No'. Loving another person can bring out the best in us, but it also makes us vulnerable. Love and Pain travel hand in hand, and if they knock at your door you will be so much the poorer if you don't let them in.

You say you dabble a little in poetry. My advice is that you continue to use this as therapy. I predict that your grief will inspire you to heights you have not yet reached, and that – who knows? – one day your published efforts may bring consolation to others. Don't worry about conventional religion for the moment; use your verses as a form of prayer and I predict that you will soon regain your faith, as well as achieving immortality for your friend, in universal memory.

You may read more about the scope and danger of pride in Milton's *Paradise Lost*. Students of sex between the classes may investigate the matter further in D.H. Lawrence's *Lady Chatterley's Lover*. Gentle-hearted readers will be glad to hear that Alfred Lord Tennyson did indeed face his grief in poetry and *In Memoriam* has brought relief to many sufferers.

A Poem by
Stanley Middleton

On a Bus

Hurrying to post letters, I glanced
At a girl in a telephone booth,
Her face vivid with delight. Those eyes
Did not meet mine, soothe
Or rouse any who could see her,
Concentrated away on the unknown
At the far end. Her vivacity burnt off
My dullness. I returned alone
To the bus stop. She followed, lined
Up to wait, face not alert now
But formal, with shaped eye-brows,
Reddened lips, dyed hair. How
The metamorphosis was managed
I do not dare guess. She did
Not catch the same bus as I. Ten
Minutes or so later we passengers slid
Past a house I knew as a child,
Date 1926, an owl on a moon, inside
A glassy semi-circle, green, silver, blue.
My father, with few years left to live, tried
To liven me. 'The owl house', he called
The place. It was beyond our means
But like the 'phoning girl freely
Presented pleasure. These has-beens,
These up-to-date trivialities of joy
Drawn tightly together here by chance
Stimulate memory and love: an unnamed girl,
Father, I and a glass owl leap, launch into dance.

Letters

Dear Editor,

Thank you for the recommendation of Marilynne Robinson's *Gilead* (*The Reader* 20 editorial). I didn't read Jane Davis's full commentary before reading the book – I stopped when persuaded to read it in case I was influenced too strongly in any particular way – but afterwards I finished her article and was pleased to find that love is the key thing in both our responses.

Gilead reminded me of Dickinson in style – simple but profound, the infinite in a domestic setting. It has a slanting, oblique angle on the world, that is really a revelation: 'You can know a thing to death but be for all purposes completely ignorant of it'. This seems to me what it is about – as the narrator says of water: 'It is easy to believe in such moments that water was made primarily for blessing, and only secondarily for growing vegetables or doing the wash'. He speaks of phrasing that will 'Call attention to a thing existing in excess of itself … a sort of purity or lavishness, something ordinary in kind but exceptional in degree'. It is about loving a thing, in a sense, it seems to me. There's a beautiful Easter hymn (17th century words, I think), 'My Song is Love Unknown'. and a line in it that always moved me: 'Love to the loveless shown / that they might lovely be'. The book gives that glow of love, calls attention, to the grey and homely little corners of our worlds, reveals them, changes them, makes them more than appear – or, maybe, shows them as they truly are, astonishes us. The narrator puts this in a sacred context – 'setting things apart so that their holiness will be perceived' – but the book doesn't entirely, it's a universal emotion, this momentary welling up of joy at the loveliness in the everyday.

Ian Carass

Dear Editor,

I just wanted to say how much I enjoyed the *Art and Life* Readers' Day held at Liverpool Medical Institute in December. Elaine Feinstein's workshop gave deep and genuine instruction. Most importantly, the day introduced me to your wonderful magazine.

Sylvia Miller

The Reader Crossword

Cassandra   No.13

Across

*1. See 26 across
5. But little Henry was bundled into the laundry receptacle (7)
*9. See 15 down
10. Thinking person and his glass (9)
11. Does achieving one's fantasy mean a lifetime in bed? (6, 3, 5)
13. Extensive desire (4)
14. Scientist discovered experimenting with tin boats (8)
17. Lubricate area of expertise where natural resources are exploited (8)
18. Cleaner fish for tea (4)
21. Widow's contribution and ceremony sound like alternative ways of achieving one's aim (2, 5, 2, 5)
23. In this eventuality upper class type, around showers, may have to take the bus (6, 3)
*24. Spaniel is cause of a sign of embarrassment (5)
25. Despotic rulers in Odessa trap sables illegally (7)
* 26 and 1 across. When greenrooms are often at their busiest (7, 3, 4)

* Clues with an asterisk have a common theme

Down

1. Kettering, for example, is understood to be involved in important ownership issues (4)
2. MP to act on email I circulated indicating strength of feeling (9, 6)
3. Final resting place is in the gift of Eric of Finisterre (6)
4. Traditionally Gallic gestures, initially seeming harmless, regularly undermine German statesmen (6)
5. Condition of some women who die of convulsions (8)
6. Lets hand complicated reference to M. Beyle (8)
*7. Attention should be given, in the main, to this flimsy-sounding structure (2, 3, 10)
8. Robert Ames devised these instruments for registering change (10)
12. Boys Brigade had tools to bring about indiscriminate slaughter (10)
*15 and 9 across. Grow F1 (hybrid) viola in compost to produce perhaps the most well-known bloom in WC1 (8, 5)
16. A description of these sub-units is to be found in the writings of Plato on scientific discovery (8)
19. Ready-made result? In part, but premiership ref above suspicion of course (6)
20. Young lady is healthy, we hear, despite being an eccentric (6)
22. First child holds its nose below this feature (4)

Buck's Quiz 21
Old Chestnuts

1. In which BC play does the heroine kill herself to avoid being buried alive?

2. Who fights and kills the monster Grendel?

3. The title of which Browning poem is derived from a brief song in *King Lear*?

4. Who says 'Me miserable! which way shall I fly/ Infinite wrath and infinite despair?/ Which way I fly is hell; myself am hell'?

5. From where did Chaucer take his story of *Troilus and Criseyde*?

6. 'Other women cloy/ The appetites they feed, but she makes hungry/ Where most she satisfies.' Who is being described?

7. Which old story is common to the works of Matthew Arnold, Richard Wagner and Alfred Tennyson?

8. In which nineteenth-century novel do Machiavelli and Savonarola appear?

9. In which twenty-first-century novel does Savonarola appear?

10. Which twentiethth-century novel is set in a fourteenth-century Franciscan monastery?

11. Who met Homer, Ovid, Horace and Lucan 'in that limbo, as it were suspended'?

12. Whose translation of Homer made Keats feel like 'some watcher of the skies' or 'stout Cortez'?

13. Who saves Rebecca from the dishonourable advances of Sir Brian de Bois-Guilbert?

14. 'If thou shouldst never see my face again,/ Pray for my soul. More things are wrought by prayer/ Than this world dreams of'. Which dying King speaks these words?

15. Which celebrated Roman poet was born in Sulmo about 43BC?

16. This novel of 1934 was to have been filmed with Charles Laughton in the title role, but when the project was abandoned it became known as 'the greatest picture never made'. What was it?

17. In which fourteenth-century poem does the narrator fall asleep and see in a dream 'a fair feeld ful of folk'?

18. Whose last words were 'Crito, we ought to offer a cock to Asclepius, see to it and don't forget'?

19. 'I met a traveller from an antique land'. Who is the poet and what did the traveller see?

20. C. S. Lewis was converted to Christianity after a night-long walk with which Anglo-Saxonist?

Contributors 21

Gary Allen was born in Ballymena, Co. Antrim. He has three collections of poetry, *Languages* (Flambard/Black Mountain, 2002), *Exile* (Black Mountain Press, 2004), *North of Nowhere* (Lagan Press, 2006) and a novel, *Cillin* (Black Mountain Press).

David Attwooll is a publishing consultant and agent (www.attwoollassociates.com). He is also Chairman of Liverpool University Press.

Dana Cairns Watson is the author of *Gertrude Stein and the Essence of What Happens* (2005), and her new writing project is on extinction. She teaches composition and science writing at UCLA.

Peter Conradi's most recent books are *Iris Murdoch: A Life* (2001) and *Going Buddhist: Panic and Emptiness, The Buddha and Me* (2004). He lives in London and Radnorshire.

David Constantine is a translator of Hölderlin, Goethe, Kleist and Brecht. *Collected Poems* was published in 2004 and a collection of stories *Under the Dam* (Comma Press) was published in 2005.

Pamela Coren has published papers on Renaissance poets, and had poems in many magazines. Her first collection *The Blackbird Inspector* was published by Laurel Books in 2005 (www.laurelbooks.co.uk). She is currently researching the modernist poets and music.

Alan Davis is Visiting Fellow to the Ruskin Programme, Lancaster University and an old friend of *The Reader*.

Philip Davis is a professor of English at the University of Liverpool. He has published *The Victorians* (Oxford University Press, 2002), edited a collection of religious verse, *All the Days of My Life* (Dent 1999), and is currently writing a biography of Bernard Malamud.

Jen Hadfield is a poet and photographer whose first collection, *Almanacs*, was published by Bloodaxe this year. Her website is http://www.rogueseeds.co.uk.

Sue Lloyd is a writer, editor (Roget's Thesaurus) and now publisher (www.gengepress.now-online.net) in Somerset. Her biography of French dramatist Edmond Rostand, *The Man who was Cyrano*, was published in 2003.

Frances Macmillan recently graduated with a first in English from Clare College, Cambridge. She is currently working as an intern at *The Reader*.

Jonathan Meades is the author of several books, among them *Filthy English, Pompey, Peter Knows What Dick Likes, The Fowler Family Business, Incest and Morris Dancing*. He has written and performed in many televisions films on topographical and architectural subjects.

Richard Meier was born in Epsom in 1970, and now lives and works in London. Some of his poems appeared in Carcanet's *Oxford Poets Anthology* 2002.

Stanley Middleton is the author of a series of highly-praised novels of contemporary provincial life including the 1974 Booker Prize winner, *Holiday*. His new novel *Mother's Boy* will be published 2006.

Bill Milner is now retired after a career in education. His poems have previously appeared in *Envoi*, *Orbis*, *The Interpreter's House* and *Tears in the Fence*.

Bel Mooney is a novelist, children's author and journalist, as well as an experienced broadcaster on television and radio. She was born and brought up in Liverpool, and is a Fellow of John Moores University.

Adam Piette is Professor of English at the University of Sheffield. He is author of *Remembering and the Sound of Words* and *Imagination at War*.

Stephen Pollington is a writer and broadcaster specialising in the earlier periods of English history. His recent books are on military history, medical manuscripts, feasting and a beginner's guide to Old English. He lives in Essex with his wife, three of his children and two cats.

Christopher Routledge is a freelance writer and editor. He is co-editor of *Key Thinkers in Linguistics and the Philosophy of Language* (Edinburgh, 2005). His website is at www.scriveners.demon.co.uk.

Carol Rumens is currently Professor in Creative Writing at the University of Hull. Her most recent volume of poems is *Poems: 1968–2004*, Bloodaxe, 2004.

Jane Shilling is a columnist at *The Times* and the author of a memoir, *The Fox in the Cupboard*, published by Penguin. She is currently working on a book about middle age.

Ann Stapleton is a freelance writer from Ohio whose work has appeared or is forthcoming in *Alaska Quarterly Review*, *The Dark Horse*, and *The Weekly Standard*.

Simon Starkey is a retired Church of England vicar living in inner-city Liverpool where he has worked since 1972. He is a graduate of the part-time MA in Victorian Literature at the University of Liverpool.

Enid Stubin is Assistant Professor of English at Kingsborough Community College of the City University of New York and Adjunct Professor of Humanities at New York University's School of Continuing and Professional Studies.

Sam Trainor writes and teaches English in France. 'Hippocrene' prefigures an eponymous book using the concrete 'horse stanza' in a narrative poem. Also look out for *The Birmingham Quean* and *Choreographies*.

Mary Weston was born in Hawaii and now lives in Liverpool. She is a facilitator for the community-based project *Get Into Reading*. Her novel *The Escape Plan* was published in 2001.

Buck's Quiz 20

1.William Robert Spencer **2.** Jumble **3.** Old George **4.** The Sherlock Holmes story 'Silver Blaiz'e **5.** 'With rosted flessh, or milk and wastelbreed' **6.** Diogenes **7.** *Wuthering Heights* **8.** Argus **9.** Atticus Finch **10.** Buck, *Call of the Wild* **11.** *Black Dogs*, Ian McEwan **12.** Emily Bronte **13.** *Agnes Grey* **14.** Launce in *Two Gentlemen of Verona* **15.** *Greyfriars Bobby* **16.** Montmorency, *Three Men in a Boat* **17.** *The Tale of Little Pig Robinson* **18.** *Harry Potter and the Philosopher's Stone* **19.** John Steinbeck **20.** *Hamlet*

Prizes! Please send your answers to Buck's Quiz, The Reader, 19 Abercromby Square, Liverpool L69 7ZG

Cassandra Crossword 12

Across
9. Ischiatic **10.** Banjo **11.** Flora **12.** Leasehold **13.** Arcadia **14.** Ancient **17. Picul 19.** Ada **20.** Poste **21.** Comfort **22.** Gibbons **24.** Abandoned **26.** Aloof **28.** Negro **29.** Sketchier
Down
1. Fief **2.** Echoic **3.** Pirandello **4.** Stella **5.** McNamara **6.** Able **7.** Incomers **8.** Cold **13.** Aspic **15.** Capablanca **16.** Tress **18.** Campaign **19.** Astonish **22.** Gadjet **23.** Ozonic **24.** Aunt **25.** Doom **27.** Farm

Distribution Information

For trade orders in all territories except North America and Mexico, please contact:
Marston Book Services, PO Box 269, Abingdon, OX14 4YN, UK
Tel: +44 [0]1235 465 500   **Fax:** +44 [0]1235 465 555
Email: trade.order@marston.co.uk **Web:** www.marston.co.uk

For trade orders in North America and Mexico, please contact:
University of Chicago Press, 1427 East 60th Street, Chicago, Illinois 60637, USA
Tel: +1 800 621 2736   **Fax:** +1 800 621 8476
Email: custserv@press.uchicago.edu **Web:** www.press.uchicago.edu

For institutional subscriptions in all territories, please contact:
Sarah Preece, Subscriptions, Marston Book Services Ltd, PO Box 269, Abingdon, Oxfordshire, OX14 4YN, UK
Tel: +44 [0]1235 465 537   **Email:** subscriptions@marston.co.uk

If you have any queries regarding trade orders or institutional subscriptions, please contact Janet Smith at Liverpool University Press on +44 [0]151 794 2233 or email janmar@liv.ac.uk